The Brown
Mountain Lights

Contributions to Southern Appalachian Studies

1. *Memoirs of Grassy Creek: Growing Up in the Mountains on the Virginia–North Carolina Line.* Zetta Barker Hamby. 1998

2. *The Pond Mountain Chronicle: Self-Portrait of a Southern Appalachian Community.* Edited by Leland R. Cooper and Mary Lee Cooper. 1998

3. *Traditional Musicians of the Central Blue Ridge: Old Time, Early Country, Folk and Bluegrass Label Recording Artists, with Discographies.* Marty McGee. 2000

4. *W.R. Trivett, Appalachian Pictureman: Photographs of a Bygone Time.* Ralph E. Lentz II. 2001

5. *The People of the New River: Oral Histories from the Ashe, Alleghany and Watauga Counties of North Carolina.* Edited by Leland R. Cooper and Mary Lee Cooper. 2001

6. *John Fox, Jr., Appalachian Author.* Bill York. 2003

7. *The Thistle and the Brier: Historical Links and Cultural Parallels Between Scotland and Appalachia.* Richard Blaustein. 2003

8. *Tales from Sacred Wind: Coming of Age in Appalachia. The Cratis Williams Chronicles.* Cratis D. Williams. Edited by David Cratis Williams and Patricia D. Beaver. 2003

9. *Willard Gayheart, Appalachian Artist.* Willard Gayheart and Donia S. Eley. 2003

10. *The Forest City Lynching of 1900: Populism, Racism, and White Supremacy in Rutherford County, North Carolina.* J. Timothy Cole. 2003

11. *The Brevard Rosenwald School: Black Education and Community Building in a Southern Appalachian Town, 1920–1966.* Betty J. Reed. 2004

12. *The Bristol Sessions: Writings About the Big Bang of Country Music.* Edited by Charles K. Wolfe and Ted Olson. 2005

13. *Community and Change in the North Carolina Mountains: Oral Histories and Profiles of People from Western Watauga County.* Compiled by Nannie Greene and Catherine Stokes Sheppard. 2006

14. *Ashe County: A History; A New Edition.* Arthur Lloyd Fletcher. 2009 [2006]

15. *The New River Controversy; A New Edition.* Thomas J. Schoenbaum. Epilogue by R. Seth Woodard. 2007

16. *The Blue Ridge Parkway by Foot: A Park Ranger's Memoir.* Tim Pegram. 2007

17. *James Still: Critical Essays on the Dean of Appalachian Literature.* Edited by Ted Olson and Kathy H. Olson. 2008

18. *Owsley County, Kentucky, and the Perpetuation of Poverty.* John R. Burch, Jr. 2008

19. *Asheville: A History.* Nan K. Chase. 2007

20. *Southern Appalachian Poetry: An Anthology of Works by 37 Poets.* Edited by Marita Garin. 2008

21. *Ball, Bat and Bitumen: A History of Coalfield Baseball in the Appalachian South.* L.M. Sutter. 2009

22. *The Frontier Nursing Service: America's First Rural Nurse-Midwife Service and School.* Marie Bartlett. 2009

23. *James Still in Interviews, Oral Histories and Memoirs.* Edited by Ted Olson. 2009

24. *The Millstone Quarries of Powell County, Kentucky.* Charles D. Hockensmith. 2009

25. *The Bibliography of Appalachia: More Than 4,700 Books, Articles, Monographsand Dissertations, Topically Arranged and Indexed.* Compiled by John R. Burch, Jr. 2009

26. *Appalachian Children's Literature: An Annotated Bibliography.* Compiled by Roberta Teague Herrin and Sheila Quinn Oliver. 2010

27. *Southern Appalachian Storytellers: Interviews with Sixteen Keepers of the Oral Tradition.* Edited by Saundra Gerrell Kelley. 2010

28. *Southern West Virginia and the Struggle for Modernity.* Christopher Dorsey. 2011

29. *George Scarbrough, Appalachian Poet: A Biographical and Literary Study with Unpublished Writings.* Randy Mackin. 2011

30. *The Water-Powered Mills of Floyd County, Virginia: Illustrated Histories, 1770–2010.* Franklin F. Webb and Ricky L. Cox. 2012

31. *School Segregation in Western North Carolina: A History, 1860s–1970s.* Betty Jamerson Reed. 2011

32. *The Ravenscroft School in Asheville: A History of the Institution and Its People and Buildings.* Dale Wayne Slusser. 2014

33. *The Ore Knob Mine Murders: The Crimes, the Investigation and the Trials.* Rose M. Haynes. 2013

34. *New Art of Willard Gayheart.* Willard Gayheart and Donia S. Eley. 2014

35. *Public Health in Appalachia: Essays from the Clinic and the Field.* Edited by Wendy Welch. 2014

36. *The Rhetoric of Appalachian Identity.* Todd Snyder. 2014

37. *African American and Cherokee Nurses in Appalachia: A History, 1900–1965.* Phoebe Ann Pollitt. 2016

38. *A Hospital for Ashe County: Four Generations of Appalachian Community Health Care.* Janet C. Pittard. 2016

39. *Dwight Diller: West Virginia Mountain Musician.* Lewis M. Stern. 2016

40. *The Brown Mountain Lights: History, Science and Human Nature Explain an Appalachian Mystery.* Wade Edward Speer. 2017

41. *Richard L. Davis and the Color Line in Ohio Coal: A Hocking Valley Mine Labor Organizer, 1862–1900.* Frans H. Doppen. 2016

42. *The Silent Appalachian: Wordless Mountaineers in Fiction, Film and Television.* Vicki Sigmon Collins. 2017

The Brown Mountain Lights

History, Science and Human Nature Explain an Appalachian Mystery

Wade Edward Speer

Contributions to Southern Appalachian Studies, 40

McFarland & Company, Inc., Publishers
Jefferson, North Carolina

LIBRARY OF CONGRESS CATALOGUING-IN-PUBLICATION DATA

Names: Speer, Ed (Wade Edward), author.
Title: The Brown Mountain lights : history, science and human nature explain an Appalachian mystery / Wade Edward Speer.
Other titles: Contributions to southern Appalachian studies ; 40.
Description: Jefferson, North Carolina : McFarland & Company, Inc., Publishers, 2017 | Series: Contributions to southern Appalachian studies ; 40 | Includes bibliographical references and index.
Identifiers: LCCN 2016054832 | ISBN 9781476666761 (softcover : acid free paper) ∞
Subjects: LCSH: Curiosities and wonders—North Carolina—Burke County. | Legends—North Carolina—Burke County. | Optical illusions—North Carolina—Burke County. | Burke County (N.C.)—Description and travel. | Pisgah National Forest (N.C.)—Description and travel.
Classification: LCC F262.B96 S68 2017 | DDC 975.6/85—dc23
LC record available at https://lccn.loc.gov/2016054832

BRITISH LIBRARY CATALOGUING DATA ARE AVAILABLE

ISBN (print) 978-1-4766-6676-1
ISBN (ebook) 978-1-4766-2620-8

© 2017 Wade Edward Speer. All rights reserved

No part of this book may be reproduced or transmitted in any form or by any means, electronic or mechanical, including photocopying or recording, or by any information storage and retrieval system, without permission in writing from the publisher.

Front cover *inset* staged light test on Brown Mountain at Bear Rocks (photograph by Ed Speer); view from Wiseman's View © 2017 skisergel1 / iStock

Printed in the United States of America

*McFarland & Company, Inc., Publishers
Box 611, Jefferson, North Carolina 28640
www.mcfarlandpub.com*

To all those folks,
including my own family,
both past and present,
who have seen and been mystified by
unknown lights in the Brown Mountain area

Table of Contents

Acknowledgments	xi
Preface	1
Introduction	3
1. The Research Team, Methods Used and Data Collected	17
2. Historical Overview of the BML Phenomenon	21
3. Lack of Sightings Before Electricity	25
4. Legends, Myths and Folklore	32
5. First Sightings and Birth of the Legend	36
6. The Events of 1916	43
7. Government Investigations: 1913, 1919 and 1922	48
8. Early Photographers of the Lights	57
9. Paul Rose's 1962 Tower on Brown Mountain	63
10. Ralph Lael's 1962 Alleged Alien Encounters	69
11. Other Scientific Investigations, 1915–2011	74
12. Lack of BML Sightings from the South and East	79
13. Ghosts, Aliens, Spirits and UFOs	81
14. Pseudoscientific Explanations	83
15. Possibly Misidentified Natural Lights	96
16. Possibly Misidentified Man-Made Lights	120
17. Staged Light Tests	153
18. Appalachian State University Nightly Cameras	167
19. Morphing of the Legend	171
20. Unclassified Lights	174
21. Reality or Delusion	176
Concluding Remarks	179
Appendix A. BML Research by the Author	183

Appendix B. Light Sighting Report Form and Annotated Panoramas   197
Appendix C. Annotated Chronological List of Selected References   201
Bibliography and List of References   237
Index   245

Acknowledgments

The Brown Mountain lights research team varied over time from 10 to 15 investigators. Every member of the team contributed greatly of their time, expertise, and knowledge during the three-year investigation documented in this book; however, several members stand out for their exceptional efforts.

Alex Glover of Little Switzerland, North Carolina, was instrumental in forming the original research team in 2012 composed of multidisciplinary individuals, each with unique skills and knowledge to share. Alex shared his own vast knowledge of geology, rocks, and fireflies and continues to eagerly support the team's efforts.

Dr. Dan Caton, astrophysicist at Appalachian State University (ASU), Boone, North Carolina, began his interest in the Brown Mountain lights in 1998; he quickly agreed to join our team. Dr. Caton's practical and scientific approach to data collection and interpretation were a great help throughout the investigation, as evidenced by the two all-night remote-controlled cameras he set up for observing the lights. Graduate students working with Dr. Caton contributed many hours of research time; Annette Farrah was especially helpful in providing access to the nightly camera images. In addition, Lee Hawkins, observatory engineer at ASU, greatly assisted with the camera setups and evaluation of the images produced. Lee was also instrumental in accessing the Brown Mountain lights clippings file at the Belk Library at ASU and assisted in other ways.

The organization, inspiration, and enthusiasm of Mike Fischesser of Jonas Ridge, North Carolina, were instrumental in keeping the project moving forward, and he quickly became our team's leader. Mike's unending dedication to solving the riddle of the mystery lights resulted in many long days and nights of donated time for endless hikes, campouts, interviews, staged light tests and ATV rides. Mike arranged for the American Adventure Service Corps (AASC), a youth group he founded, to volunteer countless hours for outdoor trips in the Brown Mountain area for staged light tests and repeated searches for possible sources of the lights.

Dr. Cato Holler Jr., of Marion, North Carolina, not only spent a number of days and nights on Brown Mountain and in Linville Gorge, but he and his wife Susan also graciously hosted many of our team's planning meetings in their home. Dr. Holler's extensive private library of historical North Carolina books was helpful in tracking down many obscure references. Dr. Holler was also instrumental in introducing our team to the elusive blue ghost fireflies and first suggested the possible connection between the legend and Jules Verne's science fiction novels. In addition, Dr. Holler and his son Chris were always available for day and night hikes and campouts in search of the source of the elusive lights.

Others on the research team donated countless hours of observations, literature research, scouring the Internet for sources of information, and providing transportation for field crews.

Special thanks to Karen Speer of Marion, North Carolina, who kindly edited an early draft of the manuscript and made many helpful suggestions.

Preface

Mysterious nighttime lights in the Brown Mountain area have been North Carolina's most popular and intriguing ghost story for more than 100 years. This book is the culmination of three years of the most comprehensive team investigation of these lights ever undertaken. Contributions include the work of geologists, astronomers, biologists, university professors and administrators, medical professionals, local outdoor professionals and enthusiasts, and local historians—many of whom have themselves witnessed unknown lights in the area. History, science, and human nature were each found to play major roles in the lights people see and how those lights were interpreted.

The investigation began with a review of historical documents that established when the first unknown lights were seen, when the legend of mystery lights began and the legend's changes over time. The first-ever yearly time line of the legend is presented.

Easily misinterpreted man-made lights were documented by numerous staged light tests that proved some of the kinds of man-made lights that are frequently visible and where they can be seen. Never-before-published photographs of these highly informative staged light tests are presented herein.

A previously unsuspected natural source of light was verified by biological studies that documented the presence of luminescent flying insects that produce lights totally unknown to most visitors and local residents. Descriptions and photographs of these highly unusual lights are presented for the first time.

Finally, our team's nearly 600,000 photographs, including those from two all-night remote-controlled cameras captured a large variety of man-made and natural lights that lend themselves to misinterpretation by unknowing and unsuspecting observers and thus explain the vast majority of supposed mystery lights. For the first time ever, photographs are presented of identified but unexpected nocturnal lights from bright planets, lightning, forest fires, fireworks, vehicles, buildings, cities, towns and rural areas, airplanes (including below-mountaintop flights and low-flying medevac helicopters), as well as lights from backcountry users and pranksters in unexpected places.

Most published manuscripts on the Brown Mountain lights focused primarily on subjective evidence, such as myths, legends, superstitions, and anecdotal stories. However, this book presents compelling detailed objective evidence that suggests that misinterpretations are the primary driver of beliefs in the existence of supernormal, supernatural, or paranormal lights. The book should be highly informative to scientists, researchers, investigators, historians, storytellers, and those observers seeking information about the lights they have seen.

My fascination with the Brown Mountain lights began when I was a young boy growing up in the area. After retiring from a worldwide career in geology, I returned home and renewed my interest in the lights. This book is the story of my journey into those mystery lights.

Introduction

A myth is an image in terms of which we try to make sense of the world.
—Alan Watts, *The Nature of Consciousness*, 1960

It is difficult to let the truth get in the way of a good story.
—Adam Savage (Discovery Channel's *Myth Busters*), *Men's Health News*, May 15, 2013

*A man with a conviction is a hard man to change.
Tell him you disagree and he turns away.
Show him facts or figures and he questions your sources.
Appeal to logic and he fails to see your point.*
—Leon Festinger, c. 1955

*In the absence of sound science, incomplete information
can powerfully combine with the power of suggestion.
In fact, a common thread that runs through beliefs of all sorts
is our tendency to convince ourselves:
We overvalue the shreds of evidence that support our preferred outcome,
and ignore the facts we aren't looking for.*
—Michael Shermer, *The Good Men Project*, July 22, 2013

*Identity-Protective Cognition
Individuals subconsciously resist factual information
that threatens their defining values.
People don't reason to get the right answer;
instead they reason to get the answer that they want to be right.*
—Dan Kahan, Yale Law professor, 2014

The Legend of the Brown Mountain Lights

The legend of the Brown Mountain lights has inspired and intrigued local residents and countless visitors for over 100 years and today is North Carolina's most famous ghost story. The supposedly mystery lights occur as nighttime lights seen in the vicinity of Burke County's Brown Mountain in the western part of the state, which includes a vast area of undeveloped U.S. Forest Service land on one side and large areas of cities, towns, and densely populated rural areas on the other side. Every clear night throughout the year dozens of eager observers gather at one of several popular roadside overlooks in the area with the hope of catching a glimpse of the famous lights. In addition, numerous isolated residents, hunters, fishermen, campers, hikers, climbers, and other backcountry travelers in the area occasionally report close encounters with unknown lights. The desire to believe in supernatural, paranormal, or extra-normal causes is strong and each

Figure 1. Information sign at NC Highway 181 Brown Mountain Overlook. Can the reader spot the misinformation?

observer's personality and background plays a major role in how he interprets what he sees. Some people see surprise and danger or threat; some see the hand of superior intelligent beings; some see the work of man; some see the wonder of nature; and some see aliens or ghosts and spooks. Some are at a total loss to explain what they see. For those who come away inspired and seeking more evidence-based information to better understand what they saw, this book should help.

What Are the Brown Mountain Lights (BMLs)?

Yes, unknown lights in the Brown Mountain area are real. But in order to say that, we have to come up with a definition that relies solely on the observer's interpretations. Thus the following definition is based on the original observers' on-site, real-time interpretation, not subsequent or more-informed interpretations.

This is the definition of the Brown Mountain lights: Any nocturnal light seen in the vicinity of Brown Mountain, North Carolina, with an origin that is unknown to the observer. This definition is purposefully broad so as to include all sightings by everyone who has seen lights that they identified as unexplained in the area at any time in history. It is not the existence of nocturnal lights but rather the assumed or presumed unknown origin of such lights that makes the lights appear to be mysterious in the first place. Each person's sighting is real and important to them and none are dismissed as insignificant or not real by our study. Since the distinction of unknown origin is the determination of the observer, then all of the thousands of nocturnal lights visible in the area must be BMLs! Let me explain further.

Eyewitness Sightings

Every nocturnal light visible now or in the past in the area of Brown Mountain (and there are thousands, if not tens of thousands) probably has been called a mysterious unknown-origin light (in other words, a BML) by someone. Remember, we leave it up to each individual observer to label the light she saw as explained or unexplained. Over a recent three-year period, our research team has amassed a vast collection of BML eyewitness descriptions, including both recent and historical sightings. Although these descriptions are often conflicting and vary greatly in the details of what was seen, none are dismissed, even those that can now be easily identified by us or others as misinterpretations of otherwise normal lights. Certainly for many observers their sighting was not only memorable but also unique, fascinating, and in some cases even life-changing. Therefore, to include all light sightings as BMLs, the definition given above is based on the observers' characterization of the light as having an unidentified origin. However, just because a light's origin is unknown to an observer doesn't mean that light's origin is also unknown or unknowable to someone else.

The difference between an identified light and a mystery light is often the difference between an informed and experienced observer, and an uninformed, misinformed, or unsuspecting observer.

Nocturnal Lights Visible in the Brown Mountain Area

The vast array of nighttime lights actually visible in the Brown Mountain area can be classified as the following:

MAN-MADE LIGHTS (ESTIMATED TO BE 98 OUT OF EVERY 100 REPORTED MYSTERY LIGHTS)
    Vehicles (cars, trucks, buses, motorcycles, trains, etc.)
    Aircraft (airplanes, helicopters, etc.)
    Buildings (houses, offices, stores, schools, factories, etc.)
    Artificial satellites (International Space Station, communication and weather satellites)
    Outdoor lights (street, yard, airport/runway, advertising, etc.)
    Tower lights (communication and navigation, etc.)
    Traffic lights
    Backcountry traveler lights (handheld/headlamp lights, campfires, etc.)
    Practical joker lights (laser, fireworks, drones, exploding hydrogen balloons, etc.)
    Fires (forest, brush, vehicle, building, etc.)

NATURAL LIGHTS (ESTIMATED 1 OUT OF EVERY 100 REPORTED MYSTERY LIGHTS)
    Luminescent insects (blue ghost firefly, synchronous firefly, etc.)
    Celestial objects (stars, planets, moon, meteors, reflected sunlight, etc.)
    Lightning
    Moonlight reflecting off bare rock exposures (water, snow, ice)
    Forest/brush fires (lightning caused)
    Luminescent mushrooms (foxfire)

UNCLASSIFIED LIGHTS (ESTIMATED 1 OUT OF EVERY 100 REPORTED MYSTERY LIGHTS)
    Observed lights with insufficient information for classification
    The logical conclusion based on all objective evidence: no lights defying the laws of the universe exist, only man-made and natural lights misidentified by unsuspecting or unprepared observers.

Misinformation Abounds

As with other contemporary legends, misinformation is such an integral part of the legend of the BMLs that the legend would not exist without it. Supposedly supporting comments such as "the lights were seen before the days of electricity," "Humans can't be in those areas," and "manmade lights can't do what those lights did" are often based on misinformation that leads to incorrect opinions or perceptions of reality (delusions). The conclusion from our research is that without visible man-made lights, the legend of the BMLs would not exist. It is expressly the purpose of this book to identify and dispel the misinformation related to the BMLs.

Identified, Misidentified and Unclassified Lights

While misidentification of lights plays the largest role in the legend of the BMLs, observation of lights defying easy explanations also plays a role. However, the difference between an identified light and an unidentified light is often the difference between a properly informed and experienced observer and an uninformed, misinformed, or unsuspecting observer. One person's BML is another person's streetlight. One person's BML is another person's flashlight, headlamp, or communication tower light, airplane, campfire, car headlight, firefly, International Space Station, or planet, and so on. And yet, some lights defy all attempts to identify them by simple logic, reason or otherwise scholarly investigation. The lights that seem to defy explanation are generally from older reported sightings that lack sufficient details to classify the light; as a result, those light sightings are temporarily listed as unclassified until such time as their actual origin might be determined. This study's conclusion that 99 percent of the reported mystery lights are simply misidentifications of either man-made or natural lights delegates the remaining 1 percent of unclassified lights to statistical insignificance as far as the legend is concerned—i.e., the legend exists because of 99 percent of misidentified lights, not 1 percent of unclassified lights.

Historically Proposed Origins

Over the past 100 years, many published accounts have proposed various origins for the BMLs. The list includes the following:

MAN-MADE LIGHTS

City/town/residential electric lights
Vehicle lights (car/truck/bus, train/locomotive, airplane)
Fires (campfire, forest fire, brush fire, moonshine still fire)
Fireworks/gunshots/flares)
Explosions (military, construction)
Communication tower lights
Advertising lights
Navigation lights
Flashlights/headlights
Spotlights
Camera flash lights
Laser lights
Gas lantern lights
Arc welding lights
Rocket/missile/jet engine lights
Orbiting space vehicles/satellites
Hallucinations

NATURAL LIGHTS

Lightning (heat, ball, St. Elmo's Fire, Andes light, brush)
Bioluminescence (fireflies, glowworms, foxfire/mushroom fungi)
Celestial objects
Sun
Moonlight/moon bows
High atmosphere clouds (noctilucent, nacreous, iridescent, etc.)
Rocket/jet engine vapor trails
Man-made orbiting space vehicles
Rays (crepuscular, anti-crepuscular)
Zodiacal light
Planets (Jupiter, Venus, Mars, Saturn)
Stars
Meteors

Comets
Mirage lights (reflections of man-made or natural lights)
Phosphorescent vapors
Plasma lights
Earthquake lights
Telluric earth current lights
Radiation/radon gas lights
Volcano lights
Flammable gas (forest fires, natural gas, swamp/marsh gas—will-o'-the-wisp)
Light pillars (man-made or natural lights reflected by ice crystals in the atmosphere)

SUPERNATURAL/PARANORMAL
Alien lights
UFO lights
Ghost lights
Spirit lights

Such a long list of possible origins itself suggests that we're not all seeing the same kinds of lights, yet we are all calling the lights we see BMLs. Different observers are seeing different kinds of lights, which leads to so many different proposed origins. Our recent research finds that an estimated 99 percent of the supposedly mystery lights are actually man-made or natural. After extensive investigation in the area, no supernormal, supernatural or paranormal lights were found to exist.

To Know the BMLs, First Know the Observer

The level of each person's nighttime outdoor experience, overall familiarity with nature, and preference for critical thinking versus magical thinking vary greatly among observers, yet each of these plays a major role in how observers interpret what they see, and misinterpretations are often based on incorrect ideas or opinions. As expected, informed and experienced observers are much less likely to misinterpret what they see, while uninformed, misinformed, unprepared, or unsuspecting observers are more likely to misinterpret what they see. Of course the big problem lies in the fact that each person feels that he is informed, prepared and experienced enough to properly judge the source of the lights he sees. Unfortunately, that is seldom the case.

Lights Behaving Oddly

Many BML witnesses suggest that the unexpected or odd behavior of the light they saw is proof that it is not man-made. Such odd behavior generally includes the following: speed that is perceived to be too excessive for a man-made light; unexpected flood lights; single lights splitting into multiple lights; unexpected positions, locations, or timing; or changes in movement, size, brightness, or color. Thus most stationary distant lights are generally accepted as man-made (although some people strongly disagree!), while moving or changing lights are more commonly thought to be mysterious. "No human beings are in that area," "no manmade light acts like that," or "no manmade light can do what that light did" are oft-repeated statements in support of mysterious origins. But since the determination of odd behavior is heavily dependent on the experience or knowledge of the observer or both, as well as being greatly influenced by the observer's impaired nighttime vision, especially the usual loss of distance and size perceptions, we must ask whether behaving oddly is a valid criterion for making a judgment that the phenomenon is man-made or not. Caution is advised, especially given the sometimes extremely odd or unexpected behavior of some known man-made lights. Consider for example, the remarkable light spiral seen in the sky over Norway one night in 2009 that frightened thousands of people for days until the actual source was revealed. It turned out the unexpected light was a Russian missile spiraling out of control 1,000 miles off the coast of Norway, not an alien spaceship arriving through a worm hole to destroy the earth beginning with Norway, as many frighten residents thought. Man-made lights can and sometimes do behave in ways totally unexpected by most observers. In the Brown Mountain area itself verified yet unexpected sources of man-made lights regularly misidentified as mysterious include military airplanes practicing low-level nighttime flight training; medevac helicopters heading to or from the hospital in Lenoir; ATVs, hikers, and other backcountry users on maintained trails; isolated wilderness travelers; and yes, even pranksters.

Thus it turns out that visual clues alone often aren't enough for most observers to properly distinguish between a man-made light and a non–man-made light.

The Age of Reason Has Arrived for the Legend of the BMLs

Misidentification of nocturnal lights is a common human failing that leads to faulty beliefs, which is why not all beliefs about the BMLs are based on empirical truths. Unfortunately, the uninformed or misinformed among us are often doomed to reach unrealistic beliefs. While the scientific method (i.e., the application of reason, logic, and scholarly review of empirical evidence) is only one of man's many ways of acquiring knowledge, it is the best one we have since it is the most likely to consistently lead to correct identifications and thus result in the correct understanding of reality. This book leans heavily on what science tells us about the BMLs.

Did you know that under ideal conditions, a human being with good eyesight should be able to see a single candle flame at night as far as 30 miles away? This amazing fact is not fully appreciated by most people. But now consider that a standard household 60-watt light bulb puts out 800 candlepower and you begin to understand how distant man-made lights can play such a big role in the legend of the Brown Mountain lights!

Just like the paleontologist who meticulously reconstructs bone by bone a newly found skeleton of a previously unknown animal, the evidence-based researcher conducting a proper investigation of the BMLs starts at the beginning, determines when the legend began, follows it throughout its history to see how it has changed over time, establishes what is known by documenting what man-made and natural nocturnal lights actually do exist in the area, attempts to classify and identify all lights she and others have seen, and conducts exercises such as staged light tests and photography to confirm their findings. In this manner, during 2012, 2013, and 2014, our team conducted the most comprehensive and informative scholarly research ever undertaken on the BMLs.

Preconceived Ideas

What should we do when objective facts don't support our preconceived ideas? Change those beliefs! In his 2011 book, *The Believing Brain,* the world-renowned researcher into human beliefs, Dr. Michael Shermer, writes, "Beliefs come first; explanations for beliefs follow. Most humans live in a 'belief-dependent realism' of their own making. How can we tell the difference between what we would like to be true and what is actually true? The answer is science." Has our Brown Mountain lights research team done enough investigation to reach meaningful conclusions about the legend? Yes, we certainly have collected enough data to conclude that there is no significant empirical support for the existence of lights defying the laws of the universe in the Brown Mountain area. But of course this does not totally rule out the possibility that lights currently unknown to science actually do exist in the Brown Mountain area or somewhere else on earth, for that matter. However, our research has found that by far the vast majority of people who think they have seen such mystery lights in the Brown Mountain area are mistaken. Therefore, the legend of the Brown Mountain lights is more of a social science phenomenon than it is an earth science phenomenon.

A Complex Undertaking

In order to be successful, any investigation of the BMLs must involve elements of many different fields of study such as geology, astronomy, physics, biology, medicine, history, sociology, psychology, anthropology, neuroscience, philosophy, and the like—in other words, the study of life itself! It is probably the enormity and complexity of the issue that explains why man has not previously settled the question of the BMLs. However, the legend has already survived many past investigations that suggested misinterpretation of man-made lights, including the monumental 1922 study by the United States Geological Survey. The legend will probably survive the current investigations as well.

The Beginnings of the Legend

The legend is well entrenched in the imagination of modern people, especially local residents. However, most observed lights, including the very first ones reported in the late 1800s and early 1900s, were probably some form of normal but unexpected man-made lights. Regardless of what is often reported in the published BML literature, the lights themselves have been observed only since modern man first introduced electric lights to the area. After extensive research, we have found no evidence that any lights were seen or reported before the days of electricity in the area.

Specifically, no mystery lights were seen before 1858, when the first train in western North Carolina began regular operation including nightly runs in the area. Yet even then this single train headlight didn't receive much attention for the next 40 years until local residents started seeing multiple, long-lasting lights shining simultaneously—which happened immediately following the arrival and spread of city, town and rural electricity throughout the populated areas to the south and east of Brown Mountain in the 1890s. Nocturnal lights in the area were not previously reported by Native Americans or early settlers, as is often incorrectly mentioned in much of the published BML literature (see Chapter 3).

Although the arrival of the first train in western North Carolina in 1858 apparently resulted in the earliest authentic reports of an unexpected distant light (see Chapter 5), only a few individuals took notice until the early 1900s, after electricity had spread throughout the valleys to the south and east of Brown Mountain. The first commercial electricity in western North Carolina arrived in Hickory in 1888 and by 1900 had advanced throughout the adjacent populated areas of the Catawba River Valley. The actual legend of the BMLs originated between c. 1897 and c. 1912, starting with reports of recurring short flashes of a single light seen at the same place and approximately the same time each night (train headlight), followed later by sightings of multiple, long-lived lights seen all night long (town, city and rural electric lights). The first written accounts were newspaper articles that carried the story to the general public in 1912.

It is this remarkable and irrefutable coincidence between the arrival of electricity in the area and the first widespread reports of supposed unexplained lights that constitutes the single most important fact in understanding how the legend of the Brown Mountain lights began. Such a positive correlation strongly suggests that the two are related. In addition, the fact that no other significant source of light emissions has ever been found to explain the reported lights further supports misinterpretations of man-made lights as the basis for the origin of the legend. Remarkably, Jules Verne, the most widely read novelist in the world at the time, may have also played a significant role in the origin of the legend.

Did Jules Verne Inspire the Legend of the Brown Mountain Lights?

Jules Verne's 1886 novel, *Robur le Conquerant* (published in French in 1886 and in English in 1887), with its unique cigar-shaped airship sailing around the world with kidnapped citizens is credited with initiating mankind's modern UFO scares. Observers in places throughout the world visited by the fictional Robur started reporting strange objects in the sky in the 1890s (Miller, 2013). Similarly, the 1911 English version of Verne's 1904 French novel, *Master of the World*, may have actually inspired the early reports of mystery lights in the Brown Mountain area. The novel was a sequel to Verne's 1886 book and included a cigar-shaped, lighted and mysterious airship/balloon/boat/submarine/car built by the mad scientist Robur in a secret inaccessible basin atop a rocky mountain summit north of Morganton, North Carolina. The fictional story included sightings of mystery lights and reports of loud noises coming from the mountain—later determined to be Robur testing his new mystery vehicle and burning his previous prototypes and his no-longer-needed secret workshop atop the mountain. The English version of *Master of the World* came out in 1911, only one year before the first published accounts of mysterious Brown Mountain lights began appearing in local newspapers. So the question arises: "Did Verne's novel inspire the legend, or did the legend inspire the novel?" Jules Verne having never visited North Carolina, and writing before anything had ever been published about the BMLs, it seems highly unlikely that he could have learned much, if anything, about the BML legend before 1904 when the French version of his book was first published. However, it is quite possible that Verne or his heavily involved editor had read one or more of the several 1800s adventure travelogues (see Chapter 3) describing the unique isolated mountain scenery of Linville Gorge and chose Table Rock (in the book renamed the Great Eyry) as the awe-inspiring rocky summit of the opening story in Verne's fictional book. Within one year of the English publication of the book, the local mountain residents began referring to the now recently visible man-made electric city lights seen over the top of nearby Brown Mountain as mysterious—and the legend was born.

Jules Verne, with his science fiction adventure stories of the mid to late 1800s, became the most-read author of the time and probably helped set the stage for the public's fascination with mystery lights. The possibility that his novel *Master of the World* actually inspired the beginnings of the legend of the Brown Mountain lights seems likely.

The Legend Was Firmly Established by 1922

The legend was firmly established by 1922, and based on the published descriptions of the time the supposed mystery lights were described as "unknown distant lights visible to the east over the top of Brown Mountain when viewed from observation sites in the higher mountains to the west and northwest." Keys to this description are the phrases "unknown distant lights" and "observation sites in the higher mountains to the west and northwest." Note that close encounters with mystery lights in the woods were not part of the original legend, although extensive logging on and around Brown Mountain was going on at the time. Thousands of loggers worked and camped in the area, yet they reported no close encounters with mystery lights. Only in more modern times have people reported close encounters with unknown lights deep in the forests.

The fact that practically no mystery lights have ever been reported from equally high observation sites in similar mountains to the northeast, east, southeast and south of Brown Mountain is also informative in understanding the origin of the legend. For the first time ever, this book addresses this obvious bias of observation sites and offers a possible explanation that further supports the suggestion of misinterpretation of city and town lights as the primary source of the BMLs (see Chapter 12).

Remarkably, most published descriptions of unknown-light sightings before 1922 do not include mention of the actual existence of any known lights at the same time; they speak only of supposed mystery lights being visible. Yet, based on non–BML published documents of the time, lights from town, city, and rural sources were clearly visible well before 1922 over the top of Brown Mountain from the popular mystery-light observation sites. Apparently the vast majority of the early-day observers mistook the newly visible distant man-made lights for mysterious unknown lights. Yes, the legend of the Brown Mountain lights first became established during the 15-year period between 1897 and 1912 (first published accounts) and was apparently due to sightings by unsuspecting and uninformed observers of distant electric lights, including moving lights from trains and automobiles. Although unpopular with local residents, this evidence-based explanation has withstood the test of time and numerous subsequent investigations, including the investigations that generated this book.

Sightings in the early 1900s of the newly appeared distant lights over the top of Brown Mountain greatly unnerved and concerned the local residents and visitors—just as the fictional mad-scientist Robur's airship/balloon/boat/submarine/car lights caused great fear among the mountain residents near Morganton, North Carolina, in the opening chapter of Jules Verne's 1911 novel. However, the locals and visitors seeing real multiple lights over the top of Brown Mountain twice called on North Carolina's politicians between 1912 and 1922 to "do something about these mystery lights." It was the recent arrival and ever-increasing number of these lights at the time that so concerned the local residents. These were not lights that had been seen in earlier times. Twice the concern was transmitted to Congress, which subsequently requested that the U.S. Geological Survey send geologists to the area to investigate. The Geological Survey's first investigation in 1913 was conducted by the high-ranking geologist D.B. Sterrett, who visited Brown

Mountain and found nothing but a distant locomotive headlight. This was unacceptable as an explanation to the local residents, and in response to their continued urgent requests the process was repeated in 1922 with the highly experienced geologist George Rogers Mansfield's two-week detailed field investigation, which concluded man-made lights accounted for 90 percent and brush fires accounted for the remaining 10 percent of those distant lights pointed out to him at the time by the same local resident witnesses who were most responsible for reporting the mystery lights in the first place. Mansfield's conclusions dealt a major but nonfatal blow to the legend (see Chapter 7).

The Morphing of the Legend

Over time, as modern man's electric light pollution progressively increased in the ever-expanding populations in the valleys south and east of Brown Mountain (i.e., the lights from Hickory, Lenoir, Valdese, Drexel, Connelly Springs, Rutherford College, and the like), the legend morphed, or changed, from the initial reports of a single unknown light seen temporally at the same time and place every night (probably the headlight of a distant train rounding curves on its nightly run) to sightings of multiple, continuously shining distant lights seen together over a widespread area all night long throughout the year (almost certainly town, city, and rural lights). As even more time passed and it became even more obvious to more people that the distant lights were man-made, the legend morphed again to focus on less easily dismissed lights, such as those in the sky (airplanes, celestial bodies, and reflected sunlight on man-made satellites), those on the unpopulated west side of Brown Mountain (backcountry users), and those more recently being seen in nearby Linville Gorge (also backcountry users). Today, the amorphous legend even includes close encounters with nighttime lights seen throughout the area. Note that these close-encounter, Linville Gorge and high-in-the-sky versions of light sightings were not part of the original legend. The legend has morphed over time as the types and uses of man-made lights have changed and developed. In addition, misidentification of natural lights, such as those of the blue ghost firefly (see Chapter 15), have become more common as modern man has become less familiar with the outdoors.

Today, for many people, the focus of mystery-light sightings is Linville Gorge rather than Brown Mountain. This rugged river gorge lies seven to nine miles west of Brown Mountain. While the gorge is more isolated, it certainly is not impenetrable and the greatly increased number of light sightings within the gorge, which started in the early 1950s, probably reflects the equally increased backcountry use by humans as well as the arrival of more-powerful handheld lights.

Some mystery lights are also reported in areas even further from Brown Mountain or Linville Gorge. Supposed mystery lights seen from the Lost Cove Cliffs overlook on the Blue Ridge Parkway, those seen in the North Cove Valley of McDowell County, unexpected lights on Lake James, and others seen in the Wilson Creek Valley of Caldwell County are also reported to be BMLs, although Brown Mountain itself is not even visible from those places. It seems anyone who sees an unknown light anywhere within 25 miles of Brown Mountain calls it a BML, whether it is accepted by others as a BML or not. Actually, since there are no universally accepted descriptions of the BMLs, any light qualifies if the observer chooses to say it does.

In this book, we will explore the research, conclusions and sources of the lights attributed to the Brown Mountain light legend. We will review the sources of man-made lights, including the plethora of backcountry recreation usage in the area, as well as man-made aerial sources (planes, helicopters, satellites). We will also look into natural sources of lights, including the elusive blue ghost firefly, flammable gases and celestial bodies.

Some light sightings remain unclassified; however, unclassified does not prove or even suggest supernormal or paranormal, and these unclassified sightings represent far less than an estimated 1 percent of the total sightings (see Chapter 20). Some unclassified light sightings include close encounters, but note that the original legend of the Brown Mountain lights did not include stories of close encounters with mystery lights of any kind—even though thousands of loggers lived and worked in the Brown Mountain area in the early 1900s when the legend first started. However personally intriguing these unclassified sightings are, they are statistically insignificant to the original legend of the BMLs.

If any science-defying lights exist in the Brown Mountain area, they might occur within our estimated 1 percent of unclassified lights, i.e., if seen by anyone, they could not have been seen by more than 1 percent of the people reporting observations of BMLs. This book is mostly concerned with the estimated 99 percent of reported sightings that historically explain the legend of the BMLs and that come with sufficient information to allow logical investigation.

Published Misinformation

Unfortunately, most of the published BML literature is a confusing collection of stories where misinformation abounds and separating fact from fiction is practically impossible, as few authors actually checked the validity of their information, much less included references from which they took their information (see Appendix C). I call these campfire stories. For instance, the first published reference to mystery light sightings by Native Americans in the Brown Mountain area appeared in H. McAfee's 1938 newspaper article—an apparent attempt to discredit the U.S. Geological Survey's monumental 1922 investigation, which found only man-made lights. However, McAfee neglected to properly reference the source of the information, as did the countless later authors who retold the same story, often with their own added embellishments. Today we know that there is no authentic report of light sightings by Native Americans or anyone else before the introduction of electricity into the area.

The resultant collection of BML literature has thus become less informative over time and today often presents a surprisingly nonprofessional collection of misinformation where unsupported, and even wild, speculation abounds. My comprehensive review of the BML literature can be found in the Annotated Chronological List of Selected References (Appendix C).

Photography by the Author

Unless noted otherwise, photographs in this book were taken by the author with a tripod-mounted DSLR Canon EOS REBEL T3i camera with an 18 megapixel CMOS APS-C sensor (22.3 mm × 14.9 mm and 1.62 crop factor). The individual lenses used, their focal lengths, effective focal lengths, and approximate magnifications, along with the adjustable camera settings used for each exposure are given in the captions below each image. Effective focal lengths and approximate magnifications of each exposure are calculations based on the following formulas:

Effective Focal Length= (focal length of lens)
multiplied by (crop factor of digital sensor);
Approximate Magnification = (Effective Focal Length)
divided by (50); expressed by: X.

The digital sensor crop factor and the number -50- used in these formulas are based on the photographic industry's standard 50 mm focal length lenses previously used on 35 mm film cameras, which gave a field of view of the final image matched by the human eye. Approximate magnifications, expressed, for example, as 2X (two times enlarged), 10X (ten times enlarged), 50X (50 times enlarged), etc., are equivalent to similar designations found on binoculars and telescopes. Annotations on all Ed Speer images are by the author.

Photography by Appalachian State University

Many photographs in this book were taken by two stationary remote-controlled, meteor-hunting cameras that captured time-lapse images throughout each night. The two cameras were installed and operated by astrophysicist Dr. Daniel Caton of the Department of Physics and Astronomy at Appalachian State University (Boone, North Carolina). One camera (BML Cam1) is stationed at a private residence on Jonas Ridge and overlooks Brown Mountain, 7 miles to the east. The second camera (BML Cam2) is positioned at another private residence near the mouth of Linville Gorge and looks upstream encompassing the lower half of the gorge. Each camera takes up to several thousand time-lapse still images each night, which are then compiled into short videos of each nightly run and posted to the Internet (YouTube) for the public to view. Selected individual time-lapse images from these cameras, with annotations by the author, are included in this report. As of December 31, 2014, more than 575,000 time-lapse images representing more than 6,360 hours of nightly observing between 2012 and 2015 were reviewed by the author. During 2015, another one million images were produced but were not reviewed in detail by the author; however, no obvious mystery lights have been observed in any of the images.

Both of Dr. Caton's meteor cameras were built by SBIG Astronomical Instruments (model ST-402ME, 0.39 megapixels) and contain 8.1 mm-diagonal CCD digital sensors (6.9 mm X 4.3 mm) with 5.5 crop factor. Lenses used on the cameras follow below:

1. BML Cam1
    Lens 1—Arecont Vision 4.5–12 mm zoom, ½", f/1.4, 12Feb13–13May13
    Lens 2—Arecont Vision 12–40 mm zoom, ½", f/1.8, since 14May13–31Dec14
2. BML Cam2
    Lens 1—Never used
    Lens 2—Arecont Vision 4.5–12 mm zoom, ½", f/1.4, since 16Oct13–31Dec14

Annotations on all BML Cam1 or Cam2 images are by the author.

Disclaimer

While assisted by team members and volunteers who contributed over 3,000 man hours of time during this investigation, the conclusions herein are the author's alone and do not necessary reflect the opinions of everyone on the research team. The author takes full responsibility for the accuracy and truthfulness of the evidence and interpretations presented in this book.

CHAPTER 1

The Research Team, Methods Used and Data Collected

> In science, you move closer to the truth
> by seeking evidence to the contrary.
> —David McRaney

> Imagination alone is not enough,
> because the reality of nature is far more wondrous
> than anything we can imagine.
> This adventure (into the Cosmos) is made possible by generations
> of searchers strictly adhering to a simple set of rules:
> Test ideas by experiment and observations.
> Build on those ideas that pass the test.
> Reject the ones that fail.
> Follow the evidence wherever it leads; and
> Question everything.
> Accept these terms and the Cosmos is yours.
> —Neil deGrasse Tyson,
> Astrophysicist and Director of Hayden Planetarium at the
> American Museum of Natural History
> "COMOS: A Space Time Odyssey,
> Standing Up in the Milky Way," March 9, 2014

The concept of a Brown Mountain lights research team composed of scientists, outdoor enthusiasts, local residents and eyewitnesses was proposed by geologist Alex Glover after attending the first Brown Mountain Lights Symposium in Morganton, North Carolina, in February 2012. The symposium was sponsored by Burke County's Tourism Development Authority. This well-attended event sparked a lively debate between proponents of evidence-based and belief-based explanations for the mysterious lights. Glover left the symposium convinced that a full-scale scientific investigation, involving many different fields of study, could help shed light on the legend. He immediately consulted with several other geologists of his acquaintance, including the author. Beginning in April 2012, we amassed a diverse team of other scientists, area residents, naturalists, outdoor instructors, adventurers and eyewitnesses. Everyone invited to join the loosely knit team was welcome to participate in the ambitious research project and to share their knowledge and experience. Some team members participated for only short times and new members often joined the team.

Our first order of business was to place a camera overlooking Brown Mountain with the hope of documenting unexplained lights that could subsequently be investigated. Dr.

Dan Caton, astronomer at Appalachian State University, eagerly joined our team and agreed to pursue installation of the camera, a project already planned as part of his ongoing BML research (Dr. Caton's academic interest in the BMLs had begun in 1998). The first camera, BML Cam1, was installed in November 2012 on a rooftop of a house in the community of Gingercake Acres on Jonas Ridge, approximately seven miles northwest of Brown Mountain. BML Cam2 was installed adjacent to a house near the south end of Linville Gorge on October 20, 2013.

BML Cam1 and Cam2 each record short time exposures that are then compiled into time-lapse, entire-night videos and posted on the Internet (to find: search YouTube for *Caton Brown Mountain Lights Camera 1, or Camera 2*). As of December 31, 2014, more than 6,360 hours of nighttime photography producing more than 575,000 time-lapse images have been recorded and several unexpected lights have been detected, which upon later investigation turned out to be vehicle headlights, airplanes, helicopters, fireworks, hikers or campers.

In addition to the nightly videos, our team has amassed over 3,000 total man hours of investigative time since February 2012. Our investigation has involved elements of many disciplines, including folklore, philosophy, geology, physics, biology, astronomy, medicine, history, sociology, and psychology. Our research methods included:

- Direct field observations
- Staged light tests, often radio-assisted
- Field photography (still, video, telephoto, time-lapse)
- Telescope observation and photography
- Literature research
- Identification of individual lights
- Personal interviews and anecdotal stories
- Geological research
- Biological research

Members of the BML Research Team

Never before has such an experienced, knowledgeable, and diverse group of investigators come together and worked so long and so hard on the mystery of the BMLs. In addition to the author, some of the individual BML research team members are listed below. The conclusions presented in this book are those of the author and may not reflect those of all team members.

Mike Fischesser is the BML research team leader. He is also an Eagle Scout; Instructor and Program Director, NC Outward Bound School; Director, O.B. USA National Training Institute; Fellow and Life Member National Speleological Society; Life Member American Alpine Club; Safety Committee Chair NSS; Founder of the American Adventure Service Corps. He makes his home in Jonas Ridge, NC.

Alex Glover has B.S. in geology and is a professional geologist; director of Mining and Mineral Resources, Active Minerals International, LLC; GSA Fellow; chairman of the Carolina's Section of the Society of Mining Engineers; past president of the NC Mining Association; past president of the Carolina Geological Society, past commissioner of the NC Mining Commission, and past vice chair of the NC Geology Licensing Board. He lives in Little Switzerland, NC.

Dan Caton holds a PhD in astronomy and is a professor and director of Observatories, Department of Physics and Astronomy, Appalachian State University. His home is in Boone, NC.

Lee Hawkins, MS, Applied Physics, is an observatory engineer, Department of Physics and Astronomy, Appalachian State University. He is from Boone, NC.

Cato Holler, Jr., DDS, is a Fellow of the National Speleological Society; founder and director of the NC Cave Survey; Founder of the Flittermouse Grotto; Fellow of the Explorers Club, Academy of Magical Arts, International Brotherhood of Magicians. He lives in Marion, NC.

Chris Holler is the owner of Armstrong Creek Private Fishing Preserve and is a fish and wildlife biologist, and a former USFS Wilderness Ranger for Linville Gorge. His home is in Marion, NC.

Sam Rowe is retired from the Wisconsin Historical Society, Library Division, Micro Imaging Lab, and was present during construction of Roses' Tower. He is a former producer and director of radio, TV and Film. He makes his home in Madison, WS.

Ron Swofford is a retired professor of English, campus provost, and academic dean for Georgia Perimeter College and lives in Athens, GA.

Steve Woody is from Morganton, NC.

Contributing and Temporary Guests and Volunteers

Alex Glass, PhD, Lecturer and Director of Undergraduate Studies, Division of Earth and Ocean Sciences, Nicholas School of the Environment, Duke University. His home is in Durham, NC.

John Maddry, MS in Geology, Professional Geologist, Consultant. He is from Rutherfordton, NC.

Benita Soper, Home School Instructor, lives in Morganton, NC.

Will Soper, TAASC, lives in Morganton, NC.

The American Adventure Service Corps (TAASC), fostering youth leadership through outdoor adventure education and service to others, is located in Morganton, NC.

Clyde Hollifield is a resident of NC.

Henry Cantrell (NC).

Annette Farah, graduate student, Department of Physics and Astronomy, Appalachian State University (Boone, NC).

Lauren Pandolfi, graduate student, Department of Physics and Astronomy, Appalachian State University (Boone, NC).

Art Larson, Consulting Geophysicist (Evergreen, CO).

Record Your Own Observations

To assist future researchers, observers are encouraged to use the "Sighting Report Form" compiled by the author (see Appendix B). The report form suggests recording information critical for scientific review but often missing from anecdotal accounts. Information such as the exact date, time, and azimuth of observed light(s) are often overlooked by the excited observer or quickly forgotten as time passes. Yet it is precisely this type of objective information that is most critical in identifying exactly what the observed light might have been.

The Light Sighting Report Form also includes diagrams of annotated panoramas for the two most popular observation sites—Wiseman's View on NC Highway Old 105 and the Brown Mountain overlook on NC Highway 181. These diagrams give observers a better understanding of what they are seeing in the distance and allow for fairly accurate plotting of the locations of all lights seen. In addition, the diagrams provide a means for determining the approximate azimuth of observed lights, which will greatly assist future researchers. Completed report forms should be shared with future researchers.

BML Research by the Author

While the members of the BML research team worked together to collect and record information, each member was also encouraged to work independently and to share all information they collected with the rest of the team. The author alone has accumulated a vast amount of research on the BMLs (see Appendix A).

As of December 31, 2014, the author has participated in more than 93 individual expeditions while researching the BMLs, including observational and photographic visits to the popular viewing sites, library visits, meetings, hikes and campouts on Brown Mountain itself. In addition, he has taken more than 3,600 photographs of lights, landscapes, man-made structures, fireflies, and rare documents related to the BMLs. He has written nearly 700 pages of progress reports and communicated in thousands of e-mails with his fellow team members related to the research. He has compiled an extensive annotated chronological list of selected references of the history of the BMLs, reviewing published and unpublished documents, making it the most comprehensive literature review ever undertaken (Appendix C). The author's personal review of nightly video recordings from the two research cameras includes more than 575,000 individual time-lapse images representing more than 6,360 hours of observation conducted during 758 separate nights between 2012 and 2015. In November 2012, the author began the only science-based BMLs Blog on the Internet at www.brownmountainlights.blogspot.com.

Appendix A summarizes the expeditions, photographs, identified lights, and prominent landmarks and features documented by the author during this study.

Chapter 2

Historical Overview of the BML Phenomenon

The legend began immediately following the arrival of electricity in the area and less than one year following the 1911 English publication of Jules Verne's novel *Master of the World*, which included a fictional account of sudden unexpected mystery lights seen atop a mountain north of Morganton, North Carolina.

Based on a review of more than 325 published and unpublished documents, the 12 most significant, best-documented, and most-popular Brown Mountain light stories are listed below and covered in greater detail elsewhere in this book.

1. Sightings Before the Days of Electricity (Chapter 3)

Unconfirmed reports of sightings by Cherokee and Catawba Indians, AD 800 or AD 1200.

Incorrect report of sightings by De Brahm, 1771.

2. c. 1858: Fate Wiseman Sighting (Chapter 5)

First authentic reported sighting of a mystery light over Brown Mountain.

Distant single light seen repeatedly at the same place and approximate time each night from Wiseman's View.

3. 1897–1922: Sightings from Cold Springs—Birth of the Legend (Chapter 5)

Numerous distant lights visible above Brown Mountain and seen all night long.

A single light visible briefly at same time and place every night.

Jules Vern's 1912 novel, *Master of the World*, with fictional account of mystery lights that might have started the BML legend.

The legend of the BMLs based on these sightings was well established by 1922.

4. 1912: First Published Report of BMLs (Chapter 5)

R.T. Claywell's February 14, 1912, story (*Winston-Salem Western Sentinel*).

Distant mystery lights seen over the top of Brown Mountain.

5. 1913 and 1922: U.S. Geological Survey investigations (Chapter 7)

Sterrett's 1913 locomotive headlight.

Mansfield's 1922 multiple stationary and moving distant lights visible over top of Brown Mountain (90 percent electric lights—town, autos and locomotives; 10 percent brush fires).

6. 1916: Catawba River Flood (Chapter 6)

Multiple lights still visible after flood washed away roads and railroads.
Roads and RR tracks washed out along streams, but not everywhere else.

7. 1916: H.C. Martin and Dr. L.H. Coffey Encounters (Chapter 6)
The best documented and most authentic close encounter story of the time.
Multiple lights at a time briefly visible in the woods on Brown and Adams mountains—moving through the trees on sides of the mountains.

8. 1929–1958: Early Photographs of Brown Mountain Lights (Chapter 8)
1929 E.M. Ball photograph.
1958 Bob Brown photographs.

9. 1962: Close Encounters on Brown Mountain (Chapters 9 and 10)
Paul Rose's tower—close encounters w/ multiple lights visible in trees and brush.
Ralph Lael's alien encounters—close encounters with multiple lights in trees.

10. Morphing of the Legend (Chapter 19)
Various versions of the legend existed over time.
Current version drastically different from original version.

11. Linville Gorge Lights (Chapter 19)
Distant and proximal lights visible within the confines of Linville Gorge.

12. Unclassified Lights (Chapter 20)
Numerous people see mysterious lights during remarkable and highly memorable events.

A light unknown to an observer doesn't mean that same light is unknown to others.

Most observers do not record sufficient information for proper identification of what was seen.

Brown Mountain Lights Time Line

The chronological history given below summarizes the significant developments of the Brown Mountain lights legend. The time line is based on exhaustive literature research. Each development in the history of the legend is covered in greater detail throughout this book.

Brown Mountain Lights Time Line

c. 1858 Lafayette Wiseman camped at Wiseman's View and reportedly saw the first mystery light (not reported until 1961).
1858 First Western NC railroad began operation in Catawba River Valley.
1882 Mystery lights reportedly seen by J. Stokes Penland of Linville Falls, NC (reported in 1927 based on 1922 personal communication).
1888 Western NC's first electricity—Hickory, NC; spread throughout Catawba Valley during 1890s.
1897 Mystery light reportedly first seen by Joseph Loven at Cold Springs, NC (reported in 1912).

1904 Publication of Jules Verne's novel *Master of the World* in French; fictional account of mystery lights north of Morganton, NC.
1908–9 Mystery light reportedly seen by B.S. Gaither (reported in 1912).
1910 The Rev. C.E. Gregory built cottage near Cold Springs, NC, and reportedly saw mystery light (reported in 1912).
1911 Mystery light reportedly seen by numerous members of the Morganton Fishing Club (reported in 1912).
1911 English publication of Jules Verne's *Master of the World* with fictional account of mystery lights on mountain north of Morganton.
1912 (February) First published account of BMLs; Light seen in Catawba Valley over top of Brown Mountain.
1913 (October) USGS geologist D.B. Sterrett visit—light attributed to locomotive headlight.
1915 Dr. C.L. Wilson saw lights of Joy, Lenoir, Connelly Springs, and Rutherford College from Cold Springs, NC.
1916 (April) H.C. Martin's camping parties see lights from Adams and Brown mountains—dismissed by Mansfield in 1922 as fireflies.
1916 (July) Historic flood, when Catawba River reached +25' above flood level.
1916 Joseph Loven and Lafayette Wiseman reportedly saw mystery lights immediately after the flood.
1917 C.H. Hite publishes first story of ghosts on Brown Mountain (Bird Carroll story).
1919 U.S. Weather Bureau and Smithsonian Institution issue brush lightning statement.
1921 National Geographic Society Bulletin—light attributed to brush lightning, similar to St. Elmo's fire and Andes light.
1922 USGS geologist G.R. Mansfield research—attributed 90 percent to electric lights and 10 percent to brush fires.
1927 R.K. Babington publishes first reference to De Brahm's 1771 document of nitrous vapors.
1928 J.B. Derieux and A.A. Dixon, NC State College—binocular and transit study—saw Hudson town lights.
1929 E.M. Ball—first BML photo—4-hr. exposure, moon streak and lights seen above crest of Brown Mountain.
1932 F.D. Ruggles reported 100s of lights like city street lights but concluded they were burning gasses.
1936 S.M. Dugger publishes first legend of a murdered wife, which was repeated many times later.
1938 H. McAfee publishes first legend of Indian maidens searching for their braves lost in battle, a story repeated often.
1940 H.A. Whitman's research: transit triangulation and BML photo—attributed to reflected city lights.
1941 W.J. Humpheries and H. Lyman (U.S. Weather Bureau) report—attributed to Andes light.
1948 First published story of lost lover legend—repeated many times later.
1958 Bob Brown—BML photos—attributed to reflected city lights.
1959 N. Alexander publishes first report of a swamp atop Brown Mountain, a report repeated many times.

1961 S. Wiseman publishes first reference to legend of faithful slave searching for lost master.
1962 P. Rose's (tower construction) and R. Lael's (alien abduction) close encounters on Brown Mountain.
1962 S. Rowe and C. Holler, Jr.—transit survey and site visits—attributed to refracted city lights.
1965 R. Lael publishes first stories of aliens, alien abduction, and close encounters between June and October 1962.
1968 H. Bailey first published reference to UFOs flying over Brown Mountain.
1977 ORION's 500,000 candlepower light test in Lenoir (22 miles away)—seen at Wiseman's View.
1980 First published mention of sighting of lights in Linville Gorge—not published until 1995.
1981 ORION detonated dynamite atop BM—two possible lights produced??
1982 First published legend of Revolutionary War solider searching for missing family.
1995 LEMUR begins 15-year investigation of BMLs.
1998 Dr. D. Caton, astronomer at Appalachian State University, begins long-term investigation of legend.
1999 LEMUR—*The X-Files* TV show—aired May 9, 1999.
2000 November—LEMUR—Brian Irish's video of suspected BMLs.
2002 March—LEMUR—Travel Channel segment on BMLs.
2003 Dr. Greg Little of *Alternate Perceptions* magazine videotaped BMLs.
2004 LEMUR reported plasma lights from natural capacitor producing electromagnetic energy.
2006 First BML Heritage Festival hosted by Linville Falls, June 9, 10, 11.
2009 LEMUR—Dean Warsing's night vision video of BMLs.
2012 First and Second Brown Mountain Light Symposiums, Morganton, NC; Burke County Tourism Development Authority.
2012 S. Nicholson published first reference to ghosts of Civil War soldiers.
2012 BMLs research team—BML Cam1 installed November 28, staged light tests, telephoto photography, and literature research.
2012 November—BML research team's E. Speer sets up BMLs blog.
2013 BMLs research team BML Cam2 installed October 20 at south end of Linville Gorge; staged light tests; photography.
2014 BMLs research team—Staged light tests; BML Cam1 and Cam2 operating.
2015 BMLs research team—BML Cam1 and Cam2 operating. More than +1.6 million photographs with no mystery lights seen.

Chapter 3

Lack of Sightings Before Electricity

> First they ignore you
> then they laugh at you
> then they fight you
> then you win
> —Unknown

> All truth passes through three stages.
> First, it is ridiculed.
> Second, it is violently opposed.
> Third, it is accepted as being self-evident.
> —Unknown

Lack of Sightings by Native Americans Before 1800

Although mistakenly mentioned in much of the published BML literature, the BMLs were not seen by Native Americans or anyone else before the arrival of electric lights in the area, which happened in the late 19th and early 20th centuries. While many published authors claim that the lights were seen before the days of electricity, not a single author adequately documents where that information comes from, a serious omission that raises concerns about the authors' integrity and leaves the questioning scholar unconvinced. Our extensive review of Native American and early pioneer history of the area finds no support for sightings of mysterious nighttime lights in the area until the mid and late 1800s.

Not a single authentic Native American history document can be found that mentions the BMLs! This lack of sightings by Native Americans is supported by the following scholars and published documents that fail to mention Native American sightings of BMLs before the 19th century:

de la Bandera, J., 1569, *The Bandera Document; Proceeding of the Account Which Captain Juan Pardo Gave of the Entrance Which He Made into the Land of the Floridas.*

Mooney, J., 1891, *The Sacred Formulas of the Cherokees.*

Mooney, J., 1900, *Myths of the Cherokee.*

Mansfield, G.R., 1922, *Origin of the Brown Mountain Light in North Carolina.*

Brown, F.C., 1964, "Brown Mountain Lights," in *Monumental Folklore of NC*
("The Lights seem to have been noticed only after the neighboring towns had developed to a certain size with a certain amount of electric illumination.")

Phifer, W.W., Jr., 1982, *Burke—The History of a North Carolina County; 1777-1920.* none

Clark, L.R., 2003, *Indians of Burke County and Western North Carolina.* none

Dunning, B., 2010, *The Brown Mountain Lights: What's the Explanation?*
"I was unable to find any reference to such a belief outside of publications about the Brown Mountain Lights."

Whyte, T., 2013, professor of anthropology, Appalachian State University
"*The legends involving Cherokee or Catawba references to the lights were recently invented by white people in an attempt to legitimize their own beliefs. I have not been able to find any historically validated references to the lights in Indian myth*" (August 1, 2013, e-mail response).

Burgin, B., 2013, director of Archives for Native American Studies, University of South Carolina–Lancaster
"*To my knowledge there are no Catawba stories regarding the Brown Mountain Lights*" (July 30, 2013, e-mail response).

The first published reference to Native American sightings of BMLs calls on the spirits of Indian maidens searching for their dead loved ones following an epic battle on Brown Mountain. This story is first found in H. McAfee's newspaper article in the June 5, 1938, issue of the *Asheville Citizen*. Unfortunately, McAfee did not mention where the information came from; however, it presumably was not based on verifiable evidence.

In fact, the authenticity of the supposed and often mentioned great battle between the Cherokee and Catawba Indians is also in doubt. Brent Burgin, MLIS and director of Archives for Native American Studies at the University of South Carolina at Lancaster, sent the following e-mail (July 2013) in response to our team's request for information:

> The great Catawba/Cherokee battle was first "reported" by Phillip Edward Pearson in an 1842 manuscript titled Memoir of the Catawbas. Later on, Henry Schoolcraft picked this account up when he published his works on various Indian tribes and their histories. The story is usually largely discounted and often we hear researchers speaking of the "Schoolcraft Legend." The great battle story has been picked up again and again yet there seems to be no actual historical basis for it [Brent Burgin, Director of Archives for Native American Studies at the University of South Carolina at Lancaster].

Since 1938, variations of the great battle story have been published by dozens of other BML authors who either got their information from McAfee's article or, perhaps, from the same unreliable source. Further adding to the inaccuracy of the myth, retelling of the story by later authors often includes embellishments or other incorrect information not found in the original story. For instance, the date of the supposed Indian battle is variously given as either AD 800 or AD 1200, or 800 or 1,200 years ago; 800 years ago would be AD 1200, while 1,200 years ago would be AD 800. Apparently some authors were confused and didn't understand the difference between the phrase "years ago" and actual "AD" dates.

According to the published BML literature, the mysterious lights are reported to be: (1) the spirits of Indian maidens searching for their loved ones killed in battle; (2) lights carried by the maidens; (3) spirits of the dead warriors; (4) lights carried by the warriors; or (5) campfires left on the battlefield. These are the types of BML stories I call campfire stories, where spinning an entertaining yarn takes precedence over getting the facts right.

Lack of Sightings by American Settlers Before 1900

The lack of sightings by 19th-century Americans is also well documented by the writings of the following scholars, historians, and travelers who had extensive local knowledge but did not mention the BMLs in their writings:

Lanman, C., 1849, *Letters from the Allegheny Mountains.*

Colton, H., 1859, *Mountain Scenery: The Scenery of the Mountains of Western North Carolina and Northwestern South Carolina.*

Lanman, C., 1865, *Adventures in the Wilds of the United States and British American Provinces.*

Hall, E.H., 1866, *Appletos' Hand-book of American Travel: The Southern Tour.*

Zeigler, W., and B. Grosscup, 1883, *The Heart of the Alleghenies, or Western North Carolina.*

Unknown Author, 1891, "Blue Ridge Rambler: Descriptions of Local Mountains," March 13, April 23 and May 3.

Dugger, S.M., 1895, *The Balsam Groves of the Grandfather Mountain.*

Mansfield, G.R., 1922, *Origin of the Brown Mountain Light in North Carolina* (no pre-electricity sightings).

Phifer, E.W., Jr., 1982, *Burke: The History of a North Carolina County; 1777–1920 with a Glimpse Beyond* (lights not seen until after 1900).

The following review of some mid-to-late nineteenth century publications about the area around Brown Mountain is highly revealing for the lack of mention of the Brown Mountain lights. The author, Dr. Cato Holler, Jr., is a world-recognized speleological expert, a Fellow Emeritus of the Explorers Club, and a founding member of the Brown Mountain lights research team. The following is his report.

Early North Carolina Travelogues and the Brown Mountain Lights
Dr. Cato Holler, Jr.

In the 1800s, North Carolina was a land of wild intrigue that sparked the literary interest of a number of writers. Many of these visited the Linville region and the Catawba Valley and recorded their experiences for all to enjoy. Let us take a brief look at some of the most popular of these publications.

Lanman, Charles, 1849, *Letters from the Allegheny Mountains*; **New York: Geo. P. Putnam.**

In June 1848, Lanman penned the following:

> The cabin where I am stopping at the present time is located at the extreme upper end of the North Cove. It is the residence of the best guide in the country, and the most convenient lodging place for those who would visit the Hawk's Bill and Table Mountains ... as well as the Lindville [sic] Pinnacle, the Catawba Cave, the Cake Mountain, the Linville Falls, and the Roan Mountain [Lanman, Charles, 1849, *Letters from the Allegheny Mountains*].

In addition to painting vivid descriptions of the geography and geological wonders around him, Lanman shared both local history and folklore in his book. His interest in natural phenomena is also obvious as he described viewing three thunderstorms from atop Roan Mountain. Included in the book's addenda is an article by T.L. Clingman regarding earthquakes, mysterious rumblings and the reported appearance of strange fires occurring in the Fines Creek area in the early part of the nineteenth century. No mention of the Brown Mountain lights is found anywhere in the book.

Much of the above was repeated in Lanman's later book: Lanman, Charles, 1865; *Adventures in the Wilds of the United States and British American Provinces;* Philadelphia: John W. Moore.

Colton, Henry, 1859; *Mountain Scenery: The Scenery of the Mountains of Western North Carolina and Northwestern South Carolina;* **Raleigh: W.L. Pomeroy. Philadelphia: Hayes and Zell.**

Henry Colton was quite proud of his native state and was anxious to have its merits appreciated by others. In the preface to his book, Colton emphasized that it was his intent to inform the world of the beauties of western North Carolina. Colton stated:

> There are numbers of natural curiosities throughout the South which are never seen or heard of except by some adventurous traveler, and known intimately only by the intrepid mountain hunter [Colton, Henry, 1859; *Mountain Scenery*].

Like his predecessor Lanman, he selected knowledgeable guides to show him the wonders of Linville River and its Falls, Gingercake Rock, Hawksbill, Table Rock, and the Chimneys. He stayed at the home of his guide David Franklin during these excursions. He also enlisted the aid of a member of the English family to lead him through the passages of Linville Caverns. Colton's detailed description of his exploration of the cave is perhaps the most poetic ever written.

One evening, while visiting the nearby Chimneys with David Franklin, Colton was inspired to write the following:

> The eye has a full, open scope from the Grandfather Mountain entirely around the Roan, and even beyond that. The valley of the Catawba is open to the view from its origin to its end, the whole of Turkey and North Coves, with their rich fields of waving corn. In the dim, dark distance, a lone mountain rises to view, which, from its location, we suppose to be the Pilot. Just as the sun fades beneath the horizon, it casts forth a clear, red light, and you see flashing in its blaze the windows of the houses of Morganton; from the same source, a golden tinge is thrown upon every leaf, and everything is mellowed into soft loveliness in the accomplishment of nature's most splendid creation [Colton, Henry, 1859; *Mountain Scenery*].

From the above, it is interesting to note that Colton enjoyed viewing the houses of Morganton, but nowhere are the Brown Mountain lights mentioned. This omission of BML's is significant, since Colton was quite interested in unusual phenomena such as this. This is evidenced by his visit to Roan Mountain in 1878 to investigate the well-known phantom music phenomenon, which many had experienced atop this mountain.

Zeigler, Wilbur and Ben Grosscup, 1883; *The Heart of the Alleghenies, or Western North Carolina*; Raleigh: Alfred Williams and Co. Cleveland: William W. Williams.

In describing his visit to the Linville region, the author writes,

> I could have followed up the North fork, under the shadows of Humpback mountain, and by a trail, have crossed the ridge to the Linville falls; but by this route the wild scenery of the Linville canon is lost. Bryson Magee was my guide to the Burke County Road along the summit of Bynum's Bluff.... "We jist hit it," broke forth from the guide, "a minute more an' we would n't seen 'em. See, the fog's crawlin' up, slow but shore." The author continued: It was as he had said. The massed vapors in the low sunk vales were being driven upward, and a moment later they had enfolded Table Rock and Hawk-bill, and were creeping through the woods around us [Zeigler, Wilbur and Ben Grosscup, 1883, *The Heart of the Alleghenies, or Western North Carolina*].

Later that rainy evening, the author spent the night at T.C. Franklin's, one mile from Linville Falls. He and other guests dried their wet clothes by the fireside as they whiled away the night sharing tales of getting lost in the mountains, and various hunting exploits. The following morning, the author visited Linville Falls and wrote a glowing description of the impressive cataract.

This book is filled with fascinating tales of travel as well as ghost stories and local folklore. Among the more interesting is the following:

> In 1811, when known as Chimney Rock Pass, a superstitious tale of a spectre cavalry fight was widely published in the newspapers of the day. The alleged witnesses of the spectacle were an old man and his wife living in the gap before Chimney Rock fall. So much interest was created in Rutherfordton by its recital, that a public meeting was held and a delegation, headed by Generals Miller and Walton, with a magistrate and clerk, visited the old couple and took their affidavits, to this effect: For several evenings, while shadows filled the pass and sunlight still lingered on the mountain summits, they had seen, from their doorway, two bodies of cavalry

advance toward each other across the sky. They heard the charge sounded, and saw them meet in conflict, with flashing swords, groans, shouts of victory, and then disappear. Three more settlers testified as witnesses of the same vision. They were all believed trustworthy, but evidently deluded by some natural phenomenon. Giving credence to the tale, explanations were advanced, but none are satisfactory [Zeigler, Wilbur and Ben Grosscup, 1883, *The Heart of the Alleghenies, or Western North Carolina*].

It is obvious from the above that such atmospheric events were of interest to the authors, yet even with their close interaction with locals there was no mention made in the book of the Brown Mountain lights.

It is also of interest that all the above authors selected knowledgeable local guides. Also, each author was quite familiar with the nearby resort of Piedmont Springs nestled literally at the foot of Brown Mountain, and each included it in their writings, yet the mysterious lights were nowhere mentioned.

Hall, Edward Hepple; 1866, *Appletons' Hand-book of American travel. The southern tour; being a guide through Maryland, District of Columbia, Virginia, North Carolina, Georgia and Kentucky.... With maps of the leading routes of travel and of the principal cities*; New York: D. Appleton.

This last travelogue gives the following description, but again lacks any mention of the Brown Mountain lights:

> The Hawk's Bill, in Burke County, is a stupendous projecting cliff, looking down 1,500 feet upon the waters of a rushing river. The Table Rock, a few miles below the Hawk's Bill, rises cone-shaped, 2,500 feet above the valley of the Catawba River. The Ginger Cake Rock, also in Burke County, is a singular pile, upon the summit of the Ginger Cake Mountain. It is a natural stone structure, in the form of an inverted pyramid, 29 feet in height. It is crowned with a slab, 32 feet long and two feet thick, which projects half its length beyond the edge of the pyramid upon which it is so strangely poised. Though seeming just ready to fall, nothing could be more secure. A fine view down the dark ravine below is commanded at this point [Hall, E.H., 1866, *Appleton's Hand-book of American Travel*].

From our brief perusal of these nineteenth century publications and their lack of any mention of the Brown Mountain lights, one must draw the conclusion that the probability of the existence of the lights at that time was quite low. If not totally unknown, then their existence must have been appreciated by a mere handful of individuals.

Dr. Cato Holler, Jr.

Had the BMLs existed during the 19th century, surely the authors reviewed above would have included the story in their writings. Each of these travelogue authors was intimately familiar with the mountains, streams and gorges within 50 miles of Brown Mountain and several specifically wrote about other local folklore and mysterious happenings; yet not a single author mentions the existence of the BMLs. It seems highly unlikely that the BMLs could have existed in the 1800s without one or more of these authors being aware of them and writing about them. In addition, the monumental 555-page history book on Burke County by E.W. Phifer, Jr. (1982), specifically mentions that the BMLs weren't seen until after 1900.

Sightings by Europeans in 1771?

The following paragraph from the 1771 De Brahm's Report of the General Survey in the Southern District of North America is often mentioned in the published BML literature as the definitive earliest written European document verifying the existence of the BMLs:

> Although these Mountains transpire through their Tops sulphurueaous and arsenical Sublimations, yet they are too light, as to precipitate so near their Sublimitories, but are carried away by the Winds

to distant Regions. In a heavy Atmosphere, the nitrous Vapours are swallowed up through the Spiraculs of the Mountains, and thus the Country is cleared from their Corrosion; when the Atmosphere is light, these nitrous Vapours rise up to the arsenical and sulphureous (subliming through the Expiraculs of the Mountains), and when they meet with each other in Contact, the Niter inflames, vulgurates and detonates, whence the frequent Thunders, in which a most votalized Spirit of Niter ascends to purify and inspire the upper Air, and a phlogiston Regeneratum (the metallic Seed) descends to impregnate the Bowels the Earth; and as all these Mountains form so many warm Athanors which draw and absorb, especially in foggy Seasons, all corrosive Effluvia along with the heavy Air through the Registers (Spiracles) and thus cease not from that Perpetual Circulation of the Air, corroding Vapours are no sooner raised, than that they are immediately disposed of, consequently the Air in the Appalachian Mountains is extreamly pure and healthy.

The numerous published references to this passage in the BML literature are misguided, misquoted or so grossly taken out of context that they call into question the ethics of the authors. In this passage, De Brahm is describing lightning storms in the mountains and he was writing about his personal views on the health benefits of breathing the pure mountain vapors of upstate South Carolina! The passage occurs in the South Carolina chapter of his book and he does not even describe North Carolina anywhere in his 325-page book. In fact, De Brahm may not have ever even visited North Carolina! The influence on the health of the local inhabitants by breathing good air versus bad air is a repeated theme throughout De Brahm's book, and elsewhere he describes, with similar flowing words, the poor health effects of breathing pond vapors (p. 79) and swamp vapors (p. 160) and he even goes on to suggest "a prudent and moderate use of Spirits" to offset the effects of living in an area where one is constantly breathing bad air.

The first reference to De Brahm's 1771 report is found in the 1927 *Gastonia Daily Gazette* article by R.K. Babington; however, Babington failed to reference the source of his information. It also appears that many later authors picked up the same story without properly checking their references either.

Refreshingly, Brian Dunning, on a 2010 podcast on his Skeptoid.com web site questions De Brahm's report as valid evidence of the BMLs:

> Taken in context, it's clear that De Brahm's quote (nitrous vapors, 1771) has nothing whatsoever to do with the Brown Mountain Lights. This leaves us with no documentary evidence that the Lights existed at all prior to the arrival of electric lights and people in the area in the early 1900s [Brian Dunning, *The Brown Mountain Lights*, episode # 226, October 5, 2010, www.Skeptoid.com].

First Verified Light Sighting, c. 1858

A single, newly appeared, regularly reappearing distant light seen briefly at the same place and approximate time every night was first noticed c. 1858 by local resident Lafayette (Fate) Wiseman while observing from an overlook on the west rim of Linville Gorge later named Wiseman's View (see Chapter 5 for the full story of Wiseman's light).

Although his story was not written down for another 100 years, Wiseman's light is the first believable report we have found of a supposed mystery light seen in the area. Interestingly, the very first train in western North Carolina also began operating in 1858 and undoubtedly gave rise to Wiseman's sightings as the train rounded curves and pointed its extremely bright headlight directly toward Wiseman's View on its nightly runs from Salisbury to Morganton. Lights from trains on this same railway line were found by the

U.S. Geological Survey in 1922 to explain some of the lights that mystified local residents of that time.

Although new, mysterious and unknown, Wiseman's light did not generate much interest and was largely ignored for the next 40 years, and it certainly did not give rise to the legend of the Brown Mountain lights. It was only after many other lights started appearing together at the beginning of the 1900s that the legend of mystery lights originated. Commercial, municipal and residential electricity spreading throughout the populated valleys south and east of Brown Mountain in the 1890s and the early 1900s undoubtedly added fuel to the legend as unsuspecting and uninformed mountain residents who weren't yet familiar with electric lights or did not fully understood their distance-penetrating power increasingly noticed supposedly mysterious lights over the top of Brown Mountain.

Chapter 4

Legends, Myths and Folklore

The thing that makes the Brown Mountain Lights so great is that it is a blank slate upon which you can project your imagination, your dreams, your visions.
—Joshua Warren, 2013, Brown Mountain Lights Symposium, Morganton, NC

Our perceptual systems aren't built to notice absolutely everything in our environment. We take in information through all our senses but there are gaps. So when we remember an event, what our memory ultimately does is fill in those gaps by thinking about what we know about the world.
—Kimberly Wade (University of Warwick, UK),
Why Does the Human Brain Create False Memories? BBC News, September 29, 2013

Belief is the death of intelligence. As soon as one believes a doctrine of any sort, or assumes certitude, one stops thinking about that aspect of existence.
—Robert Anton Wilson

No amount of belief makes something a fact.
—The Amazing James Randi

We can't even trust our own eyes to deliver an accurate representation of reality.
—Frater Isla,
Eye of the Skeptic

Vision is a matter of guided hallucinations.
—Patrick Henry Winston

Exhaustive literature review of published documents relating to the BMLs finds gross inaccuracies in the more popular stories. Separating fact from fiction is often impossible for the uninformed reader. For instance, there is no authentic written reference to BMLs published before 1912, and the numerous stories of pre-1850 sightings common in BML documents published since 1912 are unsupported by actual historical facts. These and many other unsupported later stories are similar to campfire stories because the details of each story vary greatly according to who is telling the story. The variations in the details of each published story are amazing, yet not a single author references where they got their information. This lack of references is a clear sign that campfire stories are being told and adherence to the facts takes back seat to spinning a good yarn. The most popular of these stories are covered in the sections that follow.

Campfire Stories: Native American Sightings

As mentioned in Chapter 3, Native American Indians did not see or report seeing the BMLs, although the opposite is incorrectly mentioned in many published BML documents.

The first report of Native American BML legends appeared in the 1938 *Asheville Citizen* article by H. McAfee entitled "Mysterious Lights of Brown Mountain Seen at This Time of Year." However, McAfee failed to reference the source of the data. After extensive literature research and contacts with Native American experts, we have been unable to find any authentic written or published reference supporting BML sightings by Native Americans, except in unreferenced BML writings since McAfee's report in 1938. Thus we conclude that the varied stories are myths made up by authors since 1938 in an unprofessional attempt to enhance their BML story.

Campfire Stories: Revolutionary War Soldier Searching for Missing Family

This legend is relatively recent and first appeared in a 1982 article in the *Watauga Democrat*. As the story goes:

> A family settled in the Brown Mountain area in the 1700s. When the Revolutionary War began, the father enlisted, leaving behind his wife and three children. The war over, he returned home to find his homestead in ruins. Desperately he took to the nearby mountain range searching for his missing loved ones. Finally, he died alone and in despair atop Brown Mountain, and today his spirit continues the search [Author Unknown, "Revolutionary War Soldier," *Watauga Democrat*, February 1, 1982].

The Revolutionary War ended in 1783, presumably the year the soldier returned home to find his family missing. A children's book by Carol Crane in 2012 retells this same sad but totally untrue story. As with all other legends, myths, or folklore stories, no references were given for the sources of the information.

Campfire Stories: Civil War Soldier Sightings

A reference to the legend of spirits of Civil War soldiers appears only once: on S. Nicholson's 2012 web site at hauntedcomputer.com where he mentions Civil War soldiers wandering the mountain with candles. Unfortunately, Nicholson does not properly cite where this information comes from.

In his 2002 document, J. Baldwin ties the "Faithful Slave Searching for Lost Master" legend to the Civil War:

> Brown Mountain was named after a Brown family, who owned a lot of land during the 19th century that included this mountain. The family owned slaves, and enjoyed the reputation of treating them well.
> During the Civil War, one of the men in the Brown family fought in the Confederate army as a colonel. He was wounded in 1863 and came home. When he was well enough, he went for a day's hike and hunting on Brown Mountain, a place he knew well. He took a little food and water, and two lanterns.
> Midnight came and the colonel had not returned. His faithful slave Jim took a lantern and went to Brown Mountain to look for him. Neither Jim nor the colonel ever returned. The family and their slaves searched the entire surface of Brown Mountain, but no trace of either of them has ever been found.
> Shortly after the colonel and Jim disappeared, bobbing lights appeared on the mountain. The lights had never been seen before, and the family believed the lights were from the lanterns the colonel and Jim carried. They are trying to find their way home [Chapter 9, "Riddle of the Brown Mountain Lights," *Smoky Mountain Mysteries: Stories About Magnificent Mountain Unique People*].

However, we have been unable to find any actual written documentation of BML sightings during or immediately after the Civil War. Instead, the monumental, 555-page book on the history of Burke County (Phifer Jr., 1977, revised 1982) details all of the Civil War military actions in the area, including those on and near Brown Mountain, without noting any BML sightings. In fact, on page 12 Phifer specifically states that no BMLs were seen prior to the twentieth century.

Campfire Stories: Slave Protecting Buried Treasure

The earliest published account linking the BMLs to ghosts or spirits is C.H. Hites' 1917 article in the *Charlotte Observer* (reprinted in the *Morganton News-Herald*). Even though the mysterious BMLs had already been known for several years and they had created great excitement due to numerous newspaper stories, they were not commonly attributed to ghosts or spirits until long after Hites' story of Negro slave superstitions.

Hites reports being told stories by Negro slaves who saw a light on Brown Mountain, presumably in the years following the Civil War, that they thought was the ghost of Bird Carroll. Apparently Carroll, a slave himself, buried his life's savings under a large pine tree on Brown Mountain but died in 1865 serving in the Civil War at Wilmington, North Carolina, before he could return and retrieve it.

While Bird Carroll's story itself was seldom, if ever, retold in print, the connection between the BMLs and ghosts and spirits was destined to become a common theme in later published reports. S.M. Dugger's stories of the ghost of a murdered wife and H. McAfee's article on Native American ghosts would not be published until 1936 and 1938, respectively. Afterwards, nearly every published author included his own version of a ghost legend.

Campfire Stories: Murdered Wife and Baby

The legends of a murdered wife from the Jonas Ridge community may have predated the BMLs. However, ties to the BMLs appear in the writings of S.M. Dugger (1936–1938), R. Russell and J. Barnett (1988) and J. Baldwin (2002). The details of the story vary greatly, but apparently a husband, known to be mean, murdered his wife and buried her and her baby on either Cold Mountain or Brown Mountain. She was either pregnant or had recently given birth to their baby. It was years before the bodies were found. The BMLs supposedly are the spirits of the wife and baby. The dates of the murder vary from before the Civil War to the late 1880s. Unfortunately, none of the authors cite references for their information.

Campfire Stories: Lost Lover

The lost lover legend first appears in published documents in 1948 (*North Carolina Folklore* and the *Gastonia Gazette*) and is again mentioned in J. Baldwin's 2002 document. Unfortunately, none of the authors reference where their information came from. According to the *North Carolina Folklore* article:

A young man fell in love with a mountain girl who lived with her father on Brown Mountain. He visited her nightly, coming through the dangerous woods from his village. They agreed to marry. On the evening of their departure she lit a pine torch and went to greet him. He never returned and she took a torch out every night crossing back and forth on Brown Mountain to look for him [Unknown Author, 1948, "The Lights of Brown Mountain," *North Carolina Folklore* 1, no. 1 (June 1948)].

According to the 2002 article, Amanda lived on Brown Mountain with her widowed father about 1775. She fell in love with young Caleb, who lived in a nearby valley. On the evening he was to come and take her away to marry, she lit a pine torch to signal him, but he never came. Her spirit still searches Brown Mountain for him.

Campfire Stories: Faithful Slave Searching for Lost Master

Perhaps the most enduring legend of the BMLs has to do with the spirit of a faithful slave searching for his lost master. The legend first appeared in print in 1961 with Scotty Wiseman's folk song, the "Ballad of the Brown Mountain Light." Over the next few years the song became very popular and was recorded by various groups, while local newspaper reporter John Parris wrote the full story of Scotty's Great Uncle, Josiah Lafayette "Fate" Wiseman (1842–1932), in 1966, 1971 and 1972 articles. According to Parris:

> About 1858, Josiah Lafayette "Fate" Wiseman, then a young boy, camped on the rim of Linville Gorge and saw the BMLs—long before electric lights. Fate Wiseman became a veteran of the Civil War and he kept cattle on his land below cliffs in Conley's Cove in Linville Gorge. On a return trip with his father to sell goods in Salisbury, they camped at today's Wiseman's View & could see the lights over BM. Later, he would often watch the lights from the same spot & it came to be called Wiseman's View. Fate told of a faithful slave with lantern searching for his missing low-country hunter master. The spirit of the slave and his lantern still wander the mountain today.

In 2002, J. Baldwin elaborated on the story—see Baldwin's quote in the "Civil War Soldier Sightings" section above where he links this story to a Confederate colonel.

The Next Campfire Story

Everyone likes a good mystery and the creative storytellers among us continue to come up with new ones almost yearly. Ralph Lael's 1962 story of alien abduction on Brown Mountain has to be high on everyone's list of favorite campfire stories (see Chapter 10). What new story will appear next? I don't know, but it'll have to be really good to top the ones we've already heard.

Chapter 5

First Sightings and Birth of the Legend

The Fate Wiseman Story

As mentioned previously, the first verifiable mystery light sighting in the Brown Mountain area was by Josiah Lafayette "Fate" Wiseman (1842–1932) about 1858. Well-known Asheville newspaper reporter John Parris reconstructed the Fate Wiseman story by interviewing Fate's great nephew Scott "Scotty" Greene Wiseman (1908–1981) in 1971 (Parris, 1971, 1972).

As a young boy, Fate Wiseman camped with his father at today's Wiseman's View on the west rim of Linville Gorge. The year of Fate's sighting reportedly was *around 1854* (Parris, 1971), but how accurate is that date? The date was third-hand coming from Scotty Wiseman, who at 63 years old was remembering something his great-uncle had told him 50 years earlier when he (Scotty) was 13 years old and his Great-uncle Fate was 79 years old and remembering something that happened 67 years before that. More likely the actual date was 1858, the year the first train began operation in western North Carolina and Fate Wiseman was 16 years old.

The first train in western North Carolina began operating in the Catawba Valley between Salisbury and Morganton in 1858 and it seems likely that Fate Wiseman's light sighting might have been this train coming around a curve on its nightly runs when the locomotive headlight was directed toward Wiseman's View. Apparently this train was also responsible for numerous other mystery light sightings over the next 60 years or so (see 1911 and 1912 published accounts). If true, this would also suggest that Fate's first sighting was in 1858 instead of 1854.

Fate reportedly saw only an instantaneous flash of light within 30 minutes of the same time each night and, knowing how easy it was to miss the flash, he refused to be distracted at the critical time, instead sitting at the overlook intensely staring in the direction of the expected light. Thus the site became known as Wiseman's View. Fate's behavior, leading to the naming of the overlook, and the regular nightly appearance of the light are consistent with the distant sighting of a train's headlight on its nightly runs between Salisbury and Morganton.

Fate Wiseman's light inspired his great nephew Scotty Wiseman's popular folk song "The Legend of the Brown Mountain Lights." Following the release of the song in 1961, Fate's story of a faithful slave searching for his lost master became North Carolina's most popular ghost story.

5. First Sightings and Birth of the Legend

No Legend Yet

Unique as this first mystery light was, few if any people paid much attention to it for the next 40 years. It certainly did not generate the legend of the BMLs. In 1882, another local resident, Stokes Penland, also reported seeing a mystery light (Babington, 1927; Clark, 2013), presumably the same as Wiseman's light. But again, few people took much notice. However, after the first electricity in western North Carolina arrived in Hickory in 1888 and then quickly spread throughout the Catawba Valley during the 1890s, local residents and visitors alike began taking note of the multiple, newly appearing, long-lasting, distant, stationary and moving lights visible throughout the night. After 1900, Loven's Hotel in the community of Cold Springs on Jonas Ridge became the favored site for observing these new lights—and here the legend of the BMLs was born.

Birth of the Legend: First Sightings from Cold Springs

After the arrival of electricity in Hickory in 1888 (a first for western North Carolina) and its spread throughout the Catawba Valley during the 1890s, local residents and visitors in the mountains overlooking Brown Mountain began taking note of the newly appearing, unexpected and supposedly mysterious lights in the valley below. Apparently during the early days of the legend moving lights were perceived to be more mysterious than stationary lights.

In the 1890s George Anderson Loven's Hotel in the community of Cold Springs on Jonas Ridge commanded a grand view looking eastward over Brown Mountain and beyond to the Catawba Valley and the South Mountains. After George Anderson died, the hotel was operated by his son Joseph L. Loven. Visitors to the hotel and nearby residents began seeing distant lights over Brown Mountain in the late 1890s and by the time the first articles about the lights were published in 1912, observers' concern, curiosity, and fear of these newly arrived lights led to the beginnings of the legend of the BMLs.

While the mountain residents themselves didn't yet have electricity, they surely were aware that the valley residence were being electrified. So why didn't they simply attribute the newly arrived distant lights to the electric lights in the valley? I suspect that neither the mountain residents (without electricity) nor the hotel visitors (often valley residents who had electricity already) were aware of just how far electric lights could be seen at night. In fact, the distance-penetrating power of electric lights continues to be poorly appreciated even today.

Loven's family first reported seeing unknown lights as early as 1897 (Harris, 1913; Scott, 1915), 39 years after Fate Wiseman's first light sighting around 1858. But things were about to get a lot more interesting. Mystery lights were reportedly seen c. 1908–1910 by B.S. Gaither (*Salisbury Evening Post*, 1912; Scott, 1915) and sometime in 1910 or 1911 the Rev. C.E. Gregory, who built a cottage near the hotel, saw lights (*Salisbury Evening Post*, 1912; Wilson, 1915). About 1911, members of the Morganton Fishing Club reported seeing lights on a fishing expedition to the area (*Western Sentinel*, 1912; Harris, 1913). In 1912, several area newspapers carried the first published accounts and described mystery lights appearing over the top of Brown Mountain in the valley to the east (*Western Sen-*

tinel, 1912, 1912a; *Salisbury Evening Post*, 1912). Other published articles followed in 1913 (Manning, 1913; Harris, 1913). In 1915, C.L. Wilson reported that it was not one light as previously reported but rather many lights that were visible from Loven's Hotel. In 1916, H.C. Martin's camping parties on both Brown Mountain and nearby Adams Mountain saw several mystery lights at different times on the same night amongst the trees (Pearson, 1916; Mansfield, 1922). Also in 1916, M.A. Bird witnessed a bright light hovering and then moving rapidly over Brown Mountain (Bird, 1916). Other 1916 published writings report multiple lights appearing immediately after nightfall in multiple places over Brown Mountain and burning for irregular intervals (Elam, 1916; Loven, 1916).

After the monumental flood of 1916 (see Chapter 6), mystery lights were still reportedly visible from Cold Springs and Wiseman's View (Loven, 1916; Parris, 1972). Loven's Hotel continued receiving increased visitation due to the mystery lights and curious patrons flocked to his hotel to see them (Elam, 1916; Perry, 1919).

George Anderson Loven (1835–1918) built the original Loven Hotel in 1892 and was the father of Joseph L. Loven (1867–1937), who operated the hotel sometime after 1919. It was sold in 1947 and the name was changed to Cold Springs Lodge. The original Loven hotel building was destroyed by fire on November 24, 1950. A new lodge was built on the same site as the original hotel, changed owners many times and finally closed to the public in 1970 and became a family residence in 1972.

The Golden Age of the BMLs

Immediately after the first documents on the BMLs were published in 1912, the legend caught fire with the area residents and, following subsequent newspaper articles over the next 10 years, the legend's popularity rapidly expanded and caught the curiosity of the entire nation. In fact, the period between 1912 and 1922 can be considered the Golden Age of the BMLs, or, as I prefer to call it, the Age of BML Hysteria. By 1922, the legend was firmly established; however, the U.S. Geological Survey investigation that year dealt it a serious blow (Mansfield, 1922; see Chapter 7).

Area residents and visitors alike were greatly concerned about these newly appearing and rapidly increasing supposedly mystery lights, and twice within the eleven-year period between 1912 and 1922, they called on North Carolina's elected officials to do something about these lights and protect the local people. In both cases, the state's politicians took the unprecedented move to petition Congress for action, and both times Congress requested that the U.S. Geological Survey send geologists to North Carolina to find out what the lights were. This was the first time in the nation's history that Congress was requested to investigate supposedly mystery lights—a testament to the fear and concern that these lights caused the local residents at the time. Not until the worldwide UFO scares starting in the 1940s would Congress again be involved in investigating mystery sightings.

Mr. R.T. Claywell of Morganton, North Carolina, was instrumental in encouraging the U.S. Geological Survey to investigate the mystery lights in 1913. In addition, Claywell assisted again in the second Geological Survey investigation in 1922. His July 31, 1913, sighting story was published in the *Winston-Salem Journal* of September 14, 1913. Claywell's account includes a detailed description of the light he saw:

There's something ghostly and uncanny about that light that I and the folks up in the neighborhood can't fathom and we want to get a government scientist down there to discover just what it is and the causes and effect.

The night that I and a number of friends saw this strange phenomenon, I was up there with George Patterson and wife, of Concord, Miss Bell Means, niece of Colonel Paul Means, and Mr. Honeycutt of Concord, Miss Sallie Hogan, Miss Fannie Roundtree, Miss Sarah Claywell, all of Morganton, and Robert Lovin, of Cold Spring.

It was the last Thursday in July, July 31st. We were all sitting on the cottage porch in conversation, on Rattlesnake Knob, about 150 yards from the Cold Spring Hotel, at exactly 10:05 o'clock.

The first thing unusual that attracted our attention was a hazy kind of a light across the valley on Brown Mountain in two places. We all watched it intently with mixed feeling of awe and wonder, while shivers ran up and down the spine of everyone present. In a few minutes while we all directed our gaze intently on the two hazy spots, just off to the right of the light in the direction of a Morganton, we saw this brighter light appear at the foot of Brown Mountain where Upper Creek cuts it at Joy. It appeared to be swinging to and fro, pendulum like, and then went upward about a distance of 200 feet. When it first appeared it seemed to be round and yellow, and gained steadily in brightness, becoming redder and redder as it went upward. When it reached its greatest height, it appeared like a flaming red ball, but the strange thing about it was that it did not cast off a particle of light. All the air around it seemed to be as dark as ever, and that added to its ghostly appearance.

It was across the valley from us at a distance of about 12 miles. It had rained in Morganton that day and there were a few clouds still hanging about. When the light started rising again and reached a height of what seemed from our distance to be about 1200 feet, it went behind one of these clouds and we did not see it any more that night.

It was one of the strangest experiences I believe I ever had, and many of the folks were near fainting. In fact, it was with difficulty that Mrs. Patterson was revived from a faint. We had been at the cottage three days previously and every evening had gone to bed about nine o'clock but this Thursday night we stayed up later. We would probably have witnessed it the other evening had we stayed on the porch a little later [G.H. Manning, "Strange Light in Mountains Still Alarming," *Winston-Salem Journal*, September 14, 1913].

Col. Wade H. Harris, editor of the *Charlotte Daily Observer* was also instrumental in requesting that North Carolina's politicians take on the task of solving the mystery, first in 1913 and again in 1922. As editor, he was also responsible for the September 23, 1913, article, "No Explanation," in his newspaper. In part, Harris's article reads as follows:

With punctual regularity the light rises in a southeasterly direction from the point of observation just over the lower slope of Brown Mountain, first about 7:30 p.m., again about 20 or 30 minutes later and again at 10 o-clock. It looks much like a toy fire balloon, a distinct ball, with no "atmosphere" about it, and as nearly as the average observer can measure it, about the size of the toy balloon.

It is much smaller than the full moon, much larger than any star and fiery red. It rises in the far distance from beyond Brown Mountain, which is about six miles from Rattlesnake Knob, and after going up a short distance, wavers and goes out in less than one minute. The observer has to watch the sky closely at the right time, or he will miss it. It does not always appear in exactly the same place, but varies what must amount in the distance to several miles. The light is visible at all seasons, so Mr. Anderson Loven, an old and reliable resident, testifies. During the winter it appears far off to the south of the usual summer position, and is not visible from Rattlensake [sic] Knob, but is seen from a point farther down the turnpike, around the point or ridge that hides it from the Summer point of observation.

That it is no mere reflection of some other light has been disproved. Some have declared that it was some practical joker sending up a light to mystify people, but it would hardly be kept up for several years, nor would it appear miles apart within a few minutes. There seems to be no doubt that the light rises from some point in the wide, level country between Brown Mountain and the South Mountains, a distance of about 12 miles, though it is possible that it rises a still greater distance.

The U.S. Geological Survey's first investigation of the lights occurred the following month, in October 1913. The chief regional geologist, D.B. Sterrett, concluded that the light was due to a train locomotive headlight (see Chapter 7). Sterrett was heavily criticized for not interviewing eyewitnesses; instead he spent only a single night observing on Brown Mountain itself. But the legend was already firmly entrenched in the minds of the local population, who quickly dismissed Sterrett's conclusion.

Also observing from Loven's Hotel, Professor W.G. Perry of the Georgia School of Technology wrote the following description of a mystery light to the Smithsonian Institution in 1919:

> We occupied a position on a high ridge. Across several intervening ridges rose Brown Mountain, some 8 miles away. After sunset we began to watch the Brown Mountain direction. Suddenly there blazed in the sky, apparently above the mountain, near one end of it, a steadily glowing ball of light. It appeared to be about 10° above the upper line of the mountain, blazed with a slightly yellow light, lasted about half a minute, and then abruptly disappeared. It was not unlike the "star" from a bursting sky rocket or Roman candle, though brighter.
>
> We were impressed with the following facts: The region about Brown Mountain and between our location and the mountain is a wild, practically uninhabited mountain region—a confusion of mountain peaks, ridges, and valleys. Viewing the lights from a fixed position our estimate of their location was most inexact; the varying color (almost a white, yellowish, reddish) may have been due to mist in the atmosphere: the view of the lights was a direct one and not a reflection; there seemed to be no regularity in their time of appearance; they came suddenly into being, blazed steadily, and as suddenly disappeared; they appeared against the sky and not against the side of the mountain.
>
> Others who have seen this phenomenon make very different reports of their observation; and some who have seen it several times report that they have seen it in varying fashion; sometimes the light appears stationary (as was uniformly the case when I saw it); sometimes it appears to move rapidly—upward, downward, horizontally [Letter to Dr. C.G. Abbot (Smithsonian Institution), in G.R. Mansfield, 1922, USGS Cir 646, p. 7].

However, the U.S. Geological Survey's second BML investigation in 1922 was much more extensive than the first one in 1913 and nearly killed the legend (see Chapter 7).

City and Town Lights Visible from Cold Springs

The presence of city and town lights visible from Cold Springs in the early days of the legend of the BMLs is mentioned in at least two early published documents. In 1912 the *Salisbury Evening Post* reported that in addition to a mystery light seen in the direction of Connelly Springs from Loven's Hotel at Cold Springs, the city lights of Morganton, Hickory and other towns were visible. In 1915, observing from Loven's Hotel, C.L. Wilson reported seeing, in addition to unknown lights, the city lights of the Catawba Valley communities of Lenoir, Joy, Connelly Springs and Rutherford College (Wilson, 1915). Apparently some observers, such as C.L. Wilson, W.G. Perry, Col. Wade H. Harris, and M.A Bird, differentiated between the visible city and town lights and mystery lights. However, many other early observers apparently did not make this distinction and appear to have called all visible lights "mystery lights," including the city and town lights.

World War I and the Legend of the BMLs

World events during the early 20th century may have helped fuel interest in the BMLs, or at least may have helped set the stage for the mass acceptance of things unexpected. The Great War (only later called the First World War) started in mid-1914 and undoubtedly contributed to the fear and concern of informed people everywhere, including the residents of western North Carolina. The rapid and unexpected development of previously unimaginably horrible military atrocities of the war, following a long and nearly unbroken period of peace in the world, must have had profound impacts, adding to feelings of fear, insecurity, unpredictability and a world beyond understanding. After the war ended in late 1918, interest in the BMLs reached fever pitch, leading to the second request to Congress and Mansfield's Geological Survey investigation in 1922 (see Chapter 7).

Does Jules Verne Have Anything to Do with the BMLs?

Ron Miller (2013), a member of the North American Jules Verne Society, presents a convincing argument that Jules Verne's immensely popular science fiction novels of the mid- to late-1800s helped set the stage for the world's first UFO scares in the late 1890s. Miller writes:

> For a brief period during the late 1890s, a wave of UFO sightings swept across the United States. Dozens of strange objects were seen sailing through the skies from coast-to-coast.
> In November 1896 an object was reported in the night sky over Sacramento, California. It was described as a light with a dark body of some kind above it. It was seen a second time about a week later. Similar reports, usually describing only the light, came from other cities in northern California. Reported movement of the light indicated a slow motion. The dark body seen above it was variously held to be "cigar-shaped, egg-shaped or barrel-shaped."
> Other reports from the 1890s wave describe a fast-moving cigar-shaped object which glowed and made small explosions, similar to what might be expected from a gasoline engine. Another emitted colored rays of light. An unknown body—a "luminous ball of fire"—circled a mountain in Canada before speeding away. The ship described in an 1896 close encounter in California was characterized as "cigar-shaped." An object seen in Kansas in 1897 looked like a 30-foot canoe with a searchlight.
> In 1886 Verne published his 31st novel, *Robur le Conquerant*. English versions were published in Britain and the United States the next year. The book's hero, Robur, invents a first-of-its-kind giant flying machine, kidnaps three skeptics and takes them on a round-the-world flight (the first UFO abduction?) [Ron Miller, 2013, "That Time Jules Verne Caused a UFO Scare"].

Our own Brown Mountain light research team member Dr. Cato Holler, Jr., is also a board director of the North American Jules Verne Society. Dr. Holler makes an even stronger connection between Jules Verne and the BMLs. He writes about another of Verne's novels:

> The year was 1911. Jules Verne's novel, *Master of the World*, was available in English for the first time. Penned in its original French in 1904, the story was now being read and enjoyed by countless Americans.
> To quote Verne in a less-than-accurate English translation, the story began "…in the western part of our great American State of North Carolina. There, deep amid the Blue Ridge Mountains rises the crest called the Great Eyrie [sic]. Its huge rounded form is distinctly seen from the little town of Morganton on the Catawba River, and still more clearly as one approaches the mountains by way of the village of Pleasant Garden." He goes on to state that the origin of the mountain's name was uncertain.
> Local residents had become frightened by strange lights appearing over the mountain, almost flame-like in nature accompanied by the appearance of smoke and unexplainable rumblings and subterranean noises. As it turned out, these manifestations were originating from an incredible amphibious flying machine invented by the mad scientist, Robur the Conqueror, whose secret base was deep inside the mountain peak.

Although Verne had never visited North Carolina, it has been suggested by some that perhaps he or one of his colleagues had seen an early travelogue describing the region. It has also been suggested that Verne's description of the Great Eyrie (the original French spelling is Eyry), bears a close resemblance to Table Rock, which does overlook Morganton.

Master of the World was Jules Verne's sequel to his novel *Robur the Conqueror*. This science fiction novel first appeared in France in 1886 under the title *Robur-le-Conquerant*, soon to be followed by an English translation the next year. The novel is also known in England as *The Clipper of the Clouds*. It is noteworthy that UNESCO's latest worldwide list of the most translated authors of all time ranked Jules Verne as number two, exceeded only by Agatha Christie.

Following the success of Verne's previous novels, countless other authors began penning similar tales of mysterious airships, which soon flooded the book markets. For a brief period of time in the 1890's UFO sightings were being reported from coast to coast across the U.S. Descriptions ranged from vague sightings of luminous floating orbs to more vivid descriptions of propeller driven cigar-shaped aircraft reminiscent of Robur's airship, the *Albatross*. It is also interesting to note that Robur the Conqueror may have contained what would later be considered the first account of an alien abduction.

About the same time the general public began enjoying these exciting novels and as a result started spotting their own UFO's was the same time that the first reports of the Brown Mountain lights began coming in. Coincidence? Perhaps not. This literary spark, which ignited the imagination, intrigue and the public's awareness of mystery lights, is certainly worth considering [Dr. Cato Holler, Jr., 2014, "Jules Verne and the Brown Mountain Lights"].

It seems Jules Verne (1828–1905) and his unique literature-changing science fiction adventure novels may have indeed helped set the stage for the public's fascination with supposedly mystery lights like the BMLs. In fact, the uncanny timing of the publication of Verne's *Master of the World* (1904 in French and 1911 in English), which included the story of nighttime mystery lights seen above a mountain near Morganton, North Carolina (supposedly Table Rock), and the birth of the legend of the BMLs (first published documents in 1912) is curious and leads one to wonder if the BMLs inspired the story in Verne's book or if the book inspired the locals to begin their own stories of mystery lights.

While Verne never visited North Carolina, it seems unlikely that he would have heard much if he heard anything about the BMLs by 1904, the year *Master of the World* was first published; however, it's possible he or perhaps his heavily involved editor had learned of the unique mountain features of the Linville Gorge area by reading some of the travelogues previously published throughout the 1800s (see Chapter 3). These published descriptions of wild, isolated mountain scenery north of Morganton may have inspired Verne to choose Table Rock as the location for the opening chapter in his book.

Verne's fictional novel centered around the efforts of a high-ranking government investigator from Washington, D.C., who was sent to western North Carolina to try to solve the mystery of lights that had recently and suddenly appeared atop that rocky mountain north of Morganton. Could this just be a curious coincident or is it the reason the Brown Mountain area residents twice insisted between 1912 and 1922 that government experts from Washington come investigate the supposed mystery lights they were seeing?

The timing of Verne's *Master of the World*, the opening-chapter location atop a mountain north of Morganton, suddenly appearing mystery lights atop a wilderness mountain that greatly frightened the local residents, and the involvement of government investigators from Washington all suggest that Verne's book may have actually started, or at least added fuel to, the BML legend.

Chapter 6

The Events of 1916

Flood of 1916

North Carolina's Great Flood of July 14–16, 1916, was caused by a hurricane that came ashore at Charleston, South Carolina, and passed directly over western North Carolina (Bell, 1916). Many BML authors use the fact that some lights still visible immediately after the flood as proof that the mystery lights were not man-made lights, since supposedly all of the man-made lights were destroyed by the flood. But is this a valid argument?

Widespread Damage

Flooding along all streams in the area caused great damage. The Catawba River between Morganton and Salisbury reached more than 25 feet above flood stage and most railroad and highway bridges were washed away. It was the temporary halting of rail traffic, including the train locomotives with their powerful headlights, combined with the continued observation of supposed mystery lights that caught the imagination of many local residents.

The *Lenoir News* sent a letter to Mr. Joseph L. Loven of Loven's Hotel in Cold Springs asking about the status of the BMLs after the flood. In response, a letter from George Anderson Loven, dated August 29, 1916, states the following:

> The light still appears every night now, for six years since it was first seen. It shows to be some four or five miles beyond the top of Brown Mountain.
> It was supposed by some that it was a train headlight; the recent floods stopped the trains from running, but it did not stop the light from showing. We watched close and it showed every night just the same.
> It is not confined to one place; it varies sometimes from two to three miles either east or west. It seems to go up over the treetops from fifty to sixty feet ["The Brown Mountain Light Not Washed Away," *Lenoir News*, September 8, 1916].

George Anderson Loven was the father of Joseph L. Loven. His letter failed to demonstrate a distinction between known man-made lights and supposed mystery lights, either before or after the flood. Note that Loven did not specifically report that all lights disappeared after the flood except for the one mystery light he witnessed. In fact, he mentioned nothing about how many or what kinds of lights were visible before or after the flood.

Later, several authors, most notably G.R. Mansfield in 1922, pointed out that Loven's observations did not prove that mystery lights were involved; after all, many automobiles continued to operate on area highways that were not destroyed by the flood. Thus lights visible immediately after the flood may have been automobiles on roads that survived the hurricane. As for Loven's Hotel, it was receiving increased visitors due to the BML mystery and his comments may have been driven more by a profit motive than by factual observations.

Josiah Lafayette "Fate" Wiseman (1842–1932), the first man to report mystery lights nearly 60 years earlier, also apparently reported that lights were still visible immediately after the flood of 1916 (Parris, 1972). This report was second-hand information (interview with Fate Wiseman's great nephew Scotty Wiseman) and, once again, it is not clear exactly which lights were being observed—the man-made lights that survived the flood or other, unknown lights? Apparently many other local residents also saw lights immediately after the flood, but no one addresses the distinction between definite man-made lights and lights of unknown origin. The lack of this distinction suggests that all lights visible at the time were mistaken for mystery lights by most people.

Sterrett's 1913 dismissal of the BMLs as the headlights of train locomotives (see Chapter 7) was very much on everyone's mind following the Great Flood of 1916. The trains temporarily stopped running. Did the lights disappear? No, at least some lights continued to be visible. However, the argument that those lights seen immediately after the flood were proof that train locomotive headlights could not be the source of the lights is invalid. The argument, often presented in later BML publications, is invalid because it is also not proven that the lights being seen immediately before the flood were locomotive headlights—which then disappeared after the flood. It could be that the lights seen both before and after the flood were automobile or city, town, or residential lights. Unfortunately, no one at the time recorded sufficient information to settle this question.

The published BML literature between 1912 (the year of first mention of BMLs in print) and 1917, the year after the Great Flood, seldom distinguishes between known man-made lights and lights of supposed unknown origin. Apparently most people of that time attributed all of the visible lights to unknown origins, even though some historical documents of the time clearly identify the man-made lights of cities, towns and communities in the Catawba Valley visible over the top of Brown Mountain when viewed from higher observation sites to the north and west.

If anything, the flood of 1916, which apparently temporarily resulted in fewer visible lights that then slowly reappeared as rebuilding of the infrastructure progressed, adds strength to the argument that man-made city, town, automobile, or locomotive lights were the source of the lights being seen over the top of Brown Mountain.

1916 Mystery Lights

Four unusual mystery light sightings were witnessed by camping parties on both Brown Mountain and nearby Adams Mountain on the night of April 11–12, 1916. At the time, this was one of the first expeditions specifically organized to observe the BMLs in the woods, and their findings comprised the most authentic close encounters known at that time. Note that most other authors reported that the lights were not visible from Brown Mountain itself.

The eleven-person expedition was organized by Mr. H.C. Martin, who camped on

Adams Mountain, and Dr. L.H. Coffey, who camped on Brown Mountain. The *Lenoir (NC) News Herald* reported the observations of the two men in an April 27, 1916, article written by W. Pearson. Apparently an earlier article written by H.C. Martin was published in the *Lenoir Topic* on April 19, 1916; however, that article was not available for review by this investigation. G.R. Mansfield's 1922 report further details the story based on his personal interviews that year with Mr. Martin. The fact that Mansfield interviewed Martin is a testament to the significance of his observations.

The expedition group consisted of Elisha Powell, Russell Pressnell, Fred McGowan, Charley Warren, Collett Coffey, Dr. L.H. Coffey and H.C. Martin, all from Lenoir, the Rev. A.I. Haentzschel of Concordia College (Conover), and Joe S. Webb, Robey Webb, and Rube Bryson of Collettsville.

Three observation sites were occupied on Brown Mountain and two sites were set up on Adams Mountain. Pistol shots alerted each group when lights were seen. The Brown Mountain groups saw lights at 8:10 p.m., 9:45 p.m., and 5:10 a.m., either on the summit or on the south slope of Adams Mountain. The Adams Mountain groups saw lights on the east side of Brown Mountain about midnight. However, none of the groups on either mountain saw the same lights as the groups on the other mountain. Four different appearances of the lights were seen to unexpectedly appear and then disappear. Martin reports:

> Most of the appearances were of short duration and reminds one of floating globes of light, apparently about the size of ordinary street lights of Lenoir seen from a distance of a mile. One appearance which occurred a few minutes before 12 o'clock and was visible for over 20 minutes, seemed to start on the side of Brown Mountain and it appeared as two lights and moved swiftly along the side of the mountain towards the south-western end, traversing a distance of approximately two miles within ten minutes and floated in and out of the ravines which furrow the steep sides of the mountain, about one eighth of the distance from the top to the foot. They traveled on a level plane and were seemingly in among the scant timber on the side of the mountain. From our point of view [atop Adam's Knob] they seemed to be within a few yards of each other at times and after going for a certain distance in one direction seemed to turn and retrace the line back to the starting point a short way and then disappeared.
>
> Another feature that adds strength to this theory [warm/cold air currents and gasses] is that 25 to 40 years ago [1871–1896] this light was not known or seen since that time much of the land that was then in native forests, south and east of the mountain, has been cleared. This we know has had an effect on the atmosphere of the locality by exposing a greater surface to become heated during the day and in that way creating a greater contrast in the temperature of the air currents that pass up the valley of Wilson's creek [Pearson, W., 1916, "The Brown Mountain Lights—Mr. Martin Writes Interestingly of Preliminary Investigations Made Recently by Lenoir Party," *Morganton (NC) News Herald*, April 27, 1916].

Mansfield elaborates on the story based on personal interviews with Mr. Martin:

> Dr. Coffey's party saw the light over the summit of Adams Mountain at 8:10 and again at 9:45, over a point somewhat farther south. About 5:10 a.m. they saw the light again over the south end of Adams Mountain. None of these appearances was seen by Mr. Martin's party, but about 11:52 his party saw two lights (floating globes), "apparently about the size of ordinary street lamps of Lenoir seen from the distance of about 1 mile," flash out among the trees on the east side of Brown Mountain about one-eighth of the distance down from the summit. These lights moved horizontally southeastward, floating in and out of the ravines, along the mountainside past a dead pine tree in Mr. Martin's line of sight for a distance estimated at 2 miles. Then they returned northwestward about half that distance, again passing the line of the dead tree. At 12:13 the lights disappeared as suddenly as they came. These lights were not seen by Dr. Coffey's party [G.R. Mansfield, 1922, *Origin of the Brown Mountain Light in North Carolina*; U.S. Geological Survey Circular 646].

Today the thick forest cover on the summits of both mountains prevents views of the other mountain; however, clear views of Adams Mountain are possible from the rock cliffs on the north face of Brown Mountain, somewhat below the actual summit. In 1916, however, Brown Mountain and, possibly, Adams Mountain were recovering from recent logging activities and clear views from their summits may have been available.

Martin's Conclusions

Martin speculates that the lights might have been produced by atmospheric conditions related to differing densities and temperatures of overlying layers of warm and cold air. He notes that the recent forest logging on Brown Mountain left the ground susceptible to greater heating by the sun, which could give rise to adjacent layers of warm and cold air currents in the mountainous region. Rejecting the commonly accepted scientific theory of shooting stars as outer-space material caught in earth's gravity field, he wonders if the interaction of different density air currents, such as those near Brown Mountain, might produce shooting stars as well as the mystery lights observed by the expedition. He also wonders if gases in the atmosphere might have produced the lights. Martin's atmospheric-conditions ideas are the first published mention of mirages or refraction of light waves due to their passage through air layers of differing densities in the area. Several later authors, including Mansfield, expanded on these ideas and concluded that rising heat waves do indeed cause the common visual effects of dancing, wobbling, wavering, bobbing, out-of-focus, color changes, and rapid changes in brightness (including fading, disappearing, and reappearing) of the distant lights seen over the top of Brown Mountain.

Fireflies

Mansfield (1922) discusses Martin's observations and suggests fireflies:

> The lights seen by Mr. Martin from Adams Mountain can probably not be satisfactorily explained after so long a lapse of time. There is no reason to attribute to them supernatural or unusual origin and they cannot be explained as due to mirage, which is Mr. Martin's idea. The suggestion that they might have been caused by moonshiners carrying lanterns has been rejected because of the roughness of the east side of Brown Mountain and because of the distance that the lights seemed to travel in 20 minutes. They might be due to fireflies flying relatively near Mr. Martin yet appearing unduly large because his eyes were focused on the distant hillside, the appearance of going in and out of ravines being due to the intermittence in the lights, but H.S. Barber, an entomologist of the Division of Insects of the National Museum, to whom the matter was referred, states that this explanation, though possible, is improbable, chiefly because of the lateness of the hour of observation [*Origin of the Brown Mountain Light in North Carolina*; U.S. Geological Survey Circular 646]

Mansfield's explanation of Martin's observations as fireflies is the first published mention of possibly naturally occurring bioluminescent lights in the area. The explanation takes on even greater significance now that we know the rare blue ghost firefly (*Phausis reticulata*) does exist in the area and is more widespread than many would think. In 1916, the existence of this continuously illuminated firefly was not known (see Chapter 22). Martin's observations are also consistent with the woodland environment of the blue ghost firefly, as well as its habit of flying horizontally near the ground, staying lighted for a considerable flight distance (100–200 feet), instantly turning on and off unexpectedly, and wandering back and forth during its flight. The firefly's extreme light sensitivity may also explain why none of the camping parties, undoubtedly with handheld flashlights or lanterns, saw the lights on their respective mountain and only those campers at a distance saw the lights. My own observations of blue ghost fireflies also confirm the ease of misjudging the distance from the observer, and thus the size and motion of the lights, such as that explained by Mansfield.

In addition, and assuming the sky was clear, the rising of the moon (56 percent Waxing Gibbous) in the middle of the day (12:34 p.m.) on April 11 would have meant that the light from the moon might have interfered with the early-evening activity of the blue ghost fireflies, preventing them from being more active. On moon-lit nights they hide from the light and fly only in the shadows of thick brush. The moon set below the western horizon at 2:18 a.m. the morning of April 12, and the resultant darkness may have played a role in the 5:10 a.m. light sighting. Again assuming clear skies, Saturn, Venus and Mars would have been visible in the western sky that night but apparently did not play a role in the lights reported. Jupiter, a daytime event on that date, would also not likely have been involved with the sightings.

Chapter 7

Government Investigations: 1913, 1919 and 1922

> Today ... it is politically effective, and socially acceptable, to deny scientific fact. Manufactured doubt ... is replacing science and technology. Science is a tradition. And as we know from history's darkest moments, even the most enlightened traditions can be broken and lost.
> —Adam Frank, "Welcome to the Age of Denial," *New York Times*, August 22, 2013
>
> Superstitions are incorrect identifications of causal links.
> —Dr. Kevin Foster, Harvard Evolutionary Biologist
>
> Do we only see what we already know?
> SerraGlia, Architect and Visual Designer, 2013

Sterrett in 1913 (U.S. Geological Survey)

Responding to the 1913 request from Congress, the United States Geological Survey (USGS) sent one of its most highly respected geologists to investigate. D.B. Sterrett, a published author with many years of experience investigating the geology of the southeastern United States, arrived in the area in October 1913. While it is not clear where Sterrett got his information, he headed straight for Brown Mountain and apparently examined the geology of the area but found nothing of unusual interest. He spent at least part of a night observing for lights, again apparently seeing nothing of interest except perhaps the headlights of a distant train locomotive. Concluding his short investigation, he quickly returned to Washington. Being in the upper management of the USGS and presumably short on time, Sterrett did not write a formal report; instead he simply discounted the local residents' concern and announced that the mystery light was most likely due to the headlight of a distant train locomotive in the Catawba Valley. But did he actually observe such a light?

In 1913 Brown Mountain was probably undergoing extensive logging. Open views toward the Catawba Valley to the east and south may have been present and would have allowed Sterrett unobstructed views. Otherwise, the usual thick tree cover would have prevented any distant views. Certainly in later years, once the forest had recovered sufficiently from the logging in the early 1900s, many BML observers state in print that no mystery lights, including train headlights, can be seen from the mountain itself.

Brown Mountain was sold to the U.S. government in 1917 (Unknown, 1917), presumably after it was stripped of useful trees. Buying logged-over land was a common method by which the U.S. government acquired much of its Forest Service lands in the southeast. Today the forest has greatly recovered and virtually no open views are present on the mountain; but in 1913 Sterrett may have had unobstructed views that included a train locomotive headlight at night. We may never know if he actually saw a train or not.

Following his short investigation, Sterrett was heavily criticized by local residents for not conducting eyewitness interviews or spending more time actually tracking down specific mystery lights. Local residents were not only disappointed in Sterrett's investigation, they were unimpressed with government geologists as well.

Sightings Continue

Sightings of mystery lights continued. In 1915 C.L. Wilson reported that it was not one mystery light as previously reported but rather many mystery lights that were visible from Loven's Hotel at Cold Springs. In 1916 H.C. Martin's camping parties on both Brown Mountain and Adams Mountain saw several mystery lights at differing times among the trees (Pearson, 1916; Mansfield, 1922) (see Chapter 10). Also in 1916, M.A. Bird saw a bright light hovering and then moving rapidly over Brown Mountain (Bird, 1916). Other 1916 published writings report multiple lights appearing immediately after nightfall in multiple places beyond the top of Brown Mountain and burning for irregular intervals (Elam, 1916; Loven, 1916).

After the monumental flood of 1916 (see Bell, 1916) mystery lights were still reportedly visible from Cold Springs and Wiseman's View (Loven, 1916; Parris, 1972) (see Chapter 9). Loven's Hotel continued receiving increased visitation due to the mystery lights and curious patrons flocked there to see them (Elam, 1916; Perry, 1919).

Also observing from Loven's Hotel, Professor W.G. Perry of the Georgia School of Technology wrote a detailed description of mystery lights to the Smithsonian Institution in 1919 (see Perry's letter in Chapter 8).

Humphreys in 1919 (U.S. Weather Bureau)

In November 1921 the National Geographic Society (NGS) issued a bulletin quoting Dr. W.J. Humphreys, of the U.S. Weather Bureau, who investigated the mystery lights in 1919, although he apparently never visited the area. Dr. Humphreys attributed the light phenomenon to brush lightning, which he described as somewhat akin to St. Elmo's fire and the Andes light. In part, the NGS bulletin reads:

> Scientists were at first prone to cavil at the stories which came out of the mountains with the tourists thinking perhaps that Locomotive headlights or wily mountaineers were playing tricks on active imaginations—but today, Dr. W.J. Humphreys, physicist of the United States Weather Bureau, and other meteorologists of note, believe that there occurs around the mountain's crest a brush discharge of lighting, similar to the famous Andes lighting, or St. Elmo's fire, which gave rise among the ancient Greeks to the myth of Castor and Pollux. That glow which accompanied the slow discharge of electricity to the earth from the atmosphere, in southern climates, during thunderstorms, seen on the tops of masts, spires, or other pointed objects was named St. Elmo's fire by sailors after one of their patron saints, because they felt that when the sign appeared they had nothing further to fear from the storm.
>
> Perhaps the most remarkable feature of the electrical discharge which takes place either from the

earth to the clouds or from the clouds to the earth around Brown mountain is that it is silent. The same thing is true of electrical displays in the Andes, which have long been known to scientists and travelers in the South American continent as the Andes Lighting. It appears as a silent but very luminous discharge of electricity along the crest of the Cordillera Real in Chili, in a region where thunder storms are practically unknown ["Brown Mountain Light Is Coming into Its Own as Natural Wonder," *Trenton Evening Times*, November 18, 1921].

Mansfield in 1922 (U.S. Geological Survey)

By 1922, the local residents once again were expressing grave concern about the ever-increasing number of mysterious lights being seen over the top of Brown Mountain. Sill believing that most of the visible lights were not man-made lights, they assumed the lights were some form of unknown natural, possibly harmful, light and once again, for the second time in ten years, they called on the state's elected politicians for help resolve the issue. And once again, North Carolina's politicians petitioned Congress for help. And once again, Congress asked the U.S. Geological Survey to conduct another investigation. These two requests from Congress directing the U.S. Geological Survey to investigate supposed mystery lights were highly unusual at the time, had never happened before and haven't happened since. The USGS, probably rightfully irritated by the repeated requests to suspend its usual highly professional activities to investigate supposed mystery lights, proceeded to do its best to solve the mystery once and for all. This time, accomplished field geologist George Rogers Mansfield was assigned the task and was directed to take as much time as needed to conduct a proper investigation.

Mansfield arrived in March 1922 and over the next two weeks conducted the most thorough and complete scientific investigation ever undertaken on the BMLs. Mansfield's findings were published by the U.S. Geological Survey as one of their usual professional scientific serial journals: *Origin of the Brown Mountain Light in North Carolina*; U.S. Geological Survey Circular 646 (reprinted 1971).

What Was Known About the BMLs in 1922?

Just as in any major scientific investigation, Mansfield went to great lengths to verify and record what was already known about the subject under investigation. He interviewed eyewitnesses, local residents, and historical experts. In addition, he reviewed published and unpublished documents. The following time line of events is summarized from Mansfield's Circular 646:

1897 Joseph Loven of Cold Springs saw BMLs but did not report them until 1910.
1897, 1899–1903, 1905 H.L. Millner, railroad engineer, worked and vacationed in the Brown Mountain area but never saw BMLs until 1910.
1908 or 1909 BMLs reportedly seen by B.S. Gaither of Morganton.
1910 BMLs reportedly seen by the Rev. C.E. Gregory from his cottage near Loven's Hotel at Cold Springs.
1909–1912 the Rev. A. Sherrill, country pastor, never saw any BMLs although he traveled extensively in the area.
c. 1911 BMLs seen by members of Morganton Fishing Club.

1913 First published account of BMLs—September 13, *Charlotte Daily Observer* (Col. Wade H. Harris, editor).

1913 USGS geologist Sterrett study (October)—concluded lights were locomotive headlights.

1915 W.W. Scott November 10 newspaper article aroused much local interest.

1916 H.C. Martin (Adams Mtn) and Dr. L.H. Coffey (Brown Mountain) expedition (April 11), during which both parties see mystery lights.

1916 Flood on Catawba River washed out railroad bridges and tracts but BMLs still seen from Cold Springs, thus not solely locomotive headlights.

1919 Smithsonian was asked for advice—deferred to U.S. Weather Bureau—Dr. W.J. Humphreys proposed an origin analogous to Andes light.

1921 Dr. H. Lyman Andes light presentation to American Meteorological Society at U.S. Weather Bureau in Washington (April).

1921 National Geographic Society issued bulletin referring to U.S. Weather Bureau scientists quoted on BMLs as manifestation of Andes light.

Notice that Mansfield's time line, based on the most thorough and complete investigation ever undertaken, does not mention sightings by Native Americans or settlers in the area before the days of electricity. Those myths did not exist until later. In fact, such myths may have been generated in a blatant attempt by less-scientifically oriented people to counter the legend-damaging impact of Mansfield's investigation.

Mansfield further reports that the only lights that had previously been seen on Brown Mountain itself were campfires, as well as possible lights from two buildings on the mountain, one owned by the Brown Mountain Club and the other owned by the U.S. Forest Service. Mansfield elaborates on the lack of mystery light sightings by observers on Brown Mountain itself by quoting conversations with several individuals, with extensive overnight experience on the mountain, who had never seen a mystery light or lights. In addition, he reports that buildings on the "southern spurs of Brown and Adams Mountains," as well as logging camps in Upper Creek and on Ripshin Ridge might also have furnished lights that were misinterpreted as BMLs by distant observers.

Mansfield interviewed H.C. Martin and accompanied him on at least one observation trip in 1922. Mansfield attributes lights seen by Martin on April 11, 1916, from his camp on Adams Mountain to fireflies: "They might be due to fireflies flying relatively near Mr. Martin yet appearing unduly large because his eyes were focused on the distant hillside, the appearance of going in and out of ravines being due to intermittence in the lights" (G.R. Mansfield, 1922, *Origin of the Brown Mountain Light in North Carolina*, U.S. Geological Survey, Circular 646, p. 6). At the time, Martin's encounter with unknown lights in the woods was the only documented observation of lights that close; otherwise, the BMLs were universally described as distant lights seen over the top of Brown Mountain when observed from higher mountains to the west or northwest. Mansfield's suggestion of fireflies is the earliest known reference to naturally occurring bioluminescent lights possibly being mistaken for BMLs.

Mansfield lists the following eleven origins for the BMLs, which were suggested to him as possible explanations by the people he interviewed or interacted with:

Will-o'-the-wisp
Phosphorus
Phosphorescence (foxfire)

Radium emanations
Hydrogen sulfide/lead oxide chemical reaction
Blockade (illicit) liquor stills
St. Elmo's fire
Andes light
Mirage
Locomotive headlights
Automobile headlights

Mansfield's Investigation

For his investigation Mansfield relied heavily on accurate line-of-sight measurements of distant lights seen from the higher elevation sites where supposed mystery lights were reported to be observed. His equipment included:

Plane table (flat drawing board, leveled and supported on tripod legs)
Alidade (telescope sighting tube with parallel straight edge for drawing lines-of-sight)
Compasses for measuring horizontal bearings and vertical angles
Binoculars for sighting distant lights
Flashlight
Camera
Topographic maps of the region

No photographic images accompanied Mansfield's Circular 646 document; however, two of his daytime distant images of Brown Mountain are housed in the USGS photography archives (Mansfield, 1922, USGS Photography Collection, images 595 and 596).

Based on the input of eyewitnesses and his own observations, Mansfield chose three separate stations for his surveys: (A) The Rev. C.E. Gregory's cabin near Loven's Hotel at Cold Springs; (B) the east slope of Gingercake Mountain; and (C) a residence at Blowing Rock. Two nights were spent on Brown Mountain, but due to the lack of observed lights no station was established there. Mansfield noted that he was able to adequately measure only 23 lights with his instruments, while perhaps twice as many other visible lights did not remain lighted long enough for him to complete all of the required measurements. Thus, from his three viewing stations, Mansfield apparently observed approximately 69 separate lights, although he does mention that scores of other lights can be seen on clear nights.

Observations at each station began in the daytime to allow for proper orientation of the topographic maps on the plane table and the drawing of lines-of-sight to prominent distant landmarks. After dark, lines-of-sight, bearings, and vertical angles were recorded for at least 23 separate supposed mystery lights, while field descriptions were made in a notebook. Critical adjustments for temperature, refraction and the earth's curvature were determined and modifications to the map positions of lights were made after each night's observation. Mansfield noted that the line-of-sight to all 23 lights he fully measured passed several hundred feet over the top of Brown Mountain, indicating that the lights were located in the valley far beyond Brown Mountain, although some of the lights appeared to the unaided eye to be on, or even below, the crest of Brown Mountain. Mansfield's investigation was apparently the first time an image-magnifying telescope was employed.

Observing from Gregory's Cabin (Station A)

Observing from Gregory's cabin on March 29, Mansfield noted that some lights appearing as single lights to the unaided eye were found to be multiple lights when viewed through the alidade telescope. One notable light was specifically identified by Joseph L. Loven, Robert Loven, Earl Loven, and Robert Ward to be a typical mystery light because it changed brightness significantly, often disappearing completely and then reappearing and occasionally seeming to move when observed by the naked eye. However, when viewed through the telescope, it was always visible, although at times it was dim and it never moved. Joseph Loven was the owner of Loven's Hotel and at the time was considered the most knowledgeable expert on the BMLs. Robert and Earl Loven were apparently two of his sons. Other lights were found to correspond to times and positions of train locomotives on railroad track curves near Conover. Additional lights were attributed to automobile headlights.

Observing from Gingercake Mountain (Station B)

Observing from Gingercake Mountain with Joseph Loven and Robert Ward on April 1, 2 and 3, Mansfield attributed nine lights to probable automobile headlights, and three lights corresponded in time and position to train locomotives near Catawba and Drexel (times confirmed later by train agents at those train stations). In addition, Train No. 35, a westbound Southern Railway passenger train, was expected to arrive at the Connelly Springs train station at 12:25 a.m. on the morning of April 3, so Mansfield and the others waited and watched. At 12:33 a.m., a light flared over Brown Mountain and was seen through the alidade telescope to be near the Connelly Springs train station. Later examination of the train station register at Connelly Springs confirmed that Train No. 35 ran ten minutes late that night, confirming that it was indeed the light seen by Mansfield and others at 12:33 a.m.

Mansfield states Joseph Loven repeatedly said that the lights they saw from Gingercake Mountain were typical mystery lights, including those subsequently identified as car and train headlights. Was Loven convinced that the lights seen through the alidade telescope and those identified by Mansfield as train or automobile headlights were his mysterious BMLs? Perhaps he was, as he was seldom, if ever, heard from again in print regarding the BMLs.

Observing from Blowing Rock (Station C)

On the evenings of April 3 and 4, accompanied by Robert Ward and H.C. Martin (observer of suspected fireflies in 1916), Mansfield identified the following: two probable brush fires on a ridge north of Mulberry Creek; a probable locomotive headlight on the Carolina, Clinchfield and Ohio Railway about a mile southeast of Spruce Pine; an automobile headlight on the streets of Lenoir; and another locomotive headlight. However, on both nights, H.C. Martin stated that the lights seen were not the mystery lights because they did not occur over Brown Mountain and did not move laterally or obliquely as the ones he had seen in 1916 did. Numerous other lights seen from Blowing Rock were believed to be man-made city and town lights.

Observing from Brown Mountain

On April 5 Mansfield, along with F.H. May, spent the night at the Forest Service building on the summit of Brown Mountain but saw no lights. On the sixth, they were joined by Monroe Coffey of the U.S. Forest Service and conducted a hike to the hill above the head of Parke Creek, but again they saw no lights.

Mansfield's Conclusions

Mansfield found no connection to the Andes light or St. Elmo's fire—in other words, nothing related to lighting phenomenon, as had been previously suggested by the U.S. Weather Bureau. Nor did he find geologic evidence for naturally occurring lights. He did note significant refraction of distant valley lights as the light waves passed through air layers of varying density (due to differences in temperature, humidity, and dust) between the observers and the light sources. He felt that this refraction was responsible for the reddish or yellowish tints frequently observed, as well as the rapid changes in brightness of the lights. Lights seen to disappear completely to the naked eye only to reappear moments later were often found to still glow dimly when viewed through the alidade telescope. Mansfield attributed the supposed mystery lights to this refraction of otherwise stationary man-made lights (specifically the fading, brightening, and reappearing in the same place). Moving vehicle lights can show the same refraction effects but generally are a flash too brief for an observer to notice refraction. Thus Mansfield concluded that the supposed mystery lights were due to distant man-made lights influenced by atmospheric refraction. Note that atmospheric refraction was first alluded to by H.C. Martin in 1916 (see Pearson, 1916).

Mansfield correctly predicted that mystery lights could not have been seen before about 1892, when he thought electricity first arrived in the area (the actual first appearance of electricity was in 1888). He also mentions that powerful electric headlights (600,000 candlepower) on locomotives began about 1909, about the same time the Rev. C.E. Gregory and observers at Loven's Hotel at Cold Springs began reporting regular light sightings. The arrival of automobiles, many also with powerful headlights, began about this same time. Automobiles probably gave rise to the lights seen immediately after the major flood of 1916.

According to Mansfield, the supposed motion of the BMLs might be due to errors of observation: "The eye is easily deceived at night as to the stability or motion of an object, and an observer's impressions are to a considerable extent affected by his mental and physical condition at the time of observation. It is not surprising that under the circumstances different eyewitnesses give quite different accounts of the light, especially as the light may appear suddenly against a dark background with nothing nearby that can be used as a scale to determine its size or its possible motion." In conclusion, Mansfield wrote, "In summary it may be said that the Brown Mountain lights are clearly not of unusual nature or origin. About 47 percent of the lights that the writer was able to study instrumentally were due to automobile headlights, 33 percent to locomotive headlights, 10 percent to stationary lights, and 10 percent to brush fires."

Death of the Legend? Close, but Not Quite!

The publication of Mansfield's Circular 646 was a big disappointment to local residents and others who did not agree with his findings. However, the thoroughness, detail, and accuracy of the report, backed by the full prestige and investigative power of the U.S. Geological Survey, were enough to kill the legend in the minds of everyone except a few diehards. Although some local residents continued to assert otherwise, the legend was dealt a major blow and it would take another 30 years before it would recover, albeit significantly changed. In addition to the USGS's authoritative report concluding that misidentifications of man-made lights were the primary sources of the BMLs, the realization was growing that the ever-increasing human population in the valleys south and east of Brown Mountain was contributing to even more new lights every year visible over the top of the mountain. As a result, a slow but steady morphing or changing of the legend began. By the early 1950s the interest had shifted away from lights seen over the top of Brown Mountain, the very lights that gave rise to the legend in the first place, and instead interest focused on less-easily dismissed lights now being seen seven to ten miles to the west in Linville Gorge (see Chapter 27).

Following Mansfield's report, tourists visiting Loven's Hotel in Cold Springs and other hotels in Blowing Rock stopped coming just to see mystery lights. While tourism in Blowing Rock recovered on its own, Joseph Loven's Hotel did not; in fact, Joseph L. Loven (1867–1937) and his hotel, which were so instrumental in the beginning days of the legend, passed into obscurity and were seldom mentioned in print again.

After 1922, published accounts of the BMLs began mentioning previously unpublished and unconfirmed stories of pre-electricity sightings and ghost myths in apparent attempts to counter Mansfield's scientific findings and keep the legend alive. The first year some of these new stories were published appear below:

1923 Civil War sightings (F.J. Haskin)
1923 Light seen before days of automobiles (*Statesville Record*)
1927 De Brahm's 1771 sighting (R.K. Babington)
1936 Ghost of a murdered wife (S.M. Dugger)
1938 Ghosts of Indian maidens since 1200 AD battle (H. McAfee)
1948 Ghost of a lost lover (*North Carolina Folklore*)
1961 Ghost of faithful slave searching for master (S. Wiseman)

Once each of these new stories was first published, it was subsequently published again and again, often with modifications or embellishments added by each new author. While some of the popular ghost stories probably existed before 1922, they apparently were not taken seriously enough to be included in published documents until the years following Mansfield's investigation. After 1922, these and other unsubstantiated stories (such as foxfire, will-o'-the-wisp, chemical reactions, uranium, radium emissions, lightning, moonshine stills, etc.) became very common as people apparently sought support for alternative explanations. It seems Mansfield's investigation had dealt a major blow to the legend and it would be many years before it regained its former glory.

Chapter 8

Early Photographers of the Lights

1929 Ball Photograph

One of Ewart M. Ball's 1929 photographs is believed to be the oldest known image of lights purported by some to be the BMLs. Ewart M. Ball, Sr., (1894–1937) was a professional photographer from Asheville, North Carolina, who worked as a staff photographer for the Asheville newspaper. His four-hour, glass-plate, time-exposure photograph was taken at Wiseman's View. A large, very bright light streak in the image is the nearly full moon. The view is to the east and, although dark, Brown Mountain is seen as the nearly flat-top ridge in the middle distance. A horizontal band of multiple faint lights can be seen above and extending to the south of Brown Mountain.

The unpublished Ball photograph is image #N1503 in the E.M. Ball Collection in the Photography Collection at the D.H. Ramsey Library at the University of North Carolina–Asheville (UNCA) (Ball, 1929). Unfortunately, only low-resolution versions of the original image are available and they don't reproduce well enough to include here. Although unpublished, Ball's photograph was the subject of a newspaper article by J.S. Coleman, Jr., in the August 25 issue of the *Asheville Times* (now the *Asheville Citizen-Times*):

> Within the last two weeks, however, the lights have been photographed for the first time in history. The difficult work was done by E.M. Ball of the Plateau studio, Asheville, and the result was highly satisfactory, even though the picture failed utterly to explain the phenomenon.
> Mr. Ball took his pictures from a point not far distant from Marion. He exposed a very sensitive color plate one night over a period of four hours. During that time, the moon, sliding across the sky, left a bright streak on his plate, but the mysterious Brown Mountain lights had been caught in the meantime.
> One thing established by the photograph is the fact that the light appears at several parallel points along a line near the summit of Brown Mountain. Each of the points seems to be a small disk of light, though the impression given an observer is that of a blaze [J.S. Coleman, Jr., "Strange Light Continues to Mystify; Rays Visible Every Evening on Brown Mountain" *Asheville Times*, August 25, 1929].

Apparently Ball did not give his permission for his image to accompany Coleman's article; or perhaps the newspaper editor eliminated the photograph to conserve space. Why Ball himself never published his photograph is unknown, but it may have stemmed from his belief that these were not mystery lights, but rather were normal city/town/rural lights in the valley beyond Brown Mountain. Or perhaps he believed these were mystery lights but could not convince the newspaper editor to accept the photograph for publication. As an experienced photographer, Ball's interpretation of the lights that showed up in his image would have been informative. Certainly if he had published the image he could have made some money or at least enhanced his career as a professional photographer. Apparently he had no interest in additional photos and never returned to photograph the lights (at least, no additional BML images are present in the Ball Collection at UNCA).

A careful study of Ball's 1929 image reveals important information. Comparison with recent photographs by the author from Wiseman's View suggests that the focal length of Ball's camera lens was about the same as a 24 mm lens on a modern 35 mm camera. Visible landmarks include the east rim of Linville Gorge, the north slope of Table Rock Mountain, Bandy Cove Mountain and North Bandy Cove Mountain, as well as Brown Mountain. These landmarks and their positions within the field of view of the image suggest that Ball's camera was positioned at Wiseman's View, which is also the observation site indicated by the label on Ball's image in the Ramsey Library collection.

Although the specific date of Ball's photograph is not recorded, it can be deduced from the image itself. Based on the bright phase of the moon, the azimuth of the moonrise, and the angle of the moon's ascending light path, the image must have been taken on the evening of Friday, August 23, 1929. The nearly-full, 78 percent waning Gibbous moon rose at 10:06 p.m. that evening at an azimuth of 86.4° and a light-path angle of 54° from the horizontal as predicted from Wiseman's View's 36° North latitude. The full moon rose on Tuesday, three days earlier. The four-hour time exposure must have lasted until early Saturday morning. This combination of timing, moonrise location, moon phase, and angle of ascent are distinctive to the night of August 23, 1929, and, due to the moon's unique 18.6-year cycle, was previously seen only from Wiseman's View in 1910 and would not be repeated again until 1947.

Since the azimuth of the moonrise moved 7.0–7.5° farther north each night in late August 1929, the moonrise a night earlier or a night later would have been at a much different position relative to Brown Mountain than it was on the night of August 23. This data was provided by moon ephemeris tables (*The Photographer's Ephemeris and Star Walk*) and measurements by Lee Hawkins, Observatory Engineer, Appalachian State University, Department of Physics and Astronomy, Boone, North Carolina. Coleman's article about Ball's photograph was published three days later in the Sunday, August 25, edition of the *Asheville Times*.

1958 Brown Photographs

Bob Brown of Asheville, North Carolina, was a popular elementary school science instructor whose annual Bob Brown's Science Circus visited area schools with interactive demonstrations. Brown also published several books keyed to introducing kids to science and wrote newspaper articles about science.

One of Brown's BML photographs was published in Bill Sharpe's 1958 *A New Geography of North Carolina*. However, Brown specifically called the lights town lights, not mysterious lights. While the photo is credited to Bob Brown, the actual date it was taken is not mentioned; however, it seems safe to assume it was close to 1958, the publication date of the book. Unfortunately, Brown's image in Sharpe's book does not reproduce well enough to include here and original copies have not been found. The caption with the image in Sharpe's book reads, "the first picture we (the editors) have seen of the Brown Mountain Lights seems to prove that the lights do not come from the top of Brown Mountain (black profile) but from far beyond the mountain itself" (Bill Sharpe, 1958, *A New Geography of North Carolina*, vol. 2).

Remember that Ball's 1929 image was never published and apparently Sharpe's editors were not aware of any earlier photographs. In his article in Sharpe's book, Brown agrees with USGS geologist Mansfield (1922) and concludes that the lights are from the valley beyond Brown Mountain and are affected by atmospheric conditions: "This seems to be the correct solution, as our photographs indicate. When the atmospheric conditions are right, the refraction in the air and moisture cause the apparent movement and the turning on and the going off. This could also account for the change of color which is often seen" (B. Brown, 1958, "Spoke Lights," in *A New Geography of North Carolina*, vol. 2, Bill Sharpe).

Brown also mentions that he took eight separate images on July 7 from the home of Joel C. McCurry, near Loven's Hotel on Jonas Ridge, and that the prominent light streaks in the photos are those of cars on NC Hwy 181 during his time exposures. Only one of Brown's images was published in Sharpe's book; however, cropped versions of that one and others appeared ten years later in Herbert Bailey's 1968 magazine article (see below). Brown and his young son, who also accompanied him during his photography on Jonas Ridge, camped on Brown Mountain July 10 but saw no lights.

In June 1962 Bob Brown published an article, picked up by several newspapers, that described and illustrated a simple kitchen science experiment that demonstrated the refraction of light rays due to rising warm air, similar to what he believed was happening to the city/town/rural lights seen over the top of Brown Mountain (Brown, 1962; June 1, 2, 3). Brown's experiment was geared toward elementary-school kids and involved a darkened kitchen, a hot plate sitting on the kitchen table, a flashlight aimed across the hot plate and an observer on the other side of the table. The rising heat waves from the hot plate distort the light waves from the flashlight, causing the light to waver, wobble, wiggle up and down, and fade in and out—just as rising heat currents over Brown Mountain distort the lights from the valley beyond. This refraction of light rays due to rising heat waves (mirages) was previously mentioned by H.C. Martin in 1916 (Pearson, 1916) and G.R. Mansfield in 1922. However, Brown's kitchen science experiment made it clear for all to see exactly how it happened. All three men were suggesting that it was the refraction and distortion of lights from the valley beyond Brown Mountain that caused at least some of the supposed mystery lights to appear to move, change color, and fade in and out—in other words, to act as if they were "alive."

1940 Whitman Photo

Hobart A. Whitman, of Asheville, North Carolina, conducted an extensive investigation of the BMLs in 1940 and on October 11 of that year wrote a letter to the *Asheville Citizen* explaining his conclusions (Whitman, 1940). George William McCoy (1901–1962), a staff member of the *Asheville Citizen* newspaper for 37 years, including editor from 1955 until 1961, wrote an article based on Whitman's letter (McCoy, 1940) and shows one of Whitman's photographs. Unfortunately, as with other old newsprint photographs, we have been unable to find images that reproduce well enough to include here. However, the caption with the photograph reads, "Here's a view of the Brown Mountain lights from Lovens—point "A" on the map (Mansfield's 1922 map). Only two lights were visible when this photograph was taken by H.A. Whitman in June of this year. The light at the right is directly over Brown Mountain. Mr. Whitman took this photograph in a one-hour time exposure, starting at 9:30 pm, on a full moonlight night" (G. McCoy, 1940). Whitman concluded that all of the lights he saw, studied and photographed were distant man-made city/town/rural lights refracted by atmospheric conditions. See more on Whitman's very thorough scientific investigation in Chapter 15.

1962 Baity Photograph

Jim Baity's historic 1962 lightning-strike photograph shows some unusual lights. In 2013, our BML research team interviewed Mr. Baity. Later that year he attended one of our planning meetings and shared his experiences.

In 1962, Baity was a newspaper reporter and his photograph was published in his article "Brown Mountain Lights Remain a Mystery to Viewers" in the July 29, 1962, issue of the *Asheville Citizen-Times* (Baity, 1962). Information presented here comes from the 1962 newspaper article (which included the image) and personal interviews with Mr. Baity in 2013. Unfortunately, Mr. Baity's newspaper photograph does not copy well enough to reproduce here and we have been unable to find original images.

The photograph was taken looking east from Wiseman's View and shows several remarkable flashes of lightning, one of which apparently strikes the ground near the summit of Brown Mountain. The camera lens was a telephoto of about 200 mm focal length. The dark ridge in the foreground is the easily identified Bandy Cove Mountain ridge (my name) with the dome-shaped North Bandy Cove Mountain summit (my name; 2,670 feet elevation), 2.9 miles distant. This northeast-trending ridge is nearly 1.4 miles long, varies from 2.9 to 3.4 miles east of Wiseman's View, and lies between the east rim of Linville Gorge and Steels Creek to the east. The south end of the ridge, which is not shown in Baity's image, contains a higher, dome-shaped summit called Bandy Cove Mountain (2,747 feet elevation) on the U.S. Geological Survey's 1993 Chestnut Mountain (7½ minute) topographic map. This ridge, with both the lower northern summit (at 90° azimuth) and the higher southern summit (at 100° azimuth), is a common middle-foreground feature in many photographs of Brown Mountain taken from Wiseman's View.

In addition to lightning flashes, Baity's image shows six small pale grayish white spots of light, four of which appear to lie on or immediately below the southern ridgeline of Brown Mountain and two of which appear to lie on the southwestern flank well below the ridgeline. However, the true distance to these lights cannot be determined from the image. According to Mr. Baity, he and his partner, Ken Thompson, first watched spots of light, "glowing with a rainbow of colors," with the naked eye and then through a 2,000 mm tripod-mounted telephoto lens. He then used a second tripod-mounted camera with a 200 mm telephoto lens to take the time exposure. The lightning flashes were a lucky occurrence during the exposure. The following are his comments:

> This reporter (Jim Baity), accompanied by Kenneth Thompson, made an investigation. Traveling to Wiseman's View, we were able to photograph the lights and, using binoculars, we were able to count 47 lights while only eight were visible to the naked eye.
>
> The lights are distributed along the full length of the mountain above and below the crest. They appear to the eye as a lit cigarette in a dark room, glowing with a rainbow of colors. As one watches,

the lights intensify, growing to the size of a floodlight. Then they subside and disappear [Jim Baity, 1962].

The mystery lights must have been present for sufficient time for Mr. Baity to first notice them with the naked eye, then through binoculars and the big telephoto lens, and then to switch cameras and take the photograph. In addition, Baity reports that he and Thompson saw eight similar mystery lights visible to the naked eye and 47 visible with binoculars along the full length of Brown Mountain both above and through the trees on the crest.

Could Baity and Thompson have been observing the multicolored distant city, town and rural lights that usually appear immediately above the crest of Brown Mountain? Such visible lights were a normal nightly event in 1962; and binocular magnification would have easily revealed more lights than the naked eye could see—just as Baity describes. While Baity's description of the colored lights matches the description of distant city/town/rural lights known to be visible in 1962, he does not report, nor does he remember seeing or identifying, actual man-made electric lights that night.

So is it possible that the six small lights in Baity's photograph are not the same as the lights they saw with the naked eye, or through binoculars and the big telephoto lens? Baity reports that lights in the image are the same lights they saw without magnification, even though they don't fit the lights he describes or the expected city/town/rural lights.

Given the observational inconsistencies mentioned above, alternative explanations of the lights in the photograph are considered. The presence of a very active thunderstorm in the area during Baity's photography suggests three other possible interpretations: (1) ball lightning or some similar, related phenomenon; (2) internal lens flares due to the bright lightning flashes; and (3) reflections of light from the lightning flashes in raindrops on the outer surface of the camera lens.

While possible, ball lightning is easily dismissed since it is extremely rare and it does not appear to fit the size, shape or positions of the six lights in Baity's image. But can internal lens flares or water-drop reflections be dismissed so easily? Lens flares due to refraction of light waves as they travel through multi-element telephoto lenses are a common phenomenon and cannot be ruled out. In addition, reflection of the lightning flashes in water drops on the lens is also a valid possibility that fits the observed size, shape and position of the lights.

Baity's description of the lights they saw that night is consistent with the expected distant city/ town/rural lights known to be present; however, the image does not show any such obvious lights. Could it be that Baity and Thompson saw distant city/town/rural lights with magnification, interpreted them as mystery lights, and then photographed lightning flashes with resultant lens flares or water-drop reflections while the distant city/town/rural lights were blocked by low clouds?

Today, Baity continues to believe that the lights in his 1962 photograph are the same unexplained mysterious lights they saw and described that night. We may never understand exactly what produced the spots of light in Baity's photograph, but logical alternatives to mystery light interpretations do exist.

Baity and Thompson subsequently spent the next three days camping on Brown Mountain but saw no mystery lights there. They did report finding a five-acre marsh atop the mountain from which they were able to collect and ignite some bubbles of organic gas with a match. The gas burned immediately as a bright blue flame. However, due to the lack of marshes or swamps along the full length of Brown Mountain, they did

1968 Bailey Photographs

Interestingly, Bob Brown's 1958 photograph (described earlier) shows up ten years later in Herbert Bailey's "Come See the Flying Saucers!" article in the December 1968 issue of *Argosy*, a popular pulp fiction magazine of the time. While Bailey mentions not being able to properly photograph the lights during his visit, the actual photographer of the images accompanying his article is not credited. However, close inspection reveals that it is Brown's 1958 image, now cropped and enlarged. As with other old newsprint images, the *Argosy* images don't reproduce well enough to include here. The caption with the 1968 *Argosy* image reads: "Entire squadron of UFOs in flight." The caption on another image reads: "Mysterious 'lights' arrive in gathering darkness. UFOs issue from depression at left, then string out along ridge."

Bailey's contention in the *Argosy* article is that UFOs can be seen every clear night issuing from the gap between Adams and Brown mountains and then flying over the crest of Brown Mountain to gain altitude before they disappear in the distance. Bailey reports two to three hundred UFOs lined up atop Brown Mountain on the night he observed them. Obviously, today we've come a long way in understanding that these are all man-made city/town/rural lights.

Two additional images in the *Argosy* magazine article are similar to the first two and thus appear to be copies of other Bob Brown images; however, those originals have yet to be seen. Brown reports exposing eight separate images on the night he took the one above, so there might be more still to be found. Somehow, the *Argosy* magazine editors got hold of at least several of Bob Brown's photos; so it seems probable that more of Brown's photos may also have been published somewhere else that we have yet to find.

Historic Photograph Conclusions

Nearly all historic photographs of supposedly mysterious BMLs that I've seen, beginning with the first one in 1929, show the expected city/town/rural lights in the far distance over the top of Brown Mountain. Only Jim Baity's 1962 image shows a different kind of light, which may be due to lens flares or water-drop reflections.

The lack of convincing photographic evidence of supposedly mystery lights in the first 70–80 years of the legend strong suggests that misconceptions are a major factor in the existence of the legend.

But do more recent photographs give us better evidence of the existence of mystery lights? Apparently not, as the lack of convincing photographic evidence continues to this day and no one has yet been able to provide any. Note that our BML team's more than 580,000 recent photographic images also fail to document any apparently abnormal mystery lights. We'll take a look at some of these newer photos in subsequent chapters.

Chapter 9

Paul Rose's 1962 Tower on Brown Mountain

1962—The Biggest Year in Recent BML History

The year 1962 was perhaps the most momentous recent year in the legend of the BMLs, as numerous significant stories unfolded that year. Bob Brown's simple home kitchen science experiment demonstrating the effects of rising heat waves as an explanation of mysterious lights was published in numerous newspapers in June of that year (Brown, 1962), while Jim Baity's lightning-strike photograph and comprehensive personal accounts were published in late July (Baity, 1962). Paul Rose and his tower lights, Ralph Lael and his trip to Venus with aliens, and Sonny James' recording of Scotty Wiseman's popular ballad "The Legend of the Brown Mountain Lights" rounded out this eventful year.

Tower Atop Brown Mountain Catches Public's Imagination

In early August 1962, Jonas Ridge resident and nurseryman Paul Rose (1908–1972), captured the public's imagination following numerous newspaper accounts of his colorful reports of nightly close encounters with multiple supposed mystery lights by he himself and several other observers atop his hastily constructed tower on Brown Mountain (U.S. Forest Service land). Within days, thousands of cars were choking NC Highway 181 as locals and visitors arrived to see the lights. Enterprising property owners along the highway began charging visitors to park their cars, and concession stands opened (Shires, 1962). However, failing to see mystery lights, the crowds soon stopped coming.

Built without U.S. Forest Service approval, the tower was soon dismantled; however, Rose's tower and his several nights of reported close encounters with supposed mystery lights created the biggest excitement so far in the history of the approximately seventy-year-old legend. Rose instantly became famous and gave many interviews to media reporters. He also intended to capitalize on his notoriety and the mystery of the lights and subsequently petitioned the U.S. Forest Service for permission to construct roads, several towers, restaurants, and hotels on Brown Mountain; however, the Forest Service declined and the required permits were never issued. Alternate plans to build a tourist observation site along Highway 181 also failed to find financial backing.

Tower Location and Description

While the exact location of Rose's tower was apparently not recorded, our research suggests it was located near the northern summit of Brown Mountain. This location is based on the following evidence:

1. Rose's published descriptions of nearby features
2. Sam Rowe's photographs
3. Convenient site along existing access road
4. Presence of various wood artifacts in the area
5. Presence of nails and other small metal hardware in the area
6. Descriptions by people who visited the tower in 1962

Figure 2. Paul Rose on his tower atop Brown Mountain (Sam Rowe photograph, July 1962).

Figure 3. Paul Rose's tower atop Brown Mountain 1962 (Sam Rowe photograph, July 1962).

Sam Rowe's photographs of Paul Rose and his tower are highly informative. Mr. Rowe is a contributing member of our Brown Mountain lights research team and actually visited the tower in 1962.

Our research also suggests the tower was about 25 feet high, not the 60 feet often mentioned in newspaper articles. In addition, it seems doubtful the hastily constructed wooden tower was capable of supporting the weight of more than a few adults at a time.

Lack of Lights Seen by Others

Despite the fact that numerous other people apparently accompanied Rose during several of his nightly sightings, none of them has confirmed Rose's descriptions of the supposed mystery lights. Sam Rowe and Dr. Cato Holler, Jr., two members of our current research team, camped atop Rose's tower the night it was completed (probably Monday, July 30); however, they report seeing only distant car headlights, no mystery lights (Braly, 1962; personal interviews, 2013). Clyde Hollifield, who visited Paul Rose on the tower several different nights, also reports seeing distant vehicle headlights but not the supposed mystery lights reported by Rose (personal communication, 2013). Bob Underwood, who met Paul Rose following the newspaper accounts, reports spending at least one night on the tower but he saw only distant car headlights on NC Highway 181 (personal communication, 2013). Another tower guest reported seeing a floodlight but not the spots of light reported by Rose.

Light Descriptions

According to newspaper accounts, Rose clearly insinuated the lights he saw as a youth on Gingercake Mountain were the same kind of lights as those he saw some 50 years later from his tower on Brown Mountain, yet his published descriptions of the two sets of lights are vastly different. The behaviors of the lights he witnessed on Gingercake are highly suggestive of the behaviors of blue ghost fireflies (Mays, 1962). Of the Gingercake lights, Rose says, "They mostly disappear, you know, when you get real close to them. They move about through the trees, but they don't touch the trees ... and they seem to be sensitive to the human body. They move away from you" (P. Mays, 1962, "Mystery of the Haunted Mountain," Unknown newspaper, September 2, 1962).

As can be seen in the numerous following descriptions of the lights he saw on the tower on Brown Mountain, Rose seems to be describing luminous toxic gasses:

Paul Rose, a Jonas Ridge nurseryman, said a dozen men stood on a tower atop Brown Mountain Wednesday night [August 1, 1962] [and] watched the curious lights flash out of crevices below.

"One of the lights came to rest on the men on the tower," Rose said. "It gave them a static-like feeling of dizziness. When they climbed to the ground, they were unable to stand up."

Rose said of the 12 men atop the 60-foot tower, 11 complained of dizziness. The other said he felt nothing.

Rose said he believes the lights are radioactive. He said he intends to get a geologist to look into them.

Rose said he's been seeing the lights for about 40 years [Unknown Author; "Mystery of Lights Grows," *Charlotte Observer*, August 3, 1962].

Paul Rose, a Jonas Ridge nurseryman, said a dozen men stood on a tower atop Brown Mountain Wednesday night [August 1, 1962] and watched the fabled lights flash out of nearby crevices.

"They came out in circles of about three feet in diameter," said Rose, who is leading the current expedition which hopes to solve the mystery. "The lights were in colors of red, orange, and the color of the moon."

"One of the lights came to rest on the men on the tower. It gave them a static-like feeling of dizziness. When they climbed to the ground, they were unable to stand up."

Rose said of the 12 men atop the 60-foot tower, 11 felt the sense of dizziness. The other felt nothing. Rose said he believes the lights are radioactive or contain some magnetic element.

"The lights seemed to come through the trees, down the mountain under a cliff, and back up again."

Rose said he is anxious to get the opinion of a professional geologist, who may be able to determine why the lights would make people dizzy. Rose and scores of volunteers carried lumber up the mountain last Monday [July 30, 1962] and erected the tower so that viewers could look down into crevices from which the lights appeared to come.

"I still don't know that the lights are coming from the crevice," Rose said Thursday. "But if the weather stays good, I believe we'll be able to find out" [Unknown Author, 1962, "Famed Lights Cause Feeling of Dizziness," *Winston-Salem Journal*, August 3, 1962].

Paul and Jim Rose said they traced the lights Thursday night to the mouth of a small cave. The cave is beneath a cliff. On Wednesday night, 12 men stood on the tower, 11 men became ill & dizzy [Unknown Author, "Brown Mountain Lights Trace to Cave Entrance," *Asheville Citizen*, August 4, 1962].

**Paul Rose describes close encounter with the lights
on Gingercake Mountain during WWI**

"As far as I know, I'm the first one to spot them up close. They mostly disappear, you know, when you get real close to them. They move about through the trees, but they don't touch the trees ... and they seem to be sensitive to the human body. They move away from you."

**Paul Rose describes close encounter with the lights
on tower on Brown Mountain**

Suddenly, glowing balls of orange and red light, about 8 feet in diameter, bubbled up from fissures in the rock around them and soared skyward like balloons, dissipating as they rose. Rose and several of the others became nauseated as the lights neared them.

"When the lights hit us, my knees got weak and shaky. I felt like I didn't weigh two ounces and it was like the lights would pull us right off the tower" [Mays, P., "Mystery of the Haunted Mountain," *Sunday News*, Unknown Newspaper, September 2, 1962].

An underground gas which ignites as it spurts through rock layers. Rose said the flames flare up and burn out four or five times an hour. They are visible from about 9:30 p.m. to about 3 a.m., putting on their wildest show during the later hours, he said.

The gas was discovered by searchers looking for a member of their party who had become lost.

Everyone in the group described the gas as smelling "sweet as a flower" [Unknown Author, "Sweet-Smelling Gas Key to Mystery?," Associated Press 1962(?)].

The various newspaper accounts of Rose's adventures on Brown Mountain give us the following approximate time line of events: Monday, July 30, tower built; Tuesday, July 31, no reported activity; Wednesday, August 1, 12 men on tower saw lights and were dizzy; Thursday August 2 Sweet smelling gas traced to a cave. Apparently Rose's sightings continued for the next week or two (Lael, 1965).

What are we to make of Rose's close encounters with the two sets of lights he saw 50 years apart? The lack of confirmatory observations from others on his Brown Mountain tower suggests caution in accepting his descriptions of those lights. After all, his notoriety began during these observations and he was hoping to make money on the phenomenon. Could he have been embellishing the story in the hope of creating a market for tourists?

Blue Ghost Fireflies?

If both sets of lights are the same, as Rose insinuates, perhaps they were both due to blue ghost fireflies. Certainly the low height of Rose's tower suggests that he might have been seeing blue ghost fireflies, which normally fly only 2–3 feet above the ground during the peak of mating season. Remember, the tower was only about 25 feet tall, plenty tall enough to get above the fireflies for an excellent aerial view. In fact, the tower was not high enough to see much of anything else; it could not see above the treetops, suggesting he was only trying to build a viewing platform to get above something at or near the ground.

My personal experience observing the blue ghost fireflies deep in dark forests shows that the observer can develop feelings of vertigo, dizziness and a loss of balance due to the lack of visual anchoring landmarks as the mass of fireflies move in unison. Perhaps this explains the reported similar experiences of Rose and others on his tower. In addition, a few blue ghost fireflies occasionally fly higher off the ground, and some will approach humans who are being still and do not have lights burning, again perhaps explaining

Rose's similar observations (see Chapter 22 for more on the fascinating but elusive blue ghost fireflies).

The new moon occurred on July 31, 1962, meaning that the nighttime skies during Rose's observations would have been the darkest skies possible—perfect monthly timing for the blue ghost fireflies! We now know that the blue ghost fireflies are extremely sensitive to moonlight and are most active on dark moonless nights such as those during Rose's observations. It is also possible that the lack of moonlight, leading to the lack of landmarks visible to the observers atop the tower, may have contributed to their vertigo and dizziness as they watched the mesmerizing movement of firefly lights below what must have been a shaky platform.

Rose also noted that the lights occurred between 9:30 p.m. and 3:00 a.m.; which again appears to match the expected behavior of blue ghost fireflies. Sunset on August 1, 1962, occurred at 8:32, and since the light-averse blue ghost fireflies avoid twilight, they would not have started flying until about an hour after sunset, or about 9:30, which was the beginning time of light activity mentioned by Rose. The blue ghosts are also highly temperature sensitive and abruptly stop flying once the night air temperature drops below about 65°F, which presumably might have happened about 3:00 a.m., when Rose reported the end of light activity.

While several features of Rose's Brown Mountain observations may be consistent with lights of the blue ghost fireflies, including the "color of the moon," others are not. For instance, Rose's mention of flames and glowing balls of red and orange lights up to eight feet in diameter are inconsistent with fireflies. However, since flammable gases, as proposed by Rose, are highly unlikely on Brown Mountain and would not have behaved as Rose described, nor would they have been colored, we may never know for sure just what he and his team saw from the tower.

Chapter 10

Ralph Lael's 1962 Alleged Alien Encounters

Ralph Isabel Lael (1909–1978) was born in Alexander County, North Carolina, started a furniture upholstering business in Hickory in 1929, owned the Outer Space Rock Shop Museum on Highway 181 about 13 miles north of Morganton, and ran unsuccessfully for Congress in 1948 for the Progressive Party. Lael's rock shop was best known for the prominent display of a small, supposedly alien mummy in a glass case. In 1965, Lael self-published *The Brown Mountain Lights*—a small 28-page booklet describing his 1962 encounters with strange lights on Brown Mountain and his alien-accompanied trip to Venus.

Lael begins his story by establishing the mystery of the lights, mentioning various stories we now know are misconceptions, such as BMLs being visible before the days of electricity, being seen by early Native Americans, and being seen before the days of trains and automobiles. He dismisses all proposed explanations that attribute the sources to man-made lights. In support of his story, he mentions sightings by elderly residents but appears critical of the numerous recent tower sightings by Paul Rose. Lael lays out a plan to get close to the lights on Brown Mountain itself as opposed to the usual distant observations reported by most others.

Between May and October 1962 Lael describes 14 separate solo trips to an area on the northwest side of Brown Mountain suggested by experienced loggers of his acquaintance as being favorable for seeing the lights. Unfortunately, the actual dates of most of the trips are not given. However, some, if not all, of Lael's trips appear to have been on weekends.

Trip 1: Date Unknown

This was a daytime trip to mark a trail up Timbered Branch and Wild Cat Branch to the top of Wild Cat Knob, the site suggested by Lael's logging acquaintances.

Trip 2: Date Unknown

This was a daytime trip cutting a trail up Wild Cat Branch to the spring at the head of Wild Cat Branch.

Trip 3: Date Unknown

This was a daytime trip cutting a trail from the head of Wild Cat Branch to the top of Wild Cat Knob.

Trip 4: Saturday, May 19(?)

This was Lael's first nighttime trip. At about 10:45 p.m., from the summit of Wild Cat Knob, the lights were first visible on a moonlit bare rock exposure [Lael's Rock, my name] ~0.75 mi away on the northeast side of Brown Mountain. Fifteen to twenty lights were visible on Lael's Rock moving in and out of the nearby trees. Several lights moved horizontally in one direction and then returned to their starting point. Then three lights were visible only 500 feet away among the trees on the summit of Wild Cat Knob. One of these lights came very close after Lael lay down with his flashlight turned off, but the light rapidly moved away, avoiding the trees, as soon as Lael's flashlight accidently turned on. Lael was very scared. The lights on or near Lael's Rock subsequently disappeared about the same time.

Trip 5: 3 Weeks Later, Weekend of June 9/10(?)

This was a daytime trip cutting trail from Wild Cat Knob toward Lael's Rock, followed by nighttime observation from the summit of Wild Cat Knob. Lots of lights appeared in woods near the summit of Wild Cat Knob and one light approached very closely when Lael lay down; Lael took the lights to be friendly life forms, although again he was very scared.

Trip 6: Weekend of Jun 30/Jul 1(?)

This was a daytime trip cutting trail toward Lael's Rock, followed by a campout on the summit of Wild Cat Knob. Lael saw the first lights about 9 p.m. He lay down and one light came very close to him and then he followed the light a few hundred feet toward Lael's Rock. Lael then asked the light questions; the light appeared to understand and responded by moving back and forth or up and down for "no" or "yes" answers. Lael felt the lights were beckoning him to visit Lael's Rock and he told them he would be back in one week to do so. The lights visible in the distance on Lael's Rock soon disappeared.

Trip 7: One Week Later, Thursday, July 5(?)

The trail to Lael's Rock was completed during this daytime trip. Lael waited on Lael's Rock as the sun set and expected the lights to appear about an hour later. It was about 9:00 p.m. when he saw the first light, apparently materializing out of the rock. Lael said "hello" and the light moved as if beckoning him to follow, which he did until both he and the light passed through a doorway into the solid rock. The underground room was crystal clear glass that honeycombs the entire interior of Brown Mountain for miles. A voice told Lael not to fear and explained how mankind destroyed the planet Pewam and is headed toward destroying earth as well. The lights are from Venus and have chosen to enlighten Lael with the secret of how to prevent man's destruction of earth.

Trips 8, 9, and 10: July 1962

Lael next spent these three trips scouting for a shortcut to Lael's Rock. Obviously unfamiliar with Brown Mountain, Lael had already spent considerable time and effort cutting long cross-country trails to areas much easier accessed via existing logging roads. For instance, loggers had previously established a now-abandoned camp and staging area on the summit of Wildcat Knob, which was still easily accessible via logging roads. In addition, as he found out, a long-established access road along the top of Brown Mountain passed less than one-half mile east of Lael's Rock. Paul Rose's tower was built on July 30, so it is possible that during his scouting trips atop Brown Mountain, Lael drove within 30 feet of the recently constructed tower; however, he does not mention any encounters with Rose or members of his party. In his book, Lael does express contempt for Rose and his instant notoriety and, as we soon learn, the Venusians themselves expressed concern about Rose's actions and the throngs of light chasers then massing around the mountain.

Trip 11: Friday, August 3, 1962

This was a daytime trip to cut trail from Lael's Rock approximately one-half mile upslope to the old logging road on top of Brown Mountain, which is accessible by vehicle. Now Lael could avoid the hours of rugged trail walk just to reach Lael's Rock.

Trip 12: Date Unknown

Lael drove to the top of Brown Mountain via NC Highway 181/Mortimer Road (FS Rd 982)/Little Chestnut Mtn Road (FS Rd 4099)/access road on Brown Mountain (FS Trail 1B). He then hiked his recently cut trail to Lael's Rock. Reaching the rock after dark, a light greeted Lael and led him through a door into the crystal interior of Brown Mountain. The lights instructed Lael to tell the world that the cause of the BMLs is gas from chemical reactions. They offered to financially reward Lael for his help in stopping the recent arrival of light-chasing hoards following Rose's tower reports. Lael and seven other people would be saved if the Venusians were forced to destroy mankind in order to prevent the destruction of the earth. Then they took Lael on a short trip in a time machine. Lael left and soon contacted TV and newspaper media, which generated his own temporary notoriety.

According to the Venusians, Lael was to tell the world the following:

> There are two veins of ore. One iron and one sulpher that crosses under Brown Mountain. That there is a swamp on Brown Mountain and several places of mica schist on the top of the mountain. The water from the swamp seeps down and contacts the ore where they cross causing a gas to form under the mica schist and this builds up pressure. When the pressure builds up it forces the mica schist apart and shoots up in the air [Ralph Lael, 1965; *The Brown Mountain Lights*, Self-published, p. 20].

Interestingly, this explanation includes elements of several previously proposed BML ideas. Chemical reactions between iron and sulfur, swamp gas, and moonlight-reflecting gems (mica) were all popular misconceptions of the time.

Trip 13: Date Unknown

Once again Lael visited his friends the "light people" at Lael's Rock. As before, a light met him and led him underground to the crystal chamber. The leader of the lights spoke:

> Welcome, friend, you have carried out the mission to perfection. Your statement was carried by the papers and it was shown on T.V. There is not so much activity on the mountain as there was. As soon as it gets a little quieter on the mountain we will take you with us to Venus. You need not bring anything special with you as we will take of all your needs while you are with us. Your air, food and clothing will be taken care of. Also your safety will be assured. You may bring along anything you wish up to ten pounds but no more [Ralph Lael, 1965; *The Brown Mountain Lights*, Self-published, p. 20].

Trip 14: Late October 1962

Lael returned to Lael's Rock, met the lights, went inside the crystal chamber that now resembled a flying saucer, and then left earth in the space ship with the lights. Once on Venus, he met other humans from the planet Pewam who tell him the story of how their former planet was destroyed by nuclear war, which is about to happen on earth. The story included references to the Cuban Missile Crisis, biblical accounts of Noah's flood and the ark filled with selected animals, and a 6,000-year-old earth. (The international stalemate between the U.S. and Russia over the impending arrival of Russian nuclear missiles in Cuba unfolded in October 1962 and obviously was a critical world threat on everyone's minds at the time.) "Welcome, Man, for a job well done. The fever on the mountain has ceased. The people no longer swarm on or around the mountain and we are about ready to begin the trip to Venus" (Ralph Lael, 1965; *The Brown Mountain Lights*, Self-published, p. 23). Lael was returned to earth a few days later and he ends his book encouraging mankind to avoid conflict and instead embrace universal love. Since the BMLs and Lael's Venusian friends were now gone, he apparently never returned to Brown Mountain again.

Blue Ghost Fireflies?

Ralph Lael's multiple close encounters with mysterious lights in 1962 and the descriptions in his book constitute the best written details we have to date of recurring encounters with mystery lights. However, Lael failed to describe the color of the lights, leaving us to conclude they might not have been colored in the first place; in other words, they were white lights. In addition, Lael's failure to mention flashing or blinking of the lights suggests they were continuously illuminated. If these assumptions are correct, Lael's lights might have been blue ghost fireflies (BGFs). Certainly numerous other behaviors of Lael's mystery lights suggest the elusive blue ghost fireflies. Behaviors and observations of Lael's lights suggesting blue ghost fireflies include the following:

1. Summer temperatures and timing consistent with the mating flights of BGFs.
2. Continuous burning white or bluish-white lights.
3. Lights present in dense forest.
4. Lights moving near the ground.
5. Slowly moving lights.
6. Lights moving among trees but avoiding tree trunks and limbs.
7. Lights slowly approaching a person lying still on the ground.
8. Lights quickly moving away when flashlight turns on.
9. Lights moving horizontally for noticeable distances then returning to starting point.
10. Lights stop shining for the evening in unison at about the same time.
11. Lights first appeared each evening at the end of twilight about an hour after sunset.
12. Lights occurred at the same time of the year as those seen on Paul Rose's tower.
13. Lights occurred within ½ mile of those seen on Paul Rose's tower.
14. Lights spend a short "forming" period before actually moving each evening.

Each of the above features is consistent with the BGF (see Chapter 22 for more on these rare and unique fireflies).

Of course, other features of Lael's lights are not consistent with the BGFs, including his descriptions of ten-to-twelve-foot diameters, light bright enough to read a newspaper, brown centers with six hands or feelers, and, later in his narrative, paranormal behavior such as logic, speech, superior intelligence, space travel, and supernatural powers.

Lael's Observations

What are we to make of Lael's observations? Certainly no one had previously gone to this extreme effort to solve the mystery by making 14 separate solo trips, cutting trails in rugged terrain, and writing detailed descriptions of what he saw. We are greatly indebted to Lael for his efforts, as his mystery light descriptions are the best we have to date in the seventy-year-old legend.

But given that he was extremely frightened during his early solo encounters with the lights when deeply isolated in the woods, it's reasonable to expect that his descriptions may have been less than totally accurate. Yet during his later encounters, when he attributes phenomenal paranormal abilities to the lights, Lael's creditability suffers greatly and we're left wondering if hallucinations were involved. Was he suffering from hallucinations caused by the lights themselves or perhaps caused by some other unknown condition? Lael's strong religious beliefs (i.e., beliefs in the supernatural) become evident in the written account of his visit to Venus and his return. Perhaps Lael was simply trying to give meaning to scary encounters with strange lights as best he could according to his worldview, which must have been heavily influenced by his religious beliefs, the current world nuclear destruction tensions, local events such as the recent influx of light-chasers following Paul Rose's exploits, and his understanding of the existing folklore of the BMLs.

Chapter 11

Other Scientific Investigations, 1915–2011

> People always ask, "What do you think causes them to move?" But if you try to explain, they don't always want to hear the answers. People like a mystery—they like an unanswered question.
> —Allen van Valkenburg, Death Valley National Park Ranger, in *Mystery of Death Valley's "Sailing Stones" Solved*, by Marc Lallanilla, *Life's Little Mysteries* Assistant Editor, June 17, 2013

> Science is defined by analytical thinking, rational inquiry, and an objective weighing of evidence.
> —Richard Schiffman, Science Now (news.sciencemag.org), June 7, 2013

> If your "science" has no data, no one should believe you.
> TauriqMoosa, FreeThoughtBlogs.com, June 9, 2013

Scientific Investigations

Although commonly dismissed or ignored by avid promoters of the legend, numerous scholarly studies have been conducted over the past 100 years and have almost-unanimously concluded that the BMLs are misinterpretations of man-made electric lights. Only the 1919 U.S. Weather Bureau (brush lightning hypothesis) and a 1977 geologist (uranium ore hypothesis) concluded otherwise, but neither of these ideas carries any validity. Although highly unpopular with the local residents, the man-made electric light explanation has withstood the test of time and the repeated review of numerous reasoned and logical investigations. These studies include the following:

1913 U.S. Geological Survey, D.B. Sterrett: locomotive headlights.
c. 1917 Staged car headlights at Lawndale (40 mi SE) seen at Loven's Hotel at Cold Springs.
1919 U.S. Weather Bureau W.J. Humphries: brush lightning, similar to St. Elmo's fire and Andes light.
1922 U.S. Geological Survey R.G. Mansfield: 90 percent refracted man-made lights and 10 percent brush fires.
1928 NC State College physics professors: binocular and transit surveys, Hudson town lights seen.
1929 E.M. Ball, first BML photo: distant city lights.
1940 H.A. Whitman, transit triangulation survey, BML photo: refracted city lights.
1958 B. Brown, BML photos: refracted city lights; kitchen table experiment (1962).

1962 S. Rowe and C. Holler, Jr., transit surveys and site visits: reflected city lights.
1968 J. Baity and K. Thompson, lightning-strike photo; camp on BM and ignite methane bubbles.
1977 Geologist Francois Schumacher: uranium ore may be the source of the lights.
1977–88 ORION and Enigma, staged Lenoir spotlight and explosives: refracted man-made lights.
1998 Astrophysicist Dr. Daniel B. Caton, Appalachian State University, begins long-term investigation.
2012 BML research team begins scientific investigations, group of diverse researchers.

Man-Made Lights?

Each of the studies mentioned above contributed to our understanding of the BMLs. The possibility that the lights seen looking east over the top of Brown Mountain were man-made lights reflected or refracted by air layers was first mentioned in H.C. Martin's 1916 article in the *Morganton News Herald*. Martin specifically noted the presence of warm and cold air layers that he thought were due to the recent forest clear-cutting in the mountainous terrains. He felt that the density variations in these layers caused reflection and refraction of visible man-made lights. Martin also reported the first close encounter with mystery lights and was the most respected eyewitness at the time (Pearson, 1916).

In 1922, U.S. Geological Survey geologist G.R. Mansfield expanded on Martin's refracted light observations. Today, we know that it is the refraction of the city and town lights by rising heat waves (mirages) that causes the observed city/town/rural lights to dance, wiggle, wobble, vibrate, change colors, and fade in and out. Aggravatingly, this minor but very noticeable movement of the lights results in out-of-focus photographic time-lapse images of the lights and perhaps produces the "circular orbs of light" reported by some observers.

Movements of the Early Lights

Limited but noticeable horizontal or vertical movement of the lights, often reported by early distant observers and still observed today, might be due to the tiring of one's eye muscles while focusing on individual bright lights in a dark setting. The actual lack of movement is easily demonstrated by viewing the suspected light through a stationary tripod-mounted camera, binoculars, or telescope and was first reported by G.R. Mansfield in 1922 and mentioned again by professors J.B. Derieux and A.A. Dixon in 1928. Likewise, my repeated photography of the distant lights by tripod-mounted cameras set in the same spot hours, days or even weeks later also shows that the vast majority of the lights are stationary and do not change location (this current study).

Lights After the 1916 Flood

The report of mystery lights appearing immediately after the July 1916 flood that heavily damaged the Catawba Valley railroads and highways is often quoted as proof that the lights were not locomotive headlights as originally proposed by U.S. Geological Survey geologist D.B. Sterrett in 1913. In his August 29, 1916, letter to the *Lenoir News* (September 8), George Anderson Loven, owner of Loven's Hotel in Cold Springs, North Carolina, states: "The light still appears every night now, for six years since it was first seen. It shows to be some four or five miles beyond the top of Brown Mountain. It was supposed by some that it was a train headlight; the recent floods stopped the trains from running, but it did not stop the light from showing. We watched close and it showed every night just the same. It is not confined to one place; it varies sometimes from two to three miles either east or west. It seems to go up over the treetops from fifty to sixty feet."

Note that Loven refers to a single mystery light and fails to mention the presence of the numerous city lights reported to be visible from his hotel the previous year by Dr. C.L. Wilson (1915). And based on 1922 interviews with prominent eyewitnesses, U.S. Geological Survey geologist G.R. Mansfield reported that moving lights seen from Cold Springs immediately after the 1916 flood were probably automobile headlights on the roadways not washed away by the flood. Presumably these and other car headlights were also visible before the flood. If so many lights were visible from Cold Springs both before and after the flood, why did Loven mention only one light? As revealed by other newspaper articles of the time, Loven's Hotel was experiencing increased visitation from patrons wishing to see mystery lights; thus, he may have been simply embellishing the legend of the lights to enhance his income.

Lights Before Electricity

Reported BML sightings before the era of electric lights are also often mentioned in post–1922 published documents as proof that the BMLs existed before the time of man-made lights. However, these reports are not based on confirmed facts and no such light sightings have been found in any document written before 1912. Note that electric lights first became widespread in the Catawba River valley in the 1890s (see Chapter 4).

Growing Recognition of Man-Made Lights

Slowly at first, and then with increasing certainty, man-made electric lights were reported to be visible over the top of Brown Mountain. In 1912 the *Salisbury Evening Post* reported the visibility of Morganton, Hickory and other town lights as seen from Loven's Hotel at Cold Springs. In 1915 Dr. C.L. Wilson identified the community lights of Joy, Lenoir, Connelly Springs, and Rutherford College while also observing from Loven's Hotel—the site of so many mystery light sightings. Oddly enough, no one else of this early BML era mentioned being able to see city lights over the top of Brown Mountain; instead they apparently interpreted all of the visible lights to be the mysterious BMLs.

In the most comprehensive and detailed scientific study ever conducted on the BMLs to that date, geologist G.R. Mansfield reports (1922): "In summary it may be said that the Brown Mountain lights are clearly not of unusual nature or origin. About 47 percent of the lights that the writer was able to study instrumentally were due to automobile headlights, 33 percent to locomotive headlights, 10 percent to stationary lights, and 10 percent to brush fires" (*Origin of the Brown Mountain Light in North Carolina*; U.S. Geological Survey Circular 646).

In his 1923 report, F.J. Haskin wrote, "Somewhere in the broad Catawba valley or beyond was the origin of the light." In the same year, the *Statesville Landmark* (1923) reported a light (presumably a town light) visible to the east from Brown Mountain itself and located midway between the towns of Drexel and Lenoir. In 1928, Professors J.B. Derieux and A.A. Dixon, using survey equipment, identified the town lights of Hudson in the Catawba Valley, visible directly over the top of Brown Mountain. E.M. Ball's 1929 first-ever photograph of BMLs shows a band of point-source lights above Brown Mountain that resembles today's photographs of city lights in the valley beyond Brown Mountain. In 1932 F.D. Ruggles reported seeing hundreds of city streetlights along a 35-mile length but concluded they were burning gases instead. H.A. Whitman's 1940 transit triangulation survey concluded that the lights were refracted city lights. And so it goes right on through all subsequent scientific surveys.

Over time, as the increasingly electrically lit population (i.e., light pollution) increased in Catawba Valley south and east of Brown Mountain, the realization began to set in to most people that some, if not all, of the supposed mystery lights were simply man-made lights. In the early days of the BML legends (c.1897–c.1922), these distant lights were a new and mysterious phenomenon that sparked the imagination of the residents, in the mountains to the west and north of Brown Mountain, who probably lagged behind the town and city residents in the use and understanding of electric lights. Who at the time knew you could see city/town lights 20 to 40 miles away? While today these man-made lights are obvious to most observers, some still mistake them for mystery lights.

Morphing of the Legend

With the passage of even more time, the legend stayed alive by morphing as the focus of light sightings slowly moved away from distant lights seen over the top of Brown Mountain to less easily dismissed lights being seen more frequently in Linville Gorge, 5–10 miles west of Brown Mountain. Today the legend also includes close encounters with mystery lights. Note that the early legend did not include close encounters or lights in Linville Gorge (see Chapter 19).

ORION Investigations, 1977–1988

The ORION research group (Oak Ridge Isochronous Observation Network) was organized to investigate unusual or mysterious phenomenon in the 1970s and 1980s. The group was centered in Oak Ridge, Tennessee, and was primarily composed of naturalists and outdoor enthusiasts from the local area. At the time, they conducted the most complete and thorough research on the BMLs since Mansfield's work in 1922. The ORION group proposed possible explanations for the lights, devised and conducted field investigations to prove or disprove those hypotheses, and reported their results in at least 23 newsletters distributed within their membership.

The ORION research group produced significant contributions and observations including these:

1. The refraction of light passing over Brown Mountain.
2. The distance a known light can be seen (Hibriten Mountain spotlight 22 miles distant).
3. Telescope identification of specific tower lights visible from the popular observation sites.
4. Compass azimuth measurements of distant cities/towns.
5. Mirages due to cold and warm air layers over Brown Mountain.
6. Unusual fireflies.
7. Photography.
8. The possibility of misidentified lens flares.
9. The measurement of weather conditions (temperature, wind speed, humidity, etc.).
10. Instrument measurements (magnetometer, seismometer, Geiger counter, spectrometer, etc.).
11. A lack of light effects due to explosives detonated on Brown Mountain.

ORION Team Finds Blue Fireflies

David K. Hackett, the principal organizer and researcher at ORION, correctly identified a continuously blue-glowing firefly as a likely natural source of some misperceived mystery lights in the Brown Mountain area. However, apparently the taxonomic classification scheme has changed since 1981. He identified the firefly as *Lucidota corrusca*, but no such firefly is known to exist today. Today's *Lucidota atra* (the black firefly—a blinking firefly) and *Ellychnia corrusca* (one of many diurnal fireflies—day time bugs) don't quite fit Hackett's description of a small black blue-burning nocturnal firefly. However, today's blue ghost firefly (*Phausis reticulata*) does perfectly match Hackett's description (see Chapter 22). This makes the ORION group the second known research effort to date to report encounters with uncommon fireflies as possible sources of at least some of the reported mystery lights. George R. Mansfield first mentioned fireflies as possible explanations in 1922.

Dr. Caton's Investigations Ongoing since 1998

Dr. Daniel B. Caton, Professor and Director of Observatories, Department of Physics and Astronomy, Appalachian State University (Boone, North Carolina) began his long-term interest in understanding the BMLs in 1998. For the past three years, Dr. Caton, and his assistant Lee Hawkins (Observatory Engineer, Appalachian State University), have been actively involved with our Brown Mountain lights research team. In addition to many hours of their own direct observation and personal interviews, they have installed and maintained two continuously running nighttime cameras at strategic sites overlooking Brown Mountain and Linville Gorge (see Chapter 27). More than 575,000 time-lapse images representing more than 6,300 hours of nightly viewing have been captured by the cameras as of December 31, 2014. While no mystery lights have yet been caught on any image and observed firsthand, both Caton and Hawkins continue to advise the team on scientific issues and are pursuing plans for a third camera installation. Dr. Caton is often called on by newspapers, radio and TV to help explain the BMLs and his views bring balance and logic to the public discussion.

Chapter 12

Lack of BML Sightings from the South and East

Why Are There No BML Sightings from the South and East?

Essentially all historic and recent mystery light sightings over Brown Mountain have been reported from observers stationed at elevated mountainous viewing sites to the north and west of the mountain, places like Wiseman's View, Highway 181 overlook, Cold Springs, Jonas Ridge, and Gingercake Mountain. However, there are similar viewing spots overlooking Brown Mountain from equally elevated mountains to the south and east; yet these sites seldom, if ever, produce reports of supposedly mysterious lights. What's going on? Why are supposedly mysterious lights seen only from two sides of Brown Mountain and not from the other two sides of the mountain? Does this lopsided viewing area have anything to do with the mystery lights themselves or is it just a coincidence?

Nocturnal distant city and town lights are certainly visible from all of the mountains around Brown Mountain, from the north, east, south, and west; but only lights seen from the north and west are ever considered to be mysterious. Are they the same lights as those seen from the south and east, and if so, what makes them mysterious when seen from the north or west of the mountain and not mysterious when seen from the south or east? A review of the geography of the area may hold the clue.

Mirages

When viewing Brown Mountain from the higher elevations to the north or west, distant city/town lights are visible to the south and east beyond the mountain. As we've learned, it was similar man-made lights that originally gave rise to the legend of the BMLs in the early 1900s (see Chapters 4 and 8). As reported by nearly every observer, then and now, these distant lights appear to move, wobble, dance, hover, flicker, vibrate, change color, and fade in and out as if they are actually alive. We now know these effects are due to the mirage-like refractions of the light rays caused by rising heat currents—specifically involving the daytime sun-warmed air of the valley rising after dark. These mirage effects were also noted by some early researchers, including H.C. Martin in 1916, R.G. Mansfield in 1922, B. Brown in 1962, and ORION researchers in 1977 and 1978.

The mirage effects are visible no matter which side of Brown Mountain an observer is stationed on; however, perhaps observers on the north and west sides see enhanced mirage refractions versus observers on the south or east sides. Such enhanced mirage effects may be due to the passage of the distant mirage-modified light rays through the layer of cooler, denser air overlying Brown Mountain itself, which lies between the lights and the observers. Light rays from the valley cities/towns traveling to observers in the mountains to the south or east of Brown Mountain do not pass through a similar layer of cooler air, which may explain the lack of mystery light sightings from these locations.

When viewed from the mountains to the south or east, the distant city/town lights are clearly visible; but without flat-topped Brown Mountain between the observer and the lights they aren't refracted as much and thus they don't appear to be as active, wild, or alive as when observed from the north or west.

In other words, to see the distant BMLs, one has to observe from specific geographically limited vantage points. This lopsided viewing configuration suggests that the light phenomenon, especially in the early days of the legend, was influenced by the topographic and atmospheric features of the area.

Such mirage effects are clearly visible today when the lights are viewed through tripod-mounted telescopes or camera telephoto lenses, where the wobbling, wavering, dancing, throbbing, vibrating, changing colors and changes in brightness are easily discernible. However, the lights in question don't actually move and the fading out of lights, often apparent to the naked eye, is found to be replaced by much dimmer but still present lights when viewed through camera or telescope lenses.

Blurry Images

In fact, it is this in-place wavering of the lights that result in out-of-focus, blurry spots of light, which are especially aggravating when taking nocturnal time-exposure photographs.

In addition, these rising-heat-wave refractions are more pronounced during warmer summer weather and are diminished during cooler winter weather. Likewise, the refractions diminish as the nighttime air cools over the course of an individual night, which produces less rising of warm air waves. Rising heat waves are more common during calm windless conditions, while wind-driven mixing of the near-surface air reduces the refracting mirage effects—perhaps explaining the often-mentioned better viewing of the lights as the air clears of moisture and the wind settles immediately following stormy conditions.

Chapter 13

Ghosts, Aliens, Spirits and UFOs

> Consensus is the business of politics. If it's consensus, it isn't science.
> If it's science, it isn't consensus. Period.
> —Dr. Michael Crichton, "Aliens Cause Global Warming,"
> January 17, 2003, speech at the California Institute of Technology

> The plural of Anecdote isn't data.
> Unknown

> Our personal experience cannot be used as a yardstick for empirical claims of "truth."
> There is a real truth. It inhabits the space outside the brain, and regardless of how we
> perceive it, it will remain what it is. Truth is objective, and will always be truth.
> Personal truth is not a place from which we can derive objectivity.
> —Martin S. Pribble, 2013, *The Argument of Truth from Personal Experience*,
> martinspribble.com/2013/08/the-argument-of-truth-from-personal-experience

Many observers interpret some of the nocturnal lights they see around Brown Mountain as manifestations of ghosts and spirits or aliens and extraterrestrials. Generally, these opinions come from people with very strong supernatural or paranormal beliefs that influence many other aspects of their lives as well. Some have such beliefs before visiting the area and first seeing supposedly mystery lights, while some develop such beliefs following their encounter with the BMLs.

Belief-dependent Realism

The desire to believe in unexplained phenomena such as mystery lights is widespread and strong; and nonbelievers are often ridiculed and shunned or summarily dismissed by the true believers. Needless to say, belief in the legend of the BMLs is very personal, with many people expressing anger and outrage toward anyone who suggests their lights are not real. The desire to believe in something beyond the understanding of science or other scholarly inquiry is also a common human trait. "Some things just can't be explained" and "science can't explain everything" are often heard from those refusing to consider alternatives, even when the facts suggest they should.

Dr. Michael Shermer, an expert in how human beliefs are acquired, is described as one of the world's most experienced champions of scientific thinking in the face of popular delusion. Shermer cautions, "Beliefs come first. Explanations for beliefs follow. Most humans live in a 'belief-dependent realism' of their own making. How can we tell the difference between what we would like to be true and what is actually true? The answer is science" (2011, *The Believing Brain*).

The three-year scientific investigation that our Brown Mountain lights research team has undertaken includes thousands of hours of direct observations, dozens of daytime and nighttime excursions to Brown Mountain itself, extensive digital photography including the use of telephoto lenses and telescopes, numerous staged light tests, comprehensive literature review, identification of hundreds of individual lights, compilation of dozens of eyewitness interviews, and geological and biological research including repeated field excursions in the area. Our work has been shared with other scientists for their review and comments and has been posted on the Internet for all to see and review.

No Ghosts, Spirits, Aliens or UFOs

Our investigation is the most comprehensive and complete study of its kind ever undertaken; however, no supernormal, supernatural, or paranormal phenomenon has been found. Our efforts have found no evidence of ghosts, spirits, aliens or extraterrestrial UFOs. Just as no evidence of these have ever been found anywhere on earth, there is no evidence that they exist on or near Brown Mountain.

Ralph Lael's amazing story of alien encounters on Brown Mountain in 1962 is explained as encounters with the unknown-to-him blue ghost firefly and the overly active imagination of a deeply religious individual unfamiliar with the isolated forest at night, at a time of mankind's beginning space ventures and the developing world concern over possible nuclear war during the Cuban Missile Crisis (see Chapter 14).

However, many stories of ghosts and spirits concerning the BMLs do exist in the published literature (see Chapter 6). As mentioned above, we still find people today who entertain ideas of aliens, disembodied sprits, and intelligent beings to explain the lights they see or the experiences they'd had either at the popular BML observation sites or deep in the woods on or near Brown Mountain.

Chapter 14

Pseudoscientific Explanations

> The Universal Signs of Geo-Pseudoscience:
> The bogus appeal to keep an "open mind."
> Denigration of the consensus.
> Inappropriate credentials.
> Willful denial of facts.
> Slavery to the idea, not the evidence.
> —Andrew Alden, *Earth Pseudoscience*, geology.about.com, August 2, 2013

> Typical Behaviors of Pseudoscientists:
> Hostile to criticism, rather than embracing criticism as
> a mechanism of self-correction.
> Works backward from desired results through motivated reasoning.
> Cherry picks evidence.
> Relies on low grade evidence when it supports their belief;
> but dismisses rigorous evidence if it is inconvenient.
> Core principles untested or unproven, often based on single case or anecdote.
> Utilizes vague, imprecise, or ambiguous terminology, often to mimic technical jargon.
> Has the trappings of science, but lacks the true methods of science.
> Invokes conspiracy arguments to explain lack of mainstream
> acceptance (Galileo syndrome).
> Lacks caution and humility by making grandiose claims from flimsy evidence.
> Practitioners often lack proper training and present that as a virtue as it
> makes them more "open."
> —Steven Novella, 2013, *Is There a Pseudoscience Event Horizon?*
> http://theness.com/neurologicablog/?s=pseudoscience+event+horizon

> [C]aution should be implemented when offering one
> little-understood phenomenon as an explanation for another.
> —Micah Hanks, 2014, "Illuminated Omens: Rare 'Earthquake Lights'
> May Explain Some Paranormal Phenomena," mysteriousuniverse.org

Illogical explanations masquerading as scientific ones have been proposed by many individuals. Often these pseudoscientific hypotheses are heavily promoted by people who have economic reasons for furthering the mystique of the BMLs. Videos of questionable BMLs can be found on the Internet, while short articles, books and Web sites posting questionable, misleading, undocumented, and even disproven BML explanations abound. Authors often fail to distinguish between fact and fiction and elaborate extensively on their favorite ghost or pseudoscientific story, for which references are conveniently omitted. In addition, hypotheses such as stresses on geologic faults, earth lights, earth currents, ionized plasmas, luminescent gases, and radioactive minerals are proposed with no logical evidence to support them. Some of these explanations are addressed below.

The Difference Between a Theory and a Hypothesis

A HYPOTHESIS attempts to answer questions by putting forth a plausible explanation that has yet to be rigorously tested.

A THEORY, on the other hand, has already undergone extensive testing by various scientists and is generally accepted as being an accurate explanation of an observation. This doesn't mean the theory is correct; only that current testing has not yet been able to disprove it, and the evidence as it is understood, appears to support it ["What Is the Difference Between a Theory and a Hypothesis?" www.wisegeek.org/what-is-the-difference-between-a-theory-and-a-hypothesis.htm].

Rock Plasma Hypotheses

An often reported explanation for the origin of mysterious nocturnal lights such as the BMLs involves a supposed "rock-producing-piezoelectric-plasma" phenomenon. Such hypotheses are at first attractive; however, under closer scrutiny, many of the implied physical processes involved are highly questionable, if not actually impossible. According to these rock plasma hypotheses, mystery lights like the BMLs are due to the emission of piezoelectric plasmas produced by one of three natural processes:

1. Over-stressed crystals in rocks along geologic faults (tectonic strain plasmas);
2. Buildup of electric currents in rocks rich in quartz and magnetite (mineral plasmas);
3. Radioactive minerals in the rocks (radioactive plasmas).

Occasionally throughout the world, these hypotheses also include abnormal psychological experiences by observers supposedly caused by brain malfunctions or hallucinations resulting from close encounters between human brains and an electromagnetic component of the plasma energy fields (Persinger and Lafreniere, 1977). Close examination of the evidence is far from convincing.

Piezoelectric plasma emissions from stressed crystals have been observed in nature, are readily produced in the laboratory, and in fact are common, everyday occurrences in our lives; however, they don't appear to last long enough or to be strong enough to generate mystery lights such as the reported BMLs. In addition, neither naturally occurring, mineral-related, electric current luminous plasmas nor luminous radioactive plasmas have been proven to exist anywhere on earth. Brain malfunctions from exposure to electromagnetic currents, although first reported in what appeared to be valid scientific studies, have more recently been called into question.

Actual psychological phenomena are also occasionally reported by observers of the BMLs. Most sightings of the lights are from mountain-top vantage points, apparently too distant from the lights themselves to cause any noticeable psychological effect. However, some observers, especially those experiencing close encounters, do occasionally report psychological effects, such as vivid memories of life-changing, frightening, and even euphoric experiences, usually difficult to express in words (otherworldly). Of course, the extraordinary experiences reported on Brown Mountain by Ralph Lael in 1962 certainly cover the gamut of the temporal lobe transient hallucination categories mentioned above.

Is there a connection? Let's look more carefully at the various aspects of these theories.

Geologic Faults, Tectonic Strain, Plasmas and Hallucinations

This hypothesis, as presented in the popular media, goes like this:

1. Since quartz crystals are known to emit tiny, hot, piezoelectric sparks (plasmas) when placed under stresses resulting in brittle rupture; and as,
2. There are numerous large-scale geologic faults in the area; and as,
3. The tectonic forces acting on these faults are continuously rupturing the rocks and breaking innumerable quartz crystals which then are producing piezoelectric sparks (plasmas); and as,
4. These innumerable individual tiny short-lived piezoelectric spark plasmas coalesce into larger long-lived accumulations; and as,
5. Some of these larger masses of piezoelectric plasmas migrate along the faults and some eventually escape into the atmosphere and become the mystery lights observed by awed humans; and as,
6. Electromagnetic fields are known to cause temporal lobe transients (hallucinations) in human test subjects in the laboratory; and as,
7. Plasmas are known to contain electromagnetic fields; then,
8. Close encounters between BMLs and humans can produce temporal lobe transients.

But we need to take a closer look at each of these hypothesis components.

Only three of the components (numbers 1, 2, and 7) meet the criteria for acceptable scientific facts; namely, they are directly observed or measured in nature and/or in repeatable laboratory experiments. However, the remaining five hypothesis components do not meet the criteria for scientific facts; instead they require five separate quantum leaps of faith.

Piezoelectric Crystals—True

As strange as it sounds, this one is true. Two very common rock-forming minerals, quartz and tourmaline, as well as other much-less-common minerals, are geologically classified as "piezoelectric crystals." According to the American Geological Institute's *Glossary of Geology* (2005), the industry standard reference of geologic terms, "piezoelectric crystals exhibit the development of an electrical potential in certain crystallographic directions when mechanical strain is applied. Quartz and tourmaline are examples of naturally piezoelectric crystals."

Quartz (pure SiO_2, aka crystalline silica), and to a lesser extent tourmaline (a complex Na, Fe, Al, B, SiO_2 mineral), along with feldspar, make up a majority of crustal rocks. Free quartz crystals alone can account for up to 30 percent of granitic rocks like the Brown Mountain Granitic Gneiss, while other high-SiO_2 minerals make up the remainder of the rock—giving a total SiO_2 (silica) content of greater than 60 percent. It is these free quartz crystals along with the microscopic silica components of the other minerals that can give granitic rocks, and others, piezoelectric properties.

Everyone is aware of this phenomenon. Remember trying, or watching someone else trying, to start a campfire by striking two rocks together? Maybe you've seen it on

TV or in the movies. Who hasn't imagined ancient man, in the days before matches and cigarette lighters, struggling to start a campfire by striking two rocks together to produce enough hot sparks to ignite dry leaves. It is actually possible, but not easy. There are spark-producing rocks and some are better than others. The greater the amount of quartz crystals and other siliceous minerals in the rocks the better they are at producing sparks when struck together. In fact, such high-silica rocks as flint, chalcedony, agate, jasper, obsidian, chert, and siltstone all contain millions of microscopically small quartz crystals and collectively they make the best striking rocks. Ancient man probably treasured good striking rocks and may have even fought over particularly good ones or the source regions where the better rocks were found.

The impact (mechanical force) of hitting two rocks together is sufficient to cause microscopic surface ruptures (strain), often accompanied by hot sparks (plasmas, aka burning ionized matter) radiating from the point of impact. Today we employ this phenomenon in the widespread use of cigarette and gas-grill lighters, where ribbed-metal thumb wheels rotate and rub against man-made (or even natural) flints, generating sparks that are hot enough to ignite escaping low-ignition-temperature combustible gas.

Geologists are particularly familiar with this hot plasma sparking effect seen when breaking silica-rich rocks. The preparation of rock samples for laboratory chemical analysis involves breaking the rocks collected in the field into smaller and smaller pieces. The first step often involves hammer blows or mechanical splitters (with heavy chisel-like blades impressed on the rock with hydraulic-produced forces until the rock splits into smaller pieces). Another step involves mechanical crushing machines where heavy metal blocks compress and pound the rocks until they break (rupture). Hot sparks are often driven off at the moment of impact or rupture, requiring appropriate safety equipment to protect the person preparing the sample. These tiny, extremely short-lived, hot sparks are plasmas (burning ionized matter): piezoelectric plasmas, if you will.

In some cases, for the geologist, a perfect rock split is required (for two identical samples) and a rock saw is employed instead of hammers, splitters, or crushers. The diamond-embedded metal rock saw blades generate excessive heat and sparks (again our plasmas) as they cut the rocks; even more if the rocks are high in silica. However, these sparks are easily dissipated by circulating a small amount of water across the point of cutting, a practice also common, for the same reason, with similar tile, ceramic, and or concrete saws used in the construction/building industry. The ease with which these piezoelectric sparks are extinguished by circulating water has a part to play in natural geologic fault zones where, according to the proposed tectonic strain hypothesis, similar plasmas might originate.

The electrical-field-producing properties of quartz crystals also have another big impact on our everyday lives—as in silicon computer chips (semiconductors)! And remember early transistor radios with quartz crystal tuners? They were even called crystal sets. With a cat whisker and earphones, you can tune a quartz crystal and listen to your local radio station!

Geologic faults—True, Including Some Really Big Ones

CLOSE, BUT NO CIGAR!

Brown Mountain and Linville Gorge both lie within a complex faulted region with a very long geologic history of repeated fault activity. Located on the eastern edge of the

Blue Ridge province, the area has undergone multiple episodes of colossal plate-tectonic collisions with other large continent-sized landmasses. The resultant deformations are evidenced by the widespread presence of stacked, flat-lying thrust faults, resulting from continental shorting of as much as 30 miles. In addition to thrust faults, the area is bounded by one of the largest high-angle faults on the planet: the 4,000-mile-long Brevard Fault.

Accompanying the repeated continental deformations of the geologic past, the country rocks underwent extensive textural and mineralogical transformations (metamorphism). In fact, the highly deformed mountainous edges of our continent, along with most other continental margins around the world, are commonly referred to by geologists as "mobile belts." Compared to the stable, nondeformed interior of the continents, the moniker is appropriate. "Not even the wind that blows, is so unstable as the level of the crust of this Earth" (Charles Darwin, *The Voyage of the Beagle*, 1834).

Brown Mountain, a metamorphosed magmatic granitic pluton, is fault bounded, meaning that major faults form the boundaries of the mountain on several sides. By major faults, I mean that movement along the faults has been so great that different rock types now lie on either side of these faults.

Brevard Fault

The Brevard Fault (BF), stretches from Alabama to New Jersey, and, some geologists believe, on to Nova Scotia, across the North Atlantic and into Scotland. That's as much as 4,000 miles, making it one of the largest faults on the planet. The BF has as much as 5–15 miles of vertical displacement in North Carolina and it passes only a few hundred feet southeast of the southern end of Brown Mountain! Obviously the Brevard Fault is a major geological feature; in fact, it's so big that it's now a 100-foot- to one-mile-wide fractured rock zone. The BF may represent a "suture line" where portions of other continents are attached to the North American continent. Today we know that all of the land east of the Brevard Fault (such as the Carolina piedmont and the coastal plain) actually originated somewhere besides the North American continent. We call such transported crustal blocks "suspect terrains," as in, "We suspect you're not from around here, are you?" Yes, the Piedmont and coastal plain, from Marion, North Carolina, to Wilmington, North Carolina, were attached to the North American continent after they were previously created somewhere else. We stole them! Think of it this way: *North America won the big tug of war and captured some new lands after the collision with, and subsequent separation from, another continent (perhaps Africa).* So today, the majority of North Carolina may have been African plate rocks! Actually it's more complicated than that, but you get the idea.

Has anyone ever reported seeing mystery lights anywhere else along the BF? If the lights are fault related, wouldn't they be likely all along one of the largest faults on the planet? As far as I know, no one has ever reported observing mystery lights anywhere along the mighty BF. Even where it runs close to Brown Mountain the mystery lights are always reported miles away, near the other end of the mountain.

Thrust Faults

The second type of fault in the area are the flat-lying thrust faults that lie both above and below Brown Mountain itself. The overlying one is the Grandfather Mountain Thrust Fault, and the underlying one is the Linville Falls Thrust Fault. As mentioned above, these faults are due to compression and shorting of the continent due to the collision with another large landmass, perhaps Africa. Today Brown Mountain is sandwiched between these two flat-lying faults, with the nearly flat, gently southward sloping top of Brown Mountain perfectly mirroring the surface of the overlying but now eroded away Grandfather Mountain Thrust Fault. The parallel underlying Linville Falls Thrust Fault daylights, or outcrops, along Upper Creek and then trends northeast up Holley Springs Branch, thus forming a fault boundary at the base of the steep cliff-rich northwest side of the mountain. The eastern side of Brown Mountain (Wilson Creek) is defined by the outcrop of the Grandfather Mountain Thrust Fault that then passes up and over Brown Mountain, or at least it once did.

Nearby Linville Gorge, site of mystery light sightings for the past 50 years or so, is also blessed with the same stacked flat-lying thrust faults as we see around Brown Mountain.

During the times when these faults were active (250–300 million years ago during the Allegheny Orogeny), Brown Mountain and Linville Gorge, or at least the area where they now exist, would have been very dangerous earthquake-prone places indeed. However, according to geologic mapping in the area, no significant movement on any of these faults has occurred in the last 185 million years! The tectonic forces that created the faults are now completely gone and the faults are now completely inactive. While there can occasionally be gravity adjustments producing small movements on such inactive faults, none are known in the 300-year recorded history of the area (see next section).

Figure 4. Panorama of Brown Mountain. Looking Southeast from the Hwy 181 overlook. The gently sloping, nearly flat top of the mountain mirrors the trace of the overlying but now eroded away Grandfather Mountain Thrust Fault.

14. Pseudoscientific Explanations

To summarize so far, we have lots of major and very interesting geologic faults, but they aren't currently active, nor are they unique to the Brown Mountain/Linville Gorge area. Instead, similar faults occur throughout the Appalachian Mountains, from Alabama to Nova Scotia—tens of thousands of miles of fault lines. And similar faults are characteristic of most other mountainous regions around the world. So, more questions arise: "If geologic faults produce mystery lights, why aren't lights seen elsewhere in the numerous faults along the Appalachian Mountain chain or in other similarly faulted mountainous regions around the world?" and, "Why aren't mystery lights seen in areas that have currently active geologic faults?" Odd, isn't it?

Don't we have earthquakes around here? Yes, earthquakes do occur in western North Carolina as can be seen on the following diagrams. A small one even occurred near my home in McDowell County while I was writing this chapter. However, they certainly aren't common, nor are they large in magnitude. Only two earthquakes have been reported near Brown Mountain in the last 323 years! And both of these were very low-level (0.1–2.0) magnitude on the Richter scale. The epicenters (ground zero centers of the earthquakes) of the two known earthquakes were located on the Brevard Fault slightly southeast of Brown Mountain (see figure 5). Note that no earthquakes have been

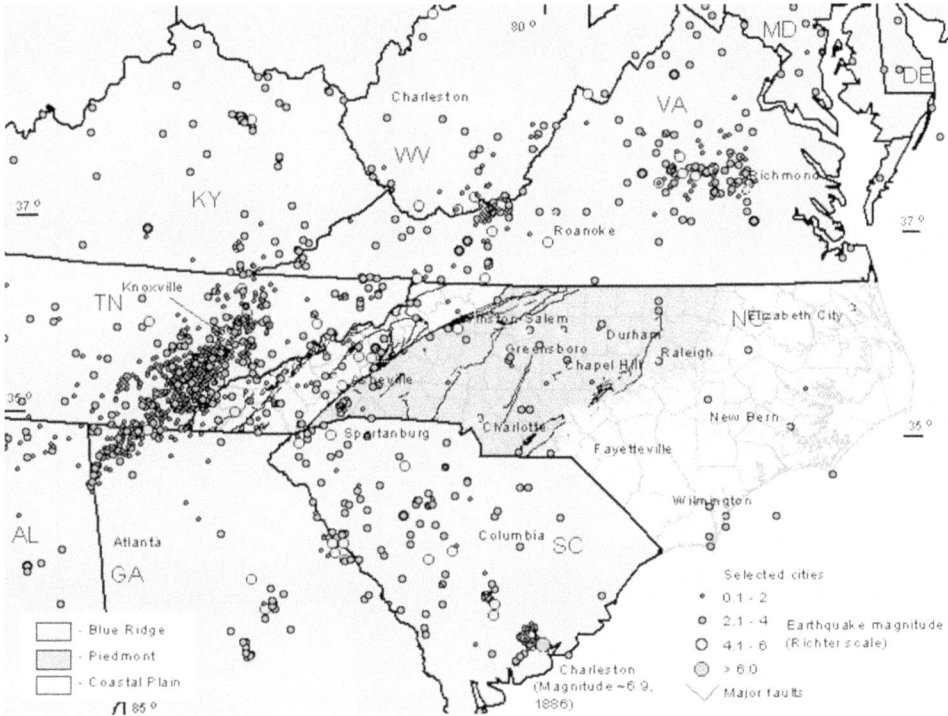

Figure 5. Earthquake epicenters in North Carolina and portions of adjacent states (1698–1997). Major geologic provinces and known major faults exposed at the surface are shown for North Carolina. Faults identified to date in North Carolina are ancient and inactive. Earthquake data before 1886 are sparse. Seismic instruments were installed in the region in the late 1920s. Prior to that time earthquake data are based on historical records. The distribution of seismograph stations did not allow for location of earthquakes with magnitudes <4 until 1962–1963. Microearthquake networks began operating in the region in the mid-1970s (Data Source: NC Geological Survey).

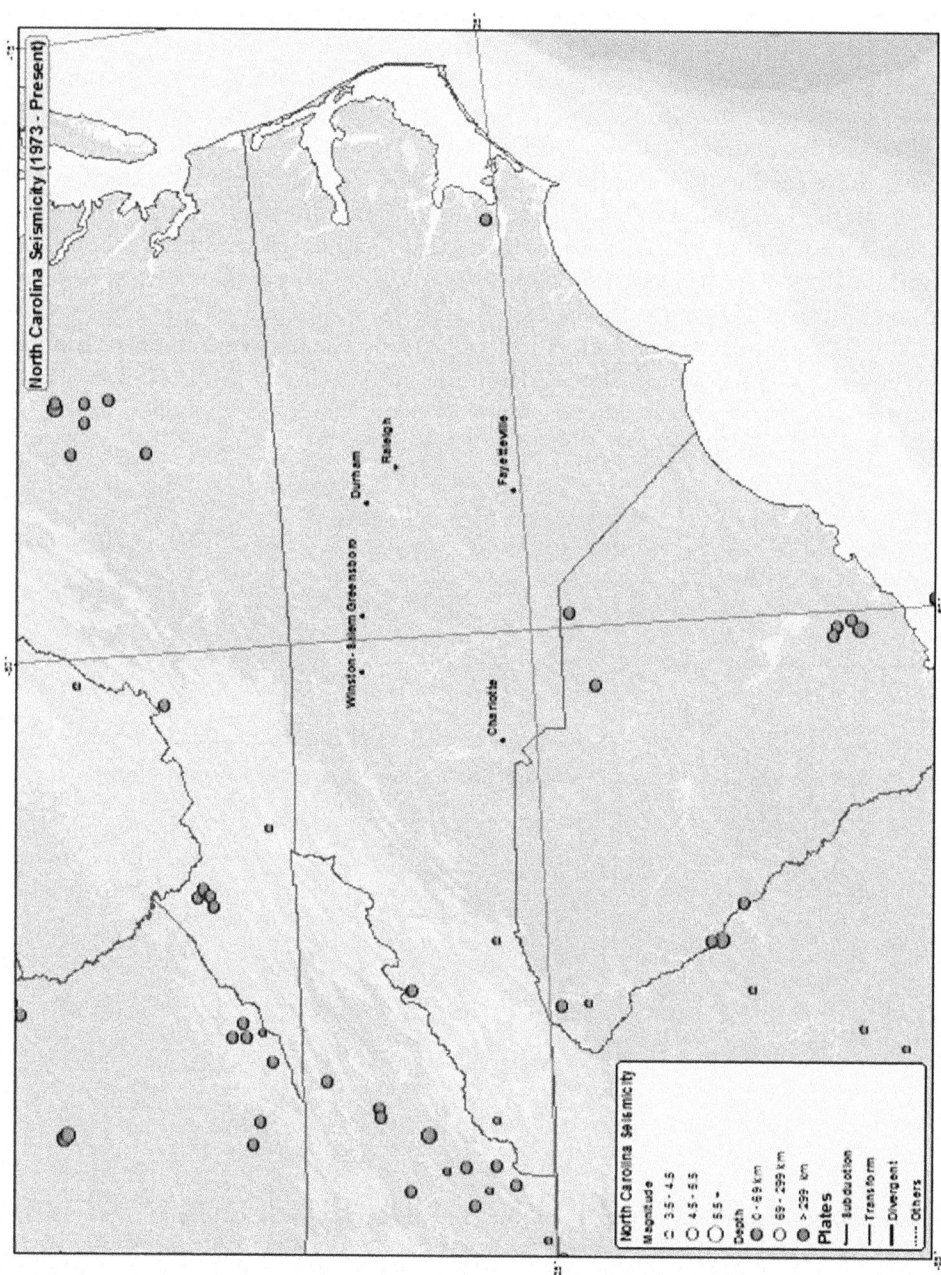

Figure 6. North Carolina earthquakes greater than magnitude 3.5, 1973–2012 (Data Source: www.earthquake.usgs.gov/earthquakes/states/north_carolina/seismicity.php).

recorded on any of the flat-lying thrust faults in the area. The second diagram below (North Carolina Earthquakes, 1973–2012) brings the information up to date and shows no earthquakes greater than 3.5 on the Richter scale in our area of interest in the last 40 years.

What are Richter scale magnitudes and what do they mean? The Richter scale is a universally accepted means of measuring the magnitude of earthquakes. Earthquakes less than about 1.8 on the scale aren't even felt by local residents, including those living at the epicenter. In addition, the Richter scale tells us that only earthquakes greater than 4 or 5 actually do any significant damage. For instance, the March 11, 2011, earthquake off the coast of Japan registered 8.9 on the Richter scale (highest ever recorded), the Great Charleston Earthquake of 1886 would have registered 7.3, and the largest earthquake ever centered in North Carolina (the 1916 Waynesville earthquake) would have registered only 5.2. On average, about 20,000 earthquakes are recorded each year on the planet, but only about 150 are greater than 5.9 on the Richter scale, which works out to about one major earthquake every other day.

But in recorded time, North Carolina has never registered a major earthquake (defined as greater than 5.9 on the Richter scale) and we get only a barely measurable low-magnitude earthquake about every 25–40 years. North Carolina, including the Brown Mountain area, is known as a tectonically inactive region. Although significant and major flat-lying thrust faults are common in the Brown Mountain-Linville Gorge area, none of them have produced measurable earthquakes in the last 323 years.

It seems safe to assume that although there are numerous large geologic faults in the area, none of them are currently active enough to produce stressed quartz. So today we have big faults but no fault movements, which mean no earthquakes and thus no tectonic stresses to produce broken quartz crystal plasmas.

This myth is busted! Without those broken quartz-crystal plasmas, we don't have anything else to research on this hypothesis. So there really is no reason to even consider the remaining six components of the Geologic Fault-Tectonic Strain Hypothesis. But, of course, I will anyway.

Plasmas, Water and Lifespan

Remember how easily water extinguished the geologists' rock saw sparks? Groundwater naturally collects and even migrates along faults, fault surfaces and fault zones, especially in our humid subtropical climate with abundant rain. The same is true of Brown Mountain. Water-well drillers in this area actually look for fault-controlled water courses to help ensure productive water wells. Even if spark plasmas could form along our geologic faults, the presence of excessive groundwater in the faults argues strongly against their survival for more than mere microseconds.

I'm a geologist, not a physicist, but what little reading I've done on plasmas suggests little ones don't combine with other little ones to make bigger ones. Little ones can become big ones only if significantly larger energy forces become available—larger energy forces as in hundreds of thousands to millions of degrees of temperature, which, if present, would melt the rocks along the faults in the first place. Note that granite melts at a mere 1,215–1,260°C (2,219–2,300°F). Little plasmas becoming big plasmas are not likely in the natural rock environment.

In addition, plasmas survive only as long as the tremendous energy that created them in the first place continues to operate; as soon as the source of the ionizing energy ends, the plasma instantly loses its luminescence and transforms back into the regular solid, liquid or gas from which it came. In other words, although ruptured quartz crystal sparks are true plasmas they are extremely short lived and do not live long enough to migrate any distance or to meet up with other distant spark plasmas.

If plasmas could live long enough to migrate along the faults and escape into the air, they would instantly disappear for the same reasons given above, unless they could somehow take their originating energy source or some new energy source with them. Neither case is likely.

As mentioned above, plasmas are hot, extremely hot, as in thousands to hundreds of thousands of degrees! If the BMLs are plasmas, then why don't they melt the rocks, set the woods on fire or burn those who get too close? Cold plasmas (whatever that is) may have been produced in the laboratory, but do they exist in nature? I don't know. I'm only a geologist, but I've never hear of one.

Earthquake Lights!

A recent publication once again drags up the Tectonic Strain Hypothesis in an attempt to explain some mystery lights and even uses the BMLs as an example. Robert Theriault and others (2014) use anecdotal evidence from 65 worldwide earthquake events over the 409-year period between 1600 and 2009 to support their poorly understood geophysical hypothesis that supposedly explains the production of visible atmospheric plasma lights arising from deeply sourced electric currents before or during continental rift-related earthquakes with Richter scale magnitudes greater than 4.0. While intriguing, the hypothesis remains unproven and even unlikely. According to the authors, earthquake lights occur during or from a few seconds to a few months before the associated earthquake and can occur unusually far from the epicenter or the trace of the earthquake fault itself.

Missing from the authors' discussion is an explanation of why the lights are generally seen only once in the weeks before each earthquake although the tectonic stresses obviously continue to build up to the time of the earthquake itself, and why the lights can appear as much as 370 miles from the epicenter or the fault rather than directly on the fault conduit that supposedly brings electric currents to the surface. Nor does the hypothesis explain why supposed earthquake lights such as the BMLs appear repeatedly in some areas of the world without any subsequent earthquakes. While only 5 percent of the world's earthquakes every year are estimated to be continental rift-related earthquakes (as reported by Theriault), an average 650 such earthquakes with magnitudes greater than 4.0 (considered the critical energy level necessary to produce earthquake lights by Theriault) occur worldwide every year (U.S. Geological Survey). Thus 266,000 such earthquakes probably occurred worldwide between 1600 and 2009 (Theriault's study period), yet Theriault and his associates found only 65 cases of earthquake-related lights during this period, suggesting a correlation rate that does not support his proposed direct earthquake-related hypothesis. In addition, Theriault's Brown Mountain light example (#7 of 27 of his North America examples) occurred 50 days after the supposedly related earthquake, which does not support his conclusion of pre- or contemporaneous earthquake lights.

Mineral Plasma Hypothesis

Another occasionally mentioned hypothesis of the supposedly remarkable plasma-producing ability of the rocks that underlie Brown Mountain doesn't involve faults at all, but instead is somehow related to ionization and electric currents due to the presence of underground water and layers of alternating quartz and magnetite in the rocks. For all the same reasons given above refuting fault-related plasmas, natural mineral-related ionized electric current plasmas are also illogical.

Also arguing against this hypothesis is the presence of some very large deposits of magnetite and quartz in the region but with no reported associated mystery lights. One of the largest massive magnetite mines in the U.S., the Cranberry Iron Mine, is located only 20 miles northwest of Brown Mountain; and although it is composed of hundreds of thousands of tons of nearly pure magnetite (Feiss et al., 1983), no mystery lights are known in that area. Likewise, some of the world's highest-purity quartz deposits are located near Spruce Pine, North Carolina (Glover et al., 2012) less than 18 miles west of Brown Mountain. But again no mystery lights are reported there. Note that high-purity quartz implies even greater piezoelectric properties than the normal quartz of granitic rocks like the Brown Mountain Gneiss.

In addition, the largest iron deposits in the world are composed of alternating thin layers of magnetite and quartz that make up deposits that are hundreds to thousands of feet thick. These deposits are so large and so common on every large continent on the planet that the host rocks have their own name—Banded Iron Formation. Yet they don't produce mystery lights either. In fact, based on his actual instrumental measurements, geophysical consultant Art Larson of Evergreen, Colorado, reports a near total lack of measurable electrical conductivity of layered magnetite/quartz deposits from around the world (personal communication, 2013). Larson reports that many other rocks are much more electrically conductive than iron deposits.

If the lights are supposedly generated by electrical currents associated with quartz and magnetite (iron oxide), wouldn't it make sense to expect that the lights would be more common where these minerals are so much more abundant or higher in purity than they are on Brown Mountain? This, too, is odd, isn't it?

In addition, the rocks beneath Brown Mountain are compositionally the same as those found elsewhere over very large areas of the earth, again with no reported mystery lights in those other areas. Collectively they are referred to as "crystalline rocks" because of their metamorphosed crustal compositions (high Si and Al and high in quartz and feldspar minerals). Brown Mountain covers only 14 square miles, while nearly 30,000 square miles of similar crystalline rocks exist elsewhere in North Carolina and 96,000 square miles of similar rocks exist throughout the entire Southern Appalachians—yet none of these produce mystery lights, due to rock-producing plasmas or anything else! Thus, naturally occurring quartz and magnetite minerals aren't the cause of the mystery lights.

Radioactive-mineral Plasmas

Even radioactive minerals in the rocks have been suspected by some to be involved in producing the BMLs. As in similar rocks around the world, trace amounts of radioactive minerals are finely disseminated throughout the Brown Mountain Granitic Gneiss but make up less than 0.001 percent of the rock. However, natural radioactive-mineral plasmas are not supported by any factual data. Nowhere on Brown Mountain are the radioactive minerals concentrated into larger masses, although such concentrations are extremely easy to identify with today's advanced radiation-detection instruments. However, a small concentration of radioactive minerals is reported on North Harper Creek, 5–7 miles northeast of Brown Mountain (Feiss et al., 1991; Wagener and McHome, 1982); but no mystery lights are reported in that area. Interestingly, extremely large deposits of highly radioactive uranium minerals are known elsewhere in the world, with the Swanson/Coles Hill deposit, one of the largest in the U.S., located near Chatham, Pittsylvania County, Virginia, less than 150 miles from Brown Mountain. Yet no mystery lights are reportedly associated with any of these deposits either. Odd, isn't it? Thus, naturally occurring radioactive minerals aren't the cause of the mystery lights. "There is nothing unique or unusual in the geology of Brown Mountain" (George Rogers Mansfield, 1922, *The Origin of the Brown Mountain Light in North Carolina*, U.S. Geological Survey Circular 646).

But how about telluric currents (aka earth currents)? Wikipedia.org gives the following explanation for Telluric Currents:

> Telluric currents are phenomena observed in the Earth's crust and mantle. The currents are primarily geo-magnetically induced currents, which are induced by changes in the outer part of the Earth's magnetic field, which are usually caused by interactions between the solar wind and the magnetosphere or solar radiation effects on the ionosphere.
>
> Telluric currents flow in the surface layers of the Earth. The electric potential on the Earth's surface can be measured at different points, enabling us to calculate the magnitudes and directions of the telluric currents and hence the Earth's conductance.
>
> These currents are known to have diurnal characteristics wherein the general direction of flow is towards the Sun. Telluric currents will move between each half of the terrestrial globe at all times. Telluric currents move equator-ward (daytime) and pole-ward (nighttime).

Since these currents affect the entire earth all at once, doesn't it seem logical that if they were involved in producing mystery lights then such lights would be seen over a much larger area or in more places than just Brown Mountain and Linville Gorge?

Telluric, or earth, currents, as described above are usually or primarily caused by the solar wind, which itself is measured and reported as the Kp index. The peak of the 11-year solar cycle corresponding to the peak of sunspot and solar storm activity was 2013 and 2014. Solar storms or winds directed toward the Earth peaked in 2013/2014 and produced some spectacular aurora displays. However, we saw no increased BML activity, nor have we observed any correlation between the BMLs and the Kp index numbers. Thus we conclude Telluric, or earth, currents resulting from solar activity do not cause the BMLs.

Plasmas and Hallucinations

Can plasmas, from any source, actually cause temporal lobe transients (hallucinations) in humans? True plasmas do contain electromagnetic fields. However, Michael Persinger's groundbreaking electromagnetic, current-induced hallucination experiments of the 1970s (Persinger and Lafreniere, 1977; Persinger, 1983) have now been discredited. The results could not be reproduced in more-tightly controlled laboratory experiments (Granqvist, 2005). Although frequently referenced in both the scientific and pseudoscientific literature, Persinger's interesting direct-correlation results were apparently due to the power of suggestion rather than the electromagnetic forces themselves.

Apparently close encounters with plasmas do not cause temporal lobe transients or hallucinations in humans.

Conclusions

Tectonic forces are no longer acting on the large faults in the area of Brown Mountain, thus there are no earthquakes and no ongoing buildup of possible fault-related, ruptured-quartz-crystal, hot-spark plasmas. Even if they could originate along the faults, ruptured-quartz-crystal, hot-spark plasmas are extremely short lived and are too low-energy to survive underwater. They apparently don't have enough energy to combine with other sparks to produce larger plasmas, nor do they have enough energy to escape into the atmosphere and live long enough to be observed as reported luminescent mystery lights.

Although mysterious once-only, daytime "glowing Earth lights" have occasionally been reported shortly before major earthquakes elsewhere in the world, the nightly BMLs are different and, as we see, are not related to geologic faults or earthquakes.

Likewise, mineral-related, ionized, electric current plasmas occurring beneath Brown Mountain don't make much sense either, especially since similar minerals in even greater purity and abundance are found elsewhere in the Southern Appalachians and around the world where no mystery lights are reported.

As for radioactive mineral plasmas, there aren't enough radioactive minerals present in the Brown Mountain Granitic Gneiss to produce anything more than the average background radioactivity present in similar crystalline rocks throughout the world, again with no reported mystery lights. Highly radioactive rocks do exist elsewhere in the world but don't produce lights; why should merely average radioactive rocks do so on Brown Mountain?

If plasmas from any source could reach the reported BML sizes (a few inches to several feet in diameter), could their electromagnetic fields adversely affect a human brain? This is highly doubtful, as recent scientific results show a lack of correlation between electromagnetic fields and hallucinations in humans.

Lastly, we've found no relationship between the BMLs and solar wind activity (Kp index), even though we had just experienced the peak of the 11-year solar cycle.

Chapter 15

Possibly Misidentified Natural Lights

Methane, Swamp Gas, Will-o'-the Wisp and Ignis Fatuus

Flammable swamp gas or marsh gas is often suggested as a possible source of the BMLs. The first published account of swamp gas comes from the 1959 Happer brothers' expedition (Alexander, 1959). However, the plausibility of burning swamp gas producing the BMLs is questionable.

Our Brown Mountain lights research team has found naturally occurring flammable organic gas (probably methane) on two creeks in McDowell County (Armstrong and Buck creeks) about 21 and 22 miles respectively southwest of Brown Mountain. The gas was collected in a partially submerged glass jar as small bubbles of the gas rose from decaying organic matter at the bottom of stagnant creek water. The lighter-than-air gas was then ignited with a match. It burned instantly with a "poof" and produced a pale blue flame. Similar flammable organic gases are reported elsewhere in the region and we have every reason to expect them to be present on Brown Mountain as well. In fact, several anecdotal stories report that it has already been seen on the mountain (among others, see Alexander, 1959, and Baity, 1962). While our team has yet to confirm this on Brown Mountain, we have no reason to doubt that it exists.

While flammable gas (probably methane) from decaying organic matter is undoubtedly present throughout many streams in the subtropical forests of the southern Appalachians, it is very rare in volumes large enough to burn and requires an ignition source. As explained above, most often that ignition source is a match, fire or spark supplied by man.

When methane is supposedly ignited by nature rather than by man, it is called swamp gas, marsh gas, jack-o'-lantern, will-o'-the-wisp, or ignis fatuus. However, the chemical or physical mechanisms whereby natural-ignition repeatedly exists have not been scientifically validated and although occasionally reported elsewhere in the world, the supposed natural phenomenon of spontaneously combusting methane is highly questionable.

Even if spontaneously combusting methane gas was possible, the small amount of gas available at any given moment would burn instantly with a pale light and would be unlikely to be the source of the distant, multicolored, long-lasting, widely-distributed, and occasionally rapidly-moving mystery lights seen in the area of Brown Mountain.

Natural Gas and Eternal Flames

Natural and continuously burning natural-gas flames (also known as eternal flames) are known elsewhere in the world. The small, single eternal flame burning beneath a steep waterfall in Chestnut Ridge Park, New York, has been known for a long time. This flame is believed to have been burning for at least several hundred years and it is unknown how it was originally ignited. Of course, lightning or lightning-caused forest fires are possible ways that such a flame could have been naturally ignited; or maybe some person ignited it! Natural gas continuously escaping from underground deposits is the source of the flammable gas in Chestnut Ridge Park. The country rocks are sedimentary rocks similar to those that host all of the world's known oil and gas deposits. In this case, a small amount of the natural gas is leaking to the surface, has been ignited and is burning under the waterfall.

Turkey is home to at least two remarkable eternal flames. Several small flames on Mount Chimaera have supposedly been burning for more than a thousand years. This is where the legend of the fire-breathing Chimaera monster originated. In addition, the Gates of Hell is a football-field sized collapsed sinkhole that developed following the gas-well extraction of a shallow natural gas deposit in the 1950s. As continued production was impossible, workmen at the time decided to burn off the escaping natural gas, expecting the burn to last only a few hours or days. But the sinkhole has been burning continuously ever since. As in the New York case, both of the Turkey eternal flames involve natural gas continuously escaping from buried oil/gas deposits hosted by sedimentary rocks. Although rare, similar natural gas eternal flames are also known in other parts of the world—but not on Brown Mountain.

There are no oil/gas deposits beneath Brown Mountain. The metamorphosed crystalline rocks that underlie Brown Mountain do not host oil or natural gas deposits. These rocks originated from hot molten intrusions that were subsequently metamorphosed under tremendous heat and pressure—conditions that not only do not produce oil or gas deposits but actually destroy any such deposits that might have originally been present. Thus, without buried oil and gas deposits beneath Brown Mountain, there is no escaping natural gas to ignite and burn at the surface.

Forest Fires, Brush Fires and Campfires

Man-made or nature-caused forest fires and brush fires obviously can produce nighttime lights. Such fires are not uncommon in the Brown Mountain area. For instance, the Table Rock Fire in November 2013 burned over 1,000 acres of pristine forest in the Linville Gorge Wilderness and the adjacent Pisgah National Forest. While such large fires are probably obvious to most observers, not everyone can distinguish between fires and mystery lights. Small forest fires have been known to confuse some people. Near the end of the Table Rock fire, when only a few isolated, widely spaced, small fires continued to burn on the lower west flank of Table Rock, several observers at Wiseman's View were overheard honestly dismissing them as "BMLs." The observers had no clue they were looking at residual hot spots from the recent large forest fire.

Campfires are also a common phenomenon visible from the popular observations sites. Numerous roadside and backcountry campsites exist in the Pisgah National Forest

Top: Figure 7. Table Rock forest fire seen from Wiseman's View on November 12, 2013. Note the airplane in the sky above Table Rock, distant city lights in the valley, and stars of constellation Orion in sky through tree branches (Canon EF 18–55 mm zoom lens set at 18 mm [29 mm effective focal length and 0.6X approx. magnification]; 7-second exposure, f/4.5, ISO-1600). *Bottom:* Figure 8. Table Rock forest fire seen from Wiseman's View on November 18, 2013. Note several isolated small residual fires on lower flank of Table Rock Mountain (Canon EF 18–55 mm zoom lens set at 18 mm [29 mm effective focal length and 0.6X approx. magnification]; 60-second exposure, f/4.5, ISO-1600).

15. Possibly Misidentified Natural Lights   99

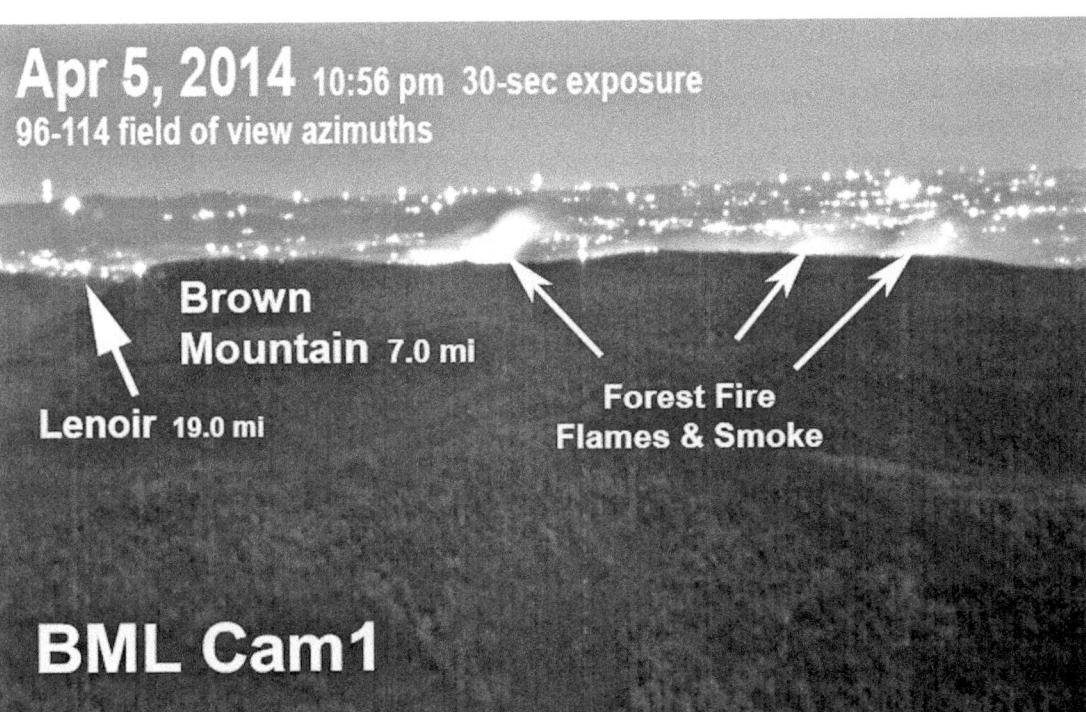

Forest fires on Brown Mountain, April 5, 2014 (Images: A. BM-04-05-06-14-056 and B. BM-04-05-06-14-168 courtesy Daniel Caton).

lands bordering Brown Mountain and within the nearby Linville Gorge Wilderness Area. Campfire lights from these campsites are often visible at night.

Natural Nighttime Celestial Lights

In our efforts to understand the possible existence of mysterious nocturnal lights in the Brown Mountain area, we must first understand all naturally occurring nighttime lights that might be visible. Today's generation is perhaps less familiar and less comfortable with the outdoor environment than our ancestors were, which may explain why today's legend of the BMLs includes sightings of mysterious nighttime sky lights, which were not part of the legend a hundred years ago. Today's observers often experience unidentified mystery lights both on the ground near Brown Mountain and high in the sky above.

Visible celestial objects, such as the moon, Venus, Jupiter, Mars, Saturn, stars, meteors, comets, and sun-related nighttime lights can confuse observers who aren't familiar with the night skies and aren't expecting to see such bright, colorful, oddly shaped, or moving lights in the sky. While we're all somewhat unfamiliar with nature, each person's cumulative outdoor experience, or lack thereof, can manifest itself as misconceptions of nighttime celestial lights visible overhead.

Many people simply aren't aware of common nighttime celestial lights such as illuminated clouds, bright stars, meteors, planets, or sunlight reflecting off of man's artificial space vehicles, much less things like light pillars, the Zodiacal light, the parhelion lights, the parhelic circle, crepuscular rays, and maybe even the aurora borealis.

On several occasions I've listened while observers at one of the popular viewing sites overlooking Brown Mountain express excitement and even fear as the International Space Station passed overhead in the night sky. For those not expecting to see such a bright object in the sky, the experience can be unnerving and worrisome, especially for those expecting to see mystery lights in the first place. Actually there are hundreds of man-made satellites that are visible to the naked eye when they reflect sunlight as they pass overhead at night. Unsuspecting or uninformed observers, beware! There are Internet Web sites and even smart phone and tablet applications that track all visible man-made satellites and space vehicles. Use of these software programs is highly recommended by anyone who plans a nighttime observation or who has already seen an unusual light in the night sky.

Bright Planets

Every year, around the world, stories arise about misinterpretations of the bright "naked-eye" planets Venus, Jupiter, Mars and Saturn. Venus, particularly, is commonly mistaken for an extraterrestrial UFO, or more recently, an enemy spy drone on the militarized border between India and Pakistan that nearly started a major battle between the warring countries. Many people aren't even aware that they can see planets with the naked eye. In the Brown Mountain area, as elsewhere, the sudden and unexpected emergence of one of these unexpectedly bright planets above a distant mountain ridge can be especially unnerving to an unsuspecting observer. The bright white light can appear to

Top: Figure 10. Jupiter rising over Hawksbill Mountain seen from Wiseman's View (Canon EF 75–300 mm zoom with 1.4X teleconverter set at 105 mm [170 mm effective focal length and 3.4X approximate magnification]; 1-second exposure, f/5.6, ISO-800). *Bottom:* Figure 11. Venus setting in trees on the north side of Hawksbill Mountain seen from NC Highway 181 Brown Mountain Overlook. Note the bright star trail in the sky (Canon EF 75–300 mm zoom set at 224 mm [363 mm effective focal length and 7.3X approximate magnification]; 20-second exposure, f/7.1, ISO-800).

Top: Figure 12. Moonrise over the north side of Table Rock Mountain, taken from Wiseman's View. Brown Mountain is the flat-topped ridge in the center of the image. Note faint city lights in the distant valley (Canon EF 18–55 mm zoom set at 24 mm [39 mm effective focal length and 0.8X approximate magnification]; 30-second exposure, f/18, ISO-200). *Bottom:* Figure 13. Moonrise over the south slope of Hawksbill Mountain, taken from Wiseman's View. Brown Mountain is the flat-topped ridge in the center of the image. Note faint city lights in the distant valley (Canon EF 18–55 mm zoom set at 18 mm [29 mm effective focal length and 0.6X approximate magnification]; 60-second exposure, f/4.5, ISO-200).

be quickly rising through the trees on the ridgeline and into the sky above. Focusing one's eye on such a bright light in an otherwise dark sky quickly results in fatigue of the eye muscles, causing the light to appear to move even more. In addition, clouds above the distant ridgeline can also move rapidly due to strong winds, creating an optical illusion that it is the bright light that is rapidly moving.

Sun-Related Nighttime Lights

While everyone is probably familiar with the moon's reflected sunlight, fewer people are familiar with the vast array of other possible sun-related nighttime lights including the following:

Moonlight
Moonbows
   Parhelic circle
   120 Parhelion light
   Night sundogs
Aurora Borealis (Northern Lights)
Zodiacal light (False Dawn)
Noctilucent clouds
Nacreous clouds
Iridescent clouds
Crepuscular and anti-Crepuscular rays
Rocket and jet aircraft vapor trails

Aurora Borealis (Northern Lights)

The rare Aurora Borealis, or Northern Lights, have occasionally been seen as far south as North Carolina. The Aurora appears when rare solar flares are directed toward earth. Note that 2013 marked the maximum of the 11-year solar sunspot activity cycle; yet, no Aurora was seen in North Carolina in 2013 or 2014. Even when seen, the Aurora Borealis is not likely to be mistaken for mysterious BMLs; however, it seems that at some time or another someone has mistaken practically every known light for a mystery light, thus the Aurora is a candidate for mistaken identity.

Zodiacal Light (False Dawn)

The Zodiacal light (false dawn in the northern hemisphere) is caused by refraction of the predawn sun by ground-level dust seen an hour or so immediately before the sun rises above the eastern horizon. It is typically seen only near the equinoxes each year and on very rare occasions can also be seen at dusk.

While unusual and interesting, the natural sun-related nighttime lights mentioned above are not likely to be candidates for misinterpretations of mysterious BMLs. They are generally rare and don't occur often enough to account for the nightly lights reported as BMLs. However, as noted above, some observers can be misled at the time of their specific sighting.

Celestial Objects Captured by BML Cam1

Bright celestial objects such as certain stars, the moon, the visible planets Jupiter, Mars, Venus, and Mercury, and even meteors have been frequently captured by BML Cam1. Some of these objects can be easily identified because they rise above the eastern horizon at predictable times and azimuths. Astronomers' ephemeris data (times and azimuths) provides the information needed for correct identification. While such sky lights are not likely to be mistaken by most people for mystery lights, as mentioned above not everyone is familiar with the night sky and we have seen some cases of mistaken identities.

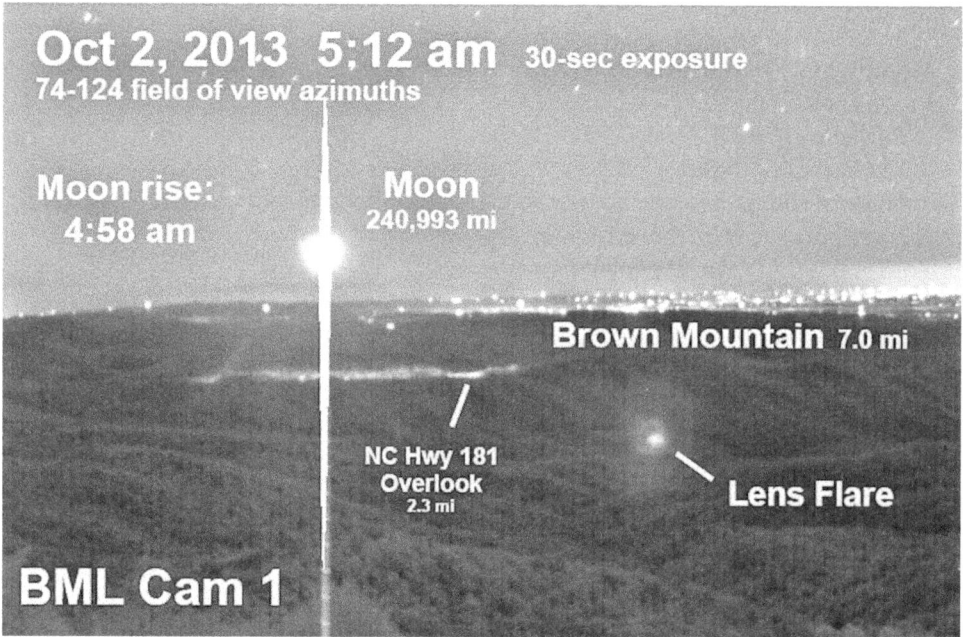

Moonrise above Brown Mountain, October 2, 2013. Notice lens flare, light rays on the moon, and vehicle lights on NC Hwy 181 (image: BM-10-01-02-13481 courtesy Daniel Caton).

Moonlight Reflecting Off Bare Rock Exposures

Several instances of moonlight reflecting off of bare rock exposures have been captured in BML Cam1 images. A small stream of water pours year-round onto the upper side of Lael's Rock and often reflects moonlight. Moonlight reflecting on snow and ice on the same rock exposure produced a remarkably bright light several nights during February 2015.

Does Lightning Play a Role in the BMLs?

The National Weather Service (National Oceanic and Atmospheric Administration, United States Department of Commerce) defines lightning as a "giant spark of electricity

Top: Figure 15. Moonrise above Brown Mountain, June 26, 2013. Notice light rays and oversaturation of light from the moon. *Bottom:* Figure 16. Lens flare from Bright Moon above Brown Mountain (both photographs courtesy Daniel Caton).

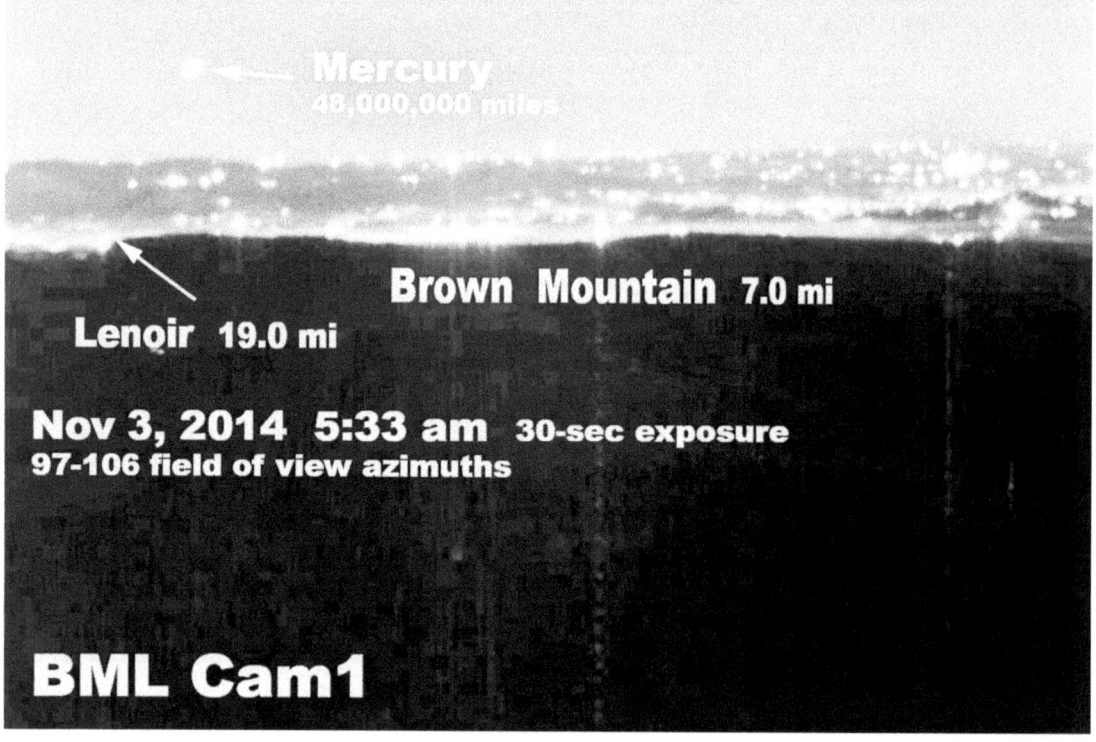

Top: Figure 17. Jupiter and the constellation Orion above Brown Mountain. *Bottom:* Figure 18. Mercury above Brown Mountain (both photographs courtesy Daniel Caton).

15. *Possibly Misidentified Natural Lights* 107

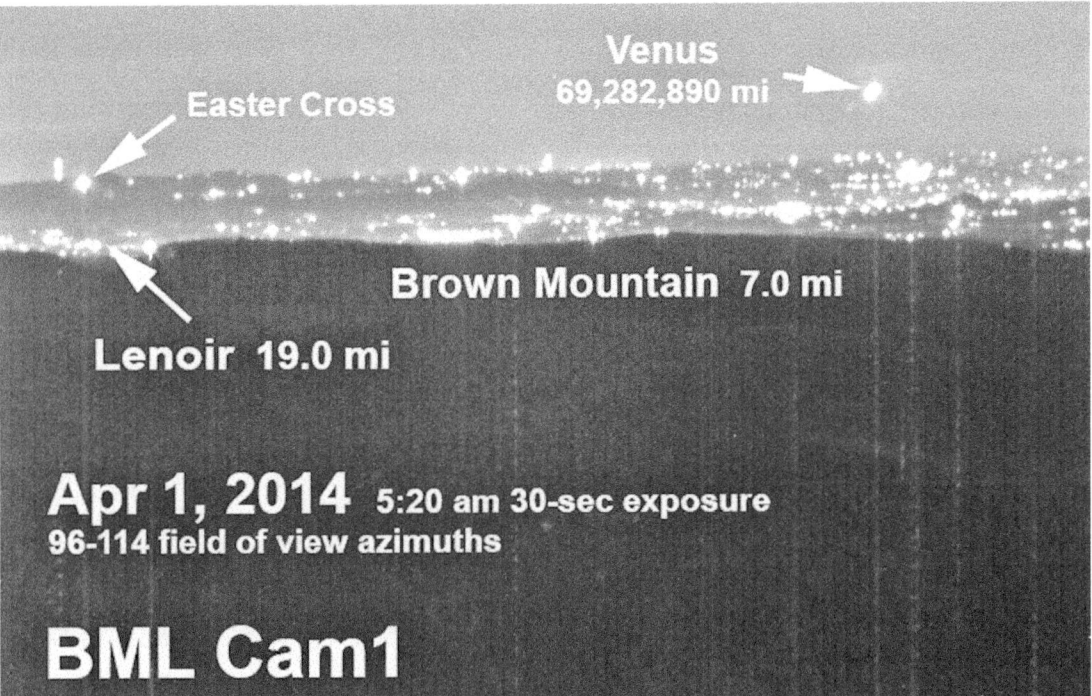

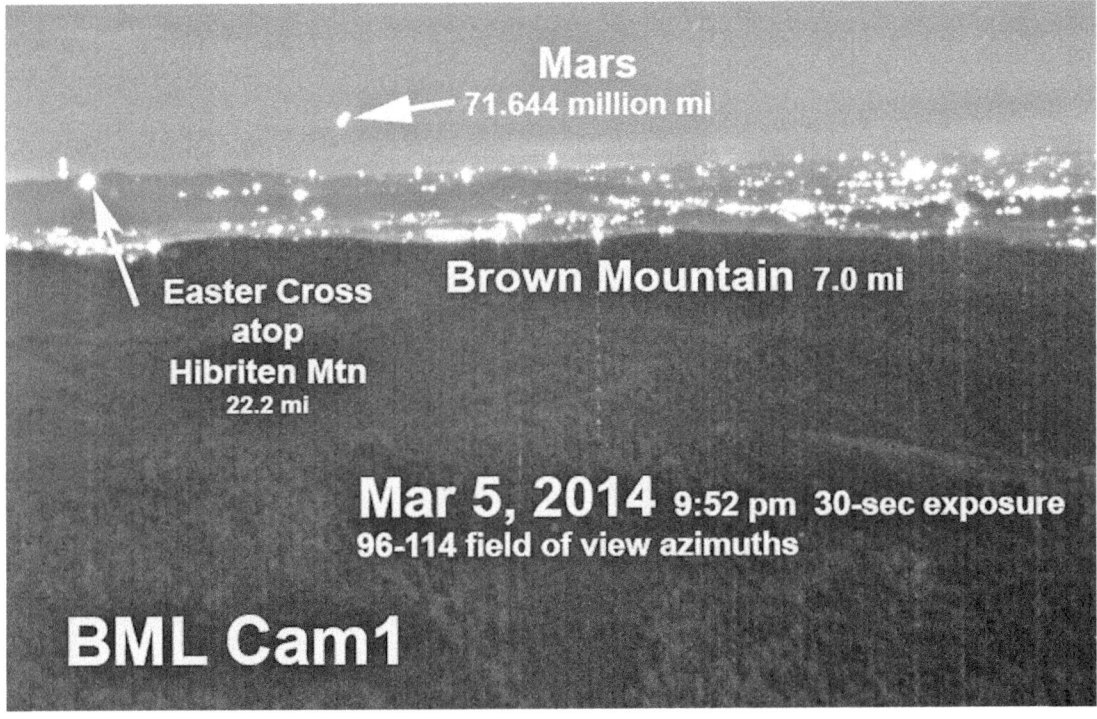

Top: Figure 19. Venus above Brown Mountain. Notice the city of Lenoir's Easter cross lighted atop Hibriten Mountain. *Bottom:* Figure 20. Mars above Brown Mountain (both photographs courtesy Daniel Caton).

Top: Figure 21. Meteor above Brown Mountain. Moonlight exposes many land features. *Bottom:* Figure 22. Moonlight reflecting on snow-covered rocks (both photographs courtesy Daniel Caton).

in the atmosphere or between the atmosphere and the ground." A more informative description is given by Wikipedia on the Internet:

> Lightning is a massive electrostatic discharge (ESD) between the electrically charged regions within clouds or between a cloud and the surface of a planet.
> The charged regions within the atmosphere temporarily equalize themselves through a lightning flash, commonly referred to as a strike if it hits an object on the ground.
> There are three primary types of lightning; from a cloud to itself (intra-cloud or IC); from one cloud to another cloud (CC); and between a cloud and the ground (CG).
> A typical cloud to ground lightning flash culminates in the formation of an electrically conducting plasma channel through the air in excess of 5 kilometers (3.1 mi) tall, from within the cloud to the ground's surface.

Thus, visible lightning is naturally occurring plasma that can produce light during the day or at night. The historical investigators of the BMLs have often considered lightning, and several manifestations of it have been proposed as a cause of at least some of the BMLs.

Brush Lightning

Brush lightning—apparently ground-level bushes glowing due to the buildup of electrical charges somewhat akin to the Andes light and St. Elmo's fire—was first proposed by W.J. Humphries of the National Weather Bureau in 1919 (Lyman, 1921 and 1941; *Trenton Evening News*, 1921; Mansfield, 1922; and Humphries, 1941). Interestingly, the same or similar glowing-brush phenomenon has been repeatedly observed by local resident Clyde Hollifield on very windy mountaintops in western North Carolina (personal communication, 2013), but apparently the lights are too small and dim to be visible from more than a few feet away and are too infrequent to offer a valid explanation for the BMLs.

Ball Lightning

Although poorly defined and understood, ball lightning has also been proposed as a cause of the mystery lights by some researchers (ORION, 1977; Kane, 1983; Caton, 1998, 2012; and Warren, 2012). Ball lightning is certainly a candidate for some mystery light sightings seen during electrical storms; however, it doesn't appear to be a contributing factor in the vast majority of mystery light sightings which are reported during non-stormy conditions.

Heat Lightning

While most people are familiar with nearby, violent, storm-related lightning with loud thunder, bright flashes and visible lightning bolts, some folks have been seen to be misled by distant lightning displays where only flashes of light are seen but no noise is heard. Such distant lightning phenomenon, generally called heat lightning, occurs so far from the observer that the true cause (distant thunder storms) is not readily apparent.

On one occasion at the Wiseman's View observation site, I quietly listened as unsuspecting and uninformed observers marveled at distant noiseless intra-cloud lightning flashes with no visible lightning bolts, wondering if that was the mysterious BMLs. They simply had never seen such a phenomenon before and since it was happening at the time and place they were expecting to see mystery lights, they naturally assumed it must be the BMLs they had heard about. This is a clear example of *Nature Deficit Disorder*, to which everyone is subject to varying degrees (Louv, 2005 and 2012). As its name implies, it is a condition that is a direct result of our usual electronic-environment lifestyles, which include limited outdoor experience.

Lightning-Caused Mystery Lights Unlikely

Lightning in any form appears to explain very few of the reported mystery lights seen during non-stormy weather, which constitute the vast majority of all reported sightings. Certainly some storm-related lights might be attributed to lightning in the sky, cloud to ground strikes (ball lightning) or the buildup of related atmospheric electrical charges (brush lightning, St. Elmo's fire, or the Andes light), but the evidence is far from conclusive.

Critters and Other Things That Glow in the Dark

Three different critters in our area naturally glow in the dark: glowworms, luminescent mushrooms, and fireflies. Can these glowing critters explain any of the BMLs?

While glowworms, mushrooms, and the common fireflies aren't likely to be mistaken for mysterious BMLs, a rare and poorly understood unique firefly in our area is a strong candidate for mistaken sightings! Called the blue ghost firefly (BGF), this continuously

Figure 23. Cloud-to-ground lightning over Brown Mountain (courtesy Daniel Caton).

15. Possibly Misidentified Natural Lights

Figure 24. Cloud-to-cloud lightning over Brown Mountain. Image transition errors are discussed in Chapter 18 (courtesy Daniel Caton).

burning, white or bluish-white light firefly is practically unknown to today's local residents, and first-time unsuspecting observers can easily be misled about what they are seeing outside. While mistakes are possible, the rarity of the BGFs suggests that somewhat less than an estimated 1 percent of all reported BMLs may be attributed to them; however, they may explain some of the biggest stories of the BML legend (see Chapters 9 and 10).

Glowworms

North America's only bioluminescent dipteral (fungus gnat) larval worm was confirmed on the rock cliffs at Wiseman's View on July 7, 2013, when several dozen specimens were observed by our research team (Cato Holler, Jr., personal communication, 2013). While known elsewhere in the Southern Appalachians, this is the first reported occurrence in our area.

Called *Orfelia fultoni*, these small half-inch larvae live in the moist moss and organic debris accumulated in recesses near the bottom of the rock cliffs to the northwest of the observation pulpits at Wiseman's View. The worms glow bluish-white and are extremely light sensitive, turning off in the presence of any artificial lights such as handheld flashlights or camera flashes. Once disturbed, they also stop glowing. The larvae can be very bright, but because of their small size, small numbers and location low on the cliffs, they aren't likely to be seen by observers at the top of the rock cliffs. Likewise, they are not likely to be mistaken for mystery lights unless their numbers greatly increase beyond their current population.

Although rare, the best-known permanent population of *Orfelia fultoni* glowworms in the Southern Appalachians occurs in Dismals Canyon in northwest Alabama. Here the numbers of glowworms can reportedly be large enough to light up the rock cliff "like a star-filled sky." Apparently the numbers at Wiseman's View have yet to get that large.

Luminescent Mushrooms (Foxfire)

Microscopic luminescent mushroom fungi can infect erect mushroom plants or decaying wood lying on or near the ground. The resultant pale to moderately bright greenish glow is fairly common and has been reported throughout the Southern Appalachians, including Brown Mountain and Linville Gorge. Local naturalist Clyde Hollifield reports that oxidization of the fungi mycelium is responsible for the luminescence, and disturbing infected dead wood exposes it to more oxygen, which often results in greater light production first noticeable up to six hours later (personal communication, 2013).

Also occasionally called foxfire, luminescent mushroom fungi are not likely to be commonly mistaken for mysterious BMLs. However, we have at least one story of just such a mistaken identification by young campers who thought they had found the mysterious BMLs—until they gathered the nerve to venture closer and found luminescent mushroom fungi in rotting logs.

Blue Ghost Fireflies: Watch Out, BML Observers!

While nearly every resident in the eastern United States is probably familiar with the common yellow-blinking eastern firefly (*Photinus pyralis*), the extremely rare and relatively unknown blue ghost firefly (*Phausis reticulata*) glows continuously with a white or bluish-white light and is so elusive that most of today's life-long local residents aren't even aware of its existence. Yet, small concentrated populations, mostly known only to entomologists and an increasing number of firefly enthusiasts, are reported in our area. Our research suggests that a small number of reported mystery light sightings may be due to the blue ghost firefly.

Unlike its yellow-blinking, summer-long active, grassland-loving cousin the eastern firefly, BGFs are active for only a few weeks each summer, are extremely sensitive to light, temperature, and air vibrations, and glow with a continuous white or bluish-white light while flying near the ground in dense forestlands.

KNOWN LOCATIONS OF BGFs

Western North Carolina sightings of BGFs known to the author include the following:

1. Smoky Mountain National Park, NC and TN (120 mi. west of Brown Mountain).
2. Wildwood Gallery, Greenville Co., SC (75 mi. southwest of Brown Mountain).
3. DuPont State Forest, Henderson and Transylvania counties, NC (71 mi. southwest of Brown Mountain).
4. Mount Pisgah, Buncombe and Haywood counties, NC (70 mi. southwest of Brown Mountain).
5. Conover, Catawba County, NC (34 mi. southeast of Brown Mountain).

6. Blue Ridge Parkway, MP 342, McDowell County, NC (25 mi. southwest of Brown Mountain).
  7. North Muddy Creek, McDowell County, NC (20 mi. southwest of Brown Mountain).
  8. Wiseman's View, Old NC Hwy 105, McDowell County, NC (8 mi. west of Brown Mountain).
  9. Hawksbill Mtn parking lot, FS Rd 210, Burke County, NC (7 mi. west of Brown Mountain).
  10. North Harper Creek, Avery County, NC (6 mi. northeast of Brown Mountain).
  11. Upper Creek, Burke County, NC (3 mi. southwest of Brown Mountain).
  12. Hwy 9, Buncombe County, NC (40 mi. southwest of Brown Mountain).
  13. McKinney Mine Road and Emerald Mine Road, Mitchell County, NC (18 mi. southwest of Brown Mountain).

In addition to the above list of specific locations, entomologists Jennifer Frick-Rupert and Joshua Rosen of the Department of Science and Math, Brevard College, Brevard, North Carolina, report collections of BGFs for their 2008 comprehensive investigation from nine counties in North Carolina (Transylvania, Avery, McDowell, Mecklenburg, Cabarrus, Davidson, Caldwell, Union, Burke, and Swain); three counties in South Carolina (Oconee, Pickens and Greenville); two counties in Tennessee (Sevier and Blount); two counties in Georgia (Clarke and Madison); and Dixie County in Florida. The BGFs are also reported to occur in Pennsylvania, Arkansas, Oklahoma, Virginia and Texas.

The various populations of BGFs seem to be isolated and possibly on the verge of dying out due to highly variable weather conditions, human encroachment, forest fires, and probably predators. It's possible that individual populations expand or contract each year in response to unknown factors and years with peak numbers may not be continuous at any given location.

BGF Mating Times

Unlike the six-month mating activity of the more-plentiful eastern firefly (*Photinus pyralis*), also known as the Big Dipper Firefly, the BGF is active for only a few weeks each summer. Also being much more sensitive to temperature, the BGF may fly only an hour or two each night before going back to the ground when the nighttime temperature drops below about 65°F, while the less-sensitive eastern firefly is often active for many more hours each night.

Peak mating activity is seen to begin once the average ground or soil temperature has risen above 65°F, which of course varies with elevation, latitude, and weather. Variables in the weather year to year mean that the mating season isn't always predictable. The season starts with a few BGFs emerging from the ground and venturing into the air for a short flight each night; and if the weather continues to warm over succeeding days and nights, these are followed by ever-increasing numbers of flying males and ever-increasing lengths of flight time. Often peak mating activity occurs over the next few nights or weeks, especially if the weather continues to warm. Unseasonable changes in the weather, such as excessive rain or sudden drops in the temperature, can seriously curtail or delay the mating activity. However, once well underway, the nightly flights may continue for one to two weeks except during heavy rain, frequent lightning, or bright moonlit nights. Mating activity slows progressively following peak mating times and may end entirely a few weeks later. However, some anecdotal stories suggest that a few solitary BGFs may actually venture into the air each night well into fall.

Peak mating times typically begin in late April to early June in western North Carolina, but as mentioned above they can occur earlier during unseasonably warm weather or later during unseasonably cold weather. Generally, the mating activity is so short in a given location that it can be easily missed by interested observers. Careful attention to the ground temperature in the area of interest is critical to observing the hatch.

The lights of the BGFs most visible to humans are those of the males, which fly two to three feet above the ground in search of the flightless females living on the ground. The far-fewer females also glow with the same white or bluish-white light, but it is much dimmer than those of the males. During peak mating times, it is possible to witness dozens to thousands of males seemingly flying in unison as gentle breezes carry them along in the same direction. The males are territorial and maintain an equal distance from each other while individually avoiding obstacles in their flight path like bushes, trees, and branches. The visual effect of a nearly continuous carpet of lights moving in unison at the same height above the ground can be mesmerizing, unforgettable, and even unnerving to the first-time observer.

BGF Burn Times

Two other major characteristics distinguish the BGF from their yellow-blinking cousins. The blue-white lights of the BGF glow continuously for up to 120 seconds as opposed to the less-than-one-second flashes of the common eastern firefly. During the burn, the BGF continues to fly and can cover up to 100 feet, giving the viewer an unexpectedly long-lived and far-traveled trail of light! In addition, the BGF is extremely sensitive to light, being most active on moonless nights and staying in the shadows on nights with subdued moonlight. They may not fly at all on full-moon nights. Although the BGFs prefer the near-total darkness of dense forests, they are also found in areas with other more-common fireflies, which can mask their presence, especially since they generally don't begin flying on any given night until about an hour after the common eastern firefly begins to fly. Often the larger numbers of eastern fireflies mask the smaller numbers of BGFs.

BGF Light Color

The bluish-white or white color of the BGF is due to an optical illusion of the human eye. The rod and cone light sensors in our eyes see light differently, with the grayscale-seeing rods sensitive to low light but the color-seeing cones insensitive to low light. Thus our eyes see the distant dim light of the BGFs as white and our brain, expecting to see some color, adds the perception of a bluish tint. Actually, when seen within a few inches of our eyes, the color of the BGF appears to be yellow or yellowish-green, nearly the same color as the larger common eastern firefly. Time-lapse photographs of flying BGFs show the true yellowish-green color, not the expected bluish-white seen by our human eyes!

One of our team members, Mr. Lee Hawkins (Observatory Engineer, Department of Physics and Astronomy, Appalachian State University, Boone, North Carolina), explains that this same phenomenon is also often seen when one looks through a telescope at a dim, far-distant, celestial object and sees only grey, while a photograph often revels more vivid colors (personal communication, 2013).

In the most definitive publication on BGFs, Frick-Ruppert and Rosen (2008) also commented on the bluish-white verses greenish color: "Difference in the apparent color of the male's glow (bluish-white at a distance but greenish up close) may result from differences in our perception of color that is affected by low light levels" (*Morphology and Behavior of* Phausis Reticulata [*Blue Ghost Firefly*]).

BGF INTELLIGENT BEHAVIOR?

Other curious reactions of the BGF happen when a flashlight is directed toward them or the viewer walks toward them. Being extremely sensitive to light and air vibrations, the fireflies will immediately turn off and fly away, avoiding the viewer. Air vibrations due to the movement of the moving observer apparently simulate those of an approaching predator and drive the firefly away. When seen glowing again, the BGF may have traveled a significant distance or another firefly is now glowing in the distance, leaving the observer with the feeling that the "light" is exhibiting intelligent behavior by playing or interacting with them. Some viewers even feel the "light" is trying to get the observer to follow them. Similarly, nearby fireflies will appear to avoid someone with a flashlight but then return or come closer after the flashlight is turned off and they have resumed glowing.

The BGFs also commonly fly in a wavering up and down or back and forth motion, traveling several feet in one direction and then appearing to turn around and retrace their path. This may explain some of Ralph Lael's encounters with mystery lights on several of his 1962 visits to Brown Mountain when he felt that the mystery lights he saw were responding to his questions with yes and no answers (1965; see also Chapter 10).

Ralph Lael (1965) also discusses a "forming" period noticed on several of his forest visits during which the mystery lights appeared to be momentarily warming up and becoming brighter near the ground before they actually started moving. This mimics the similar warming-up period of BGFs in the early evening when they first climb out on leaves on the ground or low branches, warm their wings, wait for greater darkness, and blink a few times before launching themselves into flight with continuously burning lights.

BGF MOVEMENT WITH THE WIND

The flying male BGFs are highly susceptible to wind currents and they are often seen flowing in unison in very gently moving breezes. Watching this moving carpet of light from an elevated position can lead to feelings of vertigo and dizziness, which may explain Paul Rose's 1962 reports of similar feelings by everyone observing from the top of his tower on Brown Mountain (see Chapter 9). While they generally fly only a few feet above the ground, the fireflies can be carried far above the ground when blown over steep or rugged mountain terrain.

Although low in absolute light intensity, when seen on a dark moonless night, the bluish-white light of the BGF appears shockingly bright. However, it seems unlikely that the light of the BGF can be seen by a person's naked eye more than a few hundred feet away, which greatly limits the possibility of distant misconceptions of BMLs.

BGFs MISTAKEN FOR BMLs?

In those cases when a BML observer is unaware of the presence of the BGF, the sight of this light can be misleading, especially if the observer's eye is focusing on the far distant landscape but the firefly is close by. In this manner, the nearby, small and dim BGF may be mistaken for a large, bright, distant mystery light.

Fireflies as possible sources of BMLs have been proposed before. Although the BGF was unknown at the time, the U.S. Geological Survey geologist George Rogers Mansfield wrote the following in 1922 in reference to one of the best documented BML sightings of the time: "The lights seen by Mr. Martin from Adams Mountain ... might be due to fireflies flying relatively near Mr. Martin yet appearing unduly large because his eyes were focused on the distant hillside, the appearance of going in and out of ravines being due to intermittence in the lights" (*Origin of the Brown Mountain Light in North Carolina*, U.S. Geological Survey Circular 646, 1922, Washington, DC). Mr. Martin's light encounter was originally published by W. Pearson in 1916. Martin's close encounter with lights in the woods made him the most knowledgeable witness at the time and he was specifically interviewed by Mansfield and accompanied Mansfield on several of his nightly observations in 1922.

Lighting bugs were again mentioned as possible misperceived mystery lights in 1977, 1978 and 1981. In his summary of ORION's BML research, lead researcher Dr. David K. Hackett (ORION, July 1981) reported on fireflies first observed by ORION personnel in 1977 and 1978 (ORION, May 1977; May 1978; and July 1981):

> In May 1977 an ORION team observed lightning bugs blowing by in the wind. They left lighted streaks of blue-green color, very different from the yellow-green flashes of those insects with which we are familiar.
>
> [B]luish green fireflies were seen with a constant glow, rather than blinking on and off as regular fireflies do, and groups of the fireflies flow in a "drunken" pattern of movement.
>
> A rare lightning bug, small, all black, with a bluish non-flashing light drifts by on the breezes. Coleoptera Lucidota Corrusca. A periodic peak breeding year may make this the most common coleopteran (lighted variety) in the area.
>
> Dr. D.K. Hackett,
> Oak Ridge Isochronous Observation Network (ORION),
> May 1977, May 1978, and July 1981 Newsletters

In 1992, Ron Whitworth of Morganton, North Carolina, while camping on Brown Mountain observed flying luminescent insects smaller than regular fireflies. These insects produced noticeable glows overhead (Bixler, 1992). Whitworth envisioned that a swarm of these insects (probably BGFs) could be mistaken for mystery lights.

PHOTOS OF BGFs

Photographs or videos of the BGFs are rare; however, an Internet search can lead to several better than mine. As imagined, photographs are extremely difficult to take due to the dim light of the fireflies; however, my images may give a reasonable impression of the BGFs.

Other Fireflies

A large number of different firefly species exist in western North Carolina, including the Brown Mountain area. Each lighted species displays unique characteristics such as light pattern, color, burn times, habitat, and flight and mating behavior. Most local residents are familiar with the widespread common yellow-blinking eastern firefly (*Photinus pyralis*); however, the presence of fireflies with different colors and behaviors is generally only known to a few enthusiasts and I suspect these fireflies, including the BGFs, can lead to misinterpretations by unsuspecting observers.

For instance, the synchronous firefly (*Photinus carolinus*) of Great Smoky Mountain

Top: Figure 25. Blue ghost fireflies (Phausis reticulata), DuPont State Forest, 2,550 feet elevation, Transylvania County, North Carolina (Canon EF 50 mm lens [81 mm effective focal length and 1.6X approximate magnification]; 70-second exposure, f/2.5, ISO-6400). *Bottom:* Figure 26. Two species of rare fireflies. Blue ghost fireflies (*Phausis reticulata*) are the continuous light streaks. Synchronous fireflies (*Photinus carolinus*) are the broken 6-flash light streaks. Blue Ridge Parkway, mile post 342, 3,800 feet elevation, McDowell County, North Carolina (Canon EF 50 mm lens [81 mm effective focal length and 1.6X approximate magnification]; 241-second exposure, f/2.5, ISO-6400).

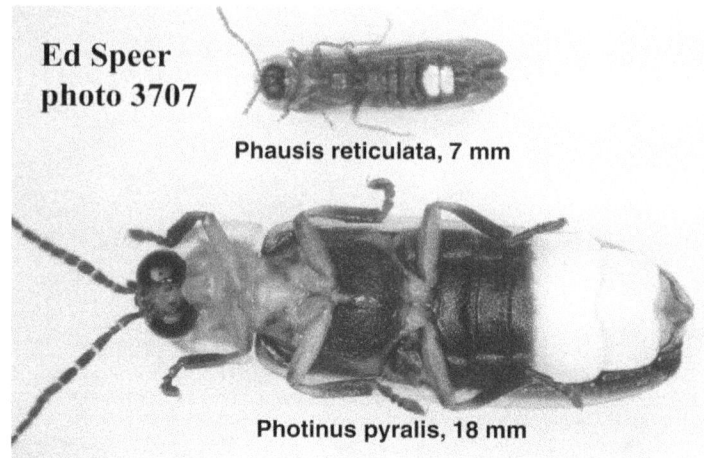

Blue ghost firefly (Phausis reticulata) and eastern firefly (Photinus pyralis). The length measurements were taken from the far end of the antennas to the tail end of each firefly (Canon EF 50 mm lens [81 mm effective focal length] and Am Scope MT trinocular zoom microscope SM-1T [11.3X approximate magnification]; $\frac{1}{60}$-second exposure, f/2.8, ISO-800).

National Park fame is a yellow-blinking firefly with the distinctive habit of flashing in unison with hundreds to thousands of other individuals of the same species! The series of six to fifteen rapid flashes typically occur with flashes less than a second apart followed by a no-flash period of up to fifteen seconds. The hundreds to thousands of individuals display a "warming-up" period when they go from flashing independently to flashing in unison; but once synchronized, they stay in unison for the rest of the night. Small populations of the synchronous firefly have recently been identified by our research team in the Brown Mountain area and we suspect that, like the BGFs, they can lead to misinterpretations by uninformed and unsuspecting observers.

Our team is on the lookout for additional firefly species that might also lead to mistaken identities.

Lightning Bugs Captured by BML Cam1

This page and following page: Figure 28 A and B. Probable lightning bugs close to the camera. Image A: BM-07-23-24-2014B-394. Image B: BM-05-30-01-2014-297 a (courtesy Daniel Caton).

15. Possibly Misidentified Natural Lights

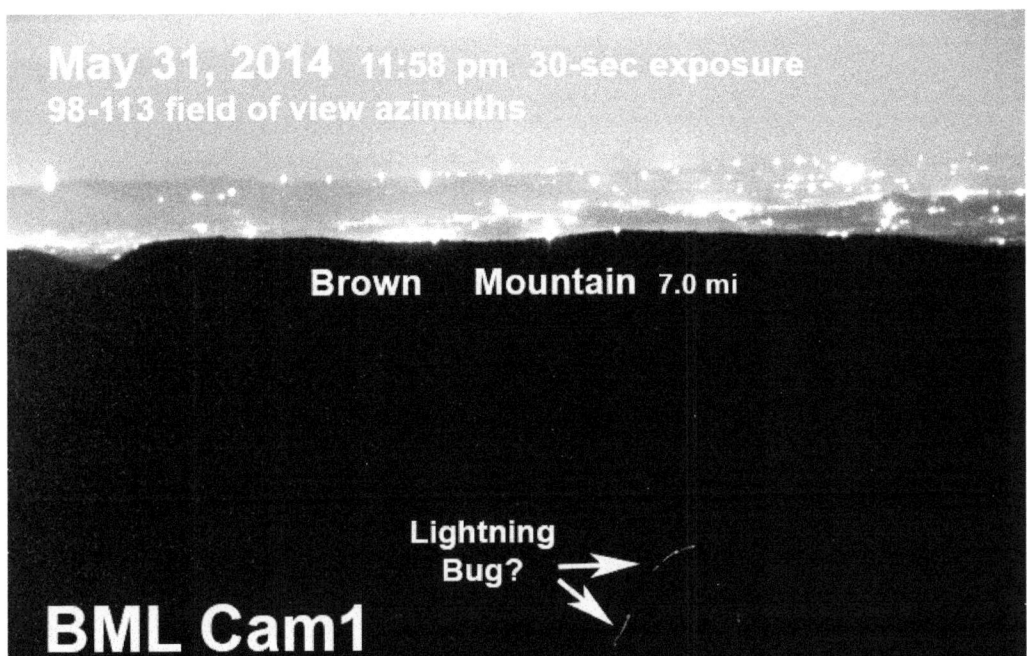

Chapter 16

Possibly Misidentified Man-Made Lights

Types of Man-Made Lights

Man-made lights often visible from the popular observation sites include the following:

Electric Lights
Vehicles
Airplanes/Helicopters
City/Town/Residential
Street/Security
Advertising
Communication Towers
Navigation
Flashlights/Headlights
Spotlights
Camera Flashes
Lasers

Other Lights
Gas Lanterns
Fireworks/Gun Shots/Flares
Fires (Forest, Brush, Camp)
Arc Welding
Explosions (Military, Construction)
Rocket/Missile/Jet Engines
Orbiting Space Vehicles/Satellites

The most commonly visible man-made lights are city/town/residential lights, communication tower lights, and vehicle lights such as those from cars, trucks, airplanes, and helicopters. While most people have no trouble correctly identifying these common man-made lights, some people have been found to mistake them for mystery lights. In addition, less-common or unexpected man-made lights have been seen to confuse an even larger number of people. When considering the visibility of nocturnal man-made lights, several facts are worth remembering:

1. Under ideal conditions, the human eye can see a single candle flame at night as far as 30 miles away.
2. Most of the popular BML observations sites are less than 10 miles from Brown Mountain.
3. Observers at the Hwy 181 Brown Mountain overlook can see about 70 miles to the far horizon.
4. Observers at Wiseman's View can see about 77 miles to the far horizon.
5. As many as 300,000 people live within view of these two most popular observation sites.

Lumen

The intensity of light visible to the human eye is measured in lumens (lm), the world's most widely used standard of light intensity. A single beeswax candle flame (1 candela or 1 candlepower in intensity) = 1 lumen (luminous flux). Some comparisons with common man-made incandescent light bulbs are informative.

- 100 watt = ~1,700 lumens
- 60 watt = ~800 lumens
- 40 watt = ~400 lumens
- 25 watt = ~180 lumens
- 4 watt = ~20 lumens

If a single 1-lumen candle flame is visible for 30 miles at night, just imagine how far a 100-watt incandescent light bulb would be visible! OK, we don't all have perfect eyesight and conditions are seldom ideal, but the distance-penetrating power of man-made lights is greatly underestimated by most people.

As you will see in Chapter 17, our staged light tests show that even small handheld lights, including the new LEDs commonly carried by backcountry travelers, are visible for many miles at night from all of the observations sites.

The purpose of this chapter is to assist the proper identification of lights by presenting actual photographs of known man-made lights as they appear from the popular observation sites. Identification of individual lights involved distant and proximal photography with telephoto and telescopic lenses, accurate measurement of line-of-sight azimuths with a Brunton Pocket Transit compass, and the careful plotting of the azimuths on aerial photographs and U.S. Geological Survey topographical maps. Helpful software programs used included *Google Earth*, *GIS Pro* (GARAFA), and *The Photographer's Ephemeris* and *The Photographer's Transit* (Crookneck Consulting LLC).

Valdese House Lights

A unique group of bright house lights visible on the skyline 21 miles from the Highway 181 Brown Mountain overlook have been identified on Rector Knob Ridge approximately two miles southwest of Valdese, North Carolina. Depending on the weather conditions, the group as seen from the overlook consists of 4 to 6 evenly spaced bright lights defining a slightly eastward-sloping row on the skyline of the South Mountains.

Top: Figure 29. House lights on skyline of South Mountains two miles southwest of Valdese, North Carolina, Rocky Road on Rector Knob Ridge looking southeast (138.5°–139.0°), 21 miles from Hwy 181 overlook (Canon EF 75–300 mm zoom lens set at 240 mm [389 mm effective focal length and 7.8X approximate magnification]; 12-second exposure, f/8, ISO-800). *Bottom:* Figure 30. House lights on skyline of South Mountains, Rocky Road on Rector Knob Ridge, two miles southwest of Valdese, North Carolina, looking southeast from a mile north of the houses (Canon EF 18–55 mm zoom lens set at 41 mm [66 mm effective focal length and 1.3X approximate magnification]; 1-second exposure, f/5.6, ISO-1600).

Top: Figure 31. Houses on the skyline of South Mountains, Rocky Road on Rector Knob Ridge, two miles southwest of Valdese, North Carolina, looking southeast from a mile north of the houses (Canon EF 18–55 mm zoom lens set at 41 mm [66 mm effective focal length and 1.3X approximate magnification]; 1/200-second exposure, f/7.1, ISO-400). *Bottom:* Figure 32. Looking northwest from a house on Rocky Road toward Brown Mountain, two miles southwest of Valdese, North Carolina (Canon EF 75–300 mm zoom lens set at 75 mm [121 mm effective focal length and 2.4X approximate magnification]; 1/200-second exposure, f/16, ISO-400).

High-Peak Communication Tower Light

The distinctive High Peak communication tower light is a single flashing white light atop the highest tower on High Peak on the skyline of the South Mountains south of Drexel, North Carolina. While up to six communications towers exist on the summit, only the tallest one is lighted at night. The 20-mile-distant light is visible from the Highway 181 overlook at azimuth 141.0°.

Figure 33. High-peak communication tower light seen from Hwy 181 Brown Mountain Overlook, 141.0° azimuth and 20 miles distant. Also the city and town lights of Drexel and Valdese (19 and 21 miles distant) can be seen (Canon EF 75–300 mm zoom lens with 1.4X teleconverter set at 300 mm [680 mm effective focal length and 13.6X approximate magnification]; 15-second exposure, f/8, ISO-800).

Hibriten Mountain Communication Tower Light

Hibriten Mountain is located on the east side of Lenoir and hosts several communication towers easily visible from both the Highway 181 overlook (98.5° azimuth and 20.0 miles distant) and Wiseman's View (91.2° azimuth and 23.3 miles distant). The summit also hosts Lenoir's very large Christmas star and Easter cross, which are lighted for about a month during the appropriate seasons. Thus the Christmas star and the Easter cross provide excellent staged light tests that are repeated each year.

Top: Figure 34. High-peak communication towers 20 miles distant, photographed through a telescope from the 181 overlook (20 miles distant). Only the tall tower is lighted at night (MEADE EXT-125EC 5" Maksutov-Cassegrain Telescope with 1,900 mm lens [3,078 mm effective focal length and 61.6X approximate magnification]; 1/60-second exposure, f/15, ISO-200).
Bottom: Figure 35. High-peak communication towers 0.5 mile distant, photographed from 0.5 mile away (Canon EF 75–300 mm zoom lens with 1.4X teleconverter set at 240 mm [544 mm effective focal length and 10.9X approximate magnification]; 1/200-second exposure, f/16, ISO-400).

Top: Figure 36. Hibriten Mountain on the skyline, photographed from Highway 181 overlook (20.0 miles distant) (Canon EF 75–300 mm zoom lens with 1.4X teleconverter set at 300 mm [680 mm effective focal length and 13.6X approximate magnification]; $\frac{1}{200}$-second exposure, f/8, ISO-400). *Bottom:* Figure 37. Telescope view of Hibriten communication towers, photographed from the Highway 181 overlook. The tall tower near the left edge of the image is the only tower lighted (slow flashing white light) (MEADE EXT-125EC 5" Maksutov-Cassegrain Telescope with 1,900 mm focal length [3,078 mm effective focal length and 61.6X approximate magnification]; $\frac{1}{60}$-second exposure, f/15, ISO-800).

Top: Figure 38. Hibriten Mountain and Lenoir's Christmas star 20 miles distant, photographed from Highway 181 overlook (20.0 miles distant). Lenoir's Christmas star is visible on the summit. The single white light to the right is the only lighted tower on the summit. Adams Mountain (6.0 miles distant) sits directly in front of Hibriten (Canon EF 75–300 mm zoom lens with 1.4X teleconverter set at 300 mm [680 mm effective focal length and 13.6X approximate magnification]; 10-second exposure, f/8, ISO-800). *Bottom:* Figure 39. Hibriten Mountain and Lenoir's Christmas star 1.9 miles distant, photographed from 1.9 miles away. Lenoir's Christmas star is visible on the summit. The single white light to the right of the summit is the only lighted tower on the mountain (Canon EF 75–300 mm zoom lens with 1.4X teleconverter set at 75 mm [170 mm effective focal length and 3.4X approximate magnification]; 20-second exposure, f/5.6, ISO-800).

Google Data Center, Lenoir

Google's Lenoir Data Center is a large building constructed in 2011 on the south side of Lenoir. The building is easily visible to the naked eye in the late afternoon sunlight from the Gingercake Acres house on Jonas Ridge where our team's BML Cam1 is located (19.2 miles distant). The building is also visible from Wiseman's View (20.1 miles distant) but not from the Highway 181 overlook.

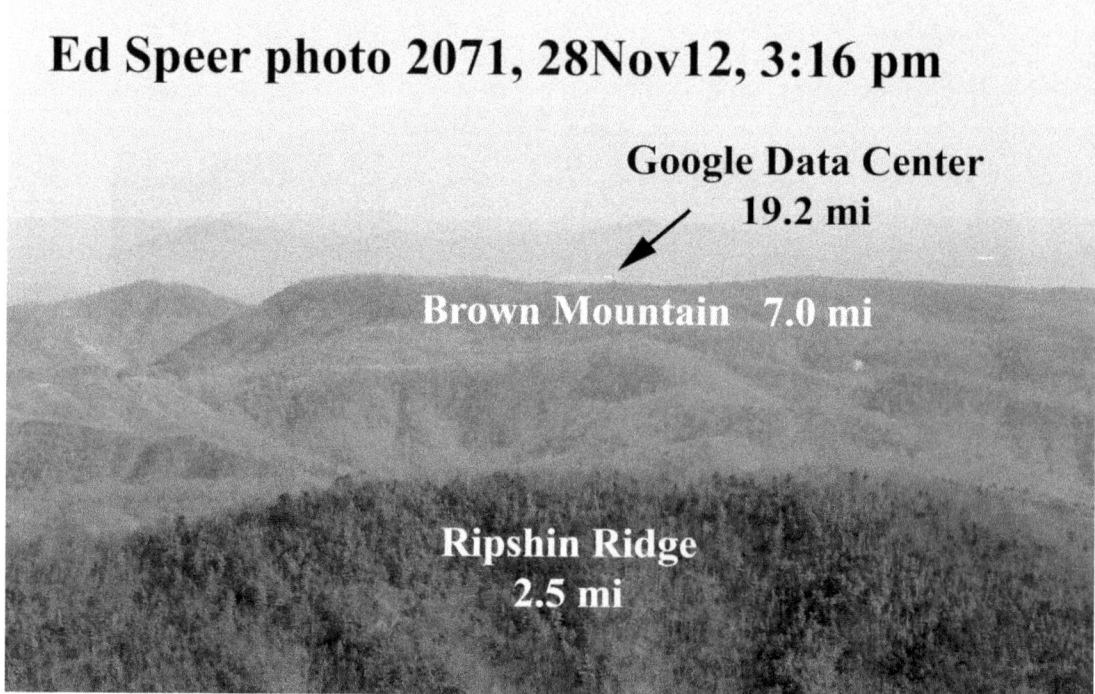

Figure 40. Google Data Center, Lenoir, above Brown Mountain. The Google Data Center building is 19.2 miles distant (Canon EF 75–300 mm zoom lens with 1.4X teleconverter set at 112 mm [181 mm effective focal length and 3.6X approximate magnification]; $1/320$-second exposure, f/8, ISO-100).

Grants Mountain Communications Tower Light

The flashing white light atop the tallest communications tower on Grants Mountain south of Marion is easily visible from Bear Rocks near the north end of Brown Mountain. The light is 21 miles distant at an azimuth of 215°.

Gingercake Acres House Lights

House lights along County Highway 1265 in the Gingercake Acres community on Jonas Ridge are readily visible from the NC Highway 181 Brown Mountain overlook and from Bear Rocks near the north end of Brown Mountain. Our BML Cam1 is located atop one of these Gingercake Acres houses.

Top: Figure 41. Google Data Center, Lenoir, enlargement. The Google Data Center building is 19.2 miles distant. Brown Mountain is the tree-covered ridge in the foreground (7.0 miles distant) (Canon EF 75–300 mm zoom lens with 1.4X teleconverter set at 300 mm [enlarged image]; $1/1000$-second exposure, f/16, ISO-800). *Bottom:* Figure 42. Lights of Lenoir, Google Data Center and Hibriten Mountain, photographed from Wiseman's View. The distant lights of Lenoir stretch across the center of the image (Canon EF 75–300 mm zoom lens with 1.4X teleconverter set at 287 mm [651 mm effective focal length and 13.0X approximate magnification]; 3-second exposure, f/6.3, ISO-800).

Top: Figure 43. Grants Mountain and Marion lights, photographed from Brown Mountain. Note the single light (slow flashing white light) atop Grants Mountain. The city lights of Marion are also visible (Canon EF 18–55 mm zoom lens set at 55 mm [89 mm effective focal length and 1.8X approximate magnification]; 102-second exposure, f/5.6, ISO-500). *Bottom:* Figure 44. Grants Mountain towers from 2 miles southeast, photographed from 2.0 miles distant. Only the tall tower is lighted at night (slow flashing white light) (Canon EF 75–300 mm zoom lens with 1.4X teleconverter set at 240 mm [544 mm effective focal length and 10.9X approximate magnification]; 1/800-second exposure, f/13, ISO-640).

Top: Figure 45. Gingercake Acres house lights seen from NC Highway 181 overlook. Gingercake Acres house lights are 2.2 miles distant at azimuth of 270°. Vehicle lights illuminate NC Highway 181 in the foreground (Canon EF 18–55 mm zoom lens set at 47 mm [76 mm effective focal length and 1.5X approximate magnification]; 19-second exposure, f/5.6, ISO-1600). *Bottom:* Figure 46. Jonas Ridge house lights seen from Brown Mountain, photographed from Bear Rocks near the north end of Brown Mountain (Canon EF 18–55 mm zoom lens set at 43 mm [70 mm effective focal length and 1.4X approximate magnification]; 120-second exposure, f/5.6, ISO-400).

Vehicle Lights

Lights from highway vehicles are readily visible from the most popular observation sites. The following images illustrate some of these lights. Note that operator changes to the field of view of BML Cam1 greatly influence which roads and highways are visible at any given time. By the end of 2013, the view field no longer included many of these roads. Vehicle traffic on NC Highway 181 is commonly visible every clear night and many vehicles stop at the Brown Mountain overlook to see the open view to the east and to look for the supposedly mysterious lights. Vehicle lights on backcountry Forest Service roads are more commonly seen on weekends and during fall hunting seasons when activity on these roads is greatest. Even during times of heavy ground fog, the headlight beams of vehicles on Highway 181 are often visible projecting into the overhead clouds; note that this happens on the east side of Ripshin Ridge where the highway is otherwise blocked from BML Cam1's view.

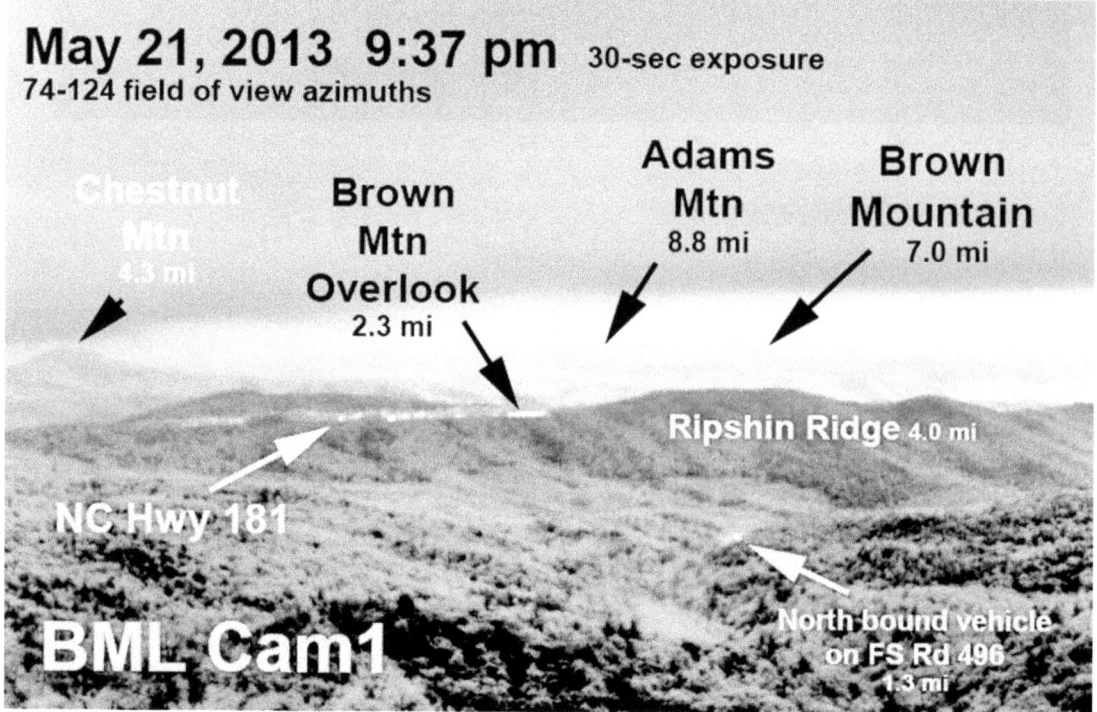

Figure 47. Vehicle lights on NC Highway 181 and Forest Service Road 496 (courtesy Daniel Caton).

City and Town Lights

While most observers know when they are looking at distant city/town lights from the popular observation sites, few understand exactly which city, town, or community they are actually seeing. Surprising to many, Morganton is hidden from view from the Highway 181 overlook and Wiseman's View, while Hickory is hidden behind Brown Moun-

16. Possibly Misidentified Man-Made Lights

Top: Figure 48. Vehicle lights on Forest Service Road 496. *Bottom:* Figure 49. Vehicle lights on NC Highway 181 and Forest Service Road 496 (both photographs courtesy Daniel Caton).

Top: Figure 50. Vehicle lights at the Brown Mountain overlook on Highway 181. *Bottom:* Figure 51. Vehicle lights reflecting in ground fog, January 2014. NC Highway 181 vehicles are on the east side of Ripshin Ridge (both photographs courtesy Daniel Caton).

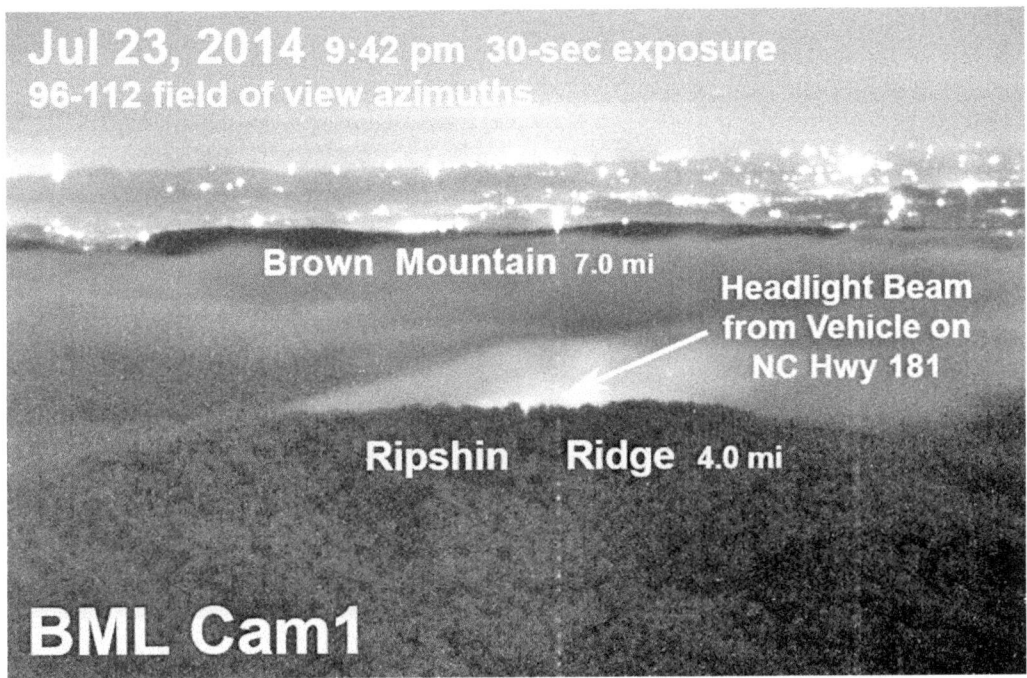

Top: Figure 52. Vehicle lights reflecting in ground fog, July 2014. NC Highway 181 vehicles are on the east side of Ripshin Ridge (courtesy Daniel Caton). *Bottom:* Figure 53. Vehicle lights on NC Highway 105 seen from Wiseman's View, photographed from Wiseman's View (approximately 0.5-mile distance at 190° azimuth) (Canon EF18–55 mm zoom lens set at 55 mm [89 mm effective focal length and 1.8X approximate magnification]; Time-lapse image composed of a stack of 3 separate time-exposure images, f/5.6, ISO-1600).

Top: Figure 54. City and town lights over the south end of Brown Mountain, photographed from NC Highway 181 Brown Mountain overlook (Canon EF 18–55 mm zoom lens set at 36 mm [58 mm effective focal length and 1.2X approximate magnification]; 180-second exposure, f/4.5, ISO-100). *Bottom:* Figure 55. City and town lights over the south end of Brown Mountain, photographed from NC Highway 181 Brown Mountain overlook (Canon EF 75–300 mm zoom lens with 1.4X teleconverter set at 300 mm [680 mm effective focal length and 13.6X approximate magnification]; 10-second exposure, f/8, ISO-1600).

16. *Possibly Misidentified Man-Made Lights* 137

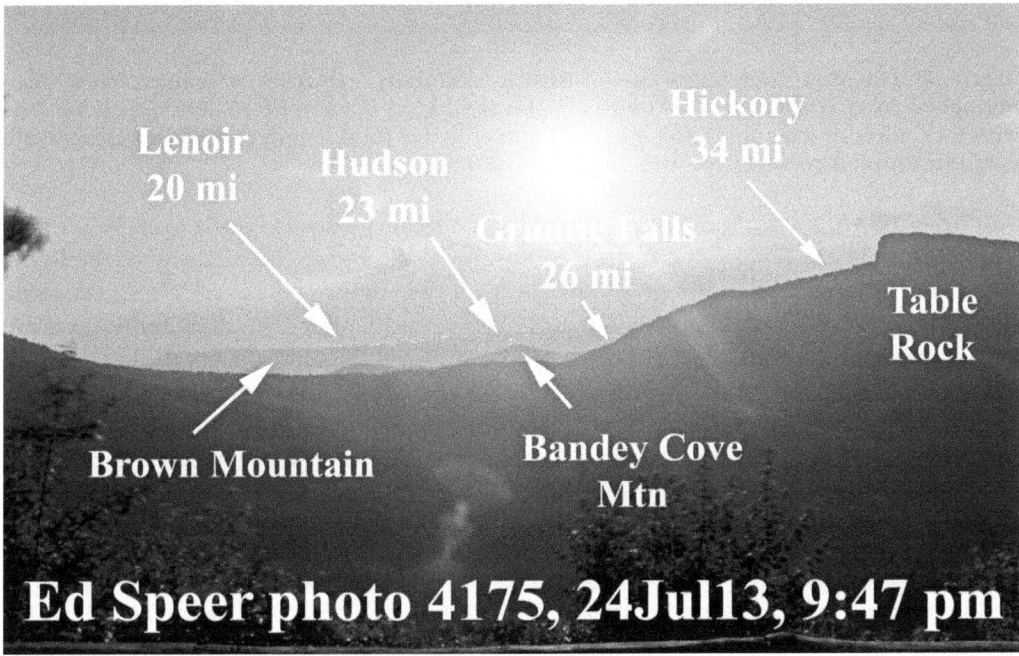

Top: Figure 56. Lights of Hickory from Gingercake Acres on Jonas Ridge, photographed from site of BML Cam1, Gingercake Acres, Jonas Ridge, North Carolina (Canon EF 75–300 mm zoom lens with 1.4X teleconverter set at 300 mm [680 mm effective focal length and 13.6X approximate magnification]; 5-second exposure, f/8, ISO-400). *Bottom:* Figure 57. City and town lights seen from Wiseman's View, photographed from Wiseman's View on NC Highway Old 105. Note the full moon (Canon EF 18–55 mm zoom lens set at18 mm [29 mm effective focal length and 0.6X approximate magnification]; 120-second exposure, f/3.5, ISO-100).

Figure 58. City and town lights east of Brown Mountain seen from Wiseman's View, photographed from Wiseman's View on NC Highway Old 105 (Canon EF 75–300 mm zoom lens with 1.4X teleconverter set at 300 mm [680 mm effective focal length and 13.6X approximate magnification]; 8-second exposure, f/8, ISO-3200).

tain from the Highway 181 overlook and only its northern edge is visible from Wiseman's View. The lights of Lenoir and nearby communities comprise the majority of the lights seen over the north end of Brown Mountain from the Highway 181 overlook. At the same time, the lights of Icard, Connelly Springs, Rutherford College, Valdese and Drexel are also visible over the south end of Brown Mountain from the same observation site. From Wiseman's View, the lights visible over the top of Brown Mountain include those of Lenoir, Hudson, Granite Falls, Hickory and Hildebran, while lights visible beyond the mouth of Linville Gorge are those of the Marion Country Club and Lake James. The annotated panoramas in Appendix C show the locations of these communities and give distances in miles and azimuths in degrees. The following photographs give an appreciation of what these lights and views look like.

Airplanes and Helicopters

At any given moment, multiple airplanes are visible in the night sky above Brown Mountain. With lighted airstrips at three nearby airports (Lenoir-Morganton, Hickory and Statesville), nighttime airplanes with bright landing lights burning are a common sight. Planes landing and taking off at the distant Statesville airport are frequently captured by BML Cam1. This airstrip is oriented toward the camera and planes landing or taking off are easily visible even 57 miles away. In addition, the runway lights can even be seen turning on moments before a takeoff or landing, then turning off a few minutes later.

The lights of unexpected airplanes flying at treetop level over Brown Mountain and even below the ridgeline have also been captured by BML Cam1. Lights of a low-flying twin-engine airplane captured on the night of December 11, 2014, were especially informative, as the author was coincidentally standing at the top of an exposed rock cliff on the west side of Brown Mountain at the exact moment the unexpected airplane flew overhead (later identified as an Air Force nighttime, low-altitude mountainous flight training mission).

Helicopters are also occasionally seen flying low over Brown Mountain at night. Medevac helicopters have been documented by BML Cam1 on numerous occasions flying northward above the mountain, landing at Caldwell Memorial Hospital heliport in Lenoir, and then taking off a few minutes later and flying back southward over Brown Mountain.

The lights of low-flying airplanes and the medevac helicopters closely match the descriptions and behaviors of some reported mystery lights. We suspect airplanes with bright landing lights, airplanes close to the ground and the medevac helicopters are commonly mistaken for mystery lights by many uninformed and unsuspecting observers.

Figure 59. Airplane lights beyond the South Mountains, photographed from NC Highway 181 Brown Mountain overlook (Canon EF 75–300 mm zoom lens with 1.4X teleconverter set at 300 mm [680 mm effective focal length and 13.6X approximate magnification]; 10-second exposure, f/8, ISO-1600).

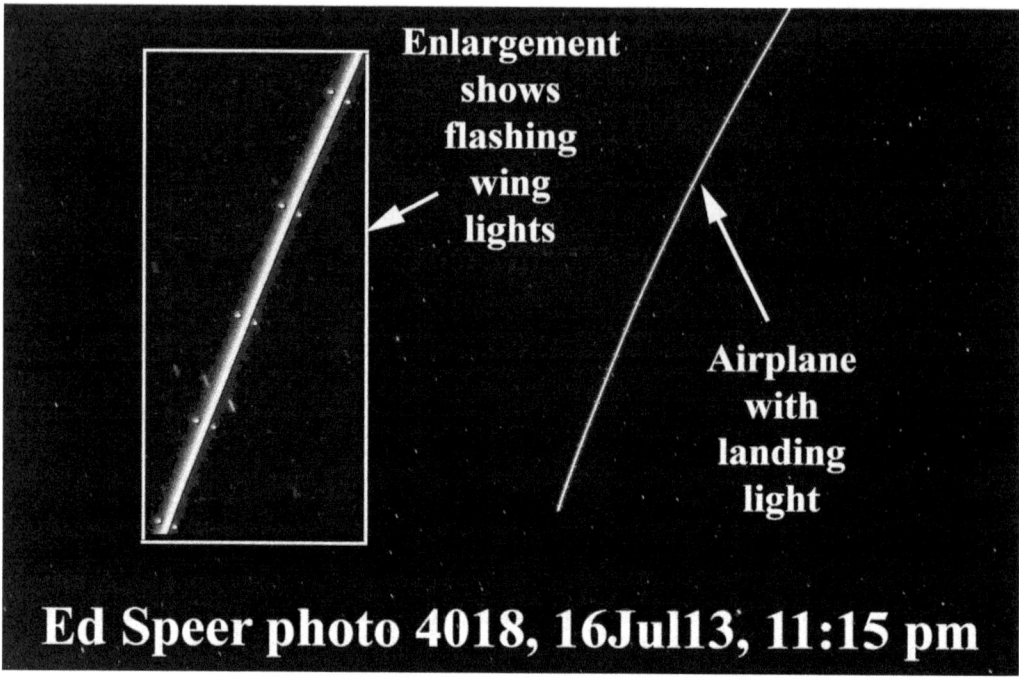

Top: Figure 60. Airplane in the sky directly above Brown Mountain, photographed from Bear Rocks near the north end of Brown Mountain. Note the continuously burning white landing light. An enlargement reveals flashing wing lights (Canon EF 18–55 mm zoom lens set at 55 mm [89 mm effective focal length and 1.8X approximate magnification]; 31-second exposure, f/5.6, ISO-400). *Bottom:* Figure 61. Three airplanes above Hawksbill Mountain, photograph taken from Wiseman's View on NC Highway Old 105. Note the short star trails in the night sky. One airplane disappeared behind Hawksbill Mountain and reappeared on the other side (Canon EF 75–300 mm zoom lens with 1.4X teleconverter set at 105 mm [168 mm effective focal length and 3.4X approximate magnification]; 33-second exposure, f/5.6, ISO-800).

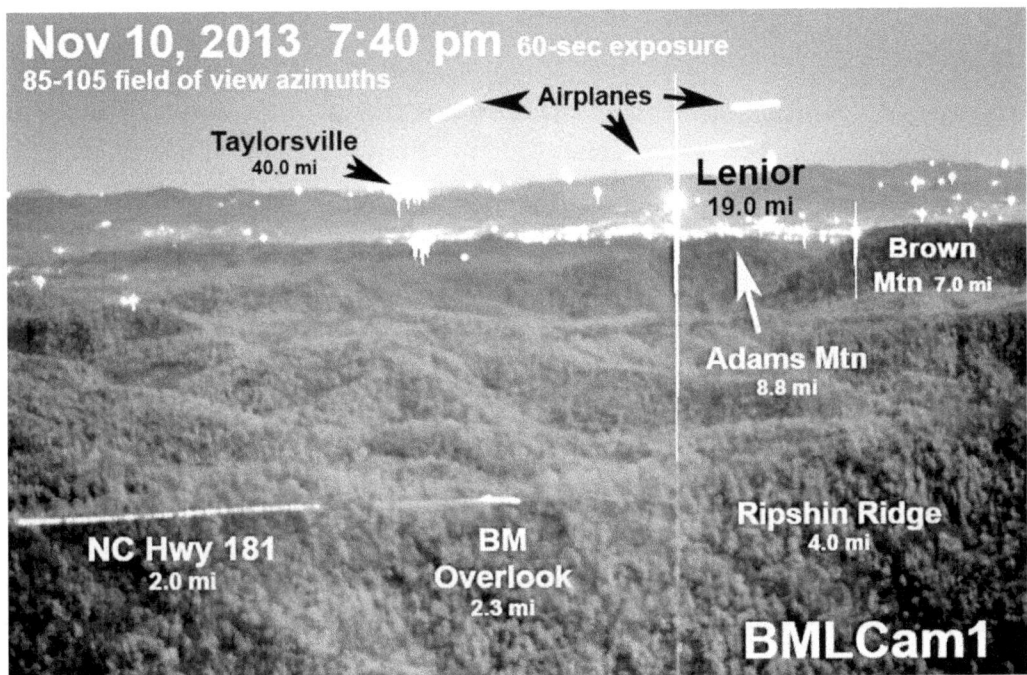

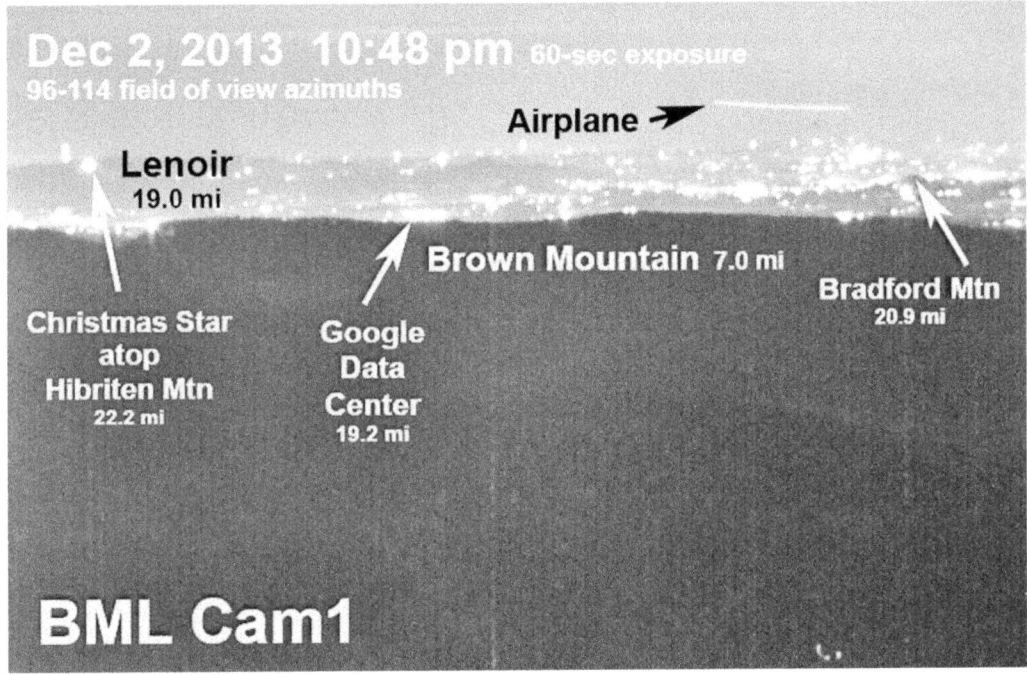

Top: Figure 62. Multiple airplanes above Brown Mountain. Notice the vehicle lights on NC Highway 181 and at the Brown Mountain overlook. *Bottom:* Figure 63. Airplane above Brown Mountain. Notice Lenoir's Christmas star atop Hibriten Mountain (both photographs courtesy Daniel Caton).

Top: Figure 64. Airplane taking off from Statesville airport. Notice Lenoir's Christmas star atop Hibriten Mountain. *Bottom:* Figure 65. Airplane flying below and east of Brown Mountain (both photographs courtesy Daniel Caton).

16. Possibly Misidentified Man-Made Lights 143

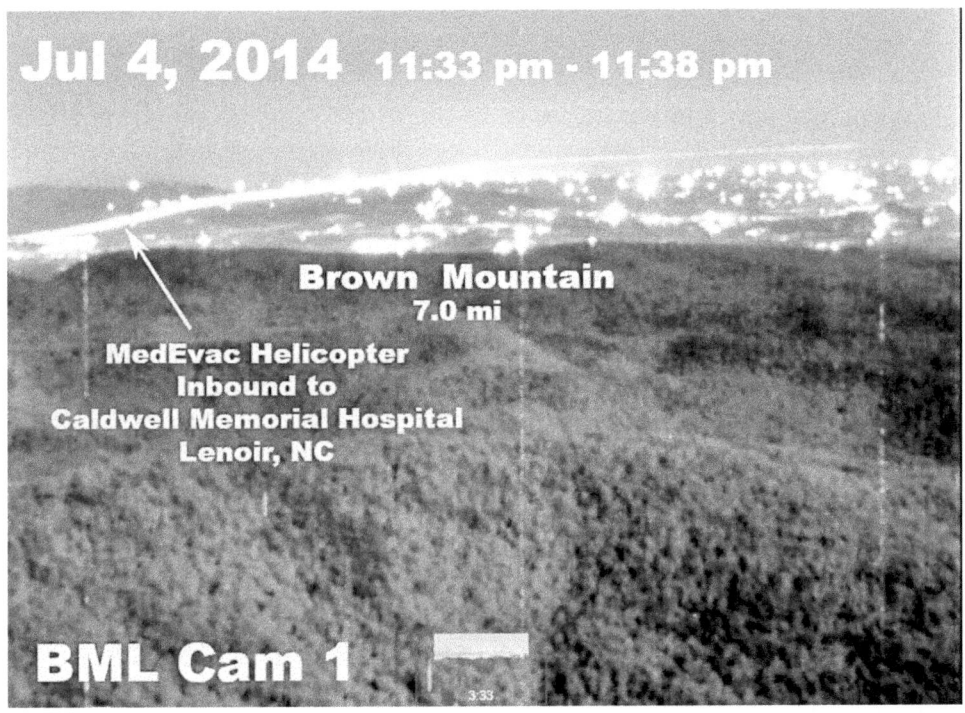

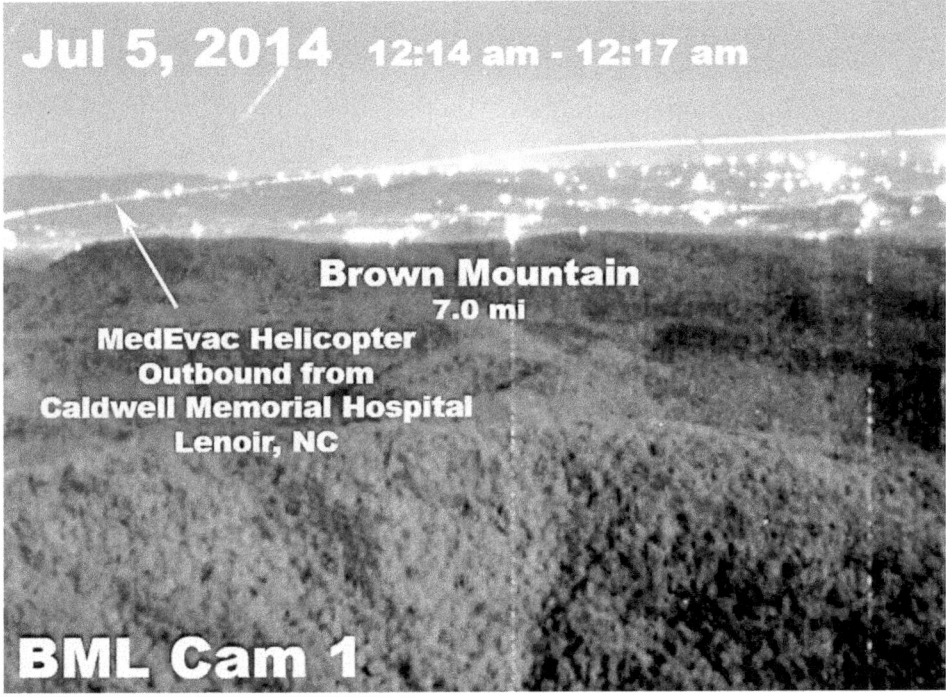

Top and bottom: Figure 66 A and B. Medevac helicopter above Brown Mountain, July 4–5, 2014. A. Five-minute time-lapse composite image created by stacking 10 individual 30-second time-exposure images. B. Three-and-½-minute time-lapse composite image created by stacking 7 individual 30-second time-exposure images (original images courtesy Daniel Caton).

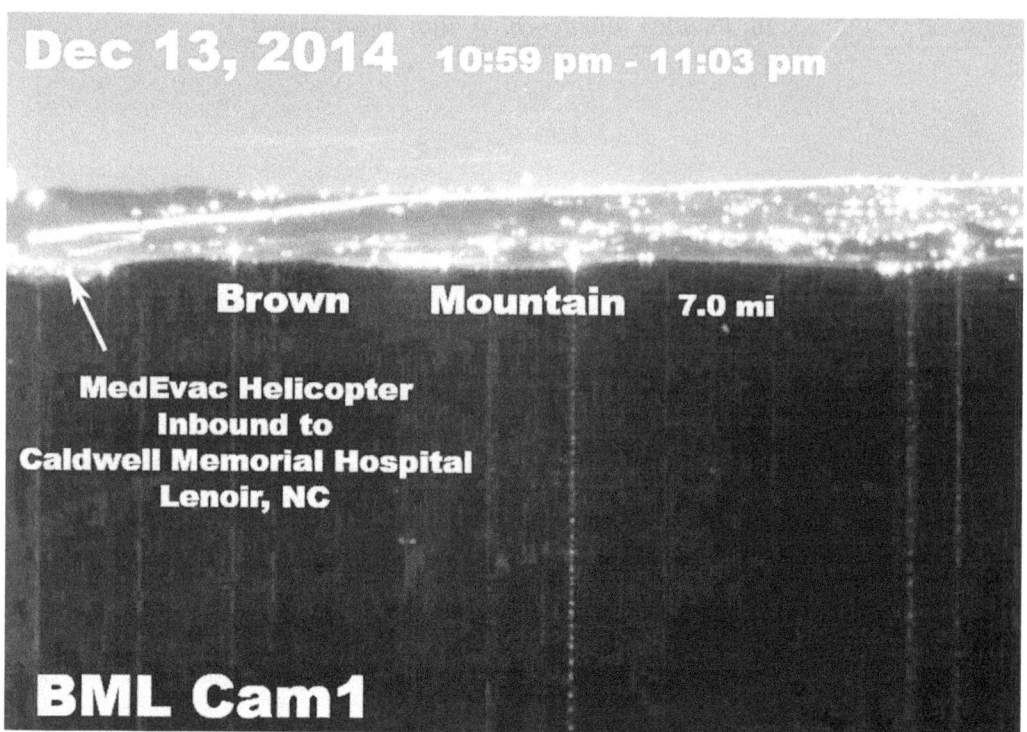

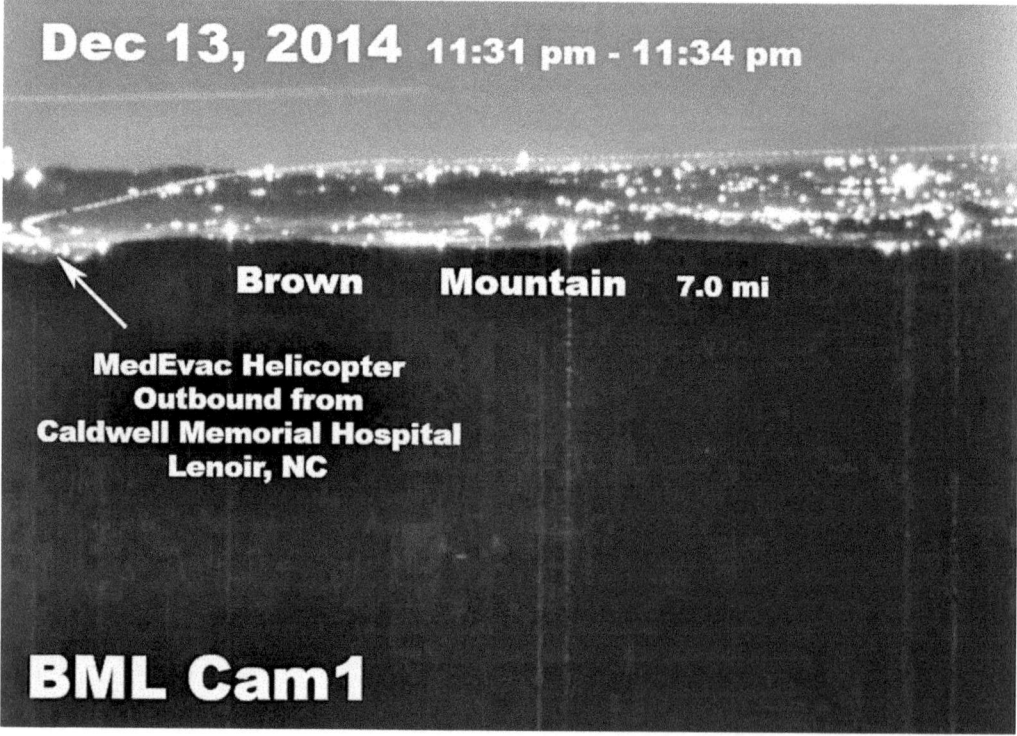

Top and bottom: Figure 67 A and B. Medevac helicopter above Brown Mountain, December 13, 2014. A. 5 ½-minute time-lapse composite image created by stacking 11 individual 30-second time-exposure images. B. Three-minute time-lapse composite image created by stacking 6 individual 30-second time-exposure images (original images courtesy Daniel Caton).

Low-flying twin-engine airplane and hiker lights. Notice Lenoir's Christmas star lighted atop Hibriten Mountain and a staged light test on the west side of Brown Mountain. The airplane was later determined to be part of the U.S. Air Force's low-altitude mountain flight training, with pilots wearing night-vision goggles. The staged hiker light was carried by the author. Image: One-minute time-lapse composite image created by stacking 2 individual 30-second time-exposure images. See Chapter 17 for a detailed discussion of this amazing image (original images courtesy Daniel Caton).

Smokestacks Beyond Brown Mountain

Nighttime emissions from several smokestacks or cooling towers are frequently seen beyond Brown Mountain. Wind occasionally distributes the smoke throughout the valley to the south or north of the stacks. The emissions appear to be coming from the south side of Lenoir and are most frequent between midnight and dawn; however, the source of these emissions has not been researched by our team.

Lights from Backcountry Users

Can lights from distant backcountry users be seen from the popular BML observations sites? Our recent research, including numerous staged light tests, suggests that such lights are not only common and easily visible, but are often mistaken for mystery lights. See Chapter 17 for some interesting photographs of such lights.

Conversations we've had or overheard at the observation sites indicate that many

Smoke Stack Emissions beyond Brown Mountain (courtesy Daniel Caton).

people are not familiar with the extent, or even the possibility, of backcountry use in the area. "It's too rugged and inaccessible for anyone to be down there" and "there's no way to get to the top of that mountain" are often-heard comments. The truth is that at any time of the day or night backcountry or wilderness users are likely to be anywhere within the field of view of the observation sites. And as our staged light tests confirm, even small handheld electric lights can be seen for great distances at night (see Chapter 17).

Backcountry Hiking Trails

This section details the vast extent of backcountry use and facilities (trails, roads, and campsites) in the areas around Brown Mountain. National Forest lands administered by the U.S. Forest Service lying within ten miles on the east, north and west sides of Brown Mountain include the most popular BML observation sites and contain over 300 miles of maintained hiking trails. In addition, there are probably more than 1,000 miles of non-maintained trails in the area.

Maintained hiking trails include 43 miles in the Linville Gorge Wilderness Area west of Brown Mountain (U.S. Forest Service Linville Gorge map R8-RG-4, 2009). Backcountry use in the wilderness area is so great that camping permits are required during summer weekends. Lights from headlamps, handheld flashlights and campfires are commonly visible from Wiseman's View, where our repeated observation shows such lights often recur at sites known to be backcountry campsites. Table Rock, site of near-nightly visible lights, is one of the most visited mountain summits in the Linville Gorge Wilderness Area, with vehicle access to within a mile of the summit and a paved trailhead parking lot that can accommodate up to 50 vehicles. At Wiseman's View, nighttime lights can also commonly be seen at a popular primitive campsite on the summit of Little Table Rock on the west flank of Table Rock Mountain.

More than 86 miles of maintained hiking trails exist in the Wilson Creek National Wild and Scenic River area immediately to the north of Brown Mountain (U.S. Forest Service Wilson Creek map R8-RG-327, 2009). This area is popular with sightseers, swimmers, hikers, campers, kayakers, and, during appropriate times of the year, hunters and fishermen. On some summer weekends, congested traffic is frequent on the access roads.

Portions of North Carolina's most popular hiking trail, the 900-mile-long Mountains-to-Sea Trail, crosses Linville River, climbs Shortoff Mountain, follows the rim of the gorge past Table Rock, turns east and passes 3.5 miles north of Brown Mountain, and then continues through the Wilson Creek Wilderness on its way to the coast. This heavily used trail includes at least four primitive backcountry campsites from which campfires and handheld lights are often seen: 1) from Wiseman's View—Top of Shortoff Mountain, Little Table Rock summit, Little Table Rock Trail # 236 near the junction with Spence Ridge Trail # 233; 2) from NC Highway 181 Brown Mountain overlook—gap located 0.5 mile north of Chestnut Mountain.

On the night of July 14, 2014, the author hiked round-trip to the summit of Shortoff Mountain via the Wolf Pit Trail. As seen in the YouTube video for BML Cam2 for that night (www.youtube.com/watch?v=bGC4l74Ibus), my handheld lights were readily visible along much of the upper section of the trail, proving that lights commonly carried by nighttime hikers on such trails are mysterious only to those unfamiliar with the location of the trails or the distance-penetrating power of even small man-made lights.

See Chapter 17 for more hiker staged light tests on Brown Mountain and in Linville Gorge.

Mountain-Climbing Areas

Table Rock and the nearby Chimneys on the east rim of Linville Gorge are only seven miles west of Brown Mountain and are two of the most popular and heavily used rock climbing sites in North Carolina. Numerous rock climbers can be found here, any time of the year, where they practice daytime and nighttime climbs and even camp on the rock cliffs, where their lights are occasionally seen from Wiseman's View.

Backcountry Roads

More than 300 miles of public-access gravel roads exist in the forested areas immediately around Brown Mountain. These popular roads allow access for sightseers, hunters, fishermen and other backcountry users, as well as residents in the communities of Mortimer and Edgemont. First built in the logging days of the late 1800s and early 1900s, these roads continue to be heavily used today. Primitive roadside campsites are common, while the larger Forest Service Mortimer Campsite can accommodate many campers.

During hunting season each fall, the Forest Service opens roads otherwise gated the rest of the year; and it is the fall, when vehicle traffic and backcountry use increase, that many mystery light sightings are reported. In addition, most of the hundreds of miles of streams in the area are designated trout waters and are maintained for backcountry sport fishing, which continues to be popular in the area.

Brown Mountain Off-Highway Vehicle Recreation Area

Unknown to many people, the East Coast's largest off-road-vehicle recreation area lies on top of Brown Mountain. With 34 miles of maintained off-road-vehicle trails, this area attracts thousands of off-road enthusiasts each year, as attested by a paved parking lot that can accommodate hundreds of vehicles at a time (U.S. Forest Service Brown Mountain Off-Highway Vehicle Area map, R8-RG-306). Nighttime use of the trails is permitted and vehicle headlights and taillights as well as driver headlamps can be seen on a few sections of some of the trails on the west side of Brown Mountain when viewed from Wiseman's View or the Highway 181 Brown Mountain overlook. Several photographs and videos of supposedly mysterious lights are posted on the Internet every year by unsuspecting observers of these off-highway vehicles. In addition, the lights of some stealth campers in the area of Bear Rocks on Brown Mountain can also be seen from the observations sites.

ATVs on Brown Mountain

Lights from all-terrain vehicles (ATVs) on Brown Mountain are frequently seen by visitors at the popular BML observation sites (Wiseman's View and Highway 181 overlook). Such lights have also been captured by BML Cam1. The ATVs are following some of the 34 miles of maintained trails of the U.S. Forest Service's Brown Mountain Off-Highway Vehicle Recreation Area. The trails are open for wheeled vehicle use from mid–March until December 31 each year but are also open for foot travel throughout the year. Approximately one mile of the north end of ATV Trail #2 falls within the current view field of BML Cam1 and the following December 31, 2014, image and the smaller trail-map image illustrate the convoluted trace of the trail. For safety reasons, this rugged trail is clearly signed in the field as one-way with motorized traffic directed north to south, or left- to-right in the image, which is the direction of movement of most of the nighttime lights captured at this spot by BML Cam1 over the past two years.

In addition, our team has conducted numerous staged light tests along ATV Trail #2 (see Chapter 17) and has established that ATV lights and backcountry user lights are visible to BML Cam1 at numerous points along the trail. Such lights are also visible at the popular viewing sites (Highway 181 Brown Mountain overlook and Wiseman's View), where we suspect numerous uninformed and unsuspecting observers mistake the lights for mystery lights.

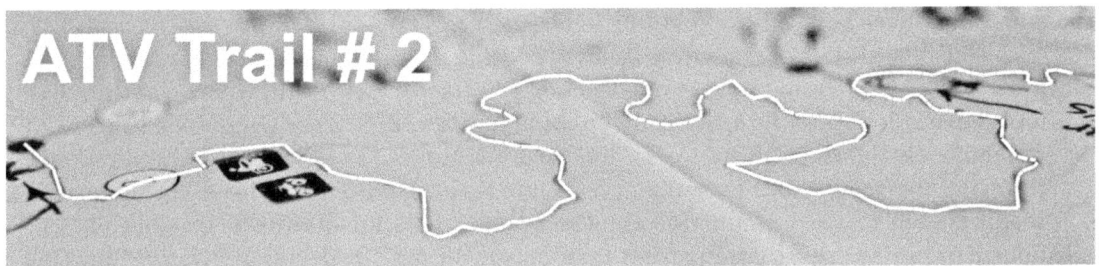

Top and Bottom: **Figure 70 A and B.** ATV lights on Trail #2 atop Brown Mountain. Notice the convoluted trace of Trail #2 as outlined by the lights in the photograph and the small topo-map image of the trail. Two separate lights moved together left to right. Image: Discontinuous thirty-three-minute time-lapse composite image created by stacking 24 individual 30-second time-exposure images (original images courtesy Daniel Caton).

Do People Purposely Try to Fool Others by Playing BMLs?

Having done so myself in the past, I can honestly answer yes to this question. In fact, I suspect that many mysterious light sightings are the result of pranksters playing BMLs. Probably every teenage boy living within 100 miles of Brown Mountain who has heard of the legend, has dreamed at one time or another of fooling others by shining unexpected lights into the night sky and actually do so every chance they get. I did it myself as a young boy growing up in the area and I know of others who have done the same. But on at least one occasion, I was the one fooled.

My own first mystery light sighting came as a young man when some friends and I were camping at Wiseman's View in the early 1960s—back in the days when that was permitted. After seeing mystery lights down in the gorge at night, our excitement was dashed the next morning when we met folks who had camped the previous night on Linville River immediately below the overlook where we camped and who, on hearing that we had camped there, asked if we had seen the lights they had pointed toward the overlook and beamed off the cliffs across the river—exactly the mystery lights we had seen the night before!

After that experience, I often make a point of asking others if they have ever played BMLs. Nearly every time I ask that question of backcountry campers in the area of Brown Mountain, they answer yes; after all, there isn't much else to do at night for fun.

Types of Lights Used by Pranksters

Possibly the ultimate BML prank was carried out by an acquaintance of mine—who shall remain unnamed. He reports that around 1972, as a young man, he and others experimented with homemade hydrogen-filled balloons with slow-burning rubber band fuses. After igniting the fuses, the released balloons would rise several hundred feet into the air before exploding with bright flashes—creating a spectacular nighttime show. Once they had perfected the process, the group launched their balloons from Table Rock! Imagine the shock and surprise of any unsuspecting observers at nearby Wiseman's View who might have seen these exploding balloons!

Many pranksters operate from easily accessible sites along roads and mountain summits. Some of the more popular sites include Wiseman's View itself, where our team has found discarded spent Roman candle tubes below the cliffs at the overlook—suggestive of pranksters shooting off fireworks and then discarding the incriminating evidence by throwing the spent tubes over the cliffs. Table Rock, Hawksbill and the Forest Service road between the two mountains are also popular sites for fireworks. In addition, the Fourth of July fireworks issuing from campers on Wilson Creek east of Brown Mountain have been reported to be quite spectacular, and to at least one unsuspecting observer at the Highway 181 overlook the source of mystery lights. Other lights probably used by pranksters include handheld flashlights, powerful spotlights, vehicle lights, Chinese lanterns, and laser pointers. The following photographs show how some of these lights might look.

Fourth of July Fireworks Above Brown Mountain

BML Cam1 captured sky rockets launched from the valley east of Brown Mountain on the night of July 4, 2014.

Top: Figure 71. Laser Pointer Light on Brown Mountain, photographed looking east from NC Highway 181 Brown Mountain overlook. The laser pointer is held by the photographer at arm's length beside the camera (Canon EF 18–55 mm zoom lens set at 55 mm [89 mm effective focal length and 1.8X approximate magnification]; 15-second exposure, f/5.6, ISO-3200). *Bottom:* Figure 72. Laser pointer light and lens flares on Brown Mountain, photographed looking east from NC Highway 181 Brown Mountain overlook. The laser pointer is held by the photographer at arm's length beside the camera (Canon EF 18–55 mm zoom lens set at 55 mm [89 mm effective focal length and 1.8X approximate magnification]; 15-second exposure, f/5.6, ISO-3200).

Top: Figure 73. Sky rocket fireworks and airplane over Hawksbill Mountain, photographed from Wiseman's View on NC Highway Old 105. Image: Discontinuous two-minute time-lapse image created by stacking 3 individual time-exposure images (31-, 35-, and 36-seconds, respectively) (Canon EF 75–300 mm zoom lens with 1.4X teleconverter set at 105 mm [170 mm effective focal length and 3.4X approximate magnification]; f/5.6, ISO-800). *Bottom:* Figure 74. Fourth of July Sky Rocket Fireworks above Brown Mountain. Image: Two-minute time-lapse composite image created by stacking 4 individual 30-second time-exposure images (original images courtesy Daniel Caton).

CHAPTER 17

Staged Light Tests

How Far Can a Man-Made Light Be Seen at Night?

Just how far a man-made light can be seen at night is one of the biggest unanswered questions and perhaps the most misunderstood phenomenon relating to the BMLs. On many occasions, we've heard people say that a particular nighttime light seen from one of the popular observation sites can't be a man-made electric light because it's too far away for electric lights to be visible. The truth is that common man-made electric lights can actually be seen for many times farther than the distance in question. This lack of appreciation for the distance-penetrating power of ordinary man-made electric lights was instrumental in the beginning of the legend of the BMLs in the early 1900s and it continues to confuse many people today.

As we learned in the previous chapter, under ideal conditions a single candle flame can be visible to the human eye as far as 30 miles away. And a 100-watt incandescent light bulb produces as much as 1,700 times more light than a candle flame! Thus, it's no wonder that man-made city/town/rural lights can be seen for hundreds of miles into space. Likewise, multiple LED lights such as those carried by today's backcountry travelers can be readily visible from all of the popular observation sites.

How Far to the Horizon?

The distance to the horizon from the popular BML observation sites is also critical in understanding how far lights are visible. The distance to the horizon is influenced by the elevation of the observation site and the curvature of the earth's surface: Gingercake Acres (3,660-feet elevation)—80.0 miles; Wiseman's View (3,400-feet elevation)—77.1 miles; and Hwy 181 overlook (2,840-feet elevation)—70.5 miles. Thus, man-made lights are visible for about 77 miles east of Wiseman's View, including the lights of Lenoir, Hudson, Granite Falls, Taylorsville, Wilkesboro, Statesville, and possibly Yadkinville. Man-made lights are also visible for about 70 miles east of the Highway 181 overlook, including the towns of Lenoir, Drexel, Valdese, Connelly Springs, Icard, Rutherford College, Granite Falls, Hudson, Taylorsville, Wilkesboro, and Statesville. Our BML Cam1 on a rooftop in Gingercake Acres can see about 80.0 miles to the far eastern horizon. The horizon distances given above are estimates based on sea level horizons; thus the actual sight distances are slightly farther than those given.

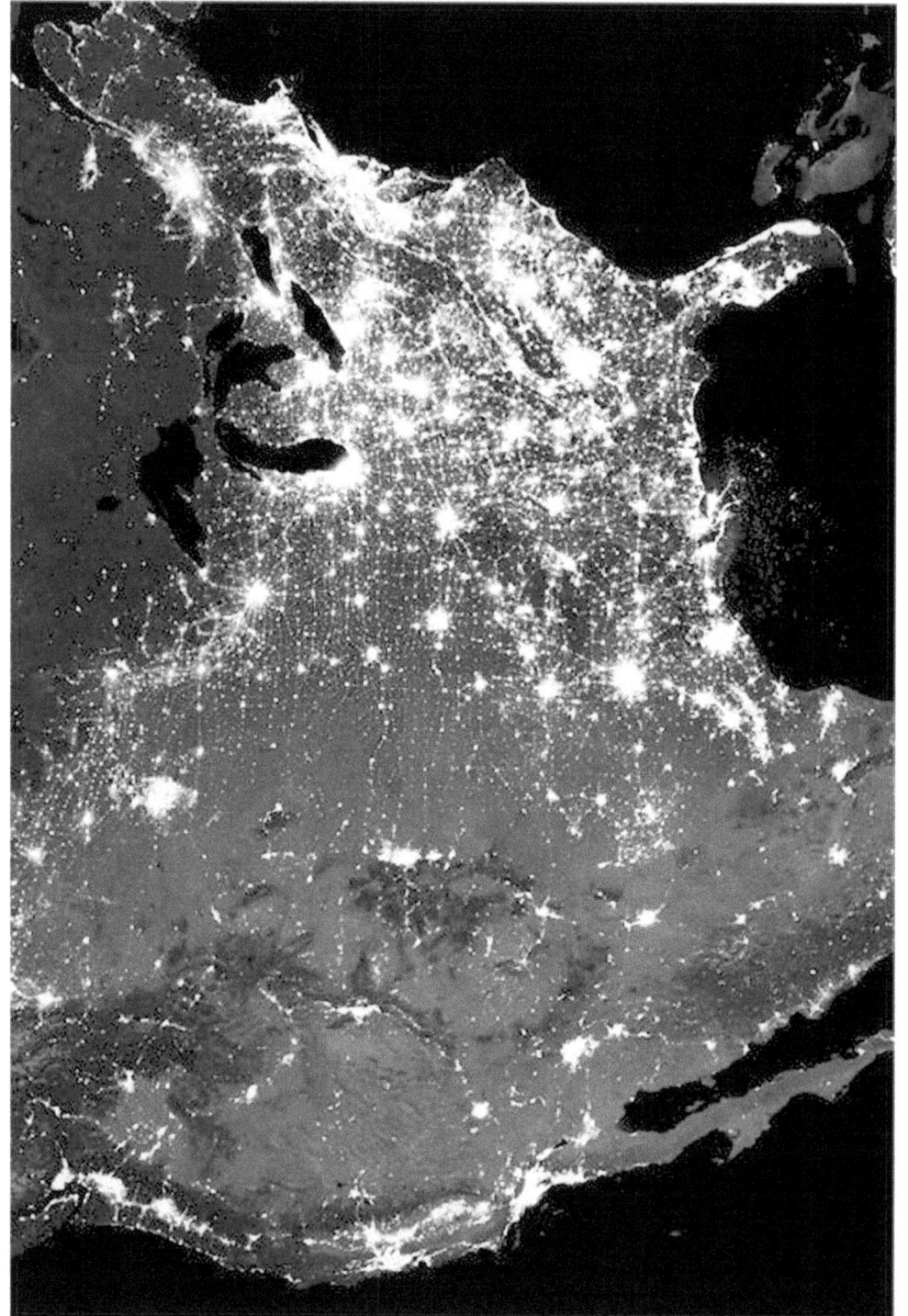

Man-made lights seen from 512 miles above earth. NASA Suomi NPP satellite photograph, 2012.

Since the legend of the BMLs began, several research investigators, including our BML research team, have conducted staged light tests to help answer the questions of distance and required brightness of visible man-made lights.

First Staged Light Test Not Seen, 1915

The first recorded staged light test was conducted in 1915 when a signal light staged by Mr. H.C. Martin at Connelly Springs was unfortunately not seen by Dr. C.L. Wilson at Loven's Hotel (Wilson, 1915). However, Wilson did report seeing electric lights from the towns of Joy, Lenoir, Connelly Springs and Rutherford College on the night of the staged light test.

1917 Staged Light Test

About 1917 another light test was apparently more successful when staged car headlights in the Catawba Valley were reportedly seen by observers at Loven's Hotel; however, the actual location of the headlights was not recorded (Babington, 1927).

ORION Staged Light Tests, 1977–1984

The Oak Ridge Isochronous Observatory Network group (ORION) staged a major light test on the evening of May 14, 1977, by placing a sealed-beam, 8"-diameter, marine spotlight (GE lamp #4715) with 500,000 candlepower, 13 VDC, 250-watt light powered by a 12v car battery on the flanks of Hibriten Mtn on the east side of Lenoir (ORION, 1977). Observers were stationed at the Highway 181 Brown Mountain overlook (19.5 miles distant; 2,840 feet elevation) and at Wiseman's View (22.5 miles distant; 3,400 feet elevation). While neither the actual location nor the elevation of the spotlight was recorded, it was apparently set on the access road somewhere below the top of Hibriten Mtn. Amateur radios provided communication between the light operators and the distant observers.

The 500,000 candlepower light was seen at Wiseman's View—22.5 miles away. However, noticeable refraction of the light beam was observed, as well as mirage-like wavering distortions due to rising heat waves between the light and the observers. The light was not seen at the Highway 181 overlook, presumably due to the lower elevation of that site and blocking of the light by the intervening Adams Mountain.

In 1978 ORION investigators conducted additional successful staged light tests from Chestnut Mountain (2.4 miles from the Highway 181 overlook) with smaller handheld electric lights and vehicle headlights (ORION, 1978). However, explosives detonated on Brown Mountain by the research group in 1981 and 1984 did not produce any noticeable lights (ORION, 1981 and 1984).

BML Research Team Staged Light Tests: 2012, 2013, 2014

Our BML research team conducted its first staged light test on August 25, 2012, with lights positioned on Brown Mountain, Sitting Bear Mountain, Hawksbill Mountain and

Table Rock. Observers with cameras and radios were stationed at the Highway 181 overlook and Wiseman's View. Additional tests were conducted periodically over the next two years. These tests conclusively demonstrated that handheld lights normally carried by backcountry users (flashlights and headlamps) can easily be seen for up to seven miles at night—well within the distance of commonly reported mystery lights seen from the popular BML observations sites. As expected, brighter vehicle lights can be seen at even greater distances.

Staged Light Tests, August 25, 2012

On the night of Saturday, August 25, and the early morning of Sunday, August 26, 2012, our BML research team, with the help of other volunteers, conducted some distant man-made light observations and photography from the Highway 181 Brown Mountain overlook and from Wiseman's View. A total of 14 people took part in the exercises and radio contact was maintained between most of the light operators and the photography crews. After dark, handheld battery-powered flashlights and a propane gas lantern were visible up to 1.6 miles from Wiseman's View and up to 4.3 miles from the Highway 181 overlook. In addition, motorcycle headlights were visible up to 3.5 miles from the Highway 181 overlook. A propane gas lantern atop Table Rock was clearly visible to the team at the highway 181 overlook at a total distance of 4.3 miles, while the Wiseman's View crew reported seeing the rechargeable 520-lumen handheld LED spotlight on Wildcat Ridge on the west flanks of Brown Mountain at an amazing 7.2 miles away!

Figure 76. **Staged light on Wildcat Ridge Trail, photographed from NC Highway 181 Brown Mountain overlook (3.7 miles distant). Stanley 520-lumen handheld LED spotlight model FL5W10 (Canon EF 75–300 mm zoom lens set at 140 mm [227 mm effective focal length and 4.5X approximate magnification]; 21-second exposure, f/5.6, ISO-200).**

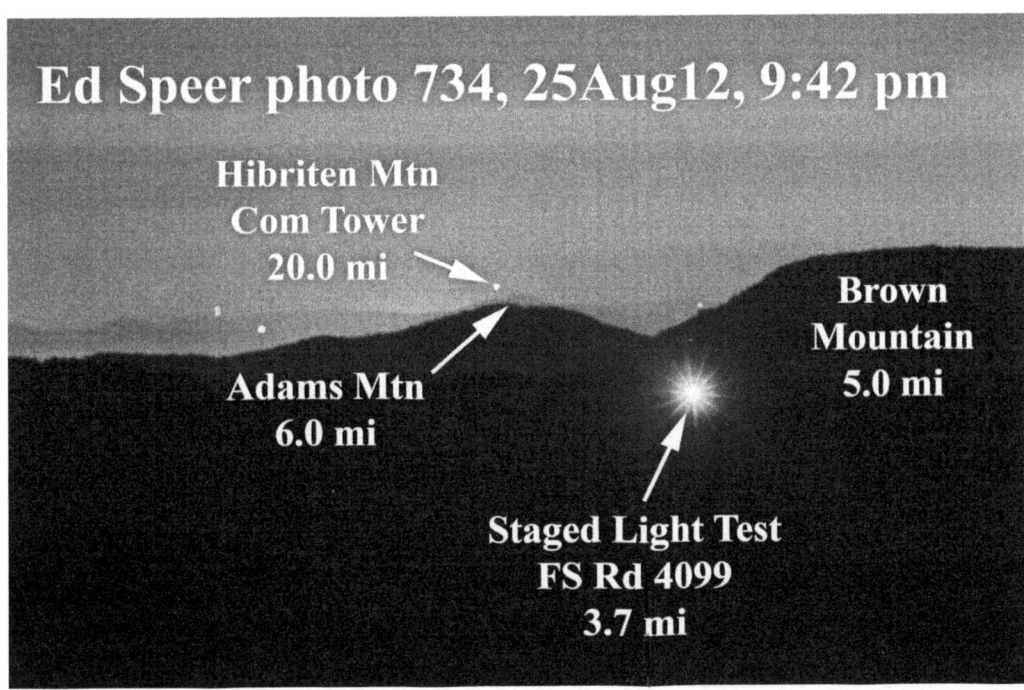

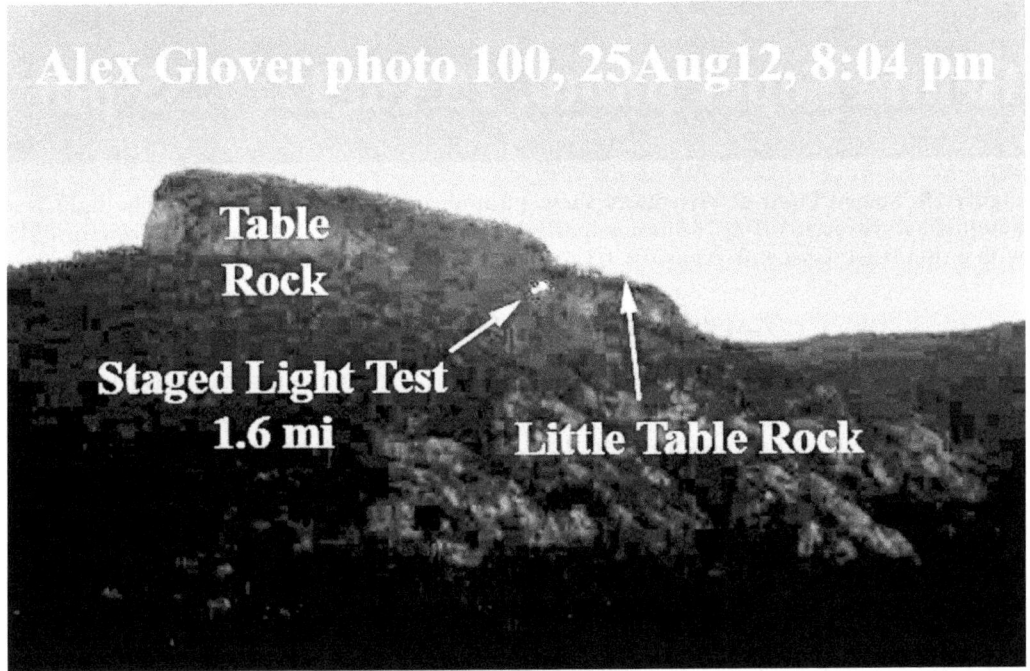

Top: Figure 77. Staged light on Forest Service Road 4099, photographed from NC Highway 181 Brown Mountain overlook. Stanley 520-lumen handheld LED spotlight model FL5W10 (Canon EF 75–300 mm zoom lens set at 140 mm [227 mm effective focal length and 4.5X approximate magnification]; 21-second exposure, f/5.6, ISO-200). *Bottom:* Figure 78. Staged lights on Table Rock, photographed from Wiseman's View (1.6 miles distant). The lights are a single-mantle Coleman propane lantern and a 30-lumen headlamp (Camera: Tripod-mounted Nikon D70S with 60 mm lens. 5-second exposure, f/4.8) (courtesy Alex Glover).

Figure 79. Staged Light at Wiseman's View, photographed from Table Rock. The light is a handheld Rayovac 16VB-2, 75-lumen spotlight (Camera: Handheld Kodak EasyShare Z915 with 6 mm lens; ⅛-second-exposure, f/3.5, ISO-1600) (courtesy Benita Soper).

Staged Light Test, October 13, 2012

The BML research team conducted staged light tests on the night of Saturday, October 13, 2012, involving small helium balloons carrying ChemLights™ and LEDs launched from Table Rock and Hawksbill Mountain. The mountain summits are 1.5 miles apart and the lights proved to be only faintly visible from one summit to the other. Commercially available 18[qm] Mylar and 9[qm] latex party balloons were combined in groups of 3 or 4 and fitted with 4[qm] Cyalume ChemLight™ glow sticks and launched from both summits. In addition, a single 9[qm] latex balloon with internal LEDs was launched from Table Rock. Radio contact between both launch crews and a team photographer stationed at Wiseman's View helped coordinate the efforts. Both launch crews were able to faintly see each other's rising balloons, especially when viewed through binoculars; however, no photographs of lights were captured by the camera at Wiseman's View. Light beams from handheld flashlights and laser pointers, when reflected off of the rising balloons by the ground crews, also produced faint lights that were visible to the crews on the adjacent mountain.

This light test demonstrated that low-intensity man-made lights like small ChemLights™ and single LEDs probably don't produce the distant lights commonly seen and reported as BMLs.

Staged Light Test, December 1, 2012

Members of our research team and other volunteers camped on Shortoff Mountain on December 1, 2012, providing yet another staged light test. Handheld radios provided communication between the light operators and the photographer, who was stationed at Wiseman's View five miles distant. Two white lights and the group's campfire were clearly visible to the photographer. Two team members with radios and 130-lumen LED headlamps moved away from the campfire and found open views toward the camera; their lights were seen at azimuths of 175° and 178°. The lights of the Marion Country Club and Lake James community were also visible beyond the mouth of Linville Gorge.

Figure 80. Staged lights on Shortoff Mountain, photographed from Wiseman's View (Canon EF 75–300 mm zoom lens with 1.4X teleconverter set at 105 mm [170 mm effective focal length and 3.4X approximate magnification]; 17-second exposure, f/5.6, ISO-800).

Staged Light Test, November 4, 2013

Our November 4, 2013, staged light test took place on Chestnut Mountain, 1.9 miles east of the Highway 181 Brown Mountain overlook. Team member Mike Fischesser drove his pickup truck along Forest Service Road #198. Lights from his vehicle headlights and a rechargeable 520-lumen LED handheld spotlight were photographed by the author from the Highway 181 overlook.

Staged Light Test, April 9, 2014

Our April 9, 2014, staged light test took place on Forest Service Road #4099 and Wildcat Knob. This was an unannounced light test when team member Mike Fischesser

Figure 81. Staged light test on Chestnut Mountain Road (FS Rd 198), photographed from NC Highway 181 overlook (1.9 miles distant). House lights from Blowing Rock are visible through the gap north of Chestnut Mountain. Image: Discontinuous compiled ten-minute time-lapse image created by stacking 3 individual select 60–66 second time-exposure images (Canon EF 18–55 mm zoom lens set at 18 mm [29 mm effective focal length and 0.6X approximate magnification]; 60- and 66-second exposures, f/4.5, ISO-1600).

rode an ATV motorcycle round-trip along the graveled Forest Service road between Chestnut Gap and Wildcat Knob. Mike's motorcycle light was captured by BML Cam1, which was 5.7 miles away. In addition, Mike hiked round-trip to the summit of Wildcat knob and his 130-lumen LED headlamp was clearly visible to BML Cam1. The following image is a time-lapse during Mike's one-hour round trip.

The day after this staged light test, our research team was contacted by a non-team observer who was at the NC Highway 181 Brown Mountain overlook on April 9, 2014, the night of the test, and reported seeing mysterious lights during the same time as Mike's ride and hike, further demonstrating that even experienced but unsuspecting people cannot distinguish between man-made lights and non-man-made lights by visual clues alone.

Staged Light Test, June 16, 2014

On the evening of June 15, 2014, team member Dr. Cato Holler, Jr., camped at Bear Rocks on Brown Mountain and his 160-lumen LED headlamp was captured by BML Cam1, which was 6.7 miles away. Dr. Holler's light was also captured at the same spot during the early morning hours of the next day. This light test not only confirmed the clear visibility of small backcountry user lights, but also established the exact location of Bear Rocks as seen in the BML Cam1 images—allowing an accurate measurement of 106.3 degrees azimuth to that known landmark.

Top: Figure 82. Staged light tests on Forest Service Road 4099. Image: Discontinuous 61-minute time-lapse image created by stacking 15 separate select 30-second time-exposure images. *Bottom:* Figure 83. Staged light test on Brown Mountain (Bear Rocks) (all original images courtesy Daniel Caton).

Staged Light Test, July 14, 2014

On the evening of July 14, 2014, the author hiked round-trip to the summit of Shortoff Mountain via the Wolf Pit and Mountain-to-Sea trails. My handheld lights included a rechargeable 520-lumen LED spotlight and a 78-lumen 4-bulb LED headlamp; both were easily captured by BML Cam2, which was located 2.8 to 3.0 miles away. This staged light test established the exact trace of those trails as seen in the BML Cam2 images and confirmed the source of similar hiker lights previously captured by the camera. The following image is a time-lapse stacked composite of 24 select 60-second time exposures during my two-hour hike.

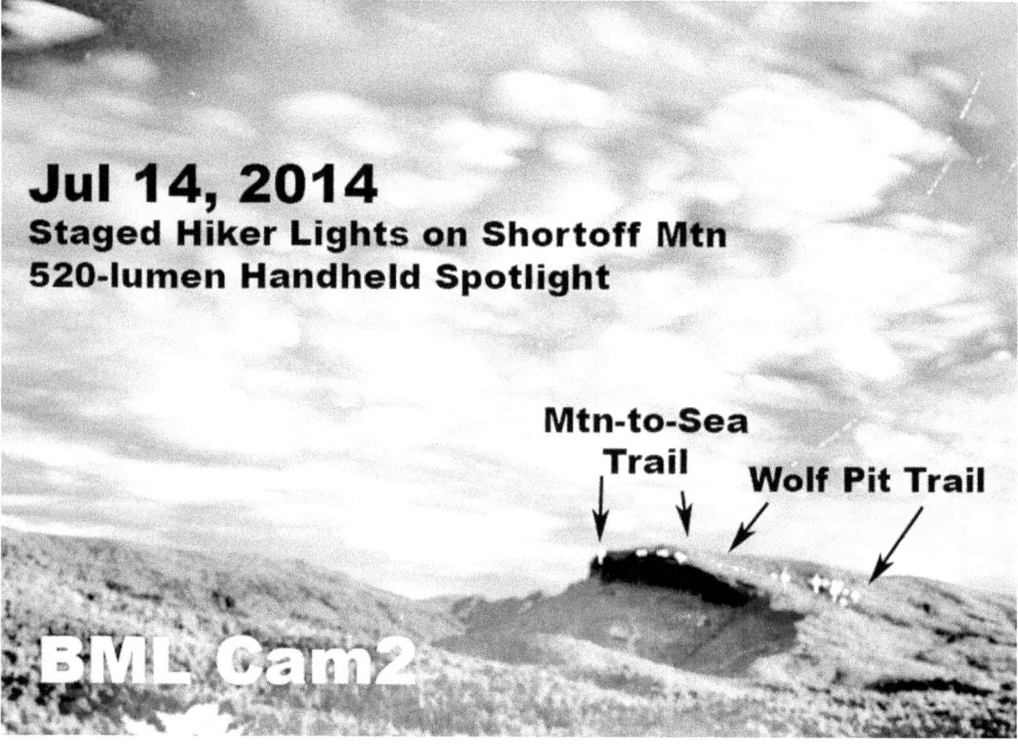

Figure 84. Staged light test on Shortoff Mountain. Image: Discontinuous composite two-hour time-lapse image created by stacking 24 separate, select 60-second time-exposure images (original images courtesy Daniel Caton).

Staged Light Test, August 13, 2014

Three BML Research Team members conducted a staged light test on Linville Gorge's Pinch-In Trail on the night of August 13, 2014. Dr. Cato Holler, Jr., his son Chris Holler, and the author hiked the trail round-trip carrying common, handheld LED spotlights (320 and 520 lumens) and LED headlamps (78 and 160 lumens). Our lights were easily captured by BML Cam2, which was 4.5 miles away. Again this staged light test confirmed the source of previously seen hiker lights on the same trail and established the exact trace of the trail as seen in the BML Cam2 images. The following image is a time-lapse during our two-hour hike.

Figure 85. Staged light test on Pinch-In Trail. Image: Discontinuous composite 30-minute time-lapse image created by stacking 12 separate select 60-second time-exposure images (original images courtesy Daniel Caton).

Staged Light Test, August 20–21, 2014

The author conducted a staged light test on Brown Mountain on the night of August 20, 2014. I rode my bicycle along FS Road #4099 from Chestnut Gap to the north base of Brown Mountain. I hiked the short connector trail between FS Rd #4099 and ATV Trail #2 and followed Trail #2 to Bear Rocks. I then looped back on ATV Trails #6, #1b, and #8 to trail #2 and the connector trail back to FS Road #4099 for a total hike of two to three miles. My rechargeable 520-lumen LED handheld spotlight was captured by BML Cam1 only at the open view at Bear Rocks (6.7 miles from Cam 1), while my 78-lumen 4-bulb LED headlamp was only visible at one point on FS Rd #4099. Leaves still on the trees apparently blocked all other views of my lights (compared to my hike on December 11, 2014, when my same lights were visible in many places). Previous lights seen on these trails during the summer of 2014 must have been much brighter than the lights I carried; presumably those previous lights were brighter ATV lights.

Staged Light Test, December 11, 2014

The author conducted a staged light test on Brown Mountain on the night of December 11, 2014. Retracing my route of August 20, 2014, I rode my bicycle along FS Road #

Figure 86. Staged light test on Brown Mountain, August 20–21, 2014. Image: Discontinuous compiled two-hour-16-minute time-lapse image created by stacking two separate select 30-second time-exposure images (original images courtesy Daniel Caton).

4099 from Chestnut Gap to the north base of Brown Mountain. I then hiked the short connector trail between road 4099 and ATV Trail #2 and followed Trail #2 to Bear Rocks. I looped back on ATV Trails #6, #1b, and #8 to trail #2 and the connector trail back to road 4099 for a total hike of two to three miles. With the leaves now off the trees, my lights were visible at many places along the trails (compared to my August 20, 2014, hike). I carried a rechargeable 520-lumen LED spotlight and a 78-lumen 4-bulb LED headlamp. BML Cam1 was located 7.0 miles west of Brown Mountain, proving once again that common backcountry user lights are readily visible at the popular observation overlooks. The following image is a time-lapse during my 4.5-hour hike. The convoluted trace of ATV Trail #2 is shown in the small insert (photographed at the same scale and angle of view as the section of Trail #2 in the Cam1 image).

The December 11, 2014, hike included a short but eventful bushwhack to Lael's Rock, the suspected site of Ralph Lael's 1962 encounter with lights he interpreted to be aliens

Opposite, top and middle: Figure 87 A and B. Staged light test on Brown Mountain, December 11, 2014. Image: Discontinuous composite 4.5-hour time-lapse image created by stacking 16 separate select 30-second time-exposure images (original images courtesy Daniel Caton). *Bottom:* Figure 88. Staged light test and low-flying airplane on Brown Mountain. Image: Composite one-minute time-lapse image created by stacking two 30-second time-exposure images (original images courtesy Daniel Caton).

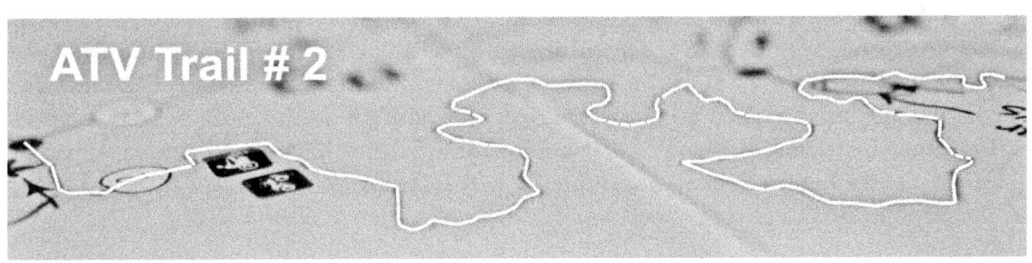

(Chapter 10). At the end of twilight, BML Cam1 captured my light on the exposed rock, establishing the exact position of that landmark in the Cam1 images and allowing the determination of an accurate azimuth of 103.1 degrees. Remarkably, only a few minutes after arriving at Lael's Rock, a twin-engine airplane flew less than 200 feet above the treetops and just to the south of my location before turning sharply to the north and flying up Upper Creek! Although this was not part of my staged light test, the coincidental flyover was captured on BML Cam1 and provided a unique opportunity to identify a most unexpected man-made light on Brown Mountain. Had I not have been on the exposed rock at the moment of the flyover and had BML Cam1 not been turned on early that night in order to capture my light during twilight, we would not have such a positive identification of this light. Figure 88 demonstrates that highly unexpected man-made lights do occur on Brown Mountain and can easily be misinterpreted by unsuspecting or uninformed observers.

Interestingly, five weeks later, on January 19, 2015, our team learned from a personal interview with one of the operators at the Hickory Regional Airport that the U.S. Air Force Special Forces out of Fort Bragg, North Carolina, conducted nighttime low-level flight training with a twin-engine De Havilland Twin Otter airplane periodically during November and December 2014. The military pilots utilized night-vision equipment and operated independently out of the Hickory airport. Undoubtedly this was the same airplane that appeared to dive-bomb me on Brown Mountain on the night of December 11, 2014. Other incidents of low-attitude nocturnal airplanes have also been captured by BML Cam1 (see Figure 65) and undoubtedly witnessed by many unsuspecting observers at the popular BML viewing sites!

Chapter 18

Appalachian State University Nightly Cameras

People's minds are changed through observation and not through argument.
—Will Rogers

In addition to our BML research team's individual personal camera photography, a major part of our research included a vast number of photographic images captured by permanently installed all-night cameras. Two modified meteor-hunting astronomical cameras overlooking Brown Mountain (BML Cam1) and Linville Gorge (BML Cam2) have captured more than 575,000 time-lapse images representing 6,300 hours of nighttime observation over 440 nights (Cam1) and 318 nights (Cam2) during 2013 and 2014. Images from both of these cameras are scattered throughout this report.

Both cameras were installed and operated by Dr. Dan Caton, Professor and Director of Observatories, Department of Physics and Astronomy, Appalachian State University, Boone, North Carolina, as part of an ongoing university-supported research project. The cameras were still running as of the end of 2015 and each day the previous night's images were compiled into short videos and posted to YouTube for public viewing and comment. To find these videos online, search YouTube for "Brown Mountain Lights Camera 1 (or Camera 2)," then search for any date you are interested in.

As expected, the nightly images from these two cameras are highly informative in recording and identifying visible lights in the Brown Mountain and Linville Gorge areas. However, contrary to the expectation suggested by the large number of reported mystery lights in these areas, no unexplained lights have been recorded by either Cam1 or Cam2 over the two-year period reviewed herein. With careful and logical evaluation, all lights recorded by these cameras as of December 31, 2014, have been identified as either manmade, natural, or internal camera flaws. This includes some highly unexpected lights like those from very low-flying airplanes and helicopters, airplanes and helicopters taking off and landing within view of the camera, backcountry users and even vehicles in supposedly inaccessible areas, vehicle headlights reflecting in ground fog, fireworks, manmade satellites and space stations, bright stars and planets, distant lightning, and even fireflies.

Let me make this perfectly clear: the author's review of more than half a million photographs taken over a period of two years has not confirmed a single mystery light; however, numerous unexpected man-made and natural lights have been documented that are known to be easily mistaken as mystery lights by uninformed or unsuspecting observers.

In the year following the author's active participation reviewing the nightly images, another 1 million images were captured and uploaded to the Internet for public inspection, but again with no obvious mystery lights. That's a total of more than 1.6 million images with no mystery lights!

A prudent person would conclude that this should be the end of the story. Unfortunately, firm believers in the existence of mystery lights discount such overwhelming non-supporting objective evidence and assume the researchers are wrong or mistaken in their evaluation. However, the challenge is on the believers in the mystery lights to provide reliable evidence supporting their hypotheses.

CCD Image Processing Errors

Throughout this report, images from BML Cam1 and Cam2 are clearly identifiable as low-resolution time-exposure images. However, understanding some of the limitations of the cameras is critical to evaluating the images they produce. These astronomical digital cameras have CCD image-producing sensors, which differ somewhat from the more common CMOS digital sensors found in normal personal cameras. CCD sensors are more sensitive to faint light but are overly sensitive to bright lights. In addition, they are prone to producing images with occasional excited pixels due to image-possessing errors internal to the cameras themselves.

Figure 89. Oversaturated bright moonlight, light ray and lens flares. Notice the vehicle lights at the Highway 181 Brown Mountain overlook (courtesy Daniel Caton).

Top: Figure 90. Double exposure and duplicate lights. Notice that the lower band of lights is a mirror image of the upper band of lights. *Bottom:* Figure 91. Smear line below bright airplane light (both photographs courtesy Daniel Caton).

Figure 92. Smear lines and duplicate lights below bright lights (courtesy Daniel Caton).

In our BML Cams, these problems are even more pronounced since we used time exposures to reduce the total number of images produced by the cameras each night. Cam1 overlooking Brown Mountain was set to capture 30-second time exposures because of the presence of numerous distant but bright city/town/rural lights in the view field; Cam2 overlooking Linville Gorge was set to capture 60-second time exposures since there are no resident bright lights in the view field. Bright lights in images from either camera are prone to overexposure, which can produce rayed stars emanating above and below the bright light, and washed-out, oversaturated lights—the longer the time exposure, the greater the problem. In addition, smear lines and double-exposure lights are often captured below bright lights as the digital image information is being transferred to the storage devices within the cameras. Cosmic rays from outer space are also often captured by CCD sensors as instantaneous tiny spots or short streaks of light. Finally, individual malfunctioning pixels can continuously register as various shades of grey. Some of these CCD sensor glitches are shown in images 89–92.

Chapter 19

Morphing of the Legend

When ignorance gets started, it knows no bounds.
—Will Rogers

Cultural influences not only played a major role in the beginning of the legend of the BMLs, but they also caused significant changes over the next 100 years. In addition, morphing of the legend reflects mankind's changing cultural values, loss of wilderness familiarity, and technological advances, as well as reactions to scientific investigations that have repeatedly found little to no support for the existence of unknown mystery lights.

First Sightings, Jules Verne and the Beginnings of the Legend

The first reliable sightings of mystery lights started around 1858 when Fate Wiseman, as a young boy, was one of the first to notice occasional nighttime flashes of light far to the east from Wiseman's View, probably from the headlight of the first train in western North Carolina, which began operation that year (see Chapter 5). However, the full legend itself actually began much later, between 1897 and 1912 when local residents and visitors began noticing multiple distant lights burning continuously throughout the night and visible from widely separated observation sites. The rapid spread of electricity in the Catawba River Valley south and east of Brown Mountain in the 1890s, after the arrival of electricity in Hickory in 1888, suggests a direct connection to the origin of the legend.

In addition, another direct cultural influence on the beginning of the legend is suggested by Jules Verne's fictional tale of mystery lights above a mountain near Morganton, North Carolina, which was the opening scene in his novel *Master of the World*. First published in French in 1904 and in English in 1911, the novel may have actually inspired the beginning of the legend of the BMLs, which first appeared in print in 1912, only one year after the English publication of Verne's book.

Apparently the science fiction adventure story in Verne's book caught the attention of the local residents at the same time distant city/town electric lights were beginning to appear over the top of Brown Mountain, and the legend was born.

Mansfield's 1922 Investigation Changed Everything

The monumental investigation by the United States Geological Survey geologist George Rogers Mansfield in 1922 found that 80 percent of the supposed mystery lights pointed out to him by prominent local citizens were in fact the lights of automobiles and train locomotives, 10 percent were stationary electric lights (houses and buildings), and the other 10 percent were brush fires. Mansfield based his conclusions on carefully compiled maps on which he plotted the locations of lights based on survey-instrument measurements he took at the time of the sightings. He subsequently visited those sites, noting the presence of houses, buildings, automobiles on roads, locomotives on train tracks, and recently burned areas. Based on interviews with eyewitnesses, Mansfield also suggested that the supposedly mystery lights reportedly seen immediately after the big flood of 1916 were probably those of automobiles still active on the undamaged roads in the distant valley.

Mansfield's conclusions dealt a serious but nonlethal blow to the legend. In fact, it would be approximately 30 years before the legend regained significant strength, this time focusing on less easily dismissed lights, then showing up for the first time in Linville Gorge, 7–10 miles west of Brown Mountain. Of course, in the 30 years following Mansfield's investigation, the realization also began to sink in to the local residents and visitors alike that most, if not all, of the distant lights seen over the top of Brown Mountain did in fact correspond to the ever-increasing electric lights in the expanding cities, towns and rural communities in the Catawba River Valley. However, the legend never completely died away and by the early 1950s it was somewhat revived, focusing on the lights of probable backcountry users and pranksters in Linville Gorge. However popular the legend is today, it has never regained the strength it had before Mansfield's report.

Linville Gorge Becomes the Place to Be

Today, many BML enthusiasts report that Brown Mountain is not the best place to see mystery lights; rather, Linville Gorge is the place to be. And Wiseman's View is mentioned as the best observation site. Ironically, this is the exact spot where the first mystery lights were sighted in the mid–1800s. However, while numerous observers over the next 100 years reported seeing distant mystery lights over Brown Mountain while observing from Wiseman's View, none reported seeing such lights down in Linville Gorge itself or along its mountainous rims until about 30 years after Mansfield's report. Since the early 1950s, anecdotal stories of mystery light sightings within the confines of Linville Gorge have abounded, while reports of mystery light sightings over Brown Mountain have diminished. Interestingly the first written record of lights seen in Linville Gorge was not published until 1995, describing events of c. 1980 (Shockley, 1995). However, Scotty Wiseman's 1961 ballad "The Legend of the Brown Mountain Lights" contains a chorus line insinuating that Fate Wiseman saw the light of the faithful slave searching for his lost master on both the top of Brown Mountain and deep in Linville Gorge. The timing would have been 100 years earlier, in the mid to late 1800s. In any event, the presence of mystery lights in Linville Gorge is apparently a fairly recent, post–Mansfield phenomenon and was not part of the original 1897–1922 legend.

Deep Woods Close Encounters

Today's version of the legend includes numerous stories of close encounters with supposed mystery lights by observers deep in the woods on and around Brown Mountain (see Chapters 9 and 10), as well as within Linville Gorge. Note that close encounters with lights of any sort were never part of the original 1897–1922 legend. The assumption that more recent close encounters with mystery lights in the woods might be due to greater backcountry use today than in the formative years of the legend is invalid, since the extensive logging of the forests on and around Brown Mountain in the late 1800s and early 1900s meant that thousands of loggers and workers were housed in remote camps in the area at the time—and apparently none of them reported close encounters. However, it is likely that backcountry use of the more isolated Linville Gorge is greater today than it was in the early 1900s, leading to more sightings of backcountry user lights. In addition, fireflies might also be playing a role!

Since the early 1960s, reports of close encounters with supposed mystery lights deep in the woods have become more common. Many of these reports have a lot of features in common with probable sightings of the rare luminescent blue ghost firefly (*Phausis reticulata*), which lights with a continuously glowing, bluish-white light as it flies near the ground in heavily wooded areas (Chapter 15). The fireflies surely existed in the forests in earlier times as well but apparently were not mistaken for mystery lights until less-informed, less-wilderness-skilled people began entering the forests.

Mysterious Sky Lights?

Today's morphed legend also includes accounts of some mysterious lights high in the sky above both Brown Mountain and Linville Gorge. Almost certainly the lights from airplanes, helicopters and man-made satellites and space vehicles, these types of lights were also never part of the original 1897–1922 legend.

When will the morphing stop? Probably never.

CHAPTER 20

Unclassified Lights

> Confirmation bias works really well to support preconceived beliefs.
> —Harriet Hall, December 31, 2013, "Doctors Are Not 'Only Out to Make Money,'" www.sciencebasedmedicine.org/doctors-are-not-only-out-to-make-money/

> A wise man proportions his belief to the evidence.
> —David Hume, 1910, An Enquiry Concerning Human Understanding

> Extraordinary claims require extraordinary evidence.
> —Carl Sagan (1934–1996)

> The weight of evidence for an extraordinary claim must be proportioned to its strangeness.
> —Pierre-Simon Lapace (1749–1827)

The 1 Percent Unclassified Lights

Not surprisingly, a small portion of reported mystery lights are not easily classified as to their origin. Some personal stories, including many close encounters, seem to defy logical explanation. Mostly these sightings are unclassified because of the lack of sufficient information to assign them an origin of any kind.

However, these unclassified sightings account for less than an estimated 1 percent of the total BML reports and are therefore statically insignificant to the legend of the BMLs. The fact that an estimated 99 percent of all BML sightings can be explained is by itself an amazing achievement; but this doesn't mean that the unclassified sightings are individually invalid, insignificant or not real.

What About the 1 Percent of Unexplained Lights?

Can it be that a portion, albeit small, of all reported light sightings are due to some physical phenomenon as yet unknown to man? Can a portion of the estimated 1 percent of unclassified lights be due to a source or sources unknown to science? This very real possibility captures and holds the attention, imagination, and curiosity of researchers, observers, and the public at large. If there are nocturnal lights in the Brown Mountain area that defy understanding, they must reside within our estimated 1 percent of unclassified BML sightings along with probable mistaken identities unclassified due to the lack of information. Thus, if they exist, science-defying lights make up less than an estimated 1 percent of all reported BML sightings. The legend of the BMLs began and continues to exist because of mistaken man-made and natural lights, not because of science-defying lights.

Chapter 21

Reality or Delusion

Memory is *not* objective; it is constructed by our own brains.
It is not burned, or ingrained, or seared into it.

Memory is not like a tape recorder
Stories are unreliable.
You need to have better evidence than eyewitness testimony to back up your claim.

Memory is something that is so often wrong that we have to face up to the reality that stories and witness accounts are the *worst* kinds of evidence upon which to base your conclusion.
—Sharon Hill, December 4, 2013,"I'm Not Making this Up: Why I'm Skeptical of Eyewitnesses," www.huffingtonpost.com/sharon-hill/im-not-making-this-up_b_4373197.html

Without independent corroboration, little can be done
to tell a false memory from a true one.
—Elizabeth Loftus, False-Memory Expert, Ph.D., Distinguished Professor
of Social Ecology and Professor of Law and Cognitive Science,
School of Social Ecology, University of California-Irvine, *New Scientist*, 2013

One must be careful when using the word "real."
—Max Planck, Discoverer of quantum physics

Can We Believe What We See with Our Own Eyes?

Many neuroscience researchers, like those quoted above and elsewhere in this book, tell us that a significant portion of what we think our eyes have seen has been recorded falsely in our brains. Since our eyes don't see every detail that unfolds in front of them, our brains compensate by filling in the gaps to compose or complete a picture of what happened based on what we expected to see, which is itself heavily influenced by our individual past experiences. Thus multiple people witnessing the same phenomenon often have widely different perceptions or beliefs about what happened. And unraveling real from false in any individual story is impossible without independent corroboration, the realization of which has recently turned the U.S. judicial system on its head regarding criminal court cases where infallible DNA data occasionally later proves the innocence of someone who was unfairly punished, or even executed, based on faulty eyewitness reports.

False memories are beyond the control of the individual and thus are independent of one's intelligence, education, honesty, or stature. Such false memories almost certainly play a role in many anecdotal stories of BML sightings, suggesting the prudent exercise of extreme caution when evaluating such stories.

What Are Delusions?

In an ideal world, we humans would first gather the correct knowledge about the world in which we live and then form beliefs based on that knowledge. If the knowledge and beliefs are correct, then our perception of reality would be correct.

Unfortunately, that's not how we generally arrive at reality. Instead, we often create beliefs first, based on incorrect or missing information, which leads to delusions and incorrect realities. In the same manner, uninformed or misinformed BML observers often form an incorrect perception of what they saw. In this book, I have attempted to present useful, accurate and dependable data that should help all BML observers avoid delusions and misperceptions.

Do You Have a BML Observation? Write It Down.

Relying on memory to record BML observations is not advisable. Over time, memories fade and are replaced with false or selected memories. A person's age, intelligence, integrity, or experience has nothing to do with the ability to remember an event correctly.

We tend to rely on our memories far too much. To remember something important, we should write it down. Often the most critical details of a light sighting are quickly lost to our memory, and over time more of the story continues to get lost. As soon as I hear someone describe an old sighting as "I remember it like it happened yesterday" I know I'm dealing with false memories. Memories fade over time, so how can someone possibly remember it like it happened yesterday? While the person might be able to describe parts of the event with apparent clarity, often one can't remember the simplest information, such as the day of the week, the month, the year or even their location when the lights were encountered. Such loss of critical information betrays the assumption that memory is perfect. Instead, what's probably happening is that individuals remember the last memory they had of the event; and in this manner, the memory of the original event changes over time without the observer's even being aware of it. Don't trust your memory with important information. Use the Light Sighting Report Form in Appendix B to write down your observations. Even writing down what is currently recalled about past sightings is useful in preventing the loss of even more critical details. I encourage everyone to use the Light Sighting Report Form to record past and future light sightings.

Concluding Remarks

Three Years of the Most Comprehensive Brown Mountain Lights Research Ever Undertaken

Our photographic research, including thousands of personal-camera photos (many with telescopic magnification), and more than 575,000 time-exposure photos from permanently mounted cameras show that no mystery lights exist. Rather, there are thousands of normal man-made lights and some rare unexpected man-made lights, all known to lend themselves to mistaken identity by many uninformed and unsuspecting observers. In addition, natural lights from celestial objects (moon, stars, planets, meteors) and storm-related lightning have been seen to confuse some people.

Our biological research has identified the presence of a rare luminescent flying insect (the blue ghost firefly, or *Phausis reticulata*) that also lends itself to misidentification by some unprepared and bewildered observers.

Our literature research finds that the legend of the BMLs started a little over 100 years ago. While a few unknown scattered lights were noticed in the area between c.1858 and c.1910, they did not give rise to a legend of mystery lights. The legend itself started after a sudden increase in the number of lights being seen beginning in 1912, a year after Jules Verne's *Master of the World,* a fictional account of mystery lights atop a mountain north of Morganton, North Carolina, was published in English. In addition, the beginnings of the legend correspond to the sudden arrival and quick spread of electric lights in this part of western North Carolina. Widespread misinformation characterizes most of the published BML literature since the first newspaper articles began appearing in 1912.

With more than 250 man-years of collective experience, our research team was heavily weighted with geologists. However, we find no earth-related source of lights in the area. Our sociological research finds that critical thinking, false memory, selected memory, unfamiliarity with the outdoors, fear of the dark, and preconceived ideas all play major roles in how observers evaluate and report what they witnessed.

Our staged light tests prove that humans can readily access the isolated wilderness locations where ground-based mystery lights are commonly reported today and in the past. They also prove that handheld lights commonly carried by backcountry users are highly visible to observers stationed miles away at the popular viewing sites. Thus our staged light tests highly suggest that common backcountry user lights can, and probably are, frequently mistaken for mystery lights by uninformed and bewildered observers.

Major Conclusions

1. The legend of the BMLs is a contemporary legend supported only by subjective anecdotal evidence.
2. The legend is more of a social science phenomenon than it is an earth science one.
3. Unexpected man-made lights are the fuel that feeds the legend and without them the legend would not exist.
4. No objective or empirical evidence supports the existence of supernormal lights in the Brown Mountain area.
5. For most observers, visual clues alone are insufficient to distinguish between man-made and non-man-made nocturnal lights.
6. The legend is only about 100 years old and closely corresponds to the 1911 publication of Jules Verne's *Master of the World* and the arrival and
   development of man-made lights in the area.
7. Misinformation plays a critical part in perpetuating the legend.
8. The mysteries lie only in the belief-dependent realities of some individuals.
9. There are no mystery lights in the Brown Mountain area, only bewildered and mystified observers.

Not everyone on our Brown Mountain research team agrees with all the conclusions I list above. While all team members are disappointed that our efforts haven't been able to find objective proof of mystery lights, some still maintain hope that such evidence may be forthcoming in the future.

What Are the Brown Mountain Lights?

Nocturnal lights seen in the vicinity of Brown Mountain in Burke County, North Carolina, have intrigued and mystified hundreds of thousands of people for more than a hundred years. A Brown Mountain light is best described as any light from an apparently unknown source seen by any mystified observer located anywhere near Brown Mountain. Thus all nighttime lights visible in the area can be called BMLs, as each has been mistaken for a mysterious light by someone recently or in the past. It is the interpretation of the sources of these lights as unexplained that is the basis for the legend of the Brown Mountain lights.

The only evidence supporting the presence of lights defying the laws of the universe in the Brown Mountain area comes from subjective anecdotal stories from uninformed, misinformed, unprepared, bewildered, and often overly excited and frightened observers who do not understand what they have seen. Properly informed and experienced observers see the same lights but see no mystery.

Thus the legend of the Brown Mountain lights is a contemporary legend supported only by unreliable subjective evidence. The available empirical evidence strongly suggests that the supposed mystery lights are primarily due to misinterpretation of man-made lights (98 percent) and natural lights (1 percent), while the remaining 1 percent are unclassified due to the lack of sufficient information. Although it is possible that the 1 percent of unclassified lights might include some lights currently unknown to science, the number is statistically insignificant and too small to account for the existence of the legend of the Brown Mountain lights; i.e., the legend began and continues to exist because of misidentified man-made and natural lights, not because of observation of actual science-defying lights.

Like most contemporary legends, the legend of the Brown Mountain lights can be described as socially accepted pseudoscience. It is pseudoscience because it is based on unsupported ideas that are refuted by empirical and objective evidence; and it is socially accepted because it is part of the local folklore that binds us all together.

The legend actually first began as misinterpretations of newly appeared distant man-made electric lights at the end of the nineteenth century and the beginning of the twentieth century. As the existence, unexpected behavior, and distance-penetrating power of these man-made lights became more obvious over the next 100 years, the legend survived by morphing and today has little to do with the types of lights originally seen and described.

Science has solved the mystery. The legend is more of a social science phenomenon than it is an earth science phenomenon.

Morphing of the Legend

Once stated, the legend significantly changed or morphed several times over the next 100 years, probably reflecting the growing realization that visible lights from distant towns and cities had greatly expanded over that time period and were contributing to the lights being observed. Also forcing the legend to change was the influence of scholarly investigations like the one detailed herein that attribute the primary sources to man-made lights. For instance, following the 1922 publication of *The Origin of the Brown Mountain Lights* by the U.S. Geological Survey, which concluded 90 percent of the lights were man-made and the remaining 10 percent were brush fires, the legend suffered greatly and over the next 80 years slowly changed to ignore the lights originally seen and reported over the top of Brown Mountain. Today the legend focuses on even more recently appearing and less easily dismissed lights being seen in nearby Linville Gorge and elsewhere. In addition, close encounters with unexpected lights by observers deep in the woods, which have been a focus of the legend since the early 1960s, were never part of the earlier legend. These close encounters may be due to luminescent insects such as the blue ghost fireflies, which are relatively unknown to today's local population but were apparently better known in the early 1900s to the area's mountain residents, who did not mistake them for mystery lights. Native Americans were also apparently not fooled by the blue ghost fireflies.

Explained Lights

To date, our research has identified only a few actual sources for nighttime lights in the area, including one major source (man-made lights) and several minor ones (natural lights). The only things "out there" producing nocturnal lights are human beings, bioluminescence, celestial objects, lightning, forest fires, and possibly flammable swamp gas. No other light sources have been found to exist.

Man-made lights, including a wide variety of lights from cities, towns, cars, trucks, airplanes and helicopters, lights carried by backcountry travelers, and lights manipulated by pranksters, probably explain greater than an estimated 98 percent of all reported mystery light observations. Reflected sunlight from mankind's artificial satellites and space vehicles above the earth are included in this category.

In addition, the bioluminescence of some rare fireflies, glowworms, and mushrooms may confuse some people. Specifically, the elusive and relatively unknown blue ghost firefly (*Phausis reticulata*) appears to explain some mystery light sightings.

Celestial bodies, such as the sun, moon, visible planets, stars, and meteors may also explain a few mysterious observations. The bright visible planets—Jupiter, Venus, Saturn, Mercury and Mars—as well as bright stars and meteors, are often mistaken throughout the world, and probably here as well, for mysterious sky lights. In addition, the sun naturally produces a vast assortment of rare nighttime lights that might easily be mistaken by an observer, including such high-altitude atmospheric effects as illuminated clouds (noctilucent, nacreous, and iridescent clouds, and rocket/jet aircraft vapor trails), sun rays (crepuscular and anti-crepuscular), moonbows, the Aurora Borealis and the Zodiacal light.

Storm-related lightning, especially distant lightning without noise (commonly referred to as heat lighting), has been seen to confuse some people, while ball lightning, although too rare to account for any significant number of all reported BML sightings, could also lead to some misconceptions.

Future of the Legend of the Brown Mountain Lights

Imagination and other forms of creative thinking are often the means by which we try to move beyond critical thinking. However, creative thinking built upon delusions too often leads to unfounded magical or wishful thinking. Critical thinking is the means by which we establish a truthful foundation upon which creative thinking can best be applied.

Critical reasoning, such as the investigation documented in this book, tells us that the vast majority of reported BMLs, both today and in the past, are misidentified man-made lights, suggesting that the legend of the BMLs is an unfounded contemporary legend. However, a very small percentage of reported BMLs cannot be so easily classified and it is this small percentage that continues to intrigue some of our team investigators. But in order for the legend to survive, it must accept and build on the objective truths established by our investigation. Additional morphing of the legend in the future is expected.

> The world needs more "badassitude"—the state of knowing you're right because you did the required research to justify it.
> —Neil deGrasse Tyson, 2014

Appendix A: BML Research by the Author

Research conducted by the author is detailed below. This is the research that directly led to the conclusions presented in this book. The information includes a summary of photographic images reviewed and specific lights and man-made structures identified from the popular observation sites.

Nightly Camera Photographs Reviewed, 2013–2014

The following table covers more than 575,000 images of Appalachian State University time-lapse photography reviewed by the author (selected images are presented throughout this report):

Camera	Year	Observation Hours	Video Hours	Total Images	# of Nights	Comments
Cam1	2013	1,162	12.76	111,610	133	Start 13Feb13
Cam1	2014	2,840	45.23	325,663	307	End 31Dec14
Cam2	2013	179	1.77	12,732	43	Start 16Oct13
Cam2	2014	2,183	17.63	126,914	275	End 31Dec14
TOTAL		6,364	77.39	576,919	758	

Personal Photographs Reviewed, 2012–2014

The following list covers more than 3,600 personal photographs taken and reviewed by the author (selected images are presented throughout this report):

NC Hwy 181 Overlook	1,479
Catawba Valley	68
Brown Mountain	202
BML Cam 1 (Jonas Ridge)	225
BML Cam 2 (Linville Gorge)	5
Sitting Bear Trail	4
Lost Cove Overlook (BRP)	9
Grant's Mtn	14
Pinnacle Mtn	8
Table Rock	76
Wiseman's View	973
Shortoff Mtn	10
Linville Gorge	50
Fireflies	176
Literature Research	338
TOTAL	3,637

BML Research Expeditions, 2012–2014

Individual expeditions carried out by the author are listed below:

2012

Jul 5	181 Overlook and Wiseman's View—Daytime observation and photography of BM
Jul 6	181 Overlook—Nighttime observation; no BMLs seen; lens flares from car headlights on NC 181 seen in binoculars while viewing eastward at night
Jul 14	181 Overlook—Nighttime observation and photography of staged lights (motorcycle and handheld lights) on BM (ATV trails 1, 2); BML research team
Jul 15	Jonas Ridge—Daytime observation of BM; inspect house for site of BML Cam 1
Jul 17	Burke County Public Library, Morganton, NC—Literature research on BMLs
Jul 19	Holly Springs Branch—Day hike exploring geology and history of area with BML research team
Aug 7	181 Overlook—Day and night photography of BM and vicinity; drive FS roads 982, 197
Aug 23	Mudcut house—Nighttime photography of distant lights and fireflies
Aug 25–26	181 Overlook—Nighttime observation and photography of radio-assisted staged lights (motorcycle lights and handheld spot light) on Little Chestnut Mtn Rd (FS 4099) and on BM; BML research team
Sep 5	181 Overlook and Jonas Ridge Cam1 site—Daytime observation and photography of BM and vicinity
Sep 19	181 Overlook—Nighttime observation and photography of distant man-made lights east of BM
Sep 22	Lost Cove Overlook (BRP)—Daytime observation and photography of BM and vicinity
Sep 27	Catawba Valley—Daytime photography of communication towers on High Peak; nighttime photography of Lenoir-Morganton Foothills Regional Airport
Sep 28	Attend Joshua Warren's celebration party in Asheville, tour his museum
Sep 29	181 Overlook—Evening and nighttime observation and photography of BM and lights to east; photography of full moon above BM
Sep 31	Visit to C. Holler library for literature research
Oct 2	Valdese, NC—Daytime and nighttime photography of Valdese house lights that are visible from 181 overlook
Oct 10	181 Overlook—Daytime observation and photography of BM and vicinity
Oct 12	BM—Day hike to summit area; Rose Tower site, Devil's Hole, etc., with BML research team
Oct 16–17	BM—Overnight campout; daytime and nighttime observation and photography, including Bear Rocks, Devil's Hole, Eggshell Rock, North Slab, Solution Pans, and Rose's Tower Slab; with BML research team and J. Maddry
Oct 17	Literature research at Wilson Creek Visitor Center
Oct 20	Meet Caton and Hawkins at Jonas Ridge house; pick up telescope
Nov 9	181 Overlook—Daytime and nighttime observation and photography of BM and vicinity, including telescope images

Nov 14	Visit to C. Holler library checking BML references
Nov 26	181 Overlook—Daytime and nighttime observation and photography of BM and vicinity, including telescope images and Christmas Star on Hibriten Mtn.
Nov 28	Jonas Ridge—Installation of BML Cam1 and daytime observation and photography of BM and vicinity
Dec 1	Wiseman's View—Daytime and nighttime observation and photography of BM and vicinity; Shortoff Mtn staged light test
Dec 12	Aruba—Daytime photography of granitic pseudokarst similar to that on Brown Mountain
Dec 18	181 Overlook—Daytime and nighttime observation; too windy for tripod photography
Dec 30	181 Overlook—Daytime and nighttime observation and photography of BM and lights to east, including telescope images

2013

Jan 5	BM—Day hike on BM; daytime photography from north face of BM; with BML research team
Jan 19	Day hike on BM with BML research team, examine erosion features
Jan 31	Literature research trip to Pack Memorial Library, Asheville, NC
Mar 22	BML research team meeting, Marion, NC
Mar 22	Pinnacle Mtn—Daytime observation and photography of Linville Gorge
Mar 23	Linville Gorge—Nighttime observation and photography from planned BML Cam2 site
Apr 17	Jonas Ridge Cam1 site—Daytime observation and photography of BM and vicinity
Apr 23	Wiseman's View—Daytime and nighttime observation; too windy for tripod photography
Apr 25	Wiseman's View—Daytime and nighttime observation and photography of BM and vicinity
May 13	Nighttime photography of blue ghost fireflies at DuPont Forest State Park, Hendersonville, NC
May 27	Nighttime photography of blue ghost fireflies at DuPont Forest State Park, Hendersonville, NC
May 29	Nighttime photography of blue ghost fireflies at DuPont Forest State Park, Hendersonville, NC
May 31	Nighttime photography of blue ghost fireflies at DuPont Forest State Park, Hendersonville, NC
Jun 1	BM—Overnight campout at Lael's Rock—observation and photography of Lael's Rock features
Jun 3	Nighttime photography of blue ghost fireflies at DuPont Forest State Park, Hendersonville, NC
Jun 4	Nighttime photography of blue ghost fireflies at DuPont Forest State Park, Hendersonville, NC
Jun 12	Overnight camp on Brown Mountain; observation and photography

Jun 14	Nighttime photography of blue ghost fireflies at Good Cemetery, BRP, McDowell Co, NC
Jun 17	Nighttime photography of blue ghost fireflies at Good Cemetery, BRP, McDowell Co, NC
Jun 17	Bakersville, NC—Don Cooper's presentation on the BMLs
Jun 18	Wiseman's View—Daytime and nighttime observation and photography of BM and vicinity
Jun 23	Wiseman's View—Daytime and nighttime observation and photography of BM and vicinity
Jun 26	Wiseman's View—Daytime and nighttime observation and photography of BM and vicinity
Jun 26	Nighttime photography of blue ghost fireflies at Good Cemetery, BRP, McDowell Co, NC
Jul 1	Wiseman's View—Daytime observation and photography of BM and vicinity
Jul 15	BML research team meeting, Marion, NC
Jul 16–17	BM—Overnight campout; daytime observation and photography of geomorphic features; nighttime observation and photography of Grants Mtn communication tower, Jonas Ridge house lights and airplane with landing light; w/ C. Holler
Jul 17	Wiseman's View—Nighttime observation and photography of distant city lights
Jul 23	Nighttime photography of blue ghost fireflies at Good Cemetery, BRP, McDowell Co, NC
Jul 24	Wiseman's View—Nighttime observation and photography of moonrise and distant city lights
Jul 24	Grants Mtn (Marion)—Daytime and nighttime photography of radio towers
Jul 26	Alex Glover and Ed Speer BML slide presentation at Little Switzerland Community Center
Jul 29	Table Rock—Daytime and nighttime observation and photography of BM and vicinity
Aug 16	Alex Glover and Ed Speer interview with the *Mitchell News-Journal*, Spruce Pine, NC
Aug 21	Wiseman's View—Daytime and nighttime observation and photography of BM and vicinity
Aug 23	Dr. Tom Whyte, Appalachian State University archeologist, presentation on Cherokee Indian sites of western NC, New River State Park
Sep 5	BM—Day hike, observation and photography of rocks on lower Parks Creek with Cato Holler; shelter caves and moonshine still ruins
Sep 10	Grants Mtn (Marion)—Daytime photography of radio towers
Sep 10	Wiseman's View—Nighttime observation and photography of BM and vicinity
Sep 18	Interview with Don Cooper in Linville Falls, NC
Sep 22	BML research team meeting, Marion, NC
Oct 15	Ed Speer BML slide presentation to Rutherford Outdoor Coalition, Isothermal Community College, Spindale, NC

Oct 16	Table Rock—Daytime and nighttime observation and photography of BM and vicinity
Oct 20	Interview with Richard and Jeff Porter, Hwy 105, Morganton, NC
Oct 23	Linville Gorge—Unsuccessful night search for luminescent mushrooms on Sitting Bear trail; reboot Cam1computer
Oct 24	Attend McDowell Co Historical Society presentation on Ghosts of McDowell Co, Marion, NC
Oct 29	181 Overlook—Nighttime observation and photography of green laser lights
Oct 30	181 Overlook—Nighttime observation and photography of ISS and distant city lights in Catawba Valley
Nov 4	181 Overlook—Nighttime observation and photography of staged light test on Chestnut Mtn Rd (FS Rd 198)
Nov 11	181 Overlook—Daytime and nighttime observation and photography, telephoto and telescope photography
Nov 12	Wiseman's View—Nighttime photography of forest fire on east rim of Linville Gorge
Nov 18	Wiseman's View—Nighttime photography of forest fire on east rim of Linville Gorge and distant lights
Dec 02	Jonas Ridge house (Cam1)—Nighttime photography of distant city lights over BM and azimuth measurements
Dec 10	Wiseman's View—Daytime and nighttime photography, including Hawksbill, Table Rock and distant city lights
Dec 13	Linville Gorge—Daytime photography of geology at Linville Falls
Dec 15	BML research team meeting, Marion, NC
Dec 16	181 Overlook—Daytime photography, panoramas of distant views

2014

Apr 22	181 Overlook—Nighttime photography, cloudy
Jul 14	Shortoff Mtn—Round-trip night hike to summit on Wolf Pit trail; headlight, handheld spotlight and laser light tests
Aug 14	Pinch-In trail—Round-trip night hike w/ Cato and Chris Holler on west side of Linville Gorge, handheld spotlight and headlamp test
Aug 20	Brown Mountain—Round-trip night hike on ATV trails 8 and 1B to Bear Rocks, return on trail 2; staged light tests
Oct 12	BML research team meeting, Marion, NC
Dec 11	BM—Round-trip night hike on ATV trails to Lael's Rock and Bear Rocks; staged light tests; low-flying airplane

Lights and Structures Observed from NC Hwy 181 BM Overlook

The following nocturnal lights and man-made structures were documented by the author from the NC Highway 181 Brown Mountain overlook. The overlook is located at 35.942N, 81.420W at 2,840-feet elevation and the distance to the far eastern horizon is approximately 70 miles:

Appendix A

Line of Sight Quadrant/ (Degrees Azimuth)	Date	Description of Lights and Structures (many seen only with magnification)
NE (43)	26Nov12	Several white and red lights on ground in gap north of Chestnut Mtn; camping hunters?
NE (43)	4Nov13	4 stationary lights on skyline ridge above north Chestnut Mtn gap 17 mi. distant; house lights
NE (43)	30Dec12	Orange light on skyline ridge above north Chestnut Mtn gap; house window reflecting sunlight?
NE (50?)	4Nov13	Several high altitude airplanes with flashing navigation lights over Chestnut Mtn; 6:46 p.m.
NE (55?)	9Nov12	Jupiter (433 million mi. distant) and airplane
NE-ESE (55–98)	4Nov13	5–8 stationary red lights widely scattered in area north of Lenoir; communication tower lights
ENE (58)	4Nov13	Staged light test, single white light from 520 lumen spotlight 1.9 miles distant
NE (60?)	4Nov13	Constellation in eastern sky over Chestnut Mtn; Pleiades, 6:46 p.m.
ENE (65)	4Nov13	Constellation in eastern sky over Chestnut Mtn; Taurus, 7:32 p.m.
ENE (84)	4Nov13	Prominent flashing light in Lenoir area; white at early twilight, red at late twilight (communication tower light)
ENE 987?)	11Nov13	Two red lights stacked vertically on communication tower
E (90)	4Nov13	Prominent flashing light n. of Lenoir; white at early twilight, red at late twilight (communication tower light)
ESE (97)	11Nov13	Two red lights stacked vertically; lights atop distant communication tower
ESE (98)	26Nov12	Large, bright orange light atop Hibriten Mtn 20 mi. distant; Lenoir's Christmas star
ESE (98)	26Nov12	Single flashing white light above Hibriten Mtn 20 mi. distant; communication tower light
ESE (98.5)	25Aug12	Staged light test, single white light (520 lumen spotlight) 3.7 mi. distant on FS Rd 4099; 8:08 p.m.
ESE (101)	11Nov13	Horizontal red streak in sky; airplane flying south over Hibriten and Brown Mountain
ESE (106)	25Aug12	Staged light test, single white light (520 lumen spotlight) 3.7 mi. distant on Wildcat Knob; 9:42 p.m.
ESE (110)	9Nov12	1,900 mm daytime image of Lael's Rock on west side of BM, 4.1 mi. distant
ESE (114)	9Nov12	1,900 mm daytime image of Bear Rocks on BM, 4.2 mi. distant; also photographed on 11Nov13
ESE (115)	18Sep12	Prominent communication tower immediately above BM ridge; at least 9 vertically stacked red lights on single tower, also some red lights on ground nearby
ESE (115)	25Aug12	Staged light test, single white light (520 lumen spotlight) 3.7 mi. distant at prospect pit on Wildcat Ridge
ESE (119?)	11Nov13	Flashing white light immediately above BM ridgeline, 5:16 p.m. communication tower
ESE (120)	9Nov12	1,900 mm daytime image of 2 water towers and a white building over top of BM
ESE (120?)	11Nov13	Flashing white light immediately above BM ridgeline, 5:15 p.m. communication tower
SE (121)	9Nov12	1,900 mm daytime image of water tower in west suburbs of Hickory over top of BM
SE (121)	26Nov12	9 evenly spaced, vertically aligned red lights immediately above BM ridge; communication tower in Catawba Valley

Line of Sight Quadrant/ (Degrees Azimuth)	Date	Description of Lights and Structures (many seen only with magnification)
SE (122)	9Nov12	1,900 mm daytime images of water tower over top of BM and valley lights in treetops of BM
SE (123?)	11Nov13	Water tower immediately above BM ridgeline, white, multiple supports; also photographed on 9Nov12 at 121 AZ
ESE (124?)	11Nov13	Baker Mtn and vicinity, multicolor lights; communication towers and city lights
ESE (124?)	11Nov13	8 or 9 vertically stacked red lights and several adjacent ground-level red lights immediately above BM ridgeline, also photographed on 9Nov12; communication tower
ESE (124?)	11Nov13	Two close-by multiple-support white water towers with adjacent building/s immediately above BM ridgeline; also photographed on 9Nov12 at 120 Az
ESE-SE (124–135)	11Nov13	Multicolored lights visible immediately above and thru treetops on BM ridgeline; communication tower and city lights
ESE-SE (124–141)	11Nov13	Prominent 10-mi.-long band of 100s–1,000s of stationary multicolored lights with a few blinking or flashing, including the towns of Hildebran, Icard, Connellys Springs, Rutherford College, Valdese and Drexel along Interstate 40 in Catawba Valley; visible on all clear-night observations; city/town/residential/communication tower lights
SE (125–140)	26Nov12	Numerous long light streaks in sky over South Mountains; airplanes
SE (128.5)	26Nov12	Numerous lights around Baker's Mtn, 32 mi distant; city/town/communication tower lights
SE (129)	30Dec12	Day and night images of Baker's Mtn and nearby buildings and lights; city/town/communication tower lights
SE (130?)	11Nov13	Moon, ~50° altitude, 60 percent Waxing Gibbous
SE (132?)	11Nov13	Two white synchronized flashing lights immediately above BM ridgeline, 5:33 p.m. may turn red in late twilight; distant communication tower
SE (133)	30Dec12	Daytime images of buildings and water tanks in Catawba Valley beyond BM
SE (133?)	11Nov13	White, single-support water tower and nearby buildings immediately above BM ridgeline, 5:42 p.m.
SE (134–138)	26Nov12	Late afternoon sun reflecting off building windows in Catawba Valley ~20 mi. distant
SE (135?)	11Nov13	4 vertically stacked white/reddish lights flashing in synch immediately above BM ridgeline, also nearby flashing red ground light; communication towers
SE (135–141)	19Sep12	100s of lights in Catawba Valley, 20–25 mi. distant; city/town/residential and communication tower lights
SE (136)	29Sep12	Flashing red light atop a communication tower in Catawba Valley, Drexel area
SE (136?)	11Nov13	Bright red flashing light above 4–5 constant red lights on ground; communication tower
SE (137?)	11Nov13	Two groups of lights: 2 vertically stacked flashing white lights above skyline peak and 5 vertically stacked red lights in far distance; communication towers
SE (138)	9Nov12	Line of close-spaced multicolor lights on skyline of South Mountains 21 mi. distant; Valdese houses
SE (138)	9Nov12	Vertically stacked red lights 21+ mi. distant; communication tower lights
SE (139)	26Nov26	Airplane over South Mountains, 7:10 p.m.

Line of Sight Quadrant/ (Degrees Azimuth)	Date	Description of Lights and Structures (many seen only with magnification)
SE (139?)	11Nov13	4 vertically stacked reddish white lights beyond South Mountains skyline; distant communication towers
SE (140?)	29Sep12	Airplane over Drexel area, 8:24 p.m.
SE (140–141)	11Nov13	2 airplanes flying east beyond South Mtn skyline
SE (141)	9Nov12	Day and night images of communication towers atop High Peak and cell tower and house on flanks, 20 mi. distant
SE (141)	4Nov13	Single flashing white light above High Peak, 20 miles distant; communication tower light
SW (218)	4Nov13	Single bright planet in evening sky above Hawksbill Mtn; Venus, 6:02 p.m.
SW (234)	11Nov13	Venus setting below ridgeline north of Hawksbill Mtn on east rim of Linville Gorge, 7:45 p.m.
SW (232?)	4Nov13	Single quick white flash well below Hawksbill Mtn on FS 210 or 496; vehicle headlight
WSW (245)	4Nov13	Moon setting over east rim of Linville Gorge; 8 percent crescent waxing; 6:18 p.m.
WSW (268)	4Nov13	Single stationary white lights on Jonas Ridge 2.3 mi distant with adjacent dim white lights; house lights
WNW (283–297)	4Nov13	8–12 Stationary lights on skyline of Jonas Ridge along Rd 1265 2.2 mi distant; house/street lights
NW (305)	4Nov13	Single isolated white lights (Cold Springs Community?); several dimmer white lights nearby; house lights
NW (318?)	11Nov13	Single isolated white light; house light
NW (323?)	11Nov13	Single isolated white light; house light
0–360	2012–13	Stars and airplanes in nighttime sky

Lights and Structures Observed from Gingercake Acres

The author has documented the following specific lights and structures visible from the location of our BML Cam1, which was mounted on the rooftop of a private residence on NC Highway 1265 on Jonas Ridge. The elevation of the house is 3,660 feet and the distance to the far eastern horizon is approximately 80 miles:

Line of Sight (Degrees Azimuth)	Date	Description of Lights and Structures (many seen only with magnification)
NE (45)	05Sep12	Maximum view to north
NE 40–50)	02Dec13	Nighttime images of distant lights on skyline; Blowing Rock, 17.8 mi.
ENE (75)	05Sep12	Summit of Chestnut Mountain; 4.3 mi.
ESE (95)	05Sep12	Brown Mountain overlook on NC Hwy 181; 2.2 mi.
ESE (98)	05Sep12	Summit of Adams Mountain; 7.9 mi.
ESE (98)	02Dec13	Nighttime image of summit of Hibriten Mountain, communication tower and Christmas star; 22.1 mi.
ESE (99)	05Sep12	Summit of Brown Mountain; 7.1 mi.
ESE (102)	28Nov12	Daytime image of large building in Lenoir over top of BM 19.2 mi. distant; Google Data Center
ESE (118)	02Dec13	Nighttime images of Hickory city lights; 33.7 mi.
SE (145)	02Dec13	Nighttime images of Morganton city lights; 17.9 mi.
SSE (175)	05Sep12	Maximum view to south

Lights and Structures Observed from Wiseman's View

The author documented the following lights and structures visible from Wiseman's View on NC Highway Old 105. Wiseman's View is located at 35.9039N, 81.9050W at 3,400-feet elevation and the distance to the far eastern horizon is approximately 77 miles:

Line of Sight (Degrees Azimuth)	Date	Description of Lights and Structures (many seen only with magnification)
NE (50)	1Dec12	Bright orange flames and small white light on Linville River, 0.5 mi. distant; campfire and headlight
NE (59)	10Dec13	Airplanes in sky above and hiker light on Hawksbill Mtn; 1 airplane with bright white landing light
NE-ESE (60–93)	1Dec12	Multiple colored lights in valleys east of BM; Lenoir and vicinity city/town lights
ENE (91)	1Dec12	Single flashing white lights on north side of summit of Hibriten Mtn, 23.5 mi. distant; communication tower
ENE (91)	1Dec12	Large yellow/orange light atop Hibriten Mtn, 23.5 mi. distant; Lenoir's Christmas star
ESE (92)	1Dec12	Line of close-spaced bright yellow/white lights over top of BM; Google Data Center building in Lenoir, 20 mi. distant
ESE (95?)	25Apr13	3 Stationary flashing white lights at early twilight; communication tower lights (may be 100 az?)
ESE (98)	21Aug13	Full moon in sky; 7:37 p.m.
ESE (115?)	25Apr13	Full moonrise in sky over Catawba Valley; 6:23 p.m.
ESE (120?)	24Jul13	Full moonrise in sky over Catawba Valley; 9:20 p.m.
SE (128)	23Jun13	Faint reddish light moving northward across sky north of Table Rock; airplane
SE (129)	23Jun13	Airplane in sky far beyond Table Rock
SE (130)	23Jun13	Several white lights atop Table Rock; hiker lights
SE (130)	24Jul13	Blinking moving white light in sky above Table Rock; airplane
SE (131)	10Sep13	Single slowly moving white light atop Table Rock; hiker light
SE (131.5)	21Aug13	Single slowly moving white light along summit trail on Table Rock; hiker light
SE (132)	21Aug13	Stationary orange and white light at campsite on Little Table Rock; campfire and camper lights
SE (135–137)	12Nov13	Forest fire on east rim of Linville Gorge immediately south of Table Rock
SSE (175–178)	1Dec12	Staged light tests on Shortoff Mtn 5 mi. distant, orange and white lights; campfire and two 130 lumen headlights
SSW (190?)		Slowly moving white lights and beams along Hwy 105 north of Dogback Mtn; vehicle headlights
SSW (208)	1Dec12	1,900 mm daytime images of communication towers on Linville Mtn, 6.4 mi. distant
S (180)	1Dec12	Numerous multicolored lights in Catawba Valley; city/town/residential lights
SE (129?)	23Jun13	Full moon in sky, 9:25 p.m.
NW-SE	23Jun13	White light slowly moving thru sky overhead; International Space Station on expected path
	25Apr13	Numerous buildings and water tanks/towers in Catawba Valley over top of BM
0–360	2012–13	Stars and airplanes in sky

Lights Observed from Bear Rocks, Brown Mountain

The author documented the following lights during an overnight visit to Brown Mountain in July 2013. Bear Rocks is an area of exposed rocks located at 39.9166N, 81.7677W at 2,520-feet elevation on the northwest side of Brown Mountain:

Line of Sight (Degrees Azimuth)	Date	Description of Lights and Structures (many seen only with magnification)
NNW (358)	17Jul13	Continuous white light moving in sky overhead; airplane with landing light
SW (220)	17Jul13	Single blinking white light above peak on skyline; Grants Mtn (Mt. Ida) communication tower
SW (222)	17Jul13	Multicolored lights and collective glow; city/town lights of Marion
SW (240)	16Jul13	Two stationary red lights stacked vertically on skyline above Linville Mtn; communication tower lights
WSW (260?)	16Jul13	Moon in sky over east rim of Linville Gorge, 11:17 p.m.
NNW (285)	16Jul13	Row of multiple multicolored lights on skyline on Jonas Ridge; house/street lights
0–360	2013	Stars and airplanes in sky

Lights Observed from Table Rock

The author documented a few of the many lights visible from the summit of Table Rock in June 2013. Table Rock is located at 35.8909N, 81.8829W at 3,920-feet elevation on the east rim of Linville Gorge:

Line of Sight (Degrees Azimuth)	Date	Description of Lights and Structures (many seen only with magnification)
unrecorded	29Jun13	Prominent row of close-spaced yellow/white lights; Google Data Center
unrecorded	29Jun13	Numerous stationary multicolored lights in Catawba Valley; city/town lights of Hickory
unrecorded	29Jun13	Numerous stationary multicolored lights in valley beyond BM; city/town lights of Lenoir
ENE (88)	29Jun13	Stationary single flashing white light above Hibriten Mtn; communication tower light
unrecorded	29Jun13	Stationary white light in woods below summit; lights of Outward Bound camp
unrecorded	16Oct13	Moon in eastern sky
0–360	2013	Stars and airplanes in sky

Prominent Landmarks and Features from NC Hwy 181 BM Overlook

The following list of azimuths and distances to some prominent landmarks and features from the NC Highway 181 Brown Mountain overlook is provided to assist researchers. Measurements were made by the author from direct personal observations and from topographic maps. Note that some features are not actually visible from the overlook. The overlook is located at 35.942N, 81.420W at 2,840 feet elevation and the distance to the far eastern horizon is approximately 70 miles:

Landmark	Azimuth (degrees)	Distance from 181 Overlook
Chestnut Mtn Summit	58.0	2.4 mi.
Sunrise @ Summer Solstice Jun 21	59.9	

Landmark	Azimuth (degrees)	Distance from 181 Overlook
Wilkesboro	68.8	40.0 mi.
Little Chestnut Mtn Summit	88.9	3.6 mi.
Taylorsville	92.1	37.0 mi.
Lenoir	96.0	17.1 mi.
Adams Mtn Summit	96.9	6.6 mi.
Hibriten Mtn (6 Towers)	98.5	20.0 mi.
Brown Mountain Summit	100.0	4.8 mi.
Statesville	101.3	54.8 mi.
Salisbury	103.3	79.1 mi. Beyond far horizon
Wildcat Knob Summit	106.0	3.7 mi.
Troutman	106.9	56.2 mi.
Hudson	108.5	20.7 mi.
Ralph Lael's Venus Rock	110.0	4.2 mi.
Mooresville	112.8	63.3 mi.
Granite Falls	113.4	25.2 mi.
Kannapolis	114.1	76.5 mi. Beyond far horizon
Conover	114.7	38.9 mi.
Wildcat Ridge Prospect Pit	116.0	3.7 mi.
Hickory	117.1	31.5 mi.
Concord	117.0	79.4 mi. Beyond far horizon
Hickory Regional Airport	118.8	29.0 mi.
Davidson	118.4	63.7 mi.
Newton	118.2	39.8 mi.
Sunrise @ Winter Solstice Dec 21	118.8	
Foothills Regional Airport	124.0	15.5 mi.
Icard	125.5	25.7 mi.
Connelly Springs	127.5	23.1 mi.
Baker's Mtn (Radio Towers)	128.7	31.5 mi.
Valdese	132.5	21.0 mi.
Drexel	135.5	18.7 mi.
South End of Brown Mountain	141.0	5.2 mi.
High Peak (6 Towers)	141.0	20.0 mi.
Morganton	149.0	16.7 mi. Beyond view to SE
Hawksbill Mtn	230.0	3.2 mi.
Sitting Bear Mtn	250.0	2.8 mi.
Gingercake Mtn	265.0	2.7 mi.

Prominent Landmarks and Features from Wiseman's View

The following list of azimuths and distances to some prominent landmarks and features from the Wiseman's View on NC Highway Old 105 (Kistler Memorial Highway) is provided to assist researchers. Measurements were made by the author from direct personal observations and from topographic maps. Note that some features are not actually visible from the overlook. Wiseman's View is located at 35.9039N, 81.9050W at 3,400-feet elevation and the distance to the far eastern horizon is approximately 77 miles:

Landmark	Azimuth (degrees)	Distance from Wiseman's View
Gingercake Mtn	18.0	2.5 mi.
Sitting Bear Mtn	25.0	2.0 mi.
Hawksbill Mtn	59.0	1.2 mi.
Sunrise @ Summer Solstice June 21	60.0	
Wilkesboro (map)	67.7	44.6 mi.
Adams Mtn (map)	76.0	9.7 mi.
Yadkinville (map)	76.8	72.0 mi. Beyond far horizon
North end of BM	77.7	8.7 mi.
Lenoir (map)	88.1	20.0 mi.

Landmark	Azimuth (degrees)	Distance from Wiseman's View
Taylorsville (map)	88.1	41.0 mi.
N. Bandy Cove Mtn (map)	89.8	2.9 mi.
Mocksville (map)	90.3	75.5 mi. Beyond far horizon
Hibriten Mtn (map)	91.2	23.3 mi.
Google Data Center (map)	92.0	20.1 mi.
Statesville (map)	98.0	58.1 mi.
Hudson (map)	99.7	23.3 mi.
Bandy Cove Mtn	100.1	3.4 mi.
Salisbury (map)	101.1	81.4 mi. Beyond far horizon
South end of BM	110.0	7.2 mi.
Granite Falls (map)	105.3	27.7 mi.
Foothill Regional Airport (map)	108.7	17.3 mi.
Conover (map)	109.1	42.1 mi.
Mooresville (map)	109.3	66.1 mi.
Hickory (map)	110.2	34.0 mi.
Kannapolis (map)	111.0	78.2 mi. Beyond far horizon
Hickory Regional Airport (map)	111.3	31.1 mi.
Newton (map)	112.7	42.0 mi.
Concord (map)	114.2	81.6 mi. Beyond far horizon
Davidson (map)	114.7	65.5 mi.
Hildebran (map)	115.5	30.0 mi.
Cornelius (map)	116.0	65.6 mi.
Rutherford College (map)	116.0	24.5 mi.
Icard (map)	116.4	27.4 mi.
Connelly Springs (map)	116.6	24.6 mi.
Sunrise @ Winter Solstice Dec 21	118.8	
Table Rock Mtn	121–134	1.6 mi.
Shortoff Mtn	160–178	5.0 mi.
Dogback Mtn	192.0	2.0 mi.
Linville Mtn Communication Towers	208.0	6.4 mi.

Prominent Landmarks and Features from Gingercake Acres

The following list of azimuths and distances to some prominent landmarks and features from the Appalachian State University camera (BML Cam1) on NC Highway 1265 on Jonas Ridge is provided to assist researchers. Measurements were made by the author from direct personal observations and from topographic maps. Note that some features are not actually visible from the overlook. The elevation of the observation site is 3,660 feet and the distance to the far eastern horizon is approximately 80 miles:

Landmark	Azimuth (degrees)	Distance from BML Cam1
Blowing Rock	40–50	17.8 mi.
Chestnut Mtn	75	4.3 mi.
181 Overlook	93	2.3 mi.
Adams Mtn	95.7	8.0 mi.
Lenoir	96.0	19.0 mi.
Hibriten Mtn	96.3	22.2 mi.
Christmas Star/Easter Cross	96.5	22.2 mi.
Caldwell Memorial Hospital	96.7	19.0 mi.
North End BM	98.1	7.1 mi.
Google Data Center	100.5	19.2 mi.
Wildcat Knob (BM)	100.6	5.9 mi.
Lick Mtn	101.0	24.2 mi.
Lael's Rock (BM)	103.1	6.3 mi.
Statesville Regional Airport	103.4	53.9 mi.

Landmark	Azimuth (degrees)	Distance from BML Cam1
Bradford Mtn	105.8	19.5 mi.
Bear Rocks (BM)	106.3	6.8 mi.
Hudson	107.0	22.7 mi.
Sawmills	111.0	24.2 mi.
Granite Falls	111.9	27.1 mi.
CMC-Northeast Stadium	112.2	79.6 mi.
Cajah Mtn	112.5	21.0 mi.
Hickory	~115	35.0 mi.
Morganton/Lenoir Airport	117	17.4 mi.
Hickory Airport	118.8	31.2 mi.
Connelly Springs	124	24.7 mi.
South end BM	130	7.9 mi.
Valdese and Drexel	~130	22.9 mi.
High Peak	136	21.6 mi.
Morganton	~145	17.8 mi.

Prominent Landmarks and Features from Bear Rocks, Brown Mountain

The following list of azimuths and distances to some prominent landmarks and features from the Bear Rocks on Brown Mountain is provided to assist researchers. Measurements were made by the author from direct personal observations and from topographic maps. Bear Rocks is an area of exposed rocks located at 39.9166N, 81.7677W at 2,520-feet elevation on the northwest side of Brown Mountain:

Landmark	Azimuth (degrees)	Distance from Bear Rocks
Marion		21.3 mi.
Grants Mtn (Mt. Ida)	215	21.0 mi.
Gingercake Acres Houses	284	6.8 mi.
Grandfather Mtn		14.0 mi.
Table Rock Mtn	252	7.0 mi.
Hawksbill Mtn	265	6.6 mi.

Prominent Landmarks and Features from Table Rock Mountain

The following list of azimuths and distances to prominent landmarks and features from Table Rock is provided to assist researchers. Measurements were made by the author from direct personal observations and from topographic maps. Table Rock is located at 35.8909N, 81.8829W at 3,920-feet elevation on the east rim of Linville Gorge:

Landmark	Azimuth (degrees)	Distance from Table Rock
Brown Mountain		
North end	70	7.6 mi.
South end	101	5.6 mi.
Far Eastern Horizon (excellent seeing)	110	76.7 mi.
Grandfather Mtn		14.2 mi.
Laurel Knob	314	2.5 mi.
Hawksbill Mtn	358	1.5 mi.
Wiseman's View	303	1.5 mi.
Hickory	280–295	34.5 mi.
Lenoir	83–91	19.7 mi.

Line-of-sight Azimuths and Compass Quadrants

Line-of-sight bearings (azimuths in degrees) as given in this appendix and throughout this book were determined with handheld and tripod-mounted compasses compensated seven degrees for west magnetic declination to give true north readings, or were taken from measurements of sight lines plotted on true-north topographical maps (USGS or USFS)—accuracy is +/- 5°. Compass quadrants listed in the previous sections are based on the following degree intervals:

0	N	North
0–30	NNE	North Northeast
31–60	NE	Northeast
61–89	ENE	East Northeast
90	E	East
91–120	ESE	East Southeast
121–150	SE	Southeast
151–179	SSE	South Southeast
180	S	South
181–210	SSW	South Southwest
211–240	SW	Southwest
241–269	WSW	West Southwest
270	W	West
271–300	WNW	West Northwest
301–330	NW	Northwest
331–359	NNW	North Northwest
360	N	North

Appendix B:
Light Sighting Report Form and Annotated Panoramas

Recording light sightings is a valuable contribution to any scholarly investigation of the BMLs. Unfortunately, most observations are not properly recorded and valuable information is lost. The human memory is not very reliable and memories commonly change or are lost over time. Recording the information at or near the time of the observation is the best way to provide critical information for future researchers. To assist in that effort, our BML research team compiled the following Light Sighting Report Form that suggests, and provides space for writing down, the critical information before it is lost or compromised by faulty memory.

The Light Sighting Report Form also includes detailed annotated panoramas of the distant views visible from two of the most popular observation sites—Wiseman's View overlook on NC Highway 105 and the Brown Mountain overlook on NC Highway 181. These diagrams provide the interested observer with detailed information about what is visible from the observation sites, including azimuth and distance measurements of the most important landmarks and distant cities and towns. With these diagrams, informed observers can accurately plot any light or lights they see, thus giving future researchers a clear understanding of the location or direction, or both, of the observed light/s.

Light Sighting Report Form

Sighting ID _____ (Use your own # system; use separate forms for each light or grouping of lights)

Date and Time of Sighting _____ am _____ pm   Date of this report _____

Observer: _____ (name, address, phone #, email)

Author of this report _____ (name, address, phone, email)

Observation Site 181 Overlook ____ Lost Cove Overlook ____ Wiseman's View ____

    Other _____

Azimuth of line of sight to light/s (if known or as determined later) ____ (degrees or N, S, E, W, NW, SSE, WNW, etc.)

Location of Light/s (if known or as determined later)_____

_____ Coordinates _____°N, _____°W (degrees Lat/Lon)

How location was determined_____

Elevation of light/s above ground _____ (vertically balled fist at arm's length = 10 degrees)

Light/s Below Horizon _____

Weather (fair, stormy, windy, clear, cloudy, partly cloudy, overcast, ground fog, rain, snow, etc.)
_____

Lightning (nearby or distant) No _____ Yes _____ Temperature _____°F

Photographed? Yes _____ No_____ Photographer _____ Image #s_____

Description of Light/s _____ # of Lights _____

    Color (white, red, orange, yellow, blue, green)_____

    Behavior (stationary, wobbling, dancing, movement, speed, constant, changing, fading, flaring, etc.) _____
_____

    Size, Shape, Burn Pattern (orb, flood, steady, flashing, beam, streak, etc.) _____
_____

    Mirage effect from rising heat waves? Yes_____No_____

    Length of burn (seconds, minutes, hours, all-night, etc.) _____

    Apparent Distance from observer _____

    Apparent Source/s of Light/s (explain why)

        Manmade

            Vehicle/s _____

            City/Town _____

            Residential _____

            Other _____

        Natural

            Celestial _____

            Bioluminescence _____

            Lightning (Nearby, Distant, Intense, etc.) _____

            Burning Gas _____

            Other _____

        Unknown _____

        Paranormal/Supernormal _____

Observational Aids

        Naked eye _____ Binoculars _____ Telephoto Lens _____ Telescope _____ Other _____

Other Witnesses _____ (name, address, phone, email)

NOTES (add more pages if needed)
_____
_____
_____

Light Sighting Report Form and Annotated Panoramas

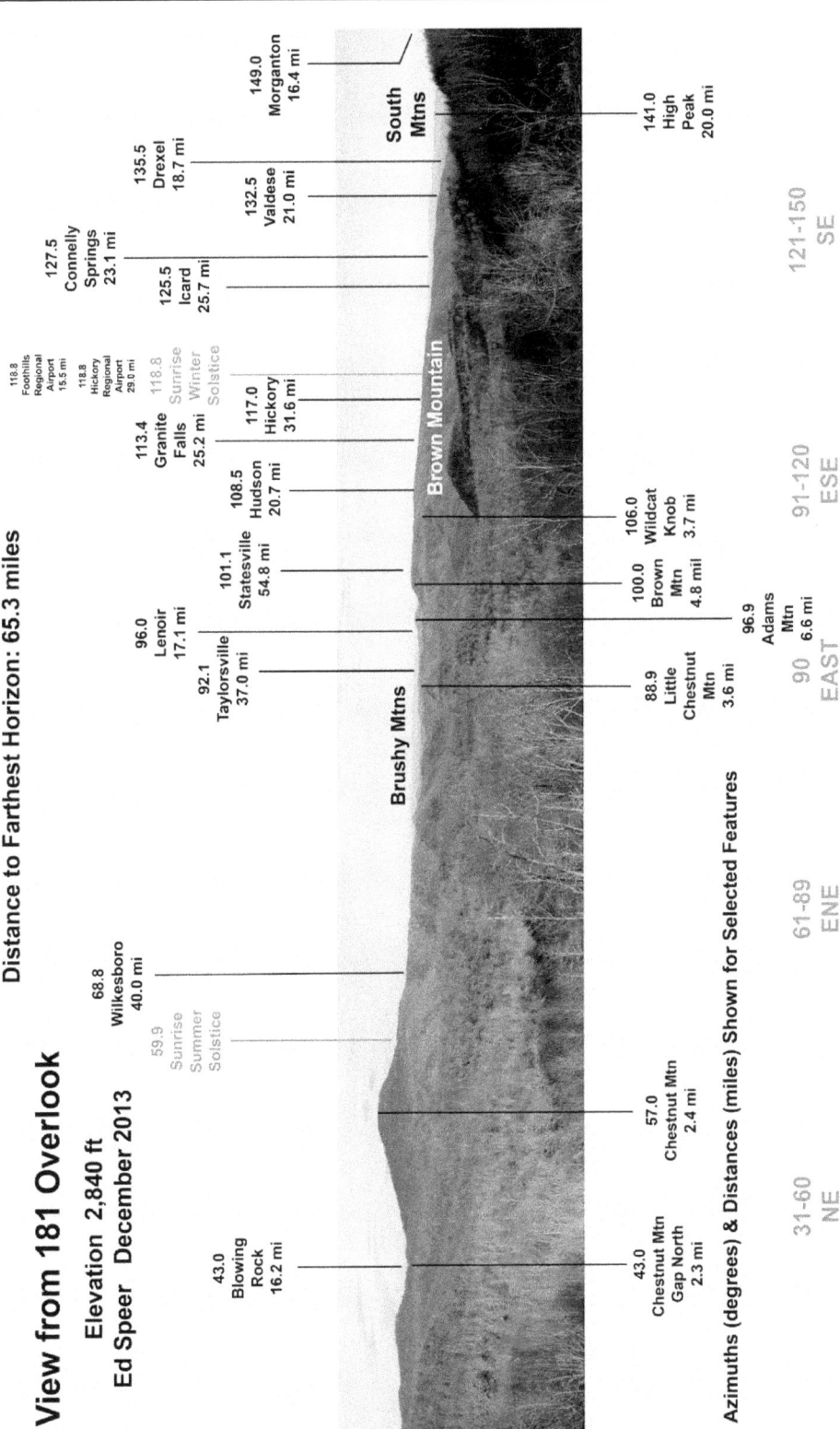

Appendix B

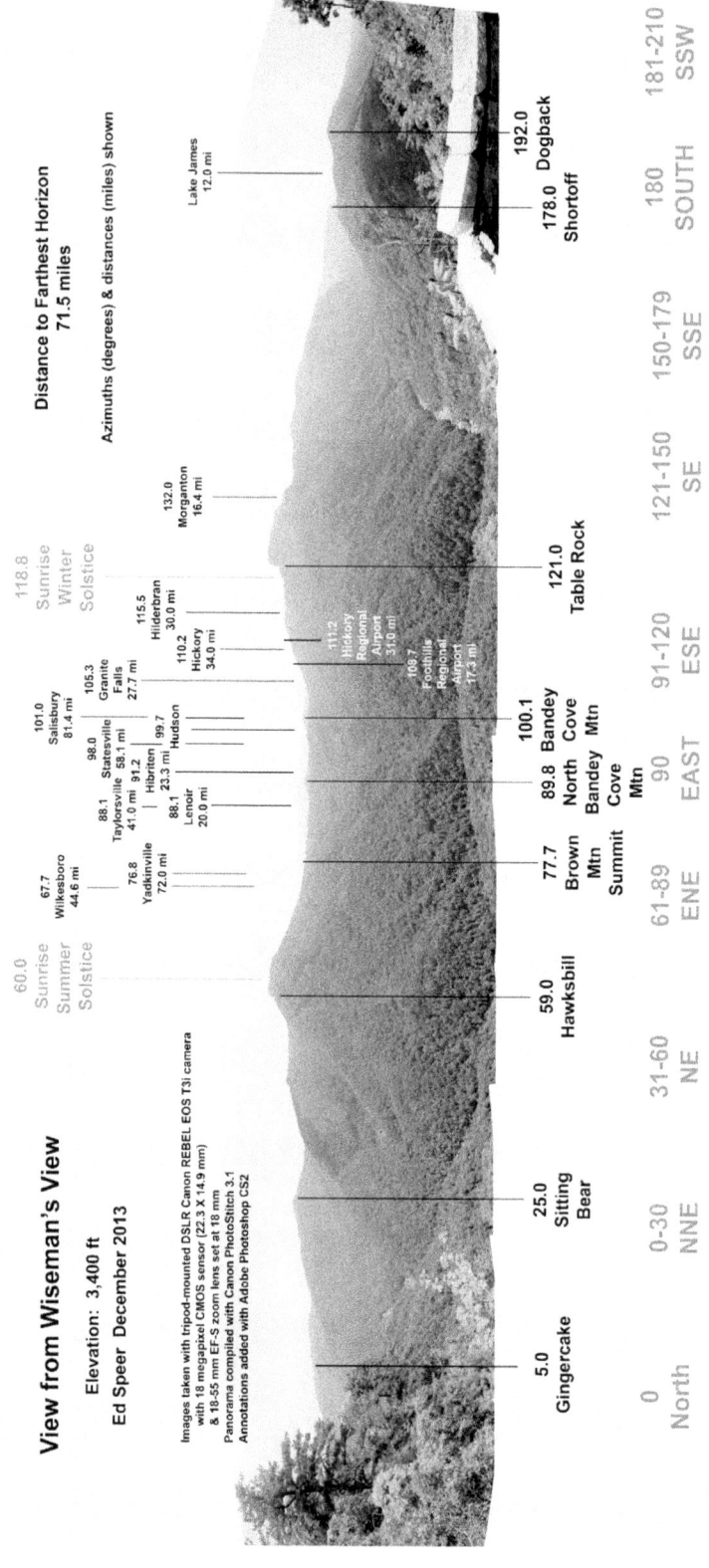

Appendix C:
Annotated Chronological List of Selected References

Brown Mountain Lights and Burke County History References (Arranged by Date)

The following documents cover many of the significant publicly available published and unpublished documents relative to the Brown Mountain lights. The references include books, historical letters, magazine and newspaper articles, and a few Internet Web sites. Annotations follow the bibliographic reference and direct quotes from the original manuscripts are given in quotation marks.

Web site documents are frequently changed or deleted altogether; however, some significant ones are included in the list of references by the date of publication. If there is no date of publication given, they are assigned the month and year they were reviewed.

Information regarding author, date, and the like is given if known.

Documents are listed chronologically by date to better facilitate the understanding of how the history of the Brown Mountain lights developed. Documents with the known year of publication but no month or day references are listed at the end of that year's collection of documents.

See Chapter 2 for a one-page summary of the history of the BMLs based on a detailed review of these and other references.

While most reviews were written by the author, the following people also contributed:

Dr. Cato Holler, Jr.
  de la Bandera, J., 1569, *The Bandera Document; Proceeding of the Account Which Captain Juan Pardo Gave of the Entrance Which He Made into the Land of the Floridas.*

Benita Soper
  Unknown Author, 1891, Blue Ridge Rambler, *Morganton* (NC) *News Herald*, March 13, April 23 and May 3, 1891.
  Scott, W.W., 1915, "Linville Gorge and the Mysterious Light on Brown Mountain," *Lenoir* (NC) *News Herald*; Lenoir, NC.

1569, April 1 de la Bandera, J. *The Bandera Document; Proceeding of the Account Which Captain Juan Pardo Gave of the Entrance Which He Made into the Land of the Floridas.*

On several different occasions during the sixteenth century, Spanish explorers passed through western North Carolina as part of their ongoing quest for gold and other precious metals. In recent years, local archaeologists have determined that the Berry Site, just northwest of

Morganton (and a few miles south of Brown Mountain), is more than likely the location of Joara, also known as Xuala. This was a very large Native American town visited briefly by Hernando de Soto in 1540 and again by Juan Pardo's expedition from 1567 to 1568. Pardo established a fort there known as Fort San Juan. This was the earliest European settlement to be established in the interior of what is now the United States (for additional information on the Berry Site see www.warren-wilson.edu/~arch/berrysite).

One of the best documentations of these early Spanish visits is an account of Pardo's second expedition. It was recorded by Juan de la Bandera (sometimes spelled Vandera), Pardo's scribe, and has become known as *The Bandera Document*. The original document is preserved in the Spanish Archivo General de Indias at Seville. In 1989, while searching the literature for possible early North Carolina cave references, I was able to order a copy of *The Bandera Document* through the North Carolina Division of Archives and History. It had been translated into English by Paul Hoffman. *The Bandera Document* is dated April 1, 1569, and is described as "proceeding of the account which Captain Juan Pardo gave of the entrance which he made into the land of the Floridas."

Bandera wrote in considerable detail about the expedition, recording their travels, contact and trade with the Indians, establishment of forts along the way, and the occasional location of "crystal mines." The document, although interesting, was written by the hand of a Spanish notary, an individual whose job it was to record hard, cold facts rather than a more readable journal of the exploration. For that reason, much of the document is somewhat tedious to absorb, as well as repetitious. Bandera carefully enumerated the specific trade items such as wedges, knives, colored fabric, and buttons left with each cacique (native chiefs) along the way in exchange for maize and the construction of wooden fortresses. With this said, the document provides a valuable insight into the daily travels of the explorers and their numerous hardships. These included dealing with Indian hostility, delays due to deep snows in the mountains, and having to wade through waist-deep icy swamps. More importantly, it provides clues as to the routes taken through our mountains.

After carefully re-reading the document, I was unable to find any reference to any phenomena that could be construed as being what we now refer to as the Brown Mountain lights.

Reviewed by Dr. Cato Holler, Jr.

1771 De Brahm, W.G. *Report of the General Survey in the Southern District of North America*. Tricentennial edition, no. 3. Columbia: University of South Carolina Press, 1971.

Although these Mountains transpire through their Tops sulphurueaous and arsenical Sublimations, yet they are too light, as to precipitate so near their Sublimitories, but are carried away by the Winds to distant Regions. In a heavy Atmosphere, the nitrous Vapours are swallowed up through the Spiraculs of the Mountains, and thus the Country is cleared from their Corrosion; when the Atmosphere is light, these nitrous Vapours rise up to the arsenical and sulphureous (subliming through the Expiraculs of the Mountains), and when they meet with each other in Contact, the Niter inflames, vulgurates and detonates, whence the frequent Thunders, in which a most votalized Spirit of Niter ascends to purify and inspire the upper Air, and a phlogiston Regeneratum (the metallic Seed) descends to impregnate the Bowels the Earth; and as all these Mountains form so many warm Athanors which draw and absorb, especially in foggy Seasons, all corrosive Effluvia along with the heavy Air through the Registers (Spiracles) and thus cease not from that Perpetual Circulation of the Air, corroding Vapours are no sooner raised, than that they are immediately disposed of, consequently the Air in the Appalachian Mountains is extreamely pure and healthy.

In this passage, De Brahm describes the health benefits of breathing the pure "Mountain Vapors" of South Carolina. The passage occurs in the South Carolina chapter of his book and he does not even describe North Carolina anywhere in the 325-page book. The influence on the health of the local inhabitants from breathing good air versus bad air is a repeated theme in the book, and elsewhere he describes, with similar flowery words, the poor health effects of breathing "Pond Vapors" (p. 79) and "Swamp Vapors" (p. 160) and goes on to suggest "a prudent and moderate use of Spirits" to offset the effects of living in an area where one is constantly breathing bad air.

1886 Verne, Jules. *Robur le Conquerant*. Originally published in French in 1886; published in English as the *Clipper of the Clouds* in Britain in 1887 and published as *Robur the Conqueror* in the United States in 1887. Various public domain versions are available online.

There is no mention of BMLs. Verne's science

fiction story includes Robur's trip around the world in his giant airship. Robur kidnapped 3 skeptical citizens and took them on the trip. In 2013 Ron Miller attributed this novel to the first-ever worldwide UFO scares and alien abductions that began in the 1890s, including mystery lights reported in California and Kansas.

1891 Unknown Author. *Morganton* (NC) *News Herald*, Blue Ridge Rambler, March 13, April 23, May 3, 1891.

These three articles describe the local mountains (including Linville Gorge and the surrounding mountain ranges) in great detail, naming and suggesting alternative Indian names for them. There is no mention of the BMLs even though the article expresses the need to "bait hooks (and hotels)" to entice tourists into the area.

1895 Dugger, S.M. *The Balsam Groves of the Grandfather Mountain: A Tale of the Western North Carolina Mountains, Together with Information Relating to the Section and Its Hotels, Also a Table Showing the Height of Important Mountains, etc.* Philadelphia: J.B. Lippincott, 1895.

There is no mention of BMLs, although later Dugger wrote and reported the first legends of a murdered wife. The book includes detailed descriptions of Grandfather Mountain and nearby mountains and rivers, including Linville River and Linville Gorge. No mention is made of murdered wife legend, as he reported elsewhere. Included is a journal of French naturalist Andre Michaux which makes no mention of BMLs.

1904 Verne, Jules. *Master of the World*. Originally published in French in 1904; published in English in 1911. Various public domain versions are available online.

Verne's science fiction story includes Robur's gigantic airship that he built inside a unique rocky-topped mountain (called the Great Ayrie) near Morganton, North Carolina (original French spelling is Eyre). Some later researchers think the Great Ayrie was actually Table Rock. According to the fictional story, locals unexpectedly began seeing mystery lights over the mountain that turned out to be those on the airship. This story was published 8 years before the first published BML stories in 1912. Thus the question arises: Did the BMLs inspire the fictional setting of Verne's *Master of the World* novel or did the novel inspire the legend of the BMLs? It seems unlikely Verne would have heard much, if anything, about the BMLs by 1904; however he may have read one or more of the 1800s travelogues that describe the unusual and unique mountain features of Linville Gorge and nearby mountains like Table Rock. Several features of the fictional story are found in later accounts of the BMLs: supposed volcano with deep crater, giant void or cave inside the mountain, danger to local residents, investigation by expert from U.S. government, noises and mystery lights, and so on. Mt. Mitchell is referred to as the Black Dome. Pleasant Garden is today's Pleasant Gardens in McDowell County, once part of Burke County. The Great Eyrie (probably Table Rock) is described as a steep-walled rock mountain never before scaled by man; it is barely over 5,000 feet in elevation. Actually Table Rock is slightly less than 4,000 feet in elevation.

1908, September 17 Unknown Author. "Strange Light in the Heavens." *Morganton* (NC) *News-Herald*.

An unknown light appeared in the sky west of Morganton on September 16, 1908, at 8 p.m. It is not known if this was a BML or not; it was not called a BML. BM is northwest of Morganton, so this light apparently appeared above the horizon toward Marion. The sky light fits the description of a meteor: "At first sight of the glow in the skies, two long bars could be seen. These gradually came together and the whole lingered for a few minutes before fading away."

1912, February 14 *Winston-Salem* (NC) *Western Sentinel*, "Asks Uncle Sam to Hunt Ghost in North Carolina."

Possibly the first published reverence to mysterious BMLs.

R.T. Claywell of Morganton wrote a letter to NC Congressman Webb asking for the government in Washington to send an expert to investigate a mysterious light. Claywell also asked that Red Buck Bryant also be sent to investigate.

A single strange light is seen every night about 9:00 p.m. from Cold Springs. "It rises up to the height of fifty feet and then gradually disappear … [and] seems to be about eight miles from Mr. Lovin's house." Rev. Gregory reported that when he saw the light last summer, it was so bright that it hurt his eyes like the sun.

Red Buck Bryant (Henry Edward Cowan Bryant, 1873–1967) was a North Carolina native who became a popular political correspondent in Washington, DC, for the *Charlotte Observer*, *New York World*, & *Boston Herald*. Upon retirement, he returned to North Carolina and wrote for the *Observer*. In 1922 & 1923, Bryant wrote about the BMLs for the *Charlotte Observer*.

1912, August 31 *Salisbury* (NC) *Evening Post*, "Mysterious Light Visible from Top of Blue Ridge" (also *Morganton Messenger*).

This is possibly the second published reference to mysterious BMLs.

Four local fishermen (E.B. Claywell, B.S. Gaither, S.R. Collett and Dr. I.P. Jeter) reported seeing a mystery light every clear night from Loving's hotel at Cold Spring. Gaither reported seeing the light two years earlier. "In appearance the light resembles a large incandescent light and is seen to shoot straight up from the earth every night about 9 o'clock, remaining stationary after reaching a high altitude, for about 15 to 20 minutes." Manmade electric lights of Morganton, Hickory and other places are reported to be plainly visible—but the mystery light is higher and brighter than the town lights.

1912, October 3 *Winston-Salem* (NC) *Western Sentinel*, "Mysterious Light in the County of Burke" (Linville Falls Dispatch to *Charlotte Observer*, Oct 3, 1912).

Possibly the third published reference to mysterious BMLs, a report is made of a single mysterious light seen just above the horizon almost every night from Rattlesnake Knob near Cold Spring. "With punctual regularity the light rises in a southeasterly direction from the point of observation, just over the lower slope of Brown mountain, first about 7:30 p.m. again about 20 or 30 minutes later and again at 10 o'clock." The light is described as being smaller than the full moon but larger than a star. Observers have to watch closely at the right time or they will miss the light. Anderson Loven reported that the light was visible in all seasons on clear nights. "There seems to be no doubt that the light rises from some point in the wide, level country between Brown mountain and the South mountains, a distance of about 12 miles, though it is possible that it rises a still greater distance."

1913, September 14 Manning, G.H. "Strange Light in Mountains Still Alarming: Remarkable Phenomenon Can Be Seen in Burke County; Spectator Gives Vivid Description." *Winston-Salem* (NC) *Journal*.

R.T. Claywell apparently played a significant role in the early development of the legend of the BMLs. He assisted in organizing the first U.S. Geological Survey investigation in 1913 (this article) and is mentioned as contributing helpful information for G.R. Mansfield's 1922 report of the second U.S. Geological Survey.

Jupiter, although visible to the SSE on the night of July 31, 1913, was probably not the light seen by the Claywell party. Jupiter rose at 5:43 p.m. and was probably about 25 degrees above the horizon to the south by 10:05 p.m. The moon set at 6:32 p.m. and thus it was a moonless night. Venus, Mars & Saturn all set in mid- to late-afternoon, before sunset, which occurred at 7:33 p.m.

Brown Mountain is only about 7–8 miles from the Cold Spring Hotel site, while the 12-mile distance to the light mentioned by Claywell would have placed it at a point in the valley to the east of Brown Mountain between Morganton and Lenoir. The community of Joy mentioned by Claywell was located at the south end of Brown Mountain only 8 miles from the Cold Spring Hotel site. Note that C.L. Wilson mentioned seeing the electric lights of Joy from Loven's Hotel in 1915 (Wilson, 1915). Claywell seems to dismiss possible fireworks, saying the light "did not cast off a particle of light"; i.e., it did not light up the surrounding landscape as a sky rocket or Roman candle would have.

The presence of one of the Loven family members (who surely made comparisons to other light sightings) and the assumption that the light occurred at the same time on previous nights suggest that this was not a one-time event; instead it apparently was a light that reappeared at the same time on successive nights. Logging was very active in the area in 1913 and may have been the source of the light. Trains had been operating in the Morganton area since the late 1850s and in the Lenoir area since the early 1880s. It's possible but not proven that the light seen by Claywell's party was a locomotive headlight on its regular nightly run.

1913, September 23 Harris, W.H., Col. "No Explanation," *Charlotte* (NC) *Daily Observer*.

This article is often incorrectly listed in the BML literature as the first written reference to the BMLs. The first U.S. Geological Survey investigation of the BMLs was conducted by D.B. Sterrett in October 1913. Colonel Wade H. Harris was the editor of the *Charlotte Daily Observer* in 1913; he also wrote a letter dated October 2, 1921, to NC senator F.M. Simmons (U.S. senator, 1901–1931) that was instrumental in persuading the U.S. Geological Survey to reinvestigate the BML legend in 1922 (Mansfield, 1922).

This document can be found online at www.dancaton.physics.appstate.edu/BML/CharObs 092413.htm.

It was first seen by members of the Morganton Fishing Club before 1911 and referred to as a single light arising from the Catawba Valley.

1913, October Sterrett, D.B. U.S. Geological Survey, Washington, DC, Unpublished Field Notes, 1913.

On a short field visit to Brown Mountain Sterrett did not interview witnesses. He determined the lights were locomotive headlights seen over the top of Brown Mountain. This explanation was not well received by locals. No report was issued.

1915, November 12 Unknown Author. "Strange Light Is Puzzle for Burke County"; Lenoir (NC) *News*, in *Mortimer, Edgemont Lenoir News, 1900–1919* by Sandra C. Coffey, Collettsville, NC: Self-published. August 1989 (revised 2004).

A peculiar night light, a ball, moves in straight lines and hovers and rises above trees. Lovill saw lights at his hotel from an unknown source. Government scientist Sterrett called it a train headlight but no one believes him.

1915, November 18 Scott, W.W. "Linville Gorge and the Mysterious Light on Brown Mountain," *Lenoir* (NC) *News Herald*.

This article describes in great detail the area in and around Linville Falls. It states the mysterious or unexplained light has been seen only from Loven's place and its appearance is limited to the two ends of the mountain. Reports had been current for nearly five years (since 1910), although Sidney Gaither of Morganton was the first to have seen them 8 or 9 years earlier (1906–1907). The light was reported to be seen most nights when the mountain was visible and although Scott was skeptical he witnessed the light on both the nights he was there.

1915, November 23 Martin, H.C. "The Brown Mountain Mysterious Light," Lenoir (NC) *Lenoir News*.

This was a general invitation to those interested in joining a BML investigative expedition. Organizational meeting set for 3:00 p.m. on November 27, 1915, at the Lenoir Drug Company store.

1915, December 14 Wilson, C.L. "Brown Mountain Light Still a Mystery and a Deeper One," Lenoir (NC) *Lenoir News*.

This was a report by C.L. Wilson to the *Lenoir News*: not a headlight, not one light, but many lights caused by some local force or combination of forces. Wilson observed from Loven's Hotel on Jonas Ridge beginning at 6:30 p.m. on December 8. The weather was cold with strong wind. Reflections of electric lights from towns of Joy near the south end of BM and Lenoir near the north end of BM could be seen at night. Previous observers believed the light rose on the east side of BM, but Wilson reported the light was visible on the west side of BM when it was first seen. The light was first seen by a party at Loven's Hotel about 10 years earlier (~1905) then was not mentioned again until about 1910 when Rev. Dr. Gregory saw the light every night from his cottage near Loven's Hotel during the summer, weather permitting. On the 8th, between 6:30 p.m. and 8:00 p.m. the light was seen by Wilson's 3-man party, including Mr. Loven, as many as 15 times, from 0.5 to 1.0 minutes each time. It resembled the morning star or a discharge from a sky-rocket or a distant person carrying a lighted lantern. Lights from Connelly Springs and Rutherford College were visible; but a signal light (by H.C. Martin) at Connelly Springs was not seen. The article discusses but dismisses the possibility that Hildebran Mountain, near Connelly Springs, is a volcano emitting flames that illuminated the entire surroundings south of Brown Mountain. Wilson believed the lights were a "bumper crop of jack o' lanterns."

1916, February 15 Bird, M.A. "Brown Mountain Light Developing into Greater Mystery," Lenoir (NC) *Lenoir News*.

Dr. Wilson is planning an expedition to BM to investigate the lights. Mr. M.A. Bird of Route 1, Morganton (near Brown Mountain), sent a letter to the *News Herald* newspaper in Morganton and it was reprinted in the *Lenoir News*.

This is the M.A. Bird story of mystery light. On night of January 19, 1916, Bird saw a light flash near the northeast end of Brown Mountain. The light sped to Table Rock mountain and then back to Brown Mountain with an obvious comet tail behind it. The light stopped moving several times and changed color and size several times. Bird and his family were totally baffled by the light. Bird reports seeing lights from a neighbor's house that night. Another time, he reports seeing another light that he thought was a train headlight.

1916, April 27 Pearson, W. "The Brown Mountain Lights—Mr. [H.C.] Martin Writes Interestingly of Preliminary Investigations Made Recently by Lenoir Party." *Morganton* (NC) *News Herald*.

Martin mentions that the BMLs have been known from sometime between 1871 and 1896. A camping party of 11 people set up 2 observation sites atop Adams's Knob and 3 sites on Brown Mountain. Four mystery lights were seen during the night of April 11–12, 1916.

All lights were seen for short durations and looked like Lenoir streetlights from a mile away. Two lights seen from Adams Mtn. at midnight were on the north slope of Brown Mountain, floating in and out of ravines and staying fairly close together, then turning around and retracing their path back to the starting point before disappearing.

The Brown Mountain parties did not see the midnight lights seen by the Adam's Knob party but did see similar lights at 8:10 p.m. 9:45 p.m. and 5:10 a.m. that were not seen by the Adam's Knob party. Martin mentions as possible sources meteors, shooting stars, contacts between warm and cold air currents, and atmospheric gases.

The description of the light behaviors suggests blue ghost fireflies.

1916, July 14–16   Bell, W.M. *The North Carolina Flood: July 14, 15, 16 1916.* Charlotte, NC: W.M. Bell, 1916.

The great flood was caused by a hurricane that came ashore at Charleston, SC, and passed directly over western North Carolina. Great damage occurred along all streams, with the Catawba River reaching more than 25 feet above flood stage. Most railroad and highway bridges were washed away.

1916, September 8   Loven, G.A. "The Brown Mountain Light Not Washed Away," Lenoir (NC) *Lenoir News*.

August 29, 1916, letter to the *Lenoir News* from G.A. Loven, Cold Springs, NC: "The light still appears every night now, for six years since it was first seen. It shows to be some four or five miles beyond the top of Brown Mountain."

Loven dismisses train headlights as the source of the light. The light varies from two to three miles either east or west and seems to go over the treetops 50 to 60 feet. Loven's letter insinuates that the light was first seen in 1910 and that it occurs beyond BM, not on BM.

1916, October 31   Elam, C. "Saw Brown Mountain Light 15 Times in Few Hours," Lenoir (NC) *Lenoir News*.

The story of Mrs. Carme Elam, of Morganton, first appeared in the *News-Herald* newspaper of Morganton, NC: Elam reports that on October 9, 1916, she and 4 others spent the night at Loven's Hotel just to look for the famous light and watched it for 6 hours. Its first appearance was 6:30 p.m. and 15 lights were seen over the next 45 minutes at 3 different places at the same time. A light was seen 4 times between 9 and 12 p.m. A full moon was shining.

1917, February 18   Unknown Author. "Brown Mt. Light now Belongs to Uncle Sam," Lenoir (NC) *Lenoir News*.

"Uncle Sam has bought the famous Brown Mountain Light, and in order to get the light, has bought the whole Brown Mountain, comprising about 4,000 acres."

1917, July 5   Houck, J. M. "Weird Explanation of a Weird Light, a New

Explanation of the Mysterious Light on Brown's Mountain—Story Narrated by John M. Huck and Copied from C.H. Hites in the *Charlotte Observer*," Morganton (NC) *News Herald*.

Bird Carroll story is that Carroll was a slave on a Wilson Creek farm. He made and sold brooms and baskets and buried the money. In 1864 and 1865, Bird and other slaves were drafted by the Confederate army. He died of disease at Wilmington, NC. Bird's mother reported learning in a dream 12 years later where Bird hid his treasure and she asked surveyor Hites to help her find it. Hites reported hearing stories from slaves who saw a mystery light on BM; they thought the light was Bird Carroll protecting his buried treasure. This is the first report of ghost lights.

1917, September 30   Duckworth, J.H. "Unknown Title," *Charlotte Observer*.

An uncanny pillar of light glows nightly on BM: phosphorescent vapor or gaseous radium emission; moonshiners.

1917, October 12   Unknown Author. "News in Condensed Form," *Shelby* (NC) *Cleveland Star*.

Brown Mountain, the site of recent mysterious light, was bought by the Federal government.

1919, December 15   Perry, W.G. "1919 Letter to Dr. C.G. Abbot of Smithsonian Institution," as reported in G.R. Mansfield, USGS Circular 646, 1922, p. 7.

We occupied a position on a high ridge. Across several intervening ridges rose Brown Mountain, some 8 miles away. After sunset we began to watch the Brown Mountain direction. Suddenly there blazed in the sky, apparently above the mountain, near one end of it, a steadily glowing ball of light. It appeared to be about 10° above the upper line of the mountain, blazed with a slightly yellow light, lasted about half a minute, and then abruptly disappeared. It was not unlike the "star" from a bursting sky rocket or Roman candle, though brighter.

We were impressed with the following facts: The region about Brown Mountain and between our location and the mountain is a wild, practically uninhabited mountain region—a confusion of mountain peaks, ridges, and valleys. Viewing the lights from a fixed position our estimate of their location was most inexact; the varying color (almost a white, yellowish, reddish) may have been due to mist in the atmosphere: the view of the lights was a direct one and not a reflection; there seemed to be no regularity in their time of appearance; they came suddenly into being, blazed steadily, and as suddenly disappeared; they appeared against the sky and not against the side of the mountain.

Others who have seen this phenomenon make very different reports of their observation; and some who have seen it several times report that they have seen it in varying fashion; sometimes the light appears stationary (as was uniformly the case when I saw it); sometimes it appears to move rapidly—upward, downward, horizontally [7].

W.G. Perry, a professor at the Georgia School of Technology at the time, was observing from Loven's Hotel in Cold Springs.

1921, April Lyman, H. "1921 Presentation to American Meteorological Society at the U.S. Weather Bureau in Washington, DC," as reported in G.R. Mansfield, USGS Circular 646, p. 5, 1922.

Dr. Herbert Lyman, of the U.S. Weather Bureau, gave a paper before the April 1921 American Meteorological Society meeting at the U.S. Weather Bureau in Washington, DC, based on concepts and ideas of Dr. W.J. Humphreys relating the BMLs to the Andes light. These ideas were later (1921) incorporated into a bulletin issued by the National Geographic Society.

1921, October 2 Harris, Col. W.H. "1921 Letter to Senator Simmons," as reported in G.R. Mansfield, USGS Circular 646, p. 4 and 7, 1922.

Light reported before the days of the Civil War.

"It is a pale white light, as one seen through a ground glass globe, and there is a faint, irregularly shaped halo around it. It is confined to a prescribed circle, appearing three or four times in quick succession, then disappearing for 20 minutes or half an hour, when it repeats within the same circle" [7].

Col Harris was the editor of the *Charlotte Daily Observer*.

1921, November 18 *Trenton* (NJ) *Evening Times*. "Brown Mountain Light Is Coming into Its Own as Natural Wonder."

A National Geographic Society bulletin quotes W.J. Humphreys (U.S. Weather Bureau) & calls the BMLs "Brush Lightning," an electrical phenomenon similar to St. Elmo's fire and Andes light.

BMLs were previously thought to be phantoms, locomotive headlights, or moonshiner fires.

1921, November 27 *Indianapolis Sunday Star*. "Mountain Light Comes into Own—North Carolina Phenomenon Once Regarded as Hoax, Electrical Fact."

This is the same news release about the National Geographic Society bulletin (brush lightning, similar to St. Elmo's fire and Andes light) reported elsewhere.

1921, December 21 *Oneonta* (NY) *Star*. "Mountain Light Is Like Aurora—Curious Electrical Display in North Carolina Excites Interest of Scientists."

This is the same news release about the National Geographic Society bulletin (brush lightning, similar to St. Elmo's fire & Andes light) reported elsewhere.

1921, December 24 *Newport* (RI) *Mercury*. "Mountain Light Is Like Aurora—Curious Electrical Display in North Carolina Excites Interest of Scientists."

This is the same news release about the National Geographic Society bulletin (brush lightning, similar to St. Elmo's fire & Andes light) reported elsewhere.

1922, January 12 *Statesville* (NC) *Record & Landmark*. "Brown Mountain Light Comes into Its Own."

This is the same news release about the National Geographic Society bulletin (brush lightning, similar to St. Elmo's fire & Andes light) reported elsewhere.

1922, January 15 Wichita [Falls] (TX) *Daily Times*. "The Flame-Clad Mountains."

This is the same news release about the National Geographic Society bulletin (brush lightning, similar to St. Elmo's fire & Andes light) reported elsewhere.

1922, March 25 Martin, H.C. "To the Editor of the Observer: Iredell County Light—Brown Mountain Light." *Charlotte* (NC) *Observer*.

Martin responds to H.W. Smith's March 21 article about an Iredell County mystery light that may be similar to the BMLs. Martin feels lights in both areas are due to refraction by air layers of differing densities.

1922, March Mansfield, G.R. "View of Brown Mountain and Vicinity, from Loven's Near Cold Spring, Morganton Quadrangle, Burke County, North Carolina, images 595 and 596." Washington, DC: U.S. Geological Survey image file, 1922. libraryphoto.cr.usgs.gov/

Two images of Brown Mountain from Mansfield's 1922 BML investigation.

1922, April 17 Unknown Author. No Title. *Statesville* (NC) *Record and Landmark*.

The last expert sent from Washington to investigate the "mysterious Brown mountain light" in Burke county has returned to Washington unenlightened as to the light. Several days and nights were spent in camp on the mountain but the mysterious light failed to light. Well, if the mystery is never solved, the people of that section of the State and others interested will have something left to imagination. If they had learned what produced the light, they would have been deprived of a talking point.

1922, April Jordan, M. Unknown Title. *Lenoir* (NC) *Davenport Weekly Record*.

"[T]he mysterious light on Brown Mountain ... has again been seen by the Burke County people." This recounts a June 8, 1908, visit by men from Morganton.

1922, May 7 Bryant, H.E.C. "Mansfield Saw Two Brown Mountain Lights—One Made by Southern Locomotive; Other Will Be Explained at a later Date." *Charlotte* (NC) *Observer*, May 7, 1922.

Washington, May 6—Mansfield arrived in Morganton on March 29 and met with Robert T. Claywell, who took him to see the light. Mansfield concluded his field works on April 7. Mansfield satisfied one light was train locomotive while another light was not a train. His report is forthcoming.

1922 Mansfield, G.R. *Origin of the Brown Mountain Light in North Carolina*; Washington, DC: U.S. Geological Survey Circular 646, 1922 (reprinted 1971).

The lights seen by Mr. Martin from Adams Mountain ... might be due to fireflies flying relatively near Mr. Martin yet appearing unduly large because his eyes were focused on the distant hillside, the appearance of going in and out of ravines being due to intermittence in the lights, but H.S. Barber, an entomologist of the Division of Insects of the National Museum, to whom the matter was referred, states that this explanation, though possible, is improbable, chiefly because of the lateness of the hour of observation [6].

There is nothing unique or unusual in the geology of Brown Mountain [2].

[N]o one has actually observed the light on Brown Mountain when he himself was on that mountain... [6].

The lights observed have nothing in common with the Andes light or with St. Elmo's fire. There is no geologic basis for the idea that the lights seen are natural wonders of any sort, but there are certain interesting surface features and atmospheric conditions that are effective in producing some of the appearances of the light [15].

The eye is easily deceived at night as to the stability or motion of an object, and an observer's impressions are to a considerable extent affected by his mental and physical condition at the time of observation. It is not surprising that under the circumstances different eyewitnesses give quite different accounts of the light, especially as the light may appear suddenly against a dark background with nothing nearby that can be used as a scale to determine its size or its possible motion [17].

In summary it may be said that the Brown Mountain lights are clearly not of unusual nature or origin. About 47 percent of the lights that the writer was able to study instrumentally were due to automobile headlights, 33 percent to locomotive headlights, 10 percent to stationary lights, and 10 percent to brush fires [18].

Mansfield's visit lasted 2 weeks in March & April 1922 and included 7 nights of observations.

Joseph Loven of Cold Springs and H.C. Martin of Lenoir were present for some of the nighttime observations.

The first written account is reported to be in the September 23, 1913, *Charlotte Daily Observer*, but we have found 1912 articles.

B.S. Gaither, a member of the fishing party mentioned in the 1913 article, reports that the lights were first seen in 1908 or 1909, not 1911 as reported in the 1913 article.

Rev. C.E. Gregory built a cottage in 1910 on Rattlesnake Knob, near Loven's Hotel at Cold Springs and was the first person to bring the lights to public notice.

Mansfield quotes several longtime residents as not seeing or hearing of the lights until 1910 & 1913. Col. Wade H. Harris, editor of the *Charlotte Daily Observer*, states in an October 2, 1921, letter to Senator Simmons that the light was seen before the Civil War.

Joseph Loven of Cold Springs reports seeing the lights in 1897 when he moved to a home near Loven's Hotel but paid then no attention until Rev. C.E. Gregory came in 1910.

There are mentions that the flood of 1916 did not stop the lights, disproving the locomotive headlight theory.

In late 1919, Smithsonian Institution and the U.S. Weather Bureau, without visiting the area, concluded the cause was an electrical discharge like the "Andes light" of South America.

Mentions of 2 buildings on BM & several more on the lower slopes indicate lights from these could be BMLs. Also, lights from lumber camp buildings in Upper Creek & Ripshin Ridge may look like BMLs.

Mansfield observed & took line-of-sight-azimuths from 3 stations: (1) C.E. Gregory's former cottage near Loven's Hotel at Cold Spring (March 29, accompanied by Joseph Loven, Robert Loven, Earl Loven, and Robert Ward); (2) a field on the east slope of Gingercake Mountain (April 1, 2, accompanied by Joseph Loven and Robert Ward); and (3) a summer residence at Blowing Rock (April 3, 4, accompanied by H.C. Martin and Robert Ward).

Although Brown Mountain was visited, no measurements were made from Brown Mountain itself.

All of the lights measured by Mansfield were located in the Catawba River Valley south of Brown Mountain, thus they appeared above the crest of the mountain.

Using a train schedule, Mansfield actually predicted the appearance of a light over Brown Mountain within 8 minutes of its actual appearance, and later confirmed the train was 8 minutes late that night. Joseph Loven declared it was one of his BMLs.

Apparently the numerous lights visible from the Blowing Rock station were manmade lights from towns beyond Brown Mountain (H.C. Martin felt they weren't the same as his BMLs).

Mansfield describes refractions of valley lights due to varying air current densities (temperature, moisture, dust, and the like) that cause color changes, wavering, extinguishing, flaring, etc.

Electric lights have been in use in the area since ~ 1892.

Powerful headlight use on locomotives began ~1909.

Recently arrived automobiles produced some of the light sightings.

Automobile headlights were the probable source of lights seen immediately after the flood of 1916.

Mansfield measured 23 lights, but he mentions twice that number were seen.

Seven measured lights were definitely locomotive headlights (up to 600,000 candlepower) based on train schedules and line of sight azimuths.

This report is one of the most scientific collections of data and explanation of the BMLs ever written.

1923, February 13 Unknown Author. "Brown Mountain Lights Simple if You Can Grasp Big Words." *Greensboro* (NC) *Daily News*.

"Charles A. Logan of Morganton says they are result from radium emanations in contact with currents—it's an occult or psychic center, being Grandfather's sister."

1923, February 17 Bryant, H.E.C. "Strange Brown Mountain Lights Divide Scientists." Washington, DC: *Washington Post*.

Mansfield's report that he found nothing unusual about the lights produced controversial: 47 percent automobile headlights, 33 percent locomotive headlights, 10 percent stationary lights, 10 percent brush fires. National Geographic Society favors "brush lightning" origin. NC senator Overman requested that the U.S. Geo Sur conduct the investigation.

1923, February 18 Bryant, H.E.C. "Mysterious Brown Mountain Lights Yet to Be Explained." *Charlotte* (NC) *Observer*.

Mansfield's report that he found nothing unusual about the lights produced controversy: 47 percent automobile headlights, 33 percent locomotive headlights, 10 percent stationary lights, 10 percent brush fires. National Geographic Society favors "brush lightning" origin. NC senator Overman requested that the United States Geological Survey conduct the 1922 investigation. Sterrett's 1913 investigation was requested by NC representative E.Y. Webb. Mansfield's report did not resolve the lights and was not be accepted by many observers.

1923, March 8 Haskin, F.J. "The Haskin Letter," *Helena* (MT) *Daily Independent*.

This article says reports of mystery lights go back to Civil War; they never did anyone harm; and lights glowed over BM with quite punctual regularity every night: "sometimes it would glow as fitfully as a firefly."

Rejected explanations include a gigantic manifestation of the will-o'-the-wisp, phosphorus, radium emanations, mineral chemical reaction, St. Elmo's fire, mirage, Andes light, and moonshine stills.

Mansfield proved the light comes from the Catawba Valley, not from Brown Mountain. He charted railroads and highways in the Catawba Valley and studied the effect of heat of the day & the cool of the night on the air currents. With alidade, telescope, camera, etc., he charted line of sight of the lights and found they matched train tracks & automobile roads.

The real solution of the mystery was Mr. Mansfield's discovery that at nightfall, the cold air currents on either side of Brown mountain crept down into the valleys, producing extraordinary atmospheric effects which resulted in refracting, magnifying, sometimes coloring and at all times distorting any light seen through this strange veil. A headlight, instead of showing a beam, as usual, would, through the veil of twisted air, show like a ball of seething light. Two automobile headlights would show as one nebulous and furtive illumination. Strange effects would be produced by the locomotives or automobiles turning curves.

1923, March 8   Haskin, F.J. "Carolina Mountain Light Called Forth Request for United States' Assistance," *Iowa City-Press*.

Same news release published in the *Helena Daily Independent*, March 8, 1923 (see above).

1923, May 14   *Statesville* (NC) *Record and Landmark*. "Camps on Brown Mountain—Brown Mountain Light Isn't on Brown Mountain."

This was originally published in the *Morganton News-Herald*, which sent reporters out to find the BMLs. "[T]he Brown Mountain light still remains a mystery. We went, and we saw, but we found difficulty in conquering."

"It ain't on Brown Mountain." The reporters saw the light from Cold Springs at azimuth south 37 degrees east. They then camped on highest peak of BM & again saw a light to the east, midway between Drexel & Lenoir. "Of course lights in the valley can be seen from the higher mountains, but we are not speaking about them. We are talking about that light seen before the time of automobiles, and during the near flood here in 1916, when there was not a train running between Salisbury and Asheville. That light has a reddish glow and seems to come from nowhere and go to the same place. From Brown Mountain we could see artificial lights plainly, but it was also easy to see that they were artificial lights."

1924, December 18   *Frederick* (MD) *News*. "How Mystery was Proven."

This is a short article describing a *Nature* magazine article about Andes light: "A few years ago American meteorologists thought they had found an example of this striking phenomenon in North Carolina, but the once mysterious 'Brown mountain lights' have been proven to be merely the beams of distant locomotive and automobile headlights or due to other human agencies."

1925, April 13   Koon, J. "Scientist Finds Explanation for Brown Mountain Lights." *Charlotte* (NC) *Observer*.

This is a report Mansfield's 1922 finding that only car, train, & manmade lights occur solves the mystery of the BMLs.

1925, May 15   *Chehalis* (WA) *Bee-Nugget*. "Light Mystery Solved."

The same short article was published in the December 18, 1924, *News* (see above).

1925, November 7   Schlosser, J. "The Queer Lights on Brown Mountain" (*Literary Digest*, November 7, 1925), in *Remarkable Luminous Phenomena in Nature: A Catalog of Geophysical Anomalies*, compiled by William R. Corliss, Sourcebook Project (Glen Arm, MD: 2001).

This is a summary of past light sightings: since about 1850; varying in size and color; rising up over the mountain before disappearing; as many as 3 lights visible at different locations at the same time; sighting frequent in fine weather but also seen in foggy conditions.

On September 17, the author saw 3 types of lights—different colors, flashes and on/off sequences.

1925, January 17   *Denton* (MD) *Journal*. "Light Mystery Solved."

This same short article was published in the December 18, 1924, *News* and the May 15, 1925, *Chehalis Bee-Nugget* (see above).

1926, May   Chater, M. "Motor-Coaching Through North Carolina: The Brown Mountain Light Mystery." *National Geographic* 49 (May 1926), 517–518.

Lights appear over the top of BM, various colors, singly or in succession, suddenly winking out, often several lights together, 15–60 seconds; also some are stationary for 10–20 minutes. The first written record was in 1913, but the lights were seen before Civil War; 1921 U.S. Weather Bureau investigation—Andes light. Other theories: phosphorescent or radium emanations, moonshine stills, St. Elmo's fire, mirage and vehicle lights. USGS investigation in 1922. Today the BMLs mysteriously appear & disappear in the Catawba Valley.

1927, February 15   Unknown Author. "Eerie Light That Plays Across Brown Mountain Mystery for 50 Years." *Asheville* (NC) *Citizen* (now *Citizen-Times*).

This contains the first mention of The Adams Mountain Light! A local resident saw light coming from a house on Adams Mountain. The article mentions USGS 1922 study, St. Elmo's fire, Andes light, phosphorous, phosphorescence, will-o'-the-wisp, radium emanations, chemical reactions hydrogen sulphide & lead oxide, whiskey stills, mirages, marsh gas, headlights, train lights, house lights. There are no references and no new information.

1927, March 7   *Statesville* (NC) *Record and Landmark*. "Brown Mountain Light Mystery— The Argument as to the Origin of the Mysterious Light Goes Merrily on Around Blowing Rock."

This is the same news release as published in February 15, 1927, *Asheville Citizen* (see above). It mentions the Adams Mountain light and says the USGS & National Geographic Society give different origins. It mentions that city lights and automobile & train headlights can be seen in Catawba Valley from Blowing Rock.

1927, May   Chater, M. "Motor-Coaching Through North Carolina." *National Geographic* (May 1927), 517-8 (also reported to be on p. 51–78 49 [1926]).

This is a general summary of past reported light sightings and says they were seen before Civil War. It also reviews the Mansfield 1922 results.

1927, December 15   Babington, R.K. "Some History of Famous Brown Mountain Light," December 13, 1927, letter to editor of the *Gastonia* (NC) *Daily Gazette*.

R.K. Babington (Atlanta, GA) BML scrapbook of newspaper articles 9 years in the making. There is a 1772 De Brahm reference, the first known reference! This reference must have come from one of Babington's newspaper articles in his scrapbook. This is amazing, as I believe the De Brahm document was a handwritten document at that time.

About 10 years earlier (c. 1917) a resident of Laundale reproduced the lights with his car headlights, which were seen by observers at Loven's Hotel.

There are references to coal vein gas; National Geographic Andes light; 1922 USGS study.

J. Penland (Linville Falls, NC) June 16, 1922, letter: Stokes saw the lights 40 years ago (c1882).

Babington ends his article with "Quod erat demonstrandum," which means "the completion of a proof," generally given as Q.E.D.

1928, April 30   *Statesville* (NC) *Record and Landmark*. "Says Light Not on Brown Mountain."

J.B. Derieux (professor of physics at NC State College, Raleigh) addressed the 27th annual meeting of the North Carolina academy of science in Chapel Hill on April 27:

The light is not on Brown Mountain, but is a light in the valley beyond. Derieux attributed the light to the town of Hudson, which is directly beyond the mountain from Cold Springs. The light was reportedly seen for the last 50 years; he mentions previous explanations such as phosphorescent gas from an old copper mine on BM, moonshiner lanterns, and gas from foliage of the trees.

With binoculars, Derieux found that the light did not come and go but instead burned steadily, and it did not move about but remained in one spot.

"With surveyor's instruments they then plotted a magnetic line directly across Brown Mountain where the light was seen. This showed that the little town of Hudson was in direct line and led them to give the explanation that it is an electric light in Hudson that is seen."

1929, August 25   Coleman, Jr., J.S. "Strange Light Continues to Mystify; Rays Visible Every Evening on Brown Mountain." *Asheville* (NC) *Times* (now the *Citizen-Times*).

The article makes reference to first known photo of the BMLs, by E.M. Ball, a photographer with Plateau Studio, Asheville.

Ball took pictures from a point not far from Marion and exposed a very sensitive color plate one night over a period of four hours.

"During that time, the moon, sliding across the sky, left a bright streak on his plate, but the mysterious Brown Mountain lights had been caught in the meantime. One thing established by the photograph is the fact that the light appears at several parallel points along a line near the summit of Brown Mountain. Each of the points seems to be a small disk of light, though the impression given an observer is that of a blaze."

Coleman goes on to mention the USGS & National Geographic Society studies and how unpopular they were with the local inhabitants. He also mentions phosphorescence, radium emanations, & gaseous discharges as possible causes.

Ball's famous first known BML photo is housed in the E.M. Ball Collection at UNC Asheville's D.H. Ramsey Library Special Collections & University Archives. It can be found online at toto.lib.unca.edu/findingaids/photo/ball/ball.htm.

1929 Ball, E.M. *Brown Mountain Lights, from Wiseman's View near Linville Falls.* Image N1503, E.M. Ball Photographic Collection (1918–1969), Special Collections, D.H. Ramsey Library, University of North Carolina at Asheville.

The photograph is believed to be to oldest known image of the Brown Mountain lights. The 4-hr time exposure on glass plate shows a full moon streak. This image was described in the August 25, 1929, *Asheville Times* article (Coleman, Jr., 1929).

1930? *The Guide to the Old North State,* Works Project Administration (WPA), Unknown reference (Info from Odenwald, S., 2001), c1930.

Mystery lights have puzzled scientists for fifty years. Reports sightings before the Civil War.

1932, September 13 Ruggles, F.D. *Charlotte* (NC) *Observer.*

Ruggles saw hundreds of lights on the side of BM, not above it.

1932, September 30 Ruggles, F.D. "Another Angle on Brown Mountain Lights Offered." *Statesville* (NC) *Record & Landmark.*

As reported in the *Charlotte Observer*, an engineer from Elizabethton, TN, Frank D. Ruggles visited and observed with field glasses from a summer home near Loven's Hotel. Then he climbed Hawk's bill & returned to the summer home in the evening to find lights:

> "You may imagine my complete surprise at finding a triple row of lights approximately thirty-five miles in length, twinkling brightly on the mountain side which we had previously found to be void of habitation."

He (Mansfield) speaks of the Brown Mountain "Light." Why not "Lights," as there were actually hundreds of them, clearly and distinctly visible to the naked eye? Looking at these lights, we found that they did not vary in intentness, though they did appear and disappear from time to time. At no one time did all of them disappear though they each one seemed to come and go at irregular intervals. Seen through the glasses they did girate at all times and not only that but appeared like strong city street lights supported on limber poles which appeared to sway (all in one direction), with a gust of wind. In fact, these lights appear to me far more like the result of fumes of some incandescent form than anything else that I can think of.

1935, March 12 Harris, W.H., Col. "Opportunity to Attract Tourists." *Hickory* (NC) *Daily Record.*

As reported in the *Sunday Charlotte Observer*, reference is made to Brown Mountain Light, not Lights. The writer suggests making BM a tourist attraction with observation towers. Senators Simmons and Overman prevailed on the U.S. Geological Survey to send geologist George Rogers Mansfield in 1922. The writer believes lights were seen before days of electricity and dismisses Mansfield's 1922 report because he did not interview everyone who had seen the light.

"Back in 1913, Congressman E. Yates Webb became interested in an editorial discussing in *The Observer* on the mysterious light and was instrumental sending Professor Sterrett, a member of the United States Geological Survey, down into the region of the light. Another thing, the Brown Mountain glow *(Light)* is but a single globe."

1936, May 7 Northrop, M. "Brown Mountain Light Is Still Creating Wonder and Speculation." *Hickory* (NC) *Daily Record.*

As originally published in *The State* magazine: The mystery light is reported differently by various observers. It mentions the USGS investigation of 1922; 1916 flood; reflected lights of Hudson; lights before electricity; Andes light; mirages due to reflected moonlight & starlight; and sulfur springs (including local spas). Burning hydrogen sulphide gas & lead oxide ore is considered the best theory.

1936, March 9 Dugger, S.M. "Letter dated March 9, 1936, to Mr. J. Marion

Saunders, Secretary of the General Alumni Association, Univ. of North Carolina, Chapel Hill, N.C.," in *The Bard of Ottary: The Life, Letters and Documents of Shepherd Monroe Dugger*, by Leslie Banner Cottingham and Carol Lowe Timblin (Banner Elk, NC: Puddingstone Press, 1979), 120–121.

Here appears the story of murdered wife, about 75 years earlier (c. 1861), Barrier's wife of Jonas Ridge went missing; 25 years ago bones were found by hunters 3 miles from Barrier's house on Cold Mtn. BMLs are believed to be her spirit leading the searchers toward her missing body.

1936, October 17 Unknown Author. "Brown Mountain Lights Amazing to Hickory Man." *Hickory* (NC) *Daily Record*.

Mystery lights were recently seen by Simon W. Long of Hickory while visiting Loven's Hotel on a clear & moonless night. It claims reflection of lights from Hudson cannot be the source and dismisses train headlights, hydrogen sulphide/lead ore gas, and mirages.

"To our utter amazement, the horizon was brilliantly illuminated for a long distance by the most famous 'Brown Mountain lights.'"

1937, August 28 Unknown Author. "Tells Legend of Brown Mountain: Shepard M. Dugger, Author of Mountain Books, Recounts Story of Superstition About Famous Lights." Blowing Rock (NC) *Blowing Rocket*.

Dugger's detailed story of the murdered wife legend is recounted.

1937, September 2 Glovier, M. "Tells Legend of Brown Mountain: Shepard M. Dugger, Author of Mountain Books, Recounts Story of Superstition About Famous Lights." Boone (NC) *Watauga Democrat*.

Dugger's detailed story of the murdered wife is given. This article is apparently a reprint of the August 28, 1937, article in the *Blowing Rocket* and the August 29, 1937, article in the *Charlotte Observer*.

1937 Dugger, S.M. "1937 Legend of Murdered Wife" (Information from Odenwald, S., 2001).

In the Jonas Ridge community, a wife was murdered c. 1887. The body was not found, and the husband was suspected. Searchers saw mystery lights and believed them to be her spirit haunting her killer. Years later a headless body was found and the lights were then believed to be the wife's soul searching with a lantern for her head.

1938, June 5 McAfee, H. "Mysterious Lights of Brown Mountain Seen at This Time of Year." *Asheville* (NC) *Citizen-Times*.

Walking toward the lights makes them disappear; spring is the best time to observe; photographs are impossible to take. The article mentions refraction of artificial lights; lights from cabins; moonshiners; jack-o'-lanterns; mineral emanations; gas; etc., and Shepherd M. Dugger's story of the murdered wife. It is possibly the first written mention of ghosts of Indian maidens after the Cherokee/Catawba battle of AD 1200.

1940, August 11 Whitman, H. "Brown Mountain Lights Have Not Disappeared." *Charlotte* (NC) *Observer*.

Same article as McCoy 1940 (see below).

1940, August 31 *Gastonia* (NC) *Daily Gazette*. "Brown Mountain Lights used as Background for Mystery Novel."

W.W. (Andy) Anderson, author of *Kill One, Kill Two*, uses BMLs as a background mystery in his novel. Various legends & Mansfield's conclusions are given.

1940, October 11 Whitman, H.A. "Letter to managing editor of the *Asheville Citizen*."

This letter is the source of the November 10, 1940, article by George W. McCoy in the *Asheville Citizen*.

1940, November 10 McCoy, G. "Study Substantiates Theory of Brown Mountain Lights." *Asheville* (NC) *Citizen*.

This article includes excerpts from Whitman's October 11, 1940, letter to the *Asheville Citizen*. BMLs caused by artificial lights influenced by atmospheric phenomena are substantiated by the most recent scientific research by Hobart A. Whitman of Asheville, NC, who found the same thing as Mansfield. The first written account was the 1913 *Charlotte Observer* article. Natural theories most favored by locals, but the exact cause is unknown. All were dismissed by Mansfield.

"There is really no mystery about the lights, only a natural phenomenon brought about by looking at artificial lights through atmospheric conditions peculiar to the area around these lights ... the lights must be artificial."

Whitman concludes the lights originate in artificial lights influenced by atmospheric phenomena. He used telescopic transit triangulation of several lights from several observation sites (Table Rock, Wiseman's View, & Grandmother Mountain), plotted on topographic maps:

The largest light ... centered over Hickory, 40 miles away; the second light intersected over Valdese, and the third light a little southwest of Morganton. The clusters of smaller lights ... line up with small towns in the large expanse of the Catawba River basin between the northern mountain ridges and South Mountains. A few lights that appeared and disappeared, always in the same location ... must originate along roadways.

By lining up the transit on the ridge of Brown Mountain while it was still daylight, I knew when the lights appeared if they were actually on Brown Mountain or somewhere beyond it. All the lights were beyond Brown Mountain and the nearby ridges when they began to show. From Wiseman's View where so many lights seem to be along the Brown Mountain ridge the actual location is somewhere beyond, and triangulation shows the lights to originate along the slopes of South mountains as in Hickory, Valdese, and Morganton. I am convinced that there are no "Brown Mountain Lights" on Brown Mountain.... Now the question is: What are the lights?

Whitman analyzed rocks on BM & found no unusual elements.

The article includes a photo by Whitman of BMLs from Loven's Hotel: one-hour time exposure (9:30–10:30 p.m.); full moon, two lights visible above BM.

Apparently a photo identical to Whitman's was taken in 1929 by an Asheville photographer (Coleman's August 25, 1929, article in the *Asheville Times* about E.M. Ball's photo?). Whitman reports that the bright light in both photos is the ballpark in Hickory: "The lights are absolutely stationary and they only appear to rise up and move around when you imagine them to do so."

He concluded magnification & refraction of the valley lights, when seen from the mountains, gives rise to the BMLs.

1941, April Humphries, W.J., Dr. "1941 Lecture before the American Meteorological Society." Unknown publication (info from Odenwald, S., 2001).

Dr. Humphries (U.S. Weather Bureau) concluded the BMLs were similar to the Andes light of South America.

1941, April Lyman, H., Sr. "1941 Lecture Before the American Meteorological Society." Unknown publication (info from Odenwald, S., 2001).

Dr. Lyman (U.S. Weather Bureau) concluded the BMLs were similar to the Andes light of South America.

1941, August 4 Weir, L. "Brown Mountain Lights Still Seen as Ghosts Walking." *The Statesville* (NC) *Record & Landmark*.

The article mentions various legends, including moonshiners, the murdered Jonas Ridge wife, Catawba & Cherokee Indian legends of the AD 1200 battle & Indian maidens searching for their husbands killed in battle, and compares BMLs to the Maco light.

1942, November 15 Chapman, A. *Charlotte Observer*.

"In the year 1200, a great battle was fought between the Catawba and Cherokee in the vicinity of Brown Mountain. 'The lights are the spirits of the Indian maidens hunting their husbands and sweethearts who died in the battle.'"

1943 Goerch, C. "The Brown Mountain Lights." *Down Home* (Raleigh, NC: Edwards & Broughton Co., 1943).

Casual observation was made at Wiseman's View. A few lights were seen, but no specific details were given.

1948, June "The Lights of Brown Mountain," in *North Carolina Folklore* 1, no. 1 (June 1948).

This is possibly the first mention of the Lost Lover legend:

A young man fell in love with a mountain girl who lived with her father on Brown Mountain. He visited her nightly, coming through the dangerous woods from his village. They agreed to marry. On the evening of their departure she lit a pine torch and went to greet him. He never returned and she took a torch out every night crossing back and forth on Brown Mountain to look for him [no date].

1948, August 11 Cobb, B. The *Gastonia* (NC) *Gazette*.

Lost Lover legend:

A long time ago a beautiful young girl and her father lived in a solitary cabin on the mountainside. A young man, in love with the girl, came every night from a nearby village, picking his way slowly through thickets full of dangerous animals.

On the night the girl agreed to marry him, the weather became cold and stormy. Nevertheless, he left for the village to prepare for the wedding, promising to return the next night. At the hour for his return, the girl carried a pine torch from the cabin to help him find his way through the darkness. However, he failed to come. He never appeared on the mountain again.

Nevertheless, the girl left her cabin with the flaming pine knot every night until she became old and died. "Folks said the lights would stop then, and they did—for awhile. Then they appeared again, faint and eerie, darting over the mountain as if by magic [no date].

1949 Harden, J. *The Devil's Tramping Grounds and Other North Carolina Mystery Stories*

(Chapel Hill: University of North Carolina Press, 1949).

The following are points taken from the book:

Brown mountain itself has no unique or distinct features.

The lights are faithful and regular.

Suddenly there will appear a light about the size of a toy balloon. It is very red in color, and it will rise over the summit of the mountain, hover there momentarily, and then disappear. In a few minutes, the light will appear again, but at another point on the mountain. And so, through the night, the lights appear, disappear, and reappear, at different points around the mountain, but nowhere else [128–9].

The lights appear stationary to some people; others see lights that move about in different directions.

Various proposed theories are recounted that include superstitions, the supernatural and mineral ores: "[T]he geologists have settled once and for all the matter of a possible geological explanation of the puzzle by announcing that Brown Mountain is composed of ordinary Cranberry granite, with no strange, weird, or interesting additions to that base" [130].

Possible causes mentioned include boyish pranks; will-o'-the-wisp; phosphorus; foxfire; pitchblende ore; hydrogen sulphide and lead oxide; moonshine stills; St. Elmo's fire; Andes light; mirage refractions of city lights or stars; locomotive headlights. The 1850 murdered wife legend is mentioned as well as the 1922 USGS study.

1951, March Bessor, J.P. "Mystery of Brown Mountain," *FATE* 4, no. 2, issue 18 (March 1951).

The lights began shortly after the Civil War. The murdered wife legend is discussed as well as reflected starlight; mineral deposits; foxfire; St. Elmo's' fire; Andes light; cars; trains; campfire on large flat rocks atop BM cracked, popped & jumped up and down; one light seen a few feet overhead, emitted a sizzling noise & hovered for a time; violent spinning of geologists' instruments. No references are given.

1952, June 29 Chapman, A. "Legend Says Brown Mountain Lights in Burke County Date Back to 1200." *Asheville* (NC) *Citizen*.

Mentions are made of flying saucers; AD 1200 Indian legend; Mansfield's 1922 study; Andes light; will-o'-wisp; foxfire; radium; chemicals, mirage, etc. Chapman presents lots of Mansfield's conclusions and agrees with him.

1954, February 9 Unknown Author. "For Real Mystery See Brown Mountain Light," *Charlotte Observer*.

This article reports that lights were seen over top of Brown Mountain, early evening, red color, hovering, disappearing, moving, stationary, bursting skyrocket. It mentions numerous possible origins. No new information is given.

1955 Paris, J. *Roaming the Mountain with John Paris* (Asheville, NC: Citizen Times Publishing Co., p. 50–52, 1955).

This is the 1913 USGS story; 1922 USGS study. It discusses the fact lights are still visible after 1916 flood and mentions possible causes: will-o'-the-wisp, foxfire, pitchblende, liquor still fires, town lights—and the Indian maiden legend and Andy Anderson mystery book *Kill One, Kill Two*. The real BMLs move around & change colors; the best observation time is during dark moon.

1956, September 14 Keever. "N.C. Folk Tales and Ghost Stories Told by Mr. Keever," *Statesville Record & Landmark*.

There are brief mention of BMLs. No details, dates or references are given.

1958 Brown, B. "Spook Lights," in *A New Geography of North Carolina*, vol. 2, by Bill Sharpe (Raleigh, NC: Sharpe Publishing, p. 662–666, 1958).

The following are discussed:

First newspaper account was in 1913 *Charlotte Observer*. Loven's Hotel on Jonas Ridge was favorite observation site. Brown and son observed from Joel C. McCurry home, near Loven's Hotel. The first light they saw appeared at 8:30 p.m. on July 7 and it changed colors, moved & disappeared. Brown and son camped on BM on July 10 but saw no lights. Possible causes of BMLs are given as radioactivity, foxfire, St. Elmo's fire, chemical reaction between hydrogen sulfide and lead oxide, and city lights from Catawba Valley. Brown concludes that city lights refracted by air & humidity cause the lights as well as the color changes & movement. Hobart A. Whitman published same conclusions in the *Asheville Citizen-Times* on November 10, 1940.

Photos by Brown were taken from the Joel C. McCurry property near Lovens on Jonas Ridge. One photo of a wide-angle nighttime view over BM shows distant city lights in Catawba Valley. A cropped version of this image was published in Bailey's 1968 *Argosy* article. Brown reports taking 8 separate photo images of the BMLs on July 7 (year uncertain).

Brown says there is no evidence to support the legend of Indian sightings of BMLs. He feels Mansfield's conclusion of the Catawba Valley lights reflected & refracted by dense air currents is the best explanation.

1959, February 5 Alexander, N. "After Generations of Superstitious Shivers, Four Young Men Provide Sensible Answer to Brown Mountain Lights," *Lenoir* (NC) *News-Herald*.

This is the first report of swamp atop BM.

William Happer and Ian Happer, Heiner Hanke, and Edward Miller are UNC students. Will-o'-wisps are from decaying organic matter in swamp. Old resident Ernest Perkins tells of a haunted area on the mountain with grass that cows refuse to graze. There is a 40–50-acre basin in headwaters of Carroll Creek. Methane gas is present. The uranium rush of 3–4 years ago brought prospectors.

1959, March 29 Wikle, J. "Many Mysterious Lights Have Been Seen in WNC," *Asheville* (NC) *Citizen-Times,* Mar 29, 1959.

This is a general discussion of mysterious lights throughout the western NC Mountains and gives possible causes as meteors, comets, Sputnik-type objects, high-flying planes, dirigibles, jack-o'-lanterns, will-o'-wisps, swamp gas, foxfire. The mineral lights or jack-o-lanterns of Cades Cove, TN, are the eerie lightning bugs that can cause consternation to many unsuspecting people, a rare mention of lightning bugs.

1961, August Krill, J. "The Lights on Brown Mountain—After a Century They Still Remain Unexplained." *Exploring the Unknown* (Robert A.W. Lowndes, editor) 2, no. 3 (August 1961).

"Since before the Civil War a strange and as yet not explained phenomenon has intrigued all people who have witnessed it."

Mention is made of the 1913 and 1922 reports and lights before 1861 and before the days of automobiles and locomotives. No references are given.

1961, September 26 "A New Explanation?," *Statesville (NC) Record & Landmark*.

Suggests the possibility that mirages might be responsible for the BMLs.

1962, June 1 Brown, B. "Science for You." *Lebanon* (PA) *Daily News*.

Bob Brown describes and illustrates a kitchen science experiment that demonstrates the refracting of light rays due to rising warm air, similar to the city lights seen over the top of Brown Mountain.

1962, June 2 Brown, B. "Practical Science," *Kingsport* (TN) *Times-News*.

Bob Brown describes and illustrates a kitchen science experiment that demonstrates the refracting of light rays due to rising warm air, similar to the city lights seen over the top of Brown Mountain.

1962, June 3 Brown, B. "Science For You." *Knoxville* (TN) *Sunday News Sentinel*.

Bob Brown describes and illustrates a kitchen science experiment that demonstrates the refracting of light rays due to rising warm air, similar to the city lights seen over the top of Brown Mountain.

1962, July 29 Baity, J. "Brown Mountain Lights Remain a Mystery to Viewers." *Asheville* (NC) *Citizen-Times*.

BMLs occur in Burke & McDowell counties; observed with Kenneth Thompson from Wiseman's View; counted 8 BMLs visible to naked eye & 47 with binoculars; along full length of BM above & below the crest; 3-day trip to BM; Andes lights were disproved as BMLs were seen with & without lighting in the area; BMLs not seen from BM itself; will-o'-the-wisp (burning marsh gas) theory rejected since there are no marshes on BM; but they did find a 5-acre marsh or swamp (inch-deep water) between the main ridge & a flash ridge; it was ignited with match and burned with a poof of bright blue flame; but swamps don't exist the full length of BM; foxfire theory also not valid as they are too weak.

Mentions other theories: radium, chemical reactions, St. Elmo's fire, mirages, the supernatural, flying saucers & Satan as well as moonshine stills.

The most likely explanation is refraction of artificial lights. BMLs were still visible after flood of 1916. B.S Gaither of Morganton saw lights in 1908 or 1909. Indian maidens' theory presented. Baity & Thompson favor light refraction of an unknown light.

The article includes 4 photographs: (1) Lighting strikes on BM with out of focus spots of light; (2) Egg Shell Rock; (3) Making camp on BM; & (4) Lumber pile.

1962, August 3 "Brown Mountain Lights May Pose Bigger Mystery." *Danville* (VA) *Register*, Aug 3, 1962.

AP press release regarding the Paul Rose tower story, the same article as the *Charlotte Observer* (August 3, 1962) & the *Winston-Salem Journal* (August 3, 1962).

1962, August 3 "Mystery of Lights Grows," *Charlotte* (NC) *Observer*.

Paul Rose, a Jonas Ridge nurseryman, said a dozen men stood on a tower atop Brown Mountain Wednesday night [August 1, 1962] and watched the curious lights flash out of crevices below.

"One of the lights came to rest on the men on the tower," Rose said. "It gave them a static-like feeling of dizziness. When they climbed to the ground, they were unable to stand up."

Rose said of the 12 men atop the 60-foot tower, 11 complained of dizziness. The other said he felt nothing. Rose said he believes the lights are radioactive. He said he intends to get a geologist to look into them. Rose said he's been seeing the lights for about 40 years.

1962, August 3 "Famed Lights Cause Feeling of Dizziness," *Winston-Salem* (NC) *Journal,* Aug 3, 1962.

Paul Rose, a Jonas Ridge nurseryman, said a dozen men stood on a tower atop Brown Mountain Wednesday night [August 1, 1962] and watched the fabled lights flash out of nearby crevices.

"They came out in circles of about three feet in diameter," said Rose, who is leading the current expedition which hopes to solve the mystery. "The lights were in colors of red, orange, and the color of the moon."

"One of the lights came to rest on the men on the tower. It gave them a static-like feeling of dizziness. When they climbed to the ground, they were unable to stand up."

Rose said of the 12 men atop the 60-foot tower, 11 felt the sense of dizziness. The other felt nothing. Rose said he believes the lights are radioactive or contain some magnetic element.

"The lights seemed to come through the trees, down the mountain under a cliff, and back up again."

Rose said he is anxious to get the opinion of a professional geologist, who may be able to determine why the lights would make people dizzy. Rose and scores of volunteers carried lumber up the mountain last Monday [July 30, 1962] and erected the tower so that viewers could look down into crevices from which the lights appeared to come.

"I still don't know that the lights are coming from the crevice," Rose said Thursday. "But if the weather stays good, I believe we'll be able to find out."

1962, August 4 "Brown Mountain Lights Traced to Cave Entrance." *Asheville* (NC) *Citizen.*

Paul & Jim Rose said they traced the lights Thursday night to the mouth of a small cave. The cave is beneath a cliff. On Wednesday night, 12 men stood on tower, 11 men became ill & dizzy.

"Word of the lights has been traced back to 1833."

This is a very short article, and no references are given.

1962, August 13 "Search Adds to Mystery of Brown Mountain Lights," *Asheville* (NC) *Citizen.*

[Paul Rose story. Rose:] "They came out in circles of about three feet in diameter. The lights were in colors of red, orange and the color of the moon. One of the lights came to rest on the men on the tower. It gave them a static-like feeling of dizziness. When they climbed to the ground, they were unable to stand up. The lights seemed to come through the trees, down the mountain, under a cliff and back up again. The lights are visible about 10 p.m. and again about 2 a.m. from highway 181."

Rose believes the lights are radioactive or contain some magnetic element; he's seen the lights for nearly 40 years. Rose & volunteers built the tower so they could look down intro crevices from which the lights appeared to come.

1962, August 16 "Brown Mountain to Be Developed," *Statesville* (NC) *Record & Landmark.*

A group of businessmen from TN & NC plan to develop Brown Mountain into a tourist attraction focused on the BMLs.

1962, August 20 Shires, W.A. "The Case of the Mysterious Lights," *Gastonia* (NC) *Gazette.*

No one really wants the mystery solved. Scientific explanations for the lights have recently been put aside as commercial interests have taken over the phenomenon. Forty-ft tower were recently constructed. New stories of close encounters in the woods are not confirmed and don't match the distant lights that gave rise to the legend.

1962, September 2 Mays, P. "Mystery of the Haunted Mountain," *Sunday News.* Unknown Newspaper.

They can be seen almost any night ... along the 20-mile ridge of BM; the lights give the impression of a city seen at a distance. Indian maidens' legend; faithful slave searching for lost master; USGS conclusions of reflected car & train lights; lights visible after flood of 1916; U.S. Weather Service lighting theory; reflected city lights. Paul Rose reports seeing close encounter with a light on Gingercake Mountain during World War I.

Rose: "As far as I know, I'm the first one to spot them up close. They mostly disappear, you know, when you get real close to them. They move about through the trees, but they don't touch the trees ... and they seem to be sensitive to the human body. They move away from you."

Geologist Dr. James McMeekin-Kerr was part of Rose's team on the tower when they saw lights. Some online research finds Dr. James McMeekin-Kerr (1908–1971) was born in Scotland, worked in TX & NC, married Frances Claire Thomas on Dec 15, 1955, & died in Jefferson, Ashe County, NC, on May 31, 1971. James & Frances had no known children.

Suddenly, Rose said, glowing balls of orange and red light, about 8 feet in diameter, bubbled up from fissures in the rock around them and soared skyward like balloons, dissipating as they rose. Rose and several of the others became nauseated as the lights neared them.

The article includes a nighttime photo of lights over the top of BM; this poor image shows numerous separate lights & two large horizontal patches of coalesced lights on a horizontal line, very similar to today's images of city lights to the east & south of BM. The photo caption reads: "But at night, its 20 mile length flickers with mysterious lights that have baffled investigators for years."

Ralph Lael is mentioned, but the rest of the article is missing.

1962, September 6 Braly, R. "Sam Rowe, Cato Holler, Jr. Explore Mystery—Marion Youths Study Brown Mt. Light." Marion (NC) *McDowell News*.

Sam began his investigation in the summer of 1961. His belief is that the BMLs are reflected light—refraction of light caused by the air itself. Sam & Cato used a transit from Wiseman's View &Table Rock to run line of sights to lights; they found lights ~ 2 miles south of BM summit, but still on the ridge. They hiked & camped on BM but never saw the lights from the mountain itself. They were present the first night that the Rose party manned the tower & using binoculars concluded that the member of the Rose party saw car lights. Sam has tape recordings of personal sightings by other people.

The first written account was 1913 *Charlotte Observer* article. U.S. Weather Bureau suggestion in 1921 of Andes light. Other causes mentioned: St. Elmo's fire, moonshine stills, vehicle headlights. Regarding the 1922 USGS study, Bob Brown agrees with Mansfield and concluded it was lights from the valley.

1962 "Sweet-Smelling Gas Key to Mystery?" Associated Press, unknown newspaper.

An underground gas which ignites as it spurts through rock layers has baffled onlookers since 1833. Rose said the flames flare up and burn out four or five times an hour. They are visible from about 9:30 p.m. to about 3 a.m., putting on their wildest show during the later hours, he said.

The gas was discovered by searchers looking for a member of their party who had become lost.

Everyone in the group described the gas as smelling "sweet as a flower."

1962 "The Legend of Brown Mountain Light." Ballad written by Scotty Wiseman; RCA Victor recording by Sonny James, 1962.

The song that reignited the legend of the Brown Mountain lights.

1962 Vincent, B. "Strolling with Bert Vincent." *Knoxville* (TN) *News-Sentinel*.

Report of a letter from Robert A. Laurence of the USGS regarding BMLs and plans for tourist development. Recounts Mansfield's 1922 conclusions.

1962 Vincent, B. "Strolling with Bert Vincent." *Knoxville* (TN) *News-Sentinel*.

Replies to earlier report of letter from Robert A. Laurence of the USGS regarding BMLs and plans for tourist development.

1962 Hartley, J.L. *The Mystery of the Brown Mountain Lights, Combined with Singing on the Mountain* (Linville, NC: J.L. Hartley, 1962).

The Great Light was first seen by Uncle John Wise, Nute Wise, & Uncle Julus Berry; they often saw the lights in 1870 from Wiseman's View. Indians saw lights in 1200. Hartley favors the theory of gases combined with uranium ore that explode in the earth & the heat casts them upward. The BMLs are one of the seven wonders of the world. Hartley reports seeing BMLs for last 70 years, as many as 25 at one time. Mr. L.C. Shell reports seeing as many as 6 lights together immediately after the flood of 1916. Robert Wiseman's great-grandfather first saw the lights during the Revolutionary War from Wiseman's View. Paul Brown reported seeing 6 lights in 1917, five lights in 1934, six lights on June 16, 1962,

& six lights in March 1963. "Let's believe God and quit wasting money," Hartley wrote at age 92.

No other published document confirms Hartley's report of lights seen during the Revolutionary War.

1963, September 9   Childress, B. "In Quest of Those Mysterious Lights," *Beckley (WV) Post*, Sep 9, 1963.

Childress attempted to see the BMLs but did not see any lights. No new information, no references.

1963, September 24   Alexander, N. "The Brown Mountain Lights—Part II." Boone (NC) *Watauga Democrat*.

Dr. H. Lyman's 1919 address to the American Meteorological Society at the Weather Bureau in Washington, DC, suggesting the lights were atmospheric phenomenon like Andes light. Reference is made to 1922 USGS study. Following 1922, locals reported lights were seen by Indians & early pioneers before the days of electricity. There is the Bird Carroll story of buried coins lost when he died fighting in Wilmington during the Civil War.

1964   Brown, F.C., Dr. "Brown Mountain Lights," in *Monumental Folklore of NC Books: The Frank C. Brown Collection of North Carolina Folklore (Collected by Dr. Frank C. Brown During 1912-1943)*. Durham, NC: Duke University Press, vol. I (of 7 vol.).

"[T]here has been adduced no legend dealing with these lights prior to the twentieth century, and no evidence that the lights themselves had appeared before that time. The Lights seem to have been noticed only after the neighboring towns had developed to a certain size with a certain amount of electric illumination" [629].

This is from the most definitive and authoritarian collection of information on North Carolina Folklore ever published, yet the author does not include the BMLs as one of the +2,000 "certified" folklores covered in the books!

1965, April 1   "Brown Mountain Lights Legend Passed Through Many Generations," Boone (NC) *Watauga Democrat*.

Mentions the story of two college students (in 1964?) who believed burning marsh gases caused the lights; S.M. Dugger's murdered wife legend as originally published in 1937; Civil War lost hunter & slave story; a shortened version of the Bird Carroll story.

"The legends of the lights will probably be passed on for generations to delight young and old alike, and because everybody loves a good mystery."

1965   Lael, R. *The Brown Mountain Lights* (Jonas Ridge, NC: Ralph Lael, 1965).

These topics are included:
Early loggers saw lights from Wildcat Knob.
From top of Wildcat Knob, at 11 p.m. he sees lights forming from large rock on BM—lights also coming from below his position.
Lael cuts trail from Wildcat Knob to rock on side of BM.
Numerous separate nights the lights come to him as he lies on ground atop Wildcat Knob.
Lights come out of solid rock and disappear into solid rock.
From planet "Pewam." The lights take him to Venus.
Date is July 1962, the same summer Paul Rose built his tower!
First legend of aliens.

1965   Lloyd, J.E. "Observations on the Biology of Three Luminescent Beetles (*Coleopters*; *Lampyridae*, *Elateridae*)." *Ann. Entomol. Soc. Amer.* 58, no. 4 (1965).

First scientific report on BGF (blue ghost firefly).

1966, June 9   Lael, R. "Mystery Brown Mountain Lights Is Topic of Volume 1." Blowing Rock (NC) *Blowing Rocket*.

First of a series of articles about Ralph Lael's 1965 book—all info comes from Lael's book. Mentions various legends & stories.

1966, June 16   Lael, R. "Brown Mountain Lights." Blowing Rock (NC) *Blowing Rocket*.

Second in a series of articles about Ralph Lael's 1965 book—all info comes from Lael's book. Mentions various legends & stories. Additional articles still to come.

1966, September 29   Parris, J. "Brown Mountain's Lights Still a Mystery," *Asheville (NC) Citizen*.

Hunter stories of scared hunting dogs on BM. Recounts USGS visits, old timers saw lights before electric lights, 1916 flood. Possible causes: foxfire, moonshine stills, Indian legends, old slave with lantern.

1968, December   Bailey, H. "Come See the Flying Saucers! You Want to See a UFO? Come Down to Brown Mountain. You Can See One Any Time—Even Take Pictures of it!" *Argosy* 367, no. 6 (December 1968), 62–65, 88.

This article gives 1858 as the date of the first published report.

Shows 3 photos of BM with numerous lights seen over the top of the ridge, which are clearly town lights, but Bailey calls them UFOs! He saw 200–300 lights lined up atop BM. The photos in the article are not Bailey's; he did not get a usable photo. The 2 photos showing lights above BM must have come from someone else. The bottom photo in this *Argosy* article is the same image published in Bob Brown's article in Sharpe's 1958 *A New Geography of North Carolina*. The source of the second BML photo in this *Argosy* article is unknown but it has features similar to Brown's 1958 photo.

There are mentions of the 1916 flood, Paul Rose & Ralph Lael, 1913 Sterrett visit, 1919 U.S. Weather Bureau, 1922 Mansfield visit, the article ignores legends of Indians, soldiers, murdered wife, etc. No references are given.

1971, June 27 Ferree, C. "Brown Mountain Light Mystery," *Winston-Salem* (NC) *Journal*.

Bob Brown's recent theory (published in *State* magazine) of the lights refracted by varying density air layers is refuted by a letter to *State* magazine by Sen. Sam Erwin, Jr., since the lights did not disappear after the 1916 flood & the lights were seen before days of electricity. Lights were supposedly seen in 1760 by Andre Michaux—but no proof is given.

1971, October 32 "Mysterious Lights Just Old Legend." *Long Beach* (CA) *Independent Press-Telegram*.

Mentions 1913 USGS study; USGS 1922 study; the 1922 USGS publication was reissued yesterday.

1971, November 4 "Brown Mountain Light Theory Reiterated," Boone (NC) *Watauga Democrat*.

USGS reissued Mansfield's 1922 report on the BMLs.

1971, November 11 Parris, J. "Roaming the Mountains—Uncle Fate Saw Ghostly Lights," *Asheville* (NC) *Citizen*.

About 1854 Fate Wiseman camped on rim of Linville Gorge and saw the mystery lights, long before electric lights. Fate grazed his cattle in Conley's Cove in Linville Gorge. The story of a low country planter who got lost and disappeared on a hunting trip to BM area is told. His slave with a lantern came looking for him and the slave's spirit with lantern still wander the mountains. Fate's nephew Sonny Wiseman recalled the story for Parris and Sonny wrote the ballad in 1961. Mentions are of USGS geologists' reports of train & electric lights; flood of 1916.

1971, November 14 Macomber, F. "Reports of Mysterious Lights Refuse to Fade," *The Brownsville* (TX) *Herald*.

USGS reissues Mansfield's 1922 report. No new information, no other references.

1971, November Helms, Jr., H.L. "America's Eerie Phantom Lights," *SAGA*.

Mentions Paul Rose's observation tower & possible nuclear radiation from the globe of light; Andes light theory; 1922 USGS study; Indian legends, De Brahm in 1771. The article also briefly describes mystery lights throughout the U.S. No references given.

1971, December 14 Avalanche-Journal. "Let's Forget About the Marfa Lights." *Lubbock* (TX) *Avalanche-Journal*.

The article ridicules Mansfield's 1922 USGS report as a waste of taxpayer's money and suggests, "Let's not do the same thing with the Marfa Lights."

1972, March 31 "Light on the Lights," *Cumberland* (ME) *News*.

Reports of the reissue of USGS 1922 report. The lights are caused by atmospheric and topographical conditions acting on explainable sources such as fires and headlights.

1972, May 9 The Daily Messenger. "Light on the Lights." *Canandaigua* (NY) *Daily Messenger*.

Reissue of USGS 1922 report. The lights are caused by atmospheric and topographical conditions acting on explainable sources such as fires and headlights.

1972 Parris, J. "Uncle Fate and the Brown Mountain Lights—Wiseman's View," in *These Storied Mountains* by John Parris (Asheville, NC: Citizen-Times Publishing, 1972).

About 1854–1858, Fate Wiseman camped on the rim of Linville Gorge and saw the BMLs—long before electric lights. Fate Wiseman was a veteran of Civil War. Fate kept cattle on his land below cliffs in Conley's Cove in Linville Gorge. On a return trip with his father to sell goods in Salisbury, they camped at what is today Wiseman's View & could see the lights over BM. Later, he would often watch the lights from the same spot & it came to be called Wiseman's View. Fate told of a faithful slave with a lantern searching for his missing low-country hunter master. Fate's grandnephew Scotty Wiseman wrote a ballad, "Legend of the Brown Mountain Lights," in 1961 & it was recorded by country music star Tommy Faile for Choice Records. Fate saw the BMLs after the 1916 flood. Parris attributes the numerous lights frequently seen over the top of BM to Uncle Fate's faithful slave's lantern.

Possibly the earliest documented sighting of the BMLs was 1858. Note that Fate Wiseman apparently did not see lights down in Linville Gorge—only over the top of BM.

Josiah Lafayette "Fate" Wiseman (1842–1932).

1973, December 13 Wadsworth, E.W. "Brown Mountain Lights," Boone (NC) *Watauga Democrat.*

He mentions lights seen nearly 200 years ago and believes lights are due to certain atmospheric conditions. Candles & campfires of early residents in communities east of BM could be the cause of early lights as light waves were bent, refracted and wiggled due to air layers of differing density. He dismisses St. Elmo's fire as the cause of lights as well as burning methane or gas, radiation & foxfire.

> The Brown Mountain Lights are a scientific phenomenon caused by the natural laws of refraction. The writer has made these observations about the lights. The lights are real and come from identifiable sources (homes, automobiles, street lights, etc.) located in Lenoir, Morganton, Hickory, Wilkesboro, and occasionally Charlotte. Although located below the normal line of vision, these lights are visible to the viewer because of the refraction of light waves. The lights can be seen when the atmosphere is clear and the humidity low. Temperature is another factor, as the air at the bottom of the mountain is at its greatest density when the temperature is lowest.

No references are given. Wadsworth was a professor at Appalachian State University.

1975, October 31 Hodge, T. "Some Serious Thinking About the Brown Mountain Lights," *Johnson City* (TN) *Press-Chronicle.*

National Park Service has erected a sign at an overlook on the Blue Ridge Parkway. The writer discusses the lights over BM; murdered wife story. The lights disappear as one gets close—phosphorescence; radium emission; ghosts & goblins; moonshiners. No references given.

1975, November 26 Hodge, T. "Elizabethton Man Tries to Spot Brown Mountain Light." *Johnson City* (TN) *Press-Chronicle.*

Stan Bentley visited Hwy 181 overlook & saw lots of lights, mostly stationary town & city light but believes some lights that moved and changed colors might be the BMLs. Hodge says yes.

1976, March 18 Harvey, R.M. "Brown Mountain Lights," Newland (NC) *Avery Journal-Times.*

The explanation for BMLs has been around for nearly 300 years and refers to a 1693 letter published in a 1975 USGS publication explaining "earthquake lights" from explosions from vapors escaping from the earth rising up & mixing with nitrous, sulphurous & other particles in the air produce lights like the BMLs.

1977, July 30 "Ghostly N.C. Lights Have Long History," *Asheville* (NC) *Citizen.*

Francois Schumacher, Geologist with the French-American Metals Corp., which is searching for uranium ore in Avery, Burke, Mitchell and Caldwell Counties, said uranium ore may be the source of the lights. "I have seen similar lights on other high mountains caused by uranium," Schumacher said.

Scott Wiseman quotes his great uncle Lafayette Wiseman who saw the lights in 1860 and thought they came from the lantern of a slave's ghost who searches the mountain for his master who had become separated from their hunting party. Lafayette Wiseman often viewed the lights from Wiseman's View.

"Other theories suggest the lights are caused by one or a combination of several minerals and gases in the area, including iron ore, copper, quartz, feldspar, mica, gold, silver and phosphorus."

First mention of uranium theory.

1977, August 3 "Theories Advanced," *Statesville* (NC) *Record & Landmark.*

This is the same article as in the July 30, 1977 issue of the *Asheville Citizen* (see above).

1977, August 22 "Brown Mountain Lights Explained?," *Hickory* (NC) *Daily Record.*

Francois Schumacher, geologist for a French company searching for uranium ore in the area, believes uranium may be the source of the lights on BM.

1977, September 20 "The Brown Mountain Lights of Western North Carolina," Raleigh, NC: Information Bulletin No. 162, Travel and Promotion Division, NC Department of Natural and Economic Resources.

The end of this document is missing. It mentions the first written account is the 1913 *Charlotte Observer* article. The most recent investigation was by Paul Rose & Howard Freeman, who reported escaping combustible underground gas. Other reported causes include radioactivity, foxfire, St. Elmo's fire, and hydrogen sulphide and lead oxide.

There are numerous referenced articles, the best references of any written article on BMLs!

The best time to see the lights is from June 1 through August, in the dark of the moon—this suggests BGFs!

1977 Persinger, M.A., and G. Lafreniere. *Space-Time Transients and Unusual Events* (Chicago, IL: Nelson-Hall).

Proposed theory of cause and effect between hallucinations and magnetic forces, later disproved by other researchers.

1980, October 9 Mast, N. "No Conclusive Explanation—Brown Mountain Lights." *Boone* (NC) *Mountain Times*.

It mentions the first published article (1913 *Charlotte Daily Observer*); various myths; USGS 1922 investigation. No references given.

1980, January 15 Hodge, T. "Brown Mountain Lights: Mystique More Important Than Source." *Johnson City* (TN) *Press-Chronicle*.

Mentions USGS 1922 investigation; 1913 USGS study; 1916 flood; 191 Weather Bureau & Smithsonian study; lights seen before days of cars & electricity.

1982, February 1 "Revolutionary War Soldier." Boone (NC) *Watauga Democrat*.

"A family settled in the Brown Mountain area in the 1700s. When the Revolutionary War began, the father enlisted, leaving behind his wife and three children. The war over, he returned home to find his homestead in ruins. Desperately he took to the nearby mountain range searching for his missing loved ones. Finally, he died alone and in despair atop Brown Mountain, and today his spirit continues the search."

No mention is made of when the light of his spirit first appeared. This is perhaps the first reference to Revolutionary War soldier legend.

1982, October Corliss, W.R. *Lightning, Auroras, Nocturnal Lights and Related Luminous Phenomena: A Catalog of Geophysical Anomalies*, compiled by William R. Corliss (Glen Arm, MD: Sourcebook Project, 1982).

Pages 173-4 briefly describe some light sightings in 1925 *Literary Digest*, 1926 *National Geographic*, & 1972 *New Horizons* magazines. Some, but not all, could be fireflies. Some lights are visible 20 miles away. Sightings were made in all types of weather. The information given is poor and lacks details, but at least Corliss gives references.

1982, December 16 Miller, H.J. "Brown Mountain Lights Continue to Fascinate Observers." Spruce Pine (NC) *Mitchell News-Journal*.

The article mentions lights might be vehicles, but lights were seen before the days of vehicles; electric power was no closer than Morganton until after World War I; best viewing is fall & winter. No references given.

1982 Phifer, Jr., E.W. *Burke: The History of a North Carolina County, 1777-1920, with a Glimpse Beyond*, revised edition (first edition 1977) (Morganton, NC: Edward William Phifer, Jr., under Sponsorship of the Burke County Historical Society, 1982).

"Just as eerie are the Brown Mountain lights which have been seen most frequently from Jonas Ridge over Brown Mountain which is located several ridges to the east. The most plausible explanation (if there is any) is that these moving lights are reflections from the headlights of trains or automobiles. That no such lights were seen prior to the twentieth century lends credence to this explanation" [12].

In chapter 15, "Wars and Acts of Violence, 1777-1920," Phifer provides great detail about the Civil War military actions in Burke County, including those on and near Brown Mountain. However, there is no mention of sightings of the BMLs by any of the soldiers.

1982 Wagener, H.D., and J.G. McHome. "Uranium Mineralization in the Wilson Creek and Cranberry Gneisses and the Grandfather Mountain Formation, North Carolina and Tennessee," Washington, D: National Uranium Resource Evaluation Report GJBX-191(82), 1982.

Detailed descriptions of uranium mineralization in areas immediately north of Brown Mountain.

1983, September and October Kane, M. "Brown Mt: Participate in a Mystery," *Carolina Outdoor Guide*.

A summary follows:

Ghosts lights seen since AD 1200; FS road 299 begins at the Adako Rd & passes over BM & continues to Chestnut Mtn. Gold can be panned in Carroll or Parks creeks; lead & uranium minerals mentioned; large granite balds occur near summit of BM; a few people have seen BMLs up close on BM itself; best observation sites are 181 overlook, WV, Table Rock, Grandfather Mtn & Hawksbill. Streetlights in Morganton & Lenoir can be seen almost every night; airplanes from Morganton-Lenoir airport can also be seen.

"Air turbulence, or refraction of light by layers of air, may cause these very ordinary lights to TWINKLE or dance."

Authentic BMLs rise up & hover over the mountain like a toy balloon, singly or several simultaneously or in succession; average 10–60 seconds; very bright, size of beach balls,

Causes: Indians saw the lights since AD 1200; spirits of Indian maidens; faithful slave looking for lost master; murdered mother & child; Ralph Lael's 1965 story; Sterret's 1913 investigation; 1916 flood didn't end the lights; 1921 U.S. Weather Bureau similar to Andes light. Other proposals include ball lightning, St. Elmo's fire, foxfire (including airborne foxfire on insects & owls), will-o'-wisp (burning methane gas reported on BM by some locals, while some scientists have found methane on the mountain). Mansfield's 1922 study mentioned. Earthquake lights mentioned (stressed quartz produces piezoelectricity) as investigated by ORION with explosives in May & July 1981 (inconclusive).

The following quote from Kane, 1983, is taken from *Remarkable Luminous Phenomena in Nature: A Catalog of Geophysical Anomalies*, compiled by William R. Corliss, Sourcebook Project (Glen Arm, MD, 2001).

An authentic Brown Mountain Light appears to rise up and hover over the mountain like a "toy balloon." The light may appear singly, or several lights may appear simultaneously or in succession. Average duration is 10–60 seconds although they have been known to endure as long as twenty minutes or more. The lights are usually described as being very bright and sometimes multicolored. Hunters and other people who have observed the lights at close range describe them as bright spheres of moving light about the size of beach balls or car tires. Although a close encounter with the lights often is a very frightening experience, no one has reported being injured by them.

1983, January 21 Marschalk, S. "Woman Explores Mystery of Burke Lights," *Hickory* (NC) *Daily Record*.

Catawba Science Center educator Marti Kane studies the lights. Tom Buchanan of Atlanta has developed a spectrograph for measuring the lights. Kane is working with ORION on fault-stressed quartz theory.

1984, February Frizzell, M.A. "Investigating the Brown Mountain Lights," *INFO*, no. 43 (January/February 1984), in *Remarkable Luminous Phenomena in Nature: A Catalog of Geophysical Anomalies*, compiled by William R. Corliss (2001) (Glen Arm, MD: Sourcebook Project, 1984).

In May 1977, ORION staged a 500,000 candlepower arc light on Hibriten Mtn in Lenoir.

When the arc light was switched on, the observers saw an orange-red orb hovering several degrees above the crest of Brown Mountain. Conclusion: at least some of the so-called Brown Mountain Lights, particularly those seen above the crest, are reflections of distant artificial lights. The real Brown Mountain Lights are those that flit through the trees well below the crest. These lights are extremely rare. Typically, they commence as a brilliant blue-white or yellow light, which tapers off to dull red before disappearing, all in 2–10 seconds. Horizontal motion is often only a degree or so, although some older reports have the lights wandering greater distances at speeds faster than a human could manage in the difficult terrain.

In an experiment to determine whether the "true" Brown Mountain Lights might be seismic in origin, ORION detonated small charges on Brown Mountain in July 1981. No artificially stimulated lights were recorded. At the present time, no one can say with any authority what the Brown Mountain Lights are.

We now know from subsequent ORION newsletters, that the team at the 181 overlook did not see the big light on Hibriten Mountain at Lenoir; however, the team at Wiseman's View did see the light.

1985, October 24 Buchanan, L. "Original Play Opens in Asheville on Friday—Brown Mountain Lights Legend Retold," *Morganton* (NC) *News Herald*.

A fictional two-part play is presented by the Smoky Mountain Repertory Theater at the Blue Ridge Parkway Folk Art Center: Young pranksters fool people then see lights themselves.

1986 Corliss, W.R. "Two Well-Known Spooklights," in *Nocturnal Lights*, chapter 1, "Luminous Phenomena," *Handbook of Unusual Natural Phenomena* (New York, NY: Arlington House, 1986).

This is a repeat of information in *National Geographic* 49 (1926), 51–78.

1988, August 1 Russell, R., and J. Barnett. "Belinda and the Brown Mountain Lights," in *Mountain Ghost Stories and Curious Tales of Western North Carolina* (Winston-Salem, NC: John F. Blair, 1988).

Mentions that the first documented sighting

was the 1771 De Brahm story, but his explanation was wrong. He then discusses the Indian battle in the 13th century and that the lights began to be observed about 10 years after the battle. A 1908 party of men from Morganton failed to see the lights. All scientific attempts have failed to explain the lights. Topics include 1913 USGS study; 1916 flood; U.S. Weather Bureau study; Marsh gases. Lights are seen atop BM. Smithsonian Institute study. Mirage. Lost lover. Moonlight reflected by rubies. Before Civil War, Belinda wed Jim, who was known to be cruel. They lived in cabin on BM. Belinda and her baby disappeared the day she gave birth. Susie immediately moved into the cabin with Jim. The lights began to appear. Grave of adult & a baby found under pile of rocks by two women guided by the lights which are the spirits of Belinda & her baby. Jim died soon after.

1989, November Jarvis, S. "The Brown Mountain Lights," in *The Uninvited: True Tales of the Unknown*, vol. II; Sharon Jarvis (ed.) (Bantam Books, 1989).

"Composed almost entirely of cranberry granite, in geological terms, Brown Mountain is not much to get excited about" [25].

This is the first mention of BMLs on Chestnut Mountain: BMLs have been" seen on and about Brown and Chestnut mountains in western North Carolina" [95].

Theories reported include swamp gas, uranium deposits, earthquake light—also folk legends include disembodied spirits of a brutally murdered housewife, young lovers, and Cherokee braves killed in battle long before white men arrived.

Controversy over when BMLs were first recorded. Earliest published account in *Charlotte Observer* September 23, 1913. Morganton Fishing Club first saw lights c. 1909. Joseph Loven saw lights in 1897.

Colonel Wade H. Harris (former editor of *Charlotte Daily Observer*) said in an October 2, 1921, letter to NC senator Simmons "there is a record that it [the light] has puzzled the people since and before the days of the Civil War." "As a direct consequence of those early sightings [early 1900s], North Carolina Representative E.Y. Webb urgently requested an investigation of the lights by the United States government. In response to Webb's request, D.B. Sterrett, a member of the U.S. Geological Survey, was sent to Brown Mountain on October 11, 1913 to observe the lights and determine their origin."

Sterrett's locomotive headlight theory was not well received and the flood of 1916 killed the idea.

Joseph Loven & C.L. Wilson story from the *Morganton News Herald* of December 16, 1915, is reviewed, as well as the 1962 Paul Rose tower story and Michael A. Frizzell of the Enigma Project investigating strange phenomena for +20 years tried but could not relocate the tower location. During 1978–1982 Frizzell's four-year Enigma Project studied the BMLs.

July 1978 was the first joint Enigma/ORION investigation. Twenty researchers with instruments spent a futile week looking for BMLs but did see a light on the north slope of Chestnut Mountain. Four more joint trips occurred from 1980 to 1984 with similar results. "Refractions of man-made lights accounts for a large portion of these sightings (BMLs)." Refractions can also cause the lights to change colors. Swamp gas is dismissed as implausible. Ball lightning also dismissed as unlikely.

About 1977, Dr. Michael Persinger (Ontario, Canada) and Dr. Brian Brady (Colorado) began research on "seismic stress lights," a new theory of earthquake-induced pressures on quartz-bearing rocks can produce piezoelectric plasma. No known connection to BMLs.

Possibility of 4-wheel-drive vehicles on logging roads at night could produce spurious BMLs to observers at 181 overlook. ORION was permitted to use Chestnut Mountain fire tower for observation & photography from 1979 until it was dismantled in 1981—no BMLs ever seen.

July 1981, ORION detonated small explosives atop BM—no lights seen at 181 overlook. Spectroscopy was unsuccessfully attempted in 1983–4 by Tom Buchanan. Sighting of true BMLs are waning and may soon disappear completely.

1991, October 30 Brewer, C. "Brown Mountain Lights; One of Nature's Unexplained Mysteries Is Right in Own Back Yard," Boone (NC) *Watauga Democrat* (reprint of a recent article in the *Blowing Rocket* (Blowing Rock, NC), which originally came from an article in the *News Sentinel* (Knoxville, TN), 1991.

This mentions various popular legends & stories; pre–Civil War murdered wife legend; USGS 1913 study; 1916 flood; 1919 Smithsonian & Weather Bureau study; USGS 1922 investigation. David Fields (ORION) never saw BMLs during 25 visits but once did see St. Elmo's Fire engulf a tree. Dugger's murdered wife story is discussed and also the 1700s Revolutionary War soldier story.

A new Indian legend says an Indian brave mourned when his maiden jumped off the cliff at Blowing Rock. He then fired lighted arrows over the cliff toward Brown Mountain to alert the gods to her misfortune; the arrows supposedly are the BMLs.

"The many legends of the Brown Mountain Lights will probably live forever."

1992, January 13 Schrum, J. "Are Brown Mountain Lights Rising Gases?," Boone (NC) *Watauga Democrat*.

John L. Burke of West Virginia reports the same lights present at the mining town of Eccles, WV, where moonlight or starlight reflect off of gas bubbles coming from decaying plant or animal matter.

1992, October Houser, S.T. "The Brown Mountain Lights—Mysterious Bright Lights Falling from a Burke County Mountain Have Dumbfounded Onlookers for Years," *State* 60, no. 5 (October 1992).

Mentions several past & recent anecdotal observations; lights seen from Lost Cove Cliffs overlook; De Brahm 1771 sighting. No references given.

1992, December 28 Bixler, M. "Legendary Lights Have Puzzled Centuries of Viewers." *Winston-Salem* (NC) *Journal*.

David Mull's sighting in 1989 is recounted. Mentions De Brahm 1771 sighting; Cherokee/Catawba battle 800 years ago; 1922 USGS study; burning gases ignited by Earth's electric currents (Charles Cook, physics professor at Lenoir-Rhyne College); fires of moonshine stills; UFOs. Ron Whitworth of Morganton camped on BM with friends & saw a luminescent insect smaller than a firefly with a powerful glow; a swarm of them could be seen for miles.

1994, September 18 Poteat, B. "The Brown Mountain Lights—Video Takes New Look at Burke County's Oldest Mystery." *Morganton* (NC) *Sunday News Herald*.

David Mull story & new video.

"There have been too many reports from too many different people for all of them to be wrong."

1994, September 28 "WNC Man Produces Video on Brown Mountain Lights." Boone (NC) *Watauga Democrat*. The story originally appeared in the *Blowing Rocket* (Blowing Rock, NC), 1994.

David Mull story & new video. Lights previously could be seen from Blowing Rock (Chateau Cloud Condo site). ORION group earthquake lights.

1995, October 27 Shockley, L. "The Legend of the Brown Mountain Lights"; this Web site is no longer available.

First published account of lights in Linville Gorge? C.W. Smith, USFS law enforcement officer, saw lights from Wiseman's View below The Chimneys about 1980 & again about 1983 or 85 below Little Table Rock.

Mentions legends of murdered wife; Revolutionary War soldier searching for missing family; faithful salve searching for lost master; USGS studies; U.S. Weather Service; ORION; stressed quartz; etc. No references given.

1996 Walser, R. *North Carolina Legends* (Raleigh: NC Division of Archives and History, 1996).

"As mountains go, low-lying Brown Mountain in Burke County is not impressive."

The lights were first seen about 1850: lost lover legend; murdered wife legend; no satisfactory scientific explanation.

1998, July 30 Garibaldi, L. "Brown Mountain Lights Continue to Fascinate Burke." *Morganton* (NC) *News Herald*.

John Brittain story: lights seen as a boy many times at Brown Mountain Baptist Church. Mentions the Cherokee/Catawba battle; slave searching for lost master. Daniel Boone saw the lights; De Brahm 1771; lights seen long before cars & trains; M.A. Bird's 1916 story; mineral deposits on BM; 1916 flood; F.W. Bricknell of Linville Falls, 1916 story; 1919 conclusions of Weather Service & Smithsonian Institute; 1921 National Geographic conclusion of lightning causes; misquote from a 1923 USGS study(??); also other anecdotal stories.

1998 Taylor, T. "The Brown Mountain Lights, Burke County, North Carolina," Unexplained America: www.prairieghosts.com/brownmt.html.

Mentions various legends, moonshine stills, will-o'-the-wisp, foxfire, phosphorus, radium, geologic anomalies, headlights, and murdered wife legend. No references given.

1999, May 26 Grizzard, G. "A Personal Experience with the Brown Mountain Lights." Boone (NC) *Watauga Democrat*.

It mentions De Braham 1771; slave searching for master; Cherokee/Catawba battle; forsaken lover; murdered wife & baby; USGS 1913 & 1922 studies; Smithsonian study; ORION; Dan Caton's work and quotes Hugh Morton on a 1930s USGS study that was inconclusive.

1999, September 12 Hudson, M.A. "Go for the Leaves, Stay for the Lights." *Charlotte* (NC) *Observer*.

This article says the mystery lights were

seen as far back as 1600s: Cherokee & Catawba battle on BM before 1750; Belinda murdered wife myth. The best viewing spots are 181 overlook, Lost Cove Cliffs overlook, & Wiseman's View. No references given.

2000   Western North Carolina Interactive. "Brown Mountain Lights." Western NC Attractions: www.westernncattractions.com/BMLights.htm.

The site says the lights seen for 100s of years: De Brahm 1771, faithful slave searching for lost master, 1850 murder of wife, AD 1200 Indian legend, radioactive minerals, phosphorus, mirages, 1916 flood. No references given.

2001, June 28   Rogers, S. "The Mystery of the Brown Mountain Lights," Blowing Rock (NC) *Blowing Rocket.*

Mentions Cherokee & Catawba battle 700 years ago; murdered wife; lost hunter; 1913 USGS investigation; 1916 flood; lights seen before electricity in area; swamp gas; may be due to seismic activity along Grandfather Mountain fault.

2001, July 2   Associated Press. "Group says it will find cause for Brown Mountain Lights." Boone, NC: *Watauga Democrat*, Jul 2, p. 3A, 2001.

Joshua Warren's group from Asheville filmed a video of supposed BMLs. Dr. Dan Caton of ASU (Boone, NC) doubts mystery lights actually exist.

2001, July 2   Dyer, L. "Group Takes on 800-year Old Mystery," *Charlotte* (NC) *Observer*, July 2, p. 1B, 2001.

Same article as above.

2001, July 3   Associated Press. "Researcher Videotapes, Tries to Explain the Legendary Brown Mountain Lights," Winston-Salem, NC: *Winston-Salem* (NC) *Journal.*

This is the same article as Dyer, L, July 2, 2001 (see above).

2001, July 3   "Asheville Group Tries to Find Explanation for N.C.'s Brown Mountain Lights," *Hickory* (NC) *Daily Record.*

Joshua Warren's group studying the lights & videotaped them in November from Hwy 181 overlook with an infrared camera. The lights occurred on the mountain in an area with no roads. D. Mull believes the video is real. Dan Caton doubts that real lights exist. Various myths are mentioned.

2001, July 3   "Group trying to explain Brown Mountain Lights," *Lenoir* (NC) *News-Topic.*

This is the same Associated Press news release as above.

2001, July 8   Associated Press. "Group Tries to Solve Mystery of Brown Mountain Lights." *Knoxville* (TN) *News-Sentinel.*

Same article as July 2, 2001 (see above).

2001, July 18   Russell, D. "The Brown Mountain Lights—New Video Evidence May Finally Provide More Clues to Potentially Solve the Mystery," *S-Project Paranormal*: www.xprojectmagazine.com/archives/paranormal/brnmntlights.html.

This site mentions lights have been seen for centuries: 800-year-old Indian legends, 1771 De Brahm, U.S. weather Bureau report, USGS 1913 and 1922 visits, other possible causes. LEMUR researchers videotaped lights in November 2000. No references given.

2001, August 13   Trivette, J. "More Letters—How About Those Brown Mtn. Lights?" Boone (NC) *Watauga Democrat.*

Here are mentions of the De Brahm 1771 story, 1913 USGS investigation, 1916 flood, 1922 USGS investigation (found the cause was flammable marsh gas), 1919 Humphries' & 1941 Lyman's Andes light, lights seen before days of Civil War, ORION 1977 spotlight in Lenoir, ORION 1881 detonations on BM, Cherokee legend from AD 1200, Cherokee/Catawba battle on BM, jilted lover story, Jim & Belinda myth. Trivette reports that the real BMLs are those seen through the trees below the crest of BM. No references given.

2001, October   Corliss, W.R. *Remarkable Luminous Phenomena in Nature: A Catalog of Geophysical Anomalies*, compiled by William R. Corliss (Glen Arm, MD: Sourcebook Project, 2001).

Corliss briefly quotes descriptions of some light sightings in 1925 *Literary Digest*, 1983 *Carolina Outdoor Guide*, 1922 USGS report, and the ORION research. He does not offer his own interpretations.

2001   Crews, E. "Mystery Mountain," *Blue Ridge Outdoors*: www.blueridgeoutdoors.com/outdoors-travel/adventures/mystery-mountain/.

Mentions 1771 De Brahm; Josh Warren's plasma theory with layers of quartz and magnetite in the rocks; 1970s ORION static electricity theory. No references given.

2001   Odenwald, S. "The Brown Mountain Lights": www.astronomycafe.net/weird/lights/brown.htm.

This is a compilation of BML literature based on Internet sites, most of which lacked references to begin with but the most complete and detailed bibliography of BML online sources to 2001: Cherokee Indian legend of spirits of maidens searching for slain husbands; De Brahm's 1771 nitrous vapors; Revolutionary War legend of distraught farmer-soldier finding his family missing; 1850 murdered wife; Souls of Indian braves killed in battle; first printed document 1913 newspaper; 1913 USGS study; 1916 flood; April 1941 lecture by Dr. W.J. Humphries (U.S. Weather Bureau) attributed lights to Andes light; Dugger legend of murdered wife c. 1887; Mike Fizzell's sighting in 1974; ORION work in 1977 & 1981.

2002, April 1   Ruggeiro, F. "ASU Prof Doesn't Buy Lights Legend." Boone (NC) *Watauga Democrat*.

Dan Caton, physics and astronomy professor at Appalachian State University, Boone, NC, observes from Wiseman's View and only sees manmade light. Caton is a "skeptical talking head." Airplanes, ATVs, campfires, cars, stars and are seen through the trees on BM and make up most sightings.

"I'd like to see documents (regarding the lights) written before electricity. Just like UFOs, about 90 percent of sightings can be explained by natural and manmade lights. You lose all ability to tell distance when points of light are in the night sky and they are more than 10 to 20 feet away. Your brain can't do it unless it has familiar objects to scale against."

2002, May 13   Sparks, J. "Skeptical Professor Tries to See the Light," *Winston-Salem* (NC) *Journal*.

Dan Caton, physics and astronomy professor at Appalachian State University, Boone, NC, searches for but can't find an actual BML; he uses the legend to teach students how to think critically. Caton is often called on by the media to help explain the lights. Caton feels 90 percent are misidentified manmade lights & 10 percent may be due to celestial sources.

2002, May 27   Sparks, J. "Professor Tries to Debunk Popular Mountain Myths," *Winston-Salem* (NC) *Journal*.

This is the same article as Sparks, May 13, 2002 (see above).

2002, August 27   Hauck, D.W. "Brown Mountain Lights," in *Haunted Places: The National Directory; Ghostly Abodes, Sacred Sites, UFO Landings and Other Supernormal Locations* (Penguin Books, revised edition, 2002).

Causes of the lights are the restless spirit of a man whose corpse was found near the bottom slope. Others could be UFOs, electromagnetic discharge; train & truck lights.

"The red and white shooting lights are only seen during the autumn months on moonless nights" and were first observed by Cherokee Indians c. 1200. De Brahm 1771; USGS 1913; ORION 1970s; Lael 1962 abduction are also discussed.

2002, September 29   Buckinger, N., and R. Holcomb. "Searching for the Brown Mountain Lights," *Focus-High Point* (NC) *Enterprise*.

Piedmont Environmental Center sponsored a two-day visit to Linville Gorge but no BMLs were seen. No references given.

2002   Baldwin, J. "Riddle of the Brown Mountain Lights," in *Smoky Mountain Mysteries: Stories About Magnificent Mountain Unique People* (Kodak, TN, and Virginia Beach, VA: Suntop Press, 2002).

This book mentions the Off Road Vehicle Area on BM; De Brahm's 1771 vapors report; D.B. Sterrett of USGS study in 1913. Flood of 1916; George R. Mansfield of USGS in 1922; 1962 work of Rose, Freeman & Lineberger.

The Scotty Wiseman Ballad is based on this story:

Brown Mountain was named after a Brown family, who owned a lot of land during the 19th century that included this mountain. The family owned slaves, and enjoyed the reputation of treating them well.

During the Civil War, one of the men in the Brown family fought in the Confederate army as a colonel. He was wounded in 1863 and came home. When he was well enough, he went for a day's hike and hunting on Brown Mountain, a place he knew well. He took a little food and water, and two lanterns.

Midnight came and the colonel had not returned. His faithful slave Jim took a lantern and went to Brown Mountain to look for him. Neither Jim nor the colonel ever returned. The family and their slaves searched the entire surface of Brown Mountain, but no trace of either of them has ever been found.

Shortly after the colonel and Jim disappeared, bobbing lights appeared on the mountain. The lights had never been seen before, and the family believed the lights were from the lanterns the colonel and Jim carried. They are trying to find their way home.

It also recounts the Cherokee and Catawba Indian legend, AD 1200, which says the lights are spirits of maidens still searching for their loved ones, and the Amanda legend: Amanda lived on BM with her widowed father about 1775. The young man Caleb lived in the valley & fell in love with Amanda. One evening he was to come and take her away to marry, and she lighted a pine torch & went out to wait for him. He never came. Her spirit still searches for Caleb.

Michael A. Frizzell, research director for Enigma Project (Maryland), joined forces with ORION (the first study was first week of July 1978) and saw 37.5 mph light on Chestnut Mountain but nothing on BM. The ORION 500,000 candlepower arc light was in Lenoir May 1977; observers at 181 overlook saw the light over the top of BM. ORION detonated charges on BM in July 1981 but no lights were produced. The LEMUR investigation in November 2000 was the first video of lights (Brian Irish video). In 2002 Travel Channel & LEMUR filmed a segment on BMLs for *Mysterious Journeys*; it aired the first time in March 2002. The May 9, 1999, segment on BMLs aired on *The X-Files* show.

2003, July 13 Little, G., Dr. "The Brown Mountain, NC Lights Videotaped: A Field Observation—July 2003." Memphis, TN: *Alternate Perceptions*, issue #70 (July 2003).

"The number of lights varies between one to literally hundreds at a time."

Little details his experience photographing hundreds of lights on July 13, 2003, over the top of Brown Mountain—so many lights that they looked like a city. He mentions various legends and theories and favors earth lights theory. Mentions M. Persinger's plasma electromagnetic forces research; reported close-up experiences of others; and possible fault-related lights. Includes a few references.

2003 Clark, L.R. *Indians of Burke County and Western North Carolina* (Morganton, NC: TimeSpan Press, 2003).

No mention is made of Indian sightings of BMLs or of Indian legends related to battles on Brown Mountain or BMLs. Extremely well researched document with extensive bibliography.

2004, February 18 Caines, R.S. *The Brown Mountain Lights and the Mesozoic Phoenix* (iUniversie, 2004).

A fictional story of two geologists and their girlfriends on a camping trip to see the BMLs, earthquakes release a Mesozoic UFO, which resumes its mission to destroy all life on earth. No factual information on BMLs. Poorly written & poor plot

2004, November 11 Warren, J.P. "Report on the Cause of the Mysterious Brown Mountain Lights," Asheville, NC: League of Energy Materialization and Unexplained Phenomena Research (L.E.M.U.R.): shadowboxent.brinkster.net/brownplasma.html.

This is also included in Joshua P. Warren's 2012 *Brown Mountain Lights Viewing Guide*.

The first reported video footage of lights (Brian Irish in 2000) mentions possible ATV headlights! The appearance of BMLs causes Geiger counter malfunctions. Erratic telluric currents are present and VLF currents detected. Correlation of BML appearances on November 4 & 11, 2000, with +5 Kp index (strong solar disruption of magnetosphere). Magnetite is common on BM (layers of quartz & magnetite capacitors?). Thrust faults are present (Reed., Jr., USGS, Pro. Paper 615). BMLs are due to natural plasma, static electrical discharges from BM to the air (ground currents &/or air currents). Electrical storms, solar flares and wood smoke combine to enhance visibility of BMLs. No supporting references given.

2004, December Adams, R., and T. Adams. *Night Lights: Golf, the Blues, and the Brown Mountain Light* (Parkway Publishers, 2004).

A fictional story of three friends' summer adventure in the Linville area, including searching for the BMLs, it is a very well written adventure story but has little to no factual data on the BMLs.

2004 Coffey, S.C. *Mortimer and Edgemont—Lenoir News, 1900–1919* (Collettsville, NC: Sandra Cloer Coffey, 1989, revised 2004).

This includes *Lenoir News* articles of historical interest to the local communities. Articles have been retyped to conform to the same print format. It includes the following articles (each listed separately elsewhere in this bibliography):
November 23, 1915, by H.C. Martin.
December 14, 1915, by C.L. Wilson
February 15, 1916, by M.A. Bird
September 8, 1916, by G.A. Lovens
October 31, 1916, by C. Elam
February 18, 1917, Brown Mountain bought by U.S. Forest Service

The *Lenoir News* and *Lenoir Topic* newspapers later consolidated into the *Lenoir News-Topic*, which today is known as the *News-Topic*.

2005, May 2 Rowe, P. "Sprites Light Up the Night with Mysterious Glow," Marion (NC) *McDowell News*.

Description of small population of blue ghost fireflies (BGFs) on North Muddy Creek, McDowell County, NC.

2005, July 3 Clabby, C. "Scientist Scrutinizes Spooky Sight—Astrophysicist Out to Explain—or Disprove—Storied Brown Mountain Lights." *Raleigh* (NC) *News & Observer*.

Appalachian State University astrophysicist Dan Caton was observing at Wiseman's View. Caton reports no sightings of lights after about 20 outings. The article mentions 1913 *Charlotte Observer* article; 1913 & 1922 USGS investigations; 1916 flood; Native American battle on BM; murdered wife; Revolutionary War soldier; Joshua Warren's plasma theory. Caton did not see any mystery lights that night & left still skeptical of their existence.

2005, July 7 Clabby, C. "Scientist Scrutinizes Spooky Sight": www.anomalyarchives.wordpress.com/2005/07/07/scientist-scrutinizes-spooky-sight.

Mentions 1913 Charlotte Observer article; 1913 USGS study; 1922 USGS study; Indian legends; Revolutionary War soldier legend; J Warren's theories.

Dr. Dan Caton, astrophysicist, Appalachian State University, observed from Wiseman's View with instruments & camera on July 7, 2005. No references given.

2005, July 10 Associated Press. "ASU Professor Chases After 'the Lights,'" *Winston-Salem* (NC) *Journal*.

Same article as Clabby, 2005 above.

2005, July 11 Beard, A. "Chasing the Legendary Brown Mountain Lights," Asheville, NC: *Asheville* (NC) *Citizen Times*.

Dan Caton, astronomer at Appalachian State University, and Lee Hawkins observe from Wiseman's View on June 22. Caton has failed to see the lights in 20 visits over the years. Joshua Warren also leads a group searching for the lights who believe the lights are plasmas that don't occur all the time.

2005, July 12 Beard, A. "Chasing the Legendary Brown Mountain Lights," *Boone* (NC) *News Herald*, Jul 12, p. 2A, 2005.

Same article as above.

2005, September 2 Huffman, S. "Brown Mountain Lights—There's Still No Clear Explanation for This Visual Phenomenon," *Salisbury* (NC) *Post*.

The lights have been visible for hundreds of years but are yet to be explained; two USGS investigations did not figure them out. De Brahm 1771; Cherokee & Catawba battle; multiple colors reported; lights occur above BM, sometimes in great numbers; best seen in September & October following rain. No references given.

2005 "The Brown Mountain Lights," Raleigh: North Carolina Museum of History: ncmuseumofhistory.org/fko/NIE/TwistedTarHeelTales/brownmountain.pdf.

There is a lack of scientific explanations. Indian legends, USGS geologists visits, murdered Belinda legend. No references given.

2005 Renegar, M. "Ghost Lights on Brown Mountain," in *Roadside Revenants* (Fairview, NC: Bright Mountain Books, 2005).

The murdered wife story from the 1850s; slave looking for lost master; 1771 De Brahm; Cherokee/Catawba battle of AD 1200; floods of 1916 & 1940. No references given.

2006, May 3–4 "Brown Mountain Lights Heritage Festival," Newland (NC) *Avery Journal-Times*.

On June 9, 10, 11 Linville Falls will host the first BML Festival.

2006, June 9 Codfelter, T. "Mountain Mystery—Light Rarely Spotted, Spark Lots of Speculation," *Winston-Salem* (NC) *Journal*.

BML Heritage Festival is this weekend. D. Mull story, producer of two videos on the lights & creator of theory of mini wormholes into other dimensions.

2006, July 14 Ruggeiro, F. "Looking for the Brown Mtn. Lights," Boone (NC) *Watauga Democrat*.

Dan Caton, astronomer at Appalachian State University, remains skeptical of mystery lights and plans to set up a webcam at Wiseman's View, but waits for U.S. Forest approval. Various legends mentioned.

2006, October Pantas, L.J. *The Ultimate Guide to Asheville & The Western North Carolina Mountains*, 3rd edition (Ultimate Guide to Asheville and Hendersonville) (Asheville, NC: R. Brent, 2006).

Discussed are the Cherokee Indian legend 1200; De Brahm; W.J. Humphries (Weather Bureau), USGS studies, as well as possible causes: nitrous vapor emissions, vehicle headlights, Andes light, marsh gas, moonshine stills, electrical phenomenon such as St. Elmo's fire, mirages, UFOs, radioactive uranium ore, atmospheric reflections from nearby towns (Hickory, Lenoir, etc.). No references given.

2006, November 4 Henderson, B. "Will You See Mountain Mystery?," *Charlotte* (NC) *Observer*.

Appalachian State University astronomer Dan Caton hopes to install a webcam at Wiseman's View to capture BMLs. Caton believes 95 percent of the reported BMLs are bogus. The article mentions De Brahm 1771; Cherokee/Catawba battle; 1922 USGS study; ball lightning; UFOs; plasma gas. Cindy Peters, owner of Parkview Lodge in Linville Falls, reports seeing the lights 30–40 times.

2006, November 12 Henderson, B. "Scientist Eyes Mysterious Mountain Lights—State Expert Hopes to Capture Images of Phenomenon." *Charlotte* (NC) *Observer*.

"Written accounts of the lights date to 1771, but they're said to have been part of Cherokee lore for centuries earlier. Some legends say the lights come from the spirits of American Indian warriors slaughtered in battle. Others say they're torches carried by the ghosts of grieving maidens."

Appalachian State University astronomer Dan Caton's video camera plans for Wiseman's View are given and the article includes a 2004 photo of bright light above Brown Mountain by Charles Braswell.

2006 Dodge, R.J. "Brown Mountain Lights," in *Encyclopedia of North Carolina* (Chapel Hill: University of North Carolina Press, 2006). ncpedia.org/brown-mountain-lights

"The lights have been documented since 1833...."

No reference is given for 1833 document. The article recounts the legend of Indian brave searching by torchlight for his lost love and mentions vehicle headlights and static electricity as possible sources. No references given.

2006 Zepke, T. "Mystery of the Brown Mountain Lights," in *Best Ghost Tales of North Carolina* (2nd ed.) (Sarasota, FL: Pineapple, 2006).

Included are stories of eyewitnesses; lights seen as early as 1850 following murdered wife (no references given); Revolutionary War soldier story; divine power; hunter lights; moonshiner lights; spirits of Indians; spirit of faithful slave. Other scientific theories dismissed include minerals, radium, will-o'-wisp, foxfire, city/town lights, Andes lights, St. Elmo's Fire, mirages.

2007 Clark, L.R. *Burke County North Carolina; Historic Tales from the Gateway to the Blue Ridge* (Charleston, SC: History, 2007).

Clark mentions the BMLs but gives no details. He also mentions De Brahm's 1771 report of nitrous vapors. It's quite shocking that Clark did not research De Brahm's report! Indian maiden legend; ghosts of Civil War Yankee soldiers killed on Winding Stairs or Ripshin Ridge.

2008 Frick-Ruppert, J., and J.J. Rosen. "Morphological and Behavior of *Phausis Reticulata* (Blue Ghost Firefly)," Jour, *North Carolina Academy Science* 124, pt. 4 (2008). This article is available online at dc.lib.unc.edu/cdm/singleitem/collection/jncas/id/3883/rec/1

This is the most scientific information available and has very detailed information on the BGF (lists populations in many North Carolina counties, including McDowell).

2009, May 5 Taylor, T. "Brown Mountain Lights," in *Weird U.S.: Your Travel Guide to America's Local Legends and Best Kept Secrets*, by Mark Moran and Mark Sceurman (Sterling, 2009).

Different people see the same lights differently. Possible origins: will-o-the-wisp, foxfire, phosphorus, radium rays, geologic gases, moonshine stills, headlights, murdered wife legend. No references given.

2009, March 11 Ruple, W. "Brown Mountain Lights," *Al Jazeera English News*: Web site no longer available.

Discusses USGS visits in 1913 & 1922, Indian legends of AD 1200, 1919 Weather Bureau report, etc.

Quotes many articles in the Asheville newspapers.

One of the best-referenced documents on the BMLs but no conclusions are reached.

2009, September 3 Mcbrayer, S. "Officials Unveil Overlook After Two Years of Removing Trees That Blocked Scenic Attraction." *News Herald*.

The city of Morganton, County of Burke, U.S. Forest Service & NC officials held opening ceremony; the overlook had been overgrown for many years with no view of BM. Signs were erected.

2009, October 13 Warsing, D. "Project UFO Night Shift": www.youtube.com/watch?v=gftfwM9_J0g.

Dean Warsing's night vision goggle video of suspected BML.

2009, December 28 Rupple, W. "Brown Mountain Lights Remain a Mystery." Web site no longer available.

Observation was made from Lost Cove overlook on the Blue Ridge Parkway. Numerous lights were seen over the top of BM. Mentions 1922 USGS Mansfield report; AD 1200 Indian legend; 1913 Sterrett USGS visit; 1916 flood; 1919 U.S. Weather Bureau; Andes light, and possible causes: will-o'-the-wisp, marsh gas, phosphorus, phosphorescent, luminous organic gas, radium, hydrogen sulfide and lead oxide reactions, whiskey stills, St. Elmo's fire, Andes light, mirage, vehicle headlights.

Mentions Whitman's 1940 research and Baity's 1962 observations and the Rose & Freeman tower observations in 1962.

2009 Casstevens, F.H. "The Brown Mountain Lights," in *Ghosts of the North Carolina Piedmont: Haunted Houses and Unexplained Events* (Charleston, SC: History, 2009).

In the 1960s Tommy Faile, musician with Arthur Smith's band, the Crackerjacks, recorded the ballad. This piece mentions Cherokee legend AD 1200. Indian maiden legend; Ghosts carrying candles; Faithful slave looking for lost planter; Murdered wife legend; De Brahm; 1771 nitrous vapors; lights reflected from Hickory and Lenoir; lights seen before Civil War; 1916 flood.

"On dark nights, the lights appear so quickly and are so numerous that it is impossible to even count them."

2010, October 5 Dunning, B. "The Brown Mountain Lights—A Ghost Light in North Carolina Has People Scratching Their Heads. What's the Explanation?" Episode 226, Skeptoid Podcast: www.skeptoid.com/episodes/4226.

Supposedly the Cherokee natives of the region believed 800 years ago that bereaved wives wandered the skies above the hills with lanterns, looking for the souls of their brave warrior husbands killed in battle.

I say "supposedly" because I was unable to find any reference to such a belief outside of publications about the Brown Mountain Lights.

Taken in context, it's clear that De Brahm's quote {nitrous vapors, 1771} has nothing whatsoever to do with the Brown Mountain Lights. This leaves us with no documentary evidence that the Lights existed at all prior to the arrival of electric lights and people in the area in the early 1900s.

Discusses Linville Gorge Lights (LGLs) on east rim of the gorge in area of popular rock climbing destinations and references the 1922 USGS report. Notes two different manifestations of the BMLs—lights appearing in the sky above Brown Mountain; and more recently, those that appear below ridge tops in Linville Gorge. Numerous references given.

2010, October 29 Tabler, D. "The Brown Mountain Lights, as Told by David Biddix," Appalachian History: appalachianhistory.net/2010/10/the-brown-mountain-lights.html.

The Lights have been seen for 100s of years; Indian legends of AD 1200; De Brahm of 1771; murdered wife of 1850; faithful slave looking for lost master; 1913 USGS visit; 1916 flood; misidentifies 1922 USGS geologist. No references given.

2010, December 21 Pitzer, S. "Brown Mountain Lights," in *Myths and Mysteries of North Carolina: True Stories of the Unsolved and Unexplained* (Myths and Mysteries Series) (Guilford, CT: Morris, 2010).

Pitzer mentions Indian legends but gives no references as well as the faithful slave searching for lost master; murdered wife about 1850; ghosts of military men carrying candles. Mention is made of Dan Caton's scientific research Web site, USGS 1913 study, De Brahm 1771 report. Possible causes include swamp gas, phosphorus, radium ore, moonshine stills. BMLs appear above BM. Pitzer ends with refreshing skepticism.

2010 Morrison, N. "The Mystery of the Brown Mountain Lights," Boone, NC: *The Mountain Times Winter Guide*, 2010.

Indian legends of AD 1200; De Brahm 177; faithful slave searching for lost master; 1913 USGS study; Scotty Wiseman's song.

2011, May 11 Pollock, V. "Brown Mountain Lights: Jim and Belinda Legend": www.thereadonwnc.ning.com/forum/topic/show?id=1972559%3ATopic%3A37654.

This is a legend as told by Mrs. Ira Vance of Pineola, NC, c. 1941. Jim murdered his wife Belinda, who was pregnant at the time. Jim was seeing another woman named Susie. Jim reported Belinda missing & locals, including Ira Vance, went looking for her. A forest fire, started by Jim, burned everything in the area. The BMLs led Ira to a rock cliff on BM where they found a pile of rocks at the base of the cliff. The pile covered the skulls of an adult & a baby. Jim got old & suffered from dementia, often seeing Belinda's ghost. No other details are given. This story supposedly occurs in F.C. Brown's *North Carolina Folklore*, v. 20, 1972. Jim's last name was Lay and his mother & father were Mattie Greene and Wash Lay.

2011 Sakowski, C. *Touring the Western North Carolina Backroads*, 3rd edition (Winston-Salem, NC: John F. Blair, 2011).

There are wildly differing versions of the lights told by observers. De Brahm's 1771 document, USGS Sterrett visit in 1913, flood of 1916, USGS Mansfield visit in 1922, Indian legends, and other legends are all discussed. It also includes a photo of the former Cold Springs Lodge, site of Loven's Hotel (destroyed by fire in 1950), on NC Highway 181.

2012, February 26 Breen, T. "Brown Mountain Lights, Mysterious Orbs in NC, Are Decades-old Mystery," *Huffington Post*: www.huffingtonpost.com/2012/02/26/brown-mountain-lights-nc_n_1302204.html.

Steve Woody story:

"Two orange orbs, just about 10 feet off the ground, floated past Steve Woody and his father as they hunted deer more than 50 years ago. The mysterious lights passed them, then dropped down the side of a gorge in the Blue Ridge foothills. 'I didn't feel anything spooky or look around for Martians or anything like that. It was just a unique situation; it's just as vivid now as when I was 12 years old.'"

No specific date given. Dan Caton's research discussed.

2012, February 9 Oakes, A. "Demystifying the Brown Mountain Lights," Boone (NC) *Watauga Democrat*.

Brief mention of legends and possible causes and the upcoming Brown Mountain Lights Symposium. No references given.

2012, February 16 Betts, J. "Still a Mystery: The Brown Mountain Lights," Rocky Knob Blog: www.rockyknobblog.blogspot.com/2012/02/still-mystery-brown-mountain-lights.html.

"The Legend of the Brown Mountain Light" by Scotty Wiseman, words to the song.

2012, February 27 Mcqueeney, K. "Mystery of the Brown Mountain Lights: Tourists Flock to See Eerie Phenomenon Which Have Baffled Residents for 100 Years," United Kingdom: *Mail Online*: www.dailymail.co.uk/news/article-2107060/Brown-Mountain-Lights-Tourists-flock-site-mysterious-phenomenon-baffles-residents-100-years.html.

This blog reports on Linville Gorge Lights (LGLs), mentions that Dan Caton plans to set up camera at Wiseman's View, and includes some YouTube videos.

No references given.

2012, February 27 "Mysterious Orbs Confound County," Shelby (NC) *Shelby Star*.

Steve Woody story, Ed Phillips & the first BML symposium in Morganton. No references given.

2012, October Jackson, S. "The Mysterious Brown Mountain Lights—There's No Explanation of Why You See Lights in These Mountains at Night": www.carolinacountry.com/index.php/carolina-stories/item/the-mysterious-brown-mountain-lights.

"According to Cherokee legend, a*round* AD 1200 a great battle was fought between the Cherokee and Catawba Indians at Brown Mountain and the mysterious lights are from the Indian maidens still searching for their men who died in battle."

"A 1913 U.S. Geological Survey concluded they were headlights from a locomotive, but when the tracks washed away three years later and people continued to see the lights that theory also was thrown out."

Includes photo of lights on ridge north of Brown Mountain. No references given.

2012, October 31 Searcy M. "Spectral Light Skepticism": blog.scienceinsociety.northwestern.edu/author/msearcy.

"The story I heard as a kid told of a terrible mine collapse in the late 1800s—dozens of miners buried alive. When word reached the town, the wives rushed up the mountain. They spent all night with their lanterns in hand searching the forest, darting off at the slightest hint of their loved ones. The Brown Mountain Lights are their ghosts endlessly searching."

There are no mines on BM, nor have there even been. There are no known mine accidents that killed dozens of miners at once anywhere in the entire history of North Carolina. This story is a myth.

2012, November 3 Washburn, M. "Brown Mountain Lights Still Enchanting," *Charlotte* (NC) *Observer*.

On November 3, 2012, BML Symposium was to be held in Morganton. Charles Braswell, Jr., October 15, 2001, photo; C.W. Smith's story; Indian legends and G.W. De Brahm, 1771 story; 1913 *Charlotte Observer* article; 1913 USGS study; 1922 USGS study; Dan Caton's 5 percent Ball Lightning theory; Les Burril story.

2012 Warren, J.P. *Brown Mountain Lights Viewing Guide: Tips on How You Can See the Lights* (Asheville, NC: Joshua P. Warren, 2012).

The earliest reports of BMLs came from Cherokee and Catawba Indians, settlers, and Civil War soldiers.

Warren gives a brief summary of past reported sightings and mentions the Brown Mountain OHV recreation area; Brian Irish's photos;

legends of the faithful slave searching for lost master; Cherokee and Catawba battle in 1200; murdered wife; UFOs; aliens, interdimensional beings; little people; fairies; conscious beings of energy who live inside the mountain; De Brahm 1771 nitrous vapors; first written document in 1913 *Charlotte Observer*; USGS 1922 study; ORION researchers.

Cranberry granite, iron & magnetite have been found on the mountain.

"The Brown Mountain Lights appear to be self-contained, concentrated balls of light which can maneuver the mountain independently while traveling, and clearly not attached to a stationary 'fuel port,' they can continue to 'burn' for a minute or more. The lights can also be extraordinarily bright (even when viewed many miles away); seemingly far too bright for known natural gas to produce. They frequently appear when the conditions are dry. Why wouldn't balls of ignited gas burn up the mountain as they move through the trees? They've never been known to start a fire."

Electrically charged plasma or some form of ball lightning are other theories.

Warren's 2004 "Report on the Cause of the Mysterious Brown Mountain Lights" is included in the 2012 guide.

2012 "The Brown Mountain Lights," Newland, NC: Avery County Historical Museum, 2012: www.averymuseum.com/brown%20mountain%20light.htm.

"The phenomenon first gained national attention in 1913 when the U.S. Geological Survey became interested in the mystery and sent scientists to study what the cause of them might be."

It also mentions the Indian maiden searching for her brave warrior killed in a bloody battle and a faithful slave searching for his missing master. No references given.

2012 "Brown Mountain Lights; Brown Mountain, North Carolina; Paranormal Phenomena, Spook Lights—Where To Find Them": www.paranormal.about.com/od/earthmysteries/ig/Spooklights—Where-to-Find-Them/Brown-Mountain-Lights.htm.

"Sightings of these lights go back at least 800 years when the native Cherokees thought them to be the spirits of slain warriors. There have been dozens of observations by explorers, some dating back to the 1700s, and by Civil War soldiers."

Includes Dean Warsing's 2009 night-vision goggle video of suspected BML. No references given.

2012 Crane, C. *The Brown Mountain Lights: A North Carolina Legend*, illustrated by Monica Wyrick (Lexington, KY: Peak City, 2012).

This is a fictional children's' book about BMLs and the story of immigrant Riley family settling first in Pennsylvania, then moving to Brown Mountain, NC. Mr. Riley served 3 years in the Revolutionary War, then returned home to find his family missing. He searched the mountains, leaving lighted torches for his family, but died without finding them. His ghost continues to search with torches to this day.

This story is identical to that in *Boone (NC) Watauga Democrat* on February 1, 1982.

The Revolutionary War ended in 1783, 100 years before BMLs were first documented.

2012 Jay, W. "The Brown Mountain Lights, Morganton, North Carolina." Wilson Jay's South. Web site no longer available.

"The local Native Americans have told of these lights for centuries. The first recorded sighting by a European settler was made by Geraud de Brahm, a German-born engineer who was exploring the area in 1771."

Included are the legend of slave with lantern searing for lost master; legend of woman murdered in 1850; U.S. Geological Survey investigation in 1913; lights seen immediately after flood of 1916; Charles Braswell's 2004 photo of bright light in sky north of Brown Mountain and links to YouTube video and still images on BrownMountainLights.com. No references given.

2012 Nicholson, S. "Brown Mountain Lights in the Spotlight": www.hauntedcomputer.com/scottst21.htm.

There are brief mentions of many legends and explanations; De Brahm; Dan Caton's dismissal of Indian legends; Josh Warren; and Civil War soldiers, etc. No references given.

2012 "The Brown Mountain Lights—North Carolina Ghost Stories and Legends": www.northcarolinaghosts.com/mountains/brownmountain.php.

Brief mention of various legends and plausible explanations. No references given.

2012 "The Brown Mountain Lights": ibiblio.org/ghosts/bmtn.html.

Brief mention of USGS visits, De Brahm 1771, 1916 flood, etc. No references given.

2012 "The Brown Mountain Lights," North Carolina Visitor Center: www.ncvisitorcenter.com/Brown_Mountain_Lights.html.

Brief mention of Indian legends, lights before 1900s, 1771 De Brahm, USGS 1913 visit, 1916 flood, murdered wife, and loyal slave looking for lost master. No references given.

2012 "The Brown Mountain Lights": www.jayboy74.tripod.com/story12.html.

Two USGS studies, De Brahm 1771 report, spirits of slain Indian warriors, lights seen since earliest times over top of BM, lights move up & down then disappear as one climbs the mountain; at times too many lights to count; 1916 flood. No references given.

2012 Warren, J. *Brown Mountain Lights: A Viewing Guide* (Morganton, NC: Burke County Tourism Development Authority, 2012). www.brownmountainlights.com

Joshua Warren is NC's most renowned paranormal researcher and promoter. While he does not offer explanations, he presents most of the stories, legends, & myths about the lights. Several photos of supposed BMLs are from his research team. There are some small caves and holes around the mountain. Warren dismisses swamp gas as illogical. He suggests the lights are related to plasmas due to natural electric capacitors (quartz & magnetite) but also mentions many other theories.

2013, July 26 Glover, A., and E. Speer. "The Real Scientific Truth of the Brown Mountain Lights," Slide presentation, Little Switzerland, NC.

Geologists Alex Glover & Ed Speer gave a slide presentation at the community center in Little Switzerland, NC, on the BML research team's 1.5-year study.

2013, August 28 Mundhenk, A. "Brown Mountain Lights Revealed," Spruce Pine (NC) *Mitchell News-Journal*.

Local scientists have identified 99 percent of reported "Lights" sightings.

Local geologists Alex Glover and Ed Speer are part of a 16-member team investigating the BMLs. Speer reports a lot of misinformation in the published literature. There have been no Indian light sightings. Fate Wiseman's story of light in 1858 was probably from a train. BMLs were seen immediately after electricity arrived in the valley. The origin of the legend is given the legend has morphed over time. Sources are: 98 percent manmade lights, 1 percent natural lights, including BGFs; 1 percent unexplained. BMLs are superstitions of the uninformed. The legend will live forever.

2013, September 7 "Couple Attacked by UFO While Watching Brown Mountain Lights," Unknown Publication. Story no longer available online.

This article appears to be a hoax. The online account has been removed, but originally showed a photo of an article as if it appeared in the *Asheville Citizen Times* newspaper; however, such an article cannot be found in that newspaper's Web site archives. The story tells of a married couple in a car that is hit by a hovering UFO. The story is vague & highly illogical. The accompanying article about the BMLs is poorly researched and contains much misinformation, such as Spanish explorers seeing the lights in the 1580s and Indian battles on BM. This story is totally unconfirmed.

2013, October 17 Mulliger, A. "What Exactly Are the Brown Mountain Lights?," *Forest City* (NC) *Daily Courier,* Local Matters. www.thedigitalcourier.com/news/x559274426/What-exactly-are-the-Brown-Mountain-Lights. see also: www.thedigitalcourier.com/news/x559273683/Legend-of-the-Brown-Mountain-Lights.

Ed Speer slide presentation was given to the Rutherford Outdoor Coalition at Isothermal Community College Library on October 15, 2013. Speer presented facts gathered by the research team over the last 1.5 years. Peer showed slides of known & unknown lights, natural nocturnal lights, staged lights tests, images from full time camera, and the earliest known photos of BMLs, etc. There are numerous sources of BMLs. Also discussed were informed observer vs. uninformed observer; BGFs; lots of manmade lights; human mind's errors; 98 percent manmade; 1 percent natural; 1 percent unclassified; first light sighting in 1858 (same year as first train). The legend of BMLs originated between 1900 and 1922, immediately following the arrival of electricity.

"Through our scientific research, the evidence strongly suggests that the BMLs are superstitions."

2013, October 31 Campbell, J. "Shedding Some Light on Brown Mountain," *Boone* (NC) *Mountain Times*.

Interview with Dr. Dan Caton, Appalachian State University astronomy professor. Two cameras were set up to catch the BMLs & images are posted on YouTube for the public (search "Brown Mountain Lights Caton").

"Part of the problem is that people are totally unfamiliar with the nightscape. They are used to being inside watching TV or on the computer at night. There are a whole range of lights people are seeing that we understand to just be normal lights. Maybe a small portion of those lights are real?"

Caton believes 95 percent of the light stories he's come across are bogus.

2013, November 22 Miller, R. "That Time Jules Verne Caused a UFO Scare": www.io9.com/that-time-jules-verne-caused-a-ufo-scare-453662253.

Miller proposes that the worldwide wave of UFO sightings in the late 1890s was the result of Jules Verne's book *Robur le Conquerant*, published in France in 1886 and in Britain and the U.S. in 1887. Previous Verne books were highly popular and *Robur* followed suit. Miller's argument appears highly probable.

2013 Clark, J. *Unexplained! Strange Sightings, Incredible Occurrences, and Puzzling Physical Phenomena*, 3rd edition (first edition, 1999) (Canton, MI: Visible Ink, 2013).

In his chapter on Ghost Lights, Clark says, "Sometimes the claim—that the lights were part of folklore even before the invention of the automobile or the locomotive—proves to be folklore."

In 1925 Robert Sparks had this to say of the Brown Mountain mystery:

The descriptions of the strange lights made by various observers do not agree. One person says that it is pale white, as is ordinarily observed through a ground-glass globe, with a faint, irregular halo encircling it. He claims that it is restricted to a prescribed circle, and appears from three to four times in rapid succession, then conceals itself for 20 minutes, when it reappears within the same circle. Another observer, who was standing about eight miles from Brown Mountain, says that suddenly after sunset there blazed into the sky above the mountain a steady glowing ball of light. To him, the light appeared yellowish, and it lasted about half a minute, when it disappeared rather abruptly. It appeared to him like a star from a bursting skyrocket, but much brighter.

To some people it appears stationary; to others, it moves sometimes upward, downward, or horizontally. A Minister says that it appeared like a ball of incandescent light in which he could observe a seething motion.

Also discussed is J. Stokes Penland's June 16, 1922, letter to R.K. Babington (*Gastonia Daily Gazette*, December 15, 1927). Penland reports seeing the BMLs 40 years earlier—c. 1882.

First printed reference was *Charlotte Daily Observer* September 13, 1913. Also included are Sterrett's visit; 1916 flood; 1921 Humphreys; 1922 Mansfield; 1977 500,000 candlepower light test; U.S. Weather Bureau; W.J. Humphreys 1921; St. Elmo's fire. J.A. reported in 1923 seeing artificial lights plainly. Frank D. Ruggles story of 1932: 100s of city street lights. Paul Devereux's earthlights.

2013 Blue Ridge Parkway, National Park Service, United States Department of the Interior, "The Brown Mountain Lights," Information Sheet reviewed in 2013 (original publishing date unknown).

This is a single sheet with short accounts of the BMLs and mentions De Brahm's 1771 description as the first scientific explanation of the lights as well as the 1913 newspaper article and the Morganton Fishing Club sighting. It refers to the U.S. government study of 1914 (Sterrett's investigation of 1913) and the flood of 1916.

"The lights had also been observed long before the days of automobiles, trains, and electricity."

Directions are given to most popular viewing sites. There are several songs about the BMLs mentioned and several books. The document reviewed included copies of 16 pages taken from Mansfield's 1922 report.

2014, January 3 Holler, C., Jr. "Jules Verne and the Brown Mountain Lights," personal communication.

E-mail post in which Dr. Holler makes the connection between Jules Verne, Table Rock, mysterious lights, and Morganton. Master of the Universe book published in 1911.

2014, January/February Theriault, R., F. St-Laurent, F.T. Freund, and J.S. Derr. "Prevalence of Earthquake Lights Associated with Rift Environments," *Seismological Research Letters* 85, no. 1 (2014). Including information in the 48-page electronic supplement to the published article available at: ftp://ftp.mrnfp.gouv.qc.ca/Public/Geologie/Robert_Theriault/SRL-D-13-0059-esupp.pdf.

The authors present anecdotal evidence of supposed earthquake lights from 65 worldwide earthquakes between 1600 and 2009 that they claim demonstrate that continental rift-related earthquakes along vertical or steep faults create or transmit electrical impulses from deep within the earth to the surface, where they produce light plasmas visible to humans. Such lights occur from a few seconds to a few months before the associated earthquake and can occur unusually far from the epicenter or the trace of the earthquake fault itself. Questionable evidence is submitted as the cause of the claimed phenomena. This is the same "Tectonic Stress Theory" for earthquake lights first proposed by Michael Persinger in the 1970s. Coauthors Freund and Derr were associates of Persinger at the time. These hypotheses have never found acceptance by experienced earth scientists. Missing from the authors' discussion is an explanation of why the lights are seen only once before each earthquake although the tectonic stresses obviously continue to build up to the time of the earthquake itself, and why the lights appear as much as 370 miles from the epicenter or the fault rather than directly on the supposed fault conduit that brings them to the surface. Nor does the hypothesis explain why supposed earthquake lights such as the BMLs appear repeatedly in some areas of the world without any subsequent earthquakes. While only 5 percent of the world's earthquakes every year are estimated to be continental rift-related earthquakes (as reported by Theriault), an average 650 such earthquakes with magnitudes greater than 4.0 (considered by Theriault critical energy levels to produce earthquake lights) occur worldwide every year (U.S. Geological Survey); thus 266,000 such earthquakes probably occurred worldwide between 1600 and 2009 (Theriault's study period), yet Theriault found only 65 cases of earthquake-related lights during this period, suggesting a correlation rate that does not support his proposed earthquake-related hypothesis. In addition, Theriault's Brown Mountain Light example (#7 of 27 of his North America examples) occurred 50 days after the supposedly related earthquake, which does not support his conclusion of pre-earthquake or contemporaneous earthquake lights.

2014, January 22 Holler, C., Jr. "Recent Investigations into North Carolina's Age-old Mystery, the Brown Mountain Lights," pre-print of an article for the online *Journal of Magic Research.*

Review of studies underway by the BML research team. De Brahm's 1771 report is about SC, not NC. Dr. Holler dismisses many proposed BML explanations as unreasonable, and it mentions that research and study are ongoing.

2014, March 24 Issacs, J. "Movie Premier—Alien Abduction; Movie Puts Supernatural Spin on Brown Mountain Lights." *Morganton* (NC) *News Herald.*

The article announces the premier April 4 at Marquee Cinemas, Morganton (director Matty Beckerman).

2014, March 27 "Morganton to Host Premier of Sci-fi Movie on 'Lights,'" Blowing Rock (NC) *Blowing Rocket.*

Fictional Alien Abduction movie to premier in Morganton on April 4, 2014. Includes interviews with Dan Caton & Joshua Warren.

2015, January Braswell, C., Jr. *Are Those the Brown Mountain Lights?: The Story of the Unexplained Lights of Brown Mountain* (Hickory, NC: Brushy Mountain Press, January 2015).

Braswell presents anecdotal accounts of his and others' encounters with mysterious lights in the BM area. He also includes his own photos & those of other people. He covers many anecdotal stories, both historic and recent.

Bibliography and List of References

About.com. "Brown Mountain Lights; Brown Mountain, North Carolina; Paranormal Phenomena, Spook Lights—Where to Find Them." 2012. www.paranormal.about.com/od/earthmysteries/ig/Spooklights—Where-to-Find-Them/Brown-Mountain-Lights.htm.

Adams, R., and T. Adams. *Night Lights: Golf, the Blues, and the Brown Mountain Light.* Parkway, 2004.

Alexander, N. "After Generations of Superstitious Shivers, Four Young Men Provide Sensible Answer to Brown Mountain Lights." *Lenoir* (NC) *News-Herald*, February 5, 1959.

____. "The Brown Mountain Lights—Part II." Boone (NC) *Watauga Democrat*, September 24, 1964, p. 6.

Asheville (NC) Citizen (now the *Citizen-Times*)
    1927, February 15, "Eerie Light That Plays Across Brown Mountain Mystery for 50 Years."
    1962, August 4, "Brown Mountain Lights Traced to Cave Entrance."
    1962, August 13, "Search Adds to Mystery of Brown Mountain Lights."
    1977, July 30, "Ghostly N.C. Lights Have Long History."

Associated Press. "Sweet-Smelling Gas Key to Mystery?" (1962).
    Lubbock (TX) *Avalanche-Journal*. "Let's Forget About the Marfa Lights," December 14, 1971.
    Newland (NC) *Avery Journal-Times*. "Brown Mountain Lights Heritage Festival," May 3–4, 2006.

Babington, R.K. "Some History of Famous Brown Mountain Light." December 13, 1927, letter to the editor of the *Gastonia* (NC) *Daily Gazette*, December 15, 1927.

Bailey, H. "Come See the Flying Saucers! You Want to See a UFO? Come Down to Brown Mountain. You Can See One Any Time—Even Take Pictures of It!" *Argosy* 367, no. 6 (December 1968).

Baity, J. "Brown Mountain Lights Remain a Mystery to Viewers." *Asheville* (NC) *Citizen-Times*, July 29, 1962.

Baldwin, J. "Chapter 9, Riddle of the Brown Mountain Lights." In *Smoky Mountain Mysteries: Stories About Magnificent Mountain Unique People.* Kodak, TN; Virginia Beach, VA: Suntop, 2002.

Ball, E.M. "*Brown Mountain Lights, from Wiseman's View Near Linville Falls.*" Image N1503 dated 1929. E.M. Ball Photographic Collection (1918–1969), Special Collections, D.H. Ramsey Library, University of North Carolina at Asheville.

Bandera, de la, J. *The Bandera Document: Proceeding of the Account Which Captain Juan Pardo Gave of the Entrance Which He Made into the Land of the Floridas* [April 1, 1569]. Translated by Paul Hoffman. Raleigh: NC Division of Archives and History.

Beard, A. "Chasing the Legendary Brown Mountain Lights." *Asheville* (NC) *Citizen Times*, July 11, 2005; *Boone* (NC) *News Herald*, July 12, 2005, p. 2A.

Bell, W.M. *The North Carolina Flood: July 14, 15, 16, 1916.* Charlotte, NC: W.M. Bell, 1916.

Bessent, M. "The Lights of Brown Mountains." *New Horizons* 1, no. 3 (1972).

Bessor, J.P. "Mystery of Brown Mountain." Evanston, Il: Clark; *FATE* 4, no. 2, issue 18 (March 1951).

Betts, J. "Still a Mystery: The Brown Mountain Lights." Rocky Knob Blog 2012. www.rockyknobblog.blogspot.com/2012/02/still-mystery-brown-mountain-lights.html

Bird, M.A. "Brown Mountain Light Developing into Greater Mystery." *Lenoir* (NC) *News*, February 15, 1916.

Bixler, M. "Legendary Lights Have Puzzled Cen-

turies of Viewers." *Winston-Salem* (NC) *Journal*, December 18, 1992, pp. 1, 4.
Blowing Rock (NC) *Blowing Rocket*
    1937, August 28, "Tells Legend of Brown Mountain: Shepard M. Dugger, Author of Mountain Books, Recounts Story of Superstition About Famous Lights."
    2014, March 27, "Morganton to Host Premier of Sci-fi Movie on 'Lights,'" p. 7.
Boone (NC) *Watauga Democrat*
    1965, April 1, "Brown Mountain Lights Legend Passed Through Many Generations."
    1971, November 4, "Brown Mountain Light Theory Reiterated."
    1982, February 1 "Revolutionary War Soldier."
    1994, September 28, "WNC Man Produces Video on Brown Mountain Lights," p. 13A.
    2001, July 2, "Group Says It Will Find Cause for Brown Mountain Lights."
Boyle, J. "Mysterious Lights Mean Big Business." *Asheville* (NC) *Citizen-Times*, July 9, 2001.
Braly, R. "Sam Rowe, Cato Holler, Jr., Explore Mystery—Marion Youths Study Brown Mt. Light." Marion (NC) *McDowell News*, September 6, 1962.
Braswell, C., Jr. *Are Those the Brown Mountain Lights?: The Story of the Unexplained Lights of Brown Mountain*. Hickory, NC: Brushy Mountain, 2015.
Breen, T. "Brown Mountain Lights, Mysterious Orbs in NC, Are Decades-old Mystery." *Huffington Post*, February 26, 2012. www.huffingtonpost.com/2012/02/26/brown-mountain-lights-nc_n_1302204.html.
Brewer, C. "Brown Mountain Lights—One of Nature's Mysteries." Knoxville (TN) *News-Sentinel*, August 12, 1984.
_____. "Brown Mountain Lights; One of Nature's Unexplained Mysteries Is Right in Own Back Yard." Boone (NC) *Watauga Democrat*, October 30, 1991, p. 11A.
Brown, B. "Again, the Brown Mountain Lights." *The State*, May 1, 1971 (Columbia, SC).
_____. "Practical Science." Kingsport (TN) *Times-News*, June 2, 1962.
_____. "Science for You."
_____. "'Spook' Lights." In *A New Geography of North Carolina*. Vol. 2. Bill Sharpe. Raleigh, NC: Sharpe, 1958; Lebanon (PA) *Daily News*, June 1, 1962; Knoxville (TN) *Sunday News Sentinel*, June 3, 1962.
Brown, F.C. (Dr.). "Brown Mountain Lights." In *Monumental Folklore of NC Books: The Frank C. Brown Collection of North Carolina Folklore (Collected by Dr. Frank C. Brown During 1912–1943)*. Vol. 1 of 7. Durham, NC: Duke University Press, 1964.
"The Brown Mountain Lights of Western North Carolina." Raleigh, NC: Information Bulletin No. 162, Travel and Promotion Division, North Carolina Department of Natural and Economic Resources, 1977.
"The Brown Mountain Lights." Raleigh: North Carolina Museum of History, 2005. www.ncmuseumofhistory.org/fko/NIE/TwistedTarHeelTales/brownmountain.pdf.
"The Brown Mountain Lights." Newland, NC: Avery County Historical Museum. www.avery-museum.com/brown%20mountain%20light.htm (posted 2012).
"The Brown Mountain Lights—North Carolina Ghost Stories and Legends." www.northcarolinaghosts.com/mountains/brownmountain.php (posted 2012).
Bryant, H.E.C. "Brown Mountain Light No Longer Mysterious." *Charlotte* (NC) *Observer*, May 20, 1922, p. 5.
_____. "Mansfield Saw Two Brown Mountain Lights—One Made by Southern Locomotive; Other Will Be Explained at a Later Date." *Charlotte* (NC) *Observer*, May 7, 1922.
_____. "Mysterious Brown Mountain Lights Yet to Be Explained." *Charlotte* (NC) *Observer*, February 18, 1923.
_____. "Strange Brown Mountain Lights Divide Scientists." *Washington Post*, February 17, 1923.
Buchanan, L. "Original Play Opens in Asheville on Friday—Brown Mountain Lights Legend Retold." *Morganton* (NC) *News Herald*, October 24, 1985, p. 11A.
Buckinger, N., and R. Holcomb. "Searching for the Brown Mountain Lights." *High Point* (NC) *Focus (High Point Enterprise)*, 2002.
Caines, R.S. *The Brown Mountain Lights and the Mesozoic Phoenix*. iUniversie, 2004.
Campbell, J. "Shedding Some Light on Brown Mountain." Boone (NC) *Mountain Times*, October 31, 2013.
Canandaigua (NY) *Daily Messenger*. "Light on the Lights," May 9, 1972.
Cantor, P. "The Brown Mountain Lights." *The Ley Hunter*, no. 100 (1986).
Casstevens, F.H. "The Brown Mountain Lights." In *Ghosts of the North Carolina Piedmont: Haunted Houses and Unexplained Events*. Charleston, SC: History, 2009.
Caton, D.B. (Dr.) "Close Encounters of the Skeptical Kind." *Charlotte* (NC) *Observer*, October 6, 1998, p. 13A.
_____. "A Scientific Investigation of the Brown Mountain Lights: Final Summary Report." Boone, NC: 1997–98 University Research Council Competitive Grants Program, Appalachian State University, October 1, 1998.
_____. Title unknown. *Winston-Salem* (NC) *Journal*, May 20, 2002.
Chapman, A. "Legend Says Brown Mountain

Lights in Burke County Date Back to 1200." *Asheville* (NC) *Citizen*, June 29, 1952.

———. Title unknown. *Charlotte* (NC) *Observer*, November 15, 1942.

Charlotte (NC) *Observer*
  1954, February 9, "For Real Mystery See Brown Mountain Light."
  1962, August 3, "Mystery of Lights Grows."

Chater, M. "Motor-Coaching Through North Carolina." *National Geographic* (May 1927).

Chehalis (WA) *Bee-Nugget*. "Light Mystery Solved," May 15, 1925.

Childress, B. "In Quest of Those Mysterious Lights." *Beckley* (WV) *Post*, September 9, 1963.

Clabby, C. "Scientist Scrutinizes Spooky Sight—Astrophysicist Out to Explain—or Disprove—Storied Brown Mountain Lights." *Raleigh* (NC) *News and Observer*, July 3, 2005, p. A1.

———. "Scientist Scrutinizes Spooky Sight." www.anomalyarchives.wordpress.com/2005/07/07/scientist-scrutinizes-spooky-sight.

Clark, J. *Unexplained!: Strange Sightings, Incredible Occurrences, and Puzzling Physical Phenomena*. 3rd ed. (1st ed. 1999). Canton, MI: Visible Ink, 2013.

Clark, L.R. *Burke County North Carolina: Historic Tales from the Gateway to the Blue Ridge*. Charleston, SC: History, 2007.

———. *Indians of Burke County and Western North Carolina*. Morganton, NC: TimeSpan, 2002.

Cobb, B. Untitled. *Gastonia* (NC) *Gazette*, August 11, 1948.

Codfelter, T. "Mountain Mystery—Light Rarely Spotted, Spark Lots of Speculation." *Winston-Salem* (NC) *Journal*, June 9, 2006, pp. E1, E2.

Coffey, S.C. *Mortimer and Edgemont: Lenoir News, 1900–1919*. 1st ed., August 1989. Collettsville, NC: Sandra Cloer Coffey, revised 2004.

Coleman, J.S., Jr. "Strange Light Continues to Mystify; Rays Visible Every Evening on Brown Mountain." *Asheville* (NC) *Times* (now *Citizen-Times*), Sunday, August 25, 1929.

Corliss, W.R. *Lightning, Auroras, Nocturnal Lights and Related Luminous Phenomena: A Catalog of Geophysical Anomalies*. Compiled by William R. Corliss. Glen Arm, MD: Sourcebook Project, 1982.

———. *Remarkable Luminous Phenomena in Nature: A Catalog of Geophysical Anomalies*. Compiled by William R. Corliss. Glen Arm, MD: Sourcebook Project, 2001.

———. "Two Well-known Spooklights." In *Nocturnal Lights*, Chapter 1, "Luminous Phenomena," *Handbook of Unusual Natural Phenomena*. New York: Arlington House, 1986.

Crane, C. *The Brown Mountain Lights: A North Carolina Legend*. Illustrated by Monica Wyrick. Lexington, KY: Peak City, 2012.

Crews, E. "Mystery Mountain." *Blue Ridge Outdoors* (2001) www.blueridgeoutdoors.com/outdoors-travel/adventures/mystery-mountain/.

Cumberland (ME) *News*. "Light on the Lights," March 31, 1972.

Danville (VA) *Register*. "Brown Mountain Lights May Pose Bigger Mystery," August 3, 1962.

De Brahm, W.G. *Report of the General Survey in the Southern District of North America*. Originally published in 1771. Tricentennial ed., no. 3. Columbia: University of South Carolina Press, 1971.

Denton (MD) *Journal*. "Light Mystery Solved," January 17, 1925.

Dodge, R.J. "Brown Mountain Lights." In *Encyclopedia of North Carolina*. Chapel Hill: University of North Carolina Press. ncpedia.org/brown-mountain-lights

Downing, B. "Searching for the Light." *Akron* (OH) *Beacon Journal*, September 15, 2002.

Duckworth, J.H. Title unknown. *Charlotte* (NC) *Observer*, September 30, 1917.

Dugger, S.M. *The Balsam Groves of the Grandfather Mountain: A Tale of the Western North Carolina Mountains; Together with Information Relating to the Section and Its Hotels; Also a Table Showing the Height of Important Mountains, etc.* Philadelphia: J.B. Lippincott, 1895.

———. "Letter dated March 9, 1936 to Mr. J. Marion Saunders, Secretary of the General Alumni Association, Univ. of North Carolina, Chapel Hill, N.C." In *The Bard of Ottary: The Life, Letters and Documents of Shepherd Monroe Dugger*, by Leslie Banner Cottingham and Carol Lowe Timblin. Banner Elk, NC: Puddingstone, 1979.

Dunning, B. "The Brown Mountain Lights—A Ghost Light in North Carolina Has People Scratching Their Heads. What's the Explanation?" Skeptoid podcast, episode 226, October 5, 2010. www.skeptoid.com/episodes/4226.

Dyer, L. "Group Takes on 800-year Old Mystery." *Charlotte* (NC) *Observer*, July 2, 2001, p. 1B.

Elam, C. "Saw Brown Mountain Light 15 Times in Few Hours." *Lenoir* (NC) *News*, October 31, 1916.

Feiss, P.G., A.H. Maybin, S.R. Riggs, and A.E. Grosz. "Mineral Resources of the Carolinas." In *The Geology of the Carolinas*. Edited by J.W. Horton, Jr., and V.A. Zullo. Knoxville: University of Tennessee Press, 1991.

Feiss, P.G., S. Goldberg, W. Ussler III, E. Bailar, and L. Myers. "The Cranberry Magnetite Deposit, Avery County, North Carolina." In *Geologic Investigations in the Blue Ridge of Northwestern North Carolina, Boone, NC, October 21–23, 1983: Carolina Geological Society Field Trip Guidebook*. Edited by S.E. Lewis. Raleigh: NC Division of Land Resources, Geological Survey Section.

Ferree, C. "Brown Mountain Light Mystery." *Winston-Salem* (NC) *Journal*, June 27, 1971.

Floyd, R. "Local Mysteries: Ghostly Lights as Common as Dew in Dixie." *Augusta* (GA) *Chronicle*, June 7, 1999.

Frederick (MD) *News*. "How Mystery Was Proven," December 18, 1924.

Frick-Ruppert, J., and J.J. Rosen. "Morphological and Behavior of *Phausis Reticulata* (Blue Ghost Firefly)." *Journal of North Carolina Academy of Science* 5, no. 124, pt. 4 (2008): 139–147. dc.lib.unc.edu/cdm/singleitem/collection/jncas/id/3883/rec/1.

Frizzell, M.A. "Investigating the Brown Mountain Lights." *INFO Journal*, no. 43 (January/February 1984): 22; In W.R. Corliss. *Remarkable Luminous Phenomena in Nature: A Catalog of Geophysical Anomalies*. Compiled by William R. Corliss. Glen Arm, MD: Sourcebook Project, 1984.

Gaddis, V.H. *Mysterious Fires and Lights*. New York: Dell, 1967.

———. "Visitors from the Void." *Amazing Science Fiction Stories* (1947), 159–161.

Garibaldi, L. "Brown Mountain Lights Continue to Fascinate Burke." *Morganton* (NC) *News Herald*, July 30, 1998, p. 10A.

Gastonia (NC) *Daily Gazette*. "Brown Mountain Lights Used as Background for Mystery Novel," August 31, 1940.

Glover, A.S., and E. Speer. "The Real Scientific Truth of the Brown Mountain Lights." Unpublished slide presentation. Little Switzerland, NC, July 26, 2013.

Glover, A.S., W.Z. Rogers, and J.E. Barton "Granitic Pegmatites: Storehouses of Industrial Minerals." Mineralogical Society of America. *Elements: An International Magazine of Mineralogy, Geochemistry, and Petrology* 8, no. 4 (August 2012).

Glovier, M. "Tells Legend of Brown Mountain: Shepard M. Dugger, Author of Mountain Books, Recounts Story of Superstition About Famous Lights." Boone (NC) *Watauga Democrat*, September 2, 1937.

———. "Tells Old Legend of Brown Mountain." *Charlotte* (NC) *Observer*, August 29, 1937.

Goerch, C. "The Brown Mountain Lights." *Down Home*. Raleigh, NC: Edwards & Broughton, 1943.

Granqvist, P., et al. "Sensed Presence and Mystical Experiences Are Predicted by Suggestibility, Not by the Application of Transcranial Weak Complex Magnetic Fields." *Neuroscience Letters* 379, no. 1 (2005), 1–6.

Greensboro (NC) *Daily News*. "Brown Mountain Lights Simple if You Can Grasp Big Words," February 13, 1923.

Grizzard, G. "A Personal Experience with the Brown Mountain Lights." Boone (NC) *Watauga Democrat*, May 26, 1999.

Harden, J. *The Devil's Tramping Grounds and Other North Carolina Mystery Stories*. Chapel Hill: University of North Carolina Press, 1949.

Harris, W.H., Col. "Letter to Senator Simmons," dated 1921; as reported in G.R. Mansfield, 1922, USGS Circular 646, pp. 4, 7.

———. "No Explanation." *Charlotte* (NC) *Daily Observer*, September 23, 1913.

———. "Opportunity to Attract Tourists." *Hickory* (NC) *Daily Record*, March 12, 1935.

Harshaw, L. Title unknown. Publicity release. Asheville, NC: Asheville Chamber of Commerce, April 1955.

Hartley, J.L. *The Mystery of the Brown Mountain Lights, Combined with Singing on the Mountain*. Linville, NC: J.L. Hartley, 1962.

Harvey, R.M. "Brown Mountain Lights." Newland (NC) *Avery Journal-Times*, March 18, 1976.

Haskin, F.J. "Carolina Mountain Light Called Forth Request for United States' Assistance." *Iowa City-Press*, March 8, 1923.

———. "The Haskin Letter." *Helena* (MT) *Daily Independent*, March 8, 1923.

Hauck, D.W. "Brown Mountain Lights." In *Haunted Places: The National Directory; Ghostly Abodes, Sacred Sites, UFO Landings and Other Supernormal Locations*. Rev. ed. Penguin, 2002.

Helms, Jr., H.L. "America's Eerie Phantom Lights." *SAGA* (November 1971).

Henderson, B. "Scientist Eyes Mysterious Mountain Lights—State Expert Hopes to Capture Images of Phenomenon." *Charlotte* (NC) *Observer*, November 12, 2006.

———. "Will You See Mountain Mystery?" *Charlotte* (NC) *Observer*, November 4, 2006, p. 1A.

Hickory (NC) *Daily Record*
    1936, October 17, "Brown Mountain Lights Amazing to Hickory Man."
    1977, "Brown Mountain Lights Explained?"
    2001, July 3, "Asheville Group Tries to Find Explanation for N.C.'s Brown Mountain Lights."

Hodge, T. "Brown Mountain Lights: Mystique More Important Than Source." *Johnson City* (TN) *Press-Chronicle*, January 15, 1980, p. 7.

———. "Elizabethton Man Tries to Spot Brown Mountain Light." *Johnson City* (TN) *Press-Chronicle*, November 26, 1975.

———. "Some Serious Thinking About the Brown Mountain Lights." *Johnson City* (TN) *Press-Chronicle*, October 31, 1975.

Holler, C., Jr. "Recent Investigations into North Carolina's Age-old Mystery, the Brown Mountain Lights." Preprint of article for the online *Journal of Magic Research*, 2014.

Houck, J. M. "Weird Explanation of a Weird Light, a New Explanation of the Mysterious Light on Brown's Mountain." *Morganton* (NC) *News Herald*, July 5, 1917. Story narrated by John M. Huck and copied from C.H. Hites in the *Charlotte Observer*.

Houser, S.T. "The Brown Mountain Lights—Mysterious Bright Lights Falling from a Burke County Mountain Have Dumbfounded Onlookers for Years." [Greensboro, NC] *The State* 60, no. 5 (October 1992).

Hudson, M.A. "Go for the Leaves, Stay for the Lights." *Charlotte* (NC) *Observer*, September 12, 1999, p. G1.

Huffman, S. "Brown Mountain Lights—There's Still No Clear Explanation for This Visual Phenomenon." *Salisbury* (NC) *Post*, September 2, 2005.

Humphries, W.J. (Dr.). Lecture before the American Meteorological Society, dated 1941 (from S. Odenwald, 2001).

Ibiblio.org. "The Brown Mountain Lights." Dated 2012. ibiblio.org/ghosts/bmtn.html.

Indianapolis (IN) *Sunday Star*. "Mountain Light Comes into Own—North Carolina Phenomenon Once Regarded as Hoax, Electrical Fact," November 27, 1921.

Issacs, J. "Movie Premier—Alien Abduction; Movie Puts Supernatural Spin on Brown Mountain Lights." *Morganton* (NC) *News Herald*, March 24, 2014, p. A1.

Jackson, S. "The Mysterious Brown Mountain Lights—There's No Explanation of Why You See Lights in These Mountains at Night." Carolinacountry.org, October 2012. www.carolinacountry.com/index.php/carolina-stories/item/the-mysterious-brown-mountain-lights.

James, S., "The Legend of Brown Mountain Light." Ballad by Scotty Wiseman. RCA Victor recording by Sonny James, 1962.

Jarvis, S. "The Brown Mountain Lights." In *The Uninvited: True Tales of the Unknown*. Vol. 2. Edited by Sharon Jarvis. Bantam, 1989.

Jessup, M.K. "The Case for the UFO." London: Arco, 1955.

Johnson, E.F., ed. *A History of Jonas Ridge*. Banner Elk, NC: Puddingstone, 1974.

Jordan, M. Title unknown. *Lenoir* (NC) *Davenport Weekly Record*, April 1922.

Kane, M. "Brown Mt: Participate in a Mystery." *Carolina Outdoor Guide* (September/October 1983).

Keever. "N.C. Folk Tales and Ghost Stories Told by Mr. Keever." *Statesville* (NC) *Record and Landmark*, September 14, 1956.

Klass, P.J. *UFOs Explained*. New York: Random House, 1974.

Knoxville (TN) *News-Sentinel*. "Group Tries to Solve Mystery of Brown Mountain Lights," July 8, 2001, p. B3.

Koon, J. "Scientist Finds Explanation for Brown Mountain Lights." *Charlotte* (NC) *Observer*, April 13, 1925.

Krill, J. "The Lights on Brown Mountain—After a Century They Still Remain Unexplained." *Exploring the Unknown* 2, no. 3 (August 1961), 77–78. Edited by Robert A.W. Lowndes.

Lael, R. *The Brown Mountain Lights*. Jonas Ridge, NC: Lael, 1965.

———. "Mystery Brown Mountain Lights Is Topic of Volume 1." Blowing Rock (NC) *Blowing Rocket*, June 9 and 16, 1966.

Lancaster, R. L. Title unknown. *Gastonia (NC) Daily Gazette*, December 9, 1927.

Lenoir (NC) *News*. "Brown Mt. Light now Belongs to Uncle Sam," February 18, 1917.

———. "Strange Light Is Puzzle for Burke County," November 12, 1915. In *Mortimer and Edgemont, Lenoir News, 1900–1919*. Edited by Sandra C. Coffey. Collettsville, NC: Self-published, August 1989 (revised 2004).

Lenoir (NC) *News-Topic*. "Group Trying to Explain Brown Mountain Lights," July 3, 2001.

"The Lights of Brown Mountain." *North Carolina Folklore* 1, no. 1 (June 1948).

Little, G. (Dr.). "The Brown Mountain, NC, Lights Videotaped: A Field Observation, July 2003." *Alternate Perceptions*, no. 70 (July 2003).

Lloyd, J.E. "Observations on the Biology of Three Luminescent Beetles (Coleopters; Lampyridae, Elateridae)." *Ann. Entomol. Soc. Amer.* 58, no. 4 (1965): 588–591.

Long Beach (CA) *Independent Press-Telegram*. "Mysterious Lights Just Old Legend," October 31, 1971.

Louv, R. *Last Child in the Woods: Saving Our Children from Nature-Deficit Disorder*. Algonquin, 2005 (updated 2008).

———. *The Nature Principle: Reconnecting with Life in a Virtual Age*. Algonquin, 2012.

Loven, G.A. "The Brown Mountain Light Not Washed Away." *Lenoir* (NC) *News*, September 8, 1916.

Lyman, H. Presentation to American Meteorological Society at the U.S. Weather Bureau in Washington, D.C., dated 1921. As reported in G.R. Mansfield, U.S. Geological Survey, Circular 646, p. 5, 1922.

Lyman, H., Sr. Lecture before the American Meteorological Society, dated 1941 [information from S. Odenwald, 2001].

Macomber, F. "Reports of Mysterious Lights Refuse to Fade." *Brownsville* (TX) *Herald*, November 4, 1971.

Manning, G.H. "Strange Light in Mountains Still Alarming: Remarkable Phenomenon Can Be Seen in Burke County; Spectator Gives Vivid Description." *Winston-Salem* (NC) *Journal*, September 14, 1913.

Mansfield, G.R. *Origin of the Brown Mountain Light in North Carolina*. Washington, D.C.: U.S. Geological Survey, Circular 646, p. 18, 1922 (reprinted 1971).

Marschalk, S. "Woman Explores Mystery of Burke Lights." *Hickory* (NC) *Daily Record*, January 21, 1983.

Martin, H.C. "The Brown Mountain Mysterious Light." *Lenoir* (NC) *News*, November 23, 1915.
_____. "To the Editor of the Observer: Iredell County Light—Brown Mountain Light." *Charlotte* (NC) *Observer*, March 25, 1922.
Mast, N. "No Conclusive Explanation—Brown Mountain Lights." *Boone* (NC) *Mountain Times*, October 9, 1980.
Mays, P. "Mystery of the Haunted Mountain." *Sunday News* [unknown location], September 2, 1962.
McAfee, H. "Mysterious Lights of Brown Mountain Seen at This Time of Year." *Asheville* (NC) *Citizen-Times*, June 5, 1938.
_____. Title unknown. *Greensboro* (NC) *Daily News*, September 9, 1945.
Mcbrayer, S. "Officials Unveil Overlook After Two Years of Removing Trees That Blocked Scenic Attraction." *Morganton* (NC) *News Herald*, September 3, 2009, p. A1, A3.
McCoy, G. "Study Substantiates Theory of Brown Mountain Lights." *Asheville* (NC) *Citizen*, November 10, 1940.
Mcqueeney, K. "Mystery of the Brown Mountain Lights: Tourists Flock to See Eerie Phenomenon Which Have Baffled Residents for 100 Years." United Kingdom *Mail Online*, February 27, 2012. dailymail.co.uk/news/article-2107060/Brown-Mountain-Lights-Tourists-flock-site-mysterious-phenomenon-baffles-residents-100-years.html.
Miller, H.J. "Brown Mountain Lights Continue to Fascinate Observers." *Spruce Pine* (NC) *Mitchell News-Journal*, December 6, 1982.
Miller, R. "That Time Jules Verne Caused a UFO Scare." Internet post, November 22, 2013. www.io9.com/that-time-jules-verne-caused-a-ufo-scare-453662253.
Mishoe, C. Title unknown. Blowing Rock (NC) *Blowing Rocket*, July 27, 1951.
Mishoe, P.B. *The Lights of Brown Mountain*. Philadelphia: Dorrance, 1972.
Morganton (NC) *News-Herald Blue Ridge Rambler*
    1891, March 13
    1891, April 23
    1891, May 3
    1908, September 17, "Strange Light in the Heavens."
Morrison, N. "The Mystery of the Brown Mountain Lights." *Boone* (NC) *Mountain Times Winter Guide* (2010), 85.
Mull, D.S. "Brown Mountain's Mysterious Lights: A Guide to the Ghostly and the Supernatural." C.V. Studios, 1998.
Mulliger, A. "What Exactly Are the Brown Mountain Lights?" *Forest City* (NC) *Daily Courier*, Local Matters, August 28, 2012.
Mundhenk, A. "Brown Mountain Lights Revealed." Spruce Pine (NC) *Mitchell News-Journal*, August 28, 2012.
National Park Service, Blue Ridge Parkway. "The Brown Mountain Lights." Information sheet, original date unknown, reviewed 2013). Washington, D.C.: National Park Service, United States Department of the Interior.
Neuendorf, K.K.E., J.P. Mehl, Jr., and J.A., Jackson, ed. *Glossary of Geology*. 5th ed. Alexandria, VA: Amer. Geol. Institute, 2005.
New Horizons. Title unknown. Summer 1972.
Newport (RI) *Mercury*. "Mountain Light Is Like Aurora—Curious Electrical Display in North Carolina Excites Interest of Scientists," December 24, 1921.
Nicholson, S. "Brown Mountain Lights in the Spotlight." Hauntedcomputer.com. 2012 post. www.hauntedcomputer.com/scottst21.htm.
North Carolina Visitor Center, 2012. "The Brown Mountain Lights." Raleigh: NCVisitorCenter.com. 2012 post. www. ncvisitorcenter.com/Brown_Mountain_Lights.html.
Northrop, M. "Brown Mountain Light Is Still Creating Wonder and Speculation." *Hickory* (NC) *Daily Record*, May 7, 1936.
Oak Ridge (TN) *Oak Ridger*. Title unknown. May 29, 1978.
Oakes, A. "Demystifying the Brown Mountain Lights." Boone (NC) *Watauga Democrat*, February 9, 2012.
Odenwald, S. "The Brown Mountain Lights." Astronomycafe.net, 2001. www.astronomycafe.net/weird/lights/brown.htm.
Oneonta (NY) *Star*. "Mountain Light Is Like Aurora—Curious Electrical Display in North Carolina Excites Interest of Scientists." December 21, 1921.
ORION Newsletters. Oak Ridge, TN: Oak Ridge Isochronous Observation Network.
    1977, May, June (#29).
    1978, April (#33), May (#34), July, August, September.
    1980, November (#63).
    1981, June (#71), July, August (#74).
    1982, January, June (#80), July (#81), August (#82), November (#85).
    1983, February (#88), July (#93), October (#96), November (#97).
    1984, September (#102).
    1985, October (#111).
    1988, March (#140), May (#141).
Painter, R. "The Brown Mountain Lights." *Search* (July 1968), 50–58.
Pantas, L.J. *The Ultimate Guide to Asheville and the Western North Carolina Mountains*. 3rd ed. "Ultimate Guide to Asheville and Hendersonville." Asheville: R. Brent, 2006.
Parris, J. "Brown Mountain's Lights Still a Mystery." *Asheville Citizen-Times*, September 29, 1966.
_____. "Roaming the Mountains—Uncle Fate Saw Ghostly Lights." *Asheville Citizen-Times*, November 11, 1971, pp. 1, 10.

_____. *Roaming the Mountains with John A. Parris.* Asheville, N.C.: Citizen-Times Pub. Co., 1955.

_____. "Uncle Fate and the Brown Mountain Lights—Wiseman's View." In *These Storied Mountains*, by John A. Parris. Asheville, N.C.: Citizen-Times Pub. Co., 1972.

Pearson, W. "The Brown Mountain Lights—Mr. [H.C.] Martin writes Interestingly of Preliminary Investigations Made Recently by Lenoir Party." *Morganton* (NC) *News Herald*, April 27, 1916.

Perry, W.G. "Letter to Dr. C.G. Abbot, Smithsonian Institution, dated 1919." As reported in G.R. Mansfield, U.S. Geological Survey, Circular 646, p. 7, 1922.

Persinger, M.A. "Religious and Mystical Experiences as Artifacts of Temporal Lobe Function: A General Hypothesis." *Perceptual and Motor Skills* 57 (1983), 1255–62.

Persinger, M.A., and G. Lafreniere. *Space-Time Transients and Unusual Events*. Chicago: Nelson-Hall, 1977.

Phifer, Jr., E.W. *Burke: The History of a North Carolina County, 1777–1920, with a Glimpse Beyond*. 1st ed. 1977, revised 1982. Morganton, NC: Edward William Phifer, Jr., under the sponsorship of the Burke County Historical Society.

Pitzer, S. "Brown Mountain Lights." In *Myths and Mysteries of North Carolina: True Stories of the Unsolved and Unexplained*. Myths and Mysteries Series. Guilford, CT: Morris, 2010.

Pollock, V. "Brown Mountain Lights, Jim and Belinda Legend." 2011 post. www.thereadonwnc.ning.com/forum/topic/show?id=1972559%3ATopic%3A37654.

Poteat, B. "The Brown Mountain Lights—Video Takes New Look at Burke County's Oldest Mystery." *Morganton* (NC) *Sunday News Herald*, September 18, 1994, Section C.

Raleigh (NC) *News and Observer*. Associated Press dispatch (Jonas Ridge dateline). August 6, 1962.

Renegar, M. "Ghost Lights on Brown Mountain." In *Roadside Revenants*. Fairview, NC: Bright Mountain, 2005.

Richardson, W. Title unknown. *Raleigh* (NC) *News and Observer*, September 8, 1952.

Roberts, N. *Southern Ghosts*. New York: Doubleday, 1979.

Rogers, S. "The Mystery of the Brown Mountain Lights." Blowing Rock (NC) *Blowing Rocket*, June 28, 2001, p. 1.

Ross, R.B., Jr., and T.M. Crandall. *Maps Showing Uranium Prospects and Mineralization in the Lost Cove and Harper Creek Roadless Areas, Avery and Caldwell Counties, North Carolina*. Washington, D.C.: U.S. Bureau of Mines, Miscellaneous Field Studies Map MF-1391-C, 1986.

Rowe, P. "Sprites Light Up the Night with Mysterious Glow." Marion (NC) *McDowell News*, May 2, 2005.

Ruggeiro, F. "ASU Prof Doesn't Buy Lights Legend." Boone (NC) *Watauga Democrat*, April 1, 2002.

_____. "Looking for the Brown Mtn. Lights." Boone (NC) *Watauga Democrat*, July 14, 2006, pp. 1, 4.

Ruggles, F.D. "Another Angle on Brown Mountain Lights Offered." *Statesville* (NC) *Record and Landmark*, September 30, 1932.

_____. Title unknown. *Charlotte* (NC) *Observer*, September 13, 1932.

Russell, D. "The Brown Mountain Lights—New Video Evidence May Finally Provide More Clues to Potentially Solve the Mystery." *S-Project Paranormal*. 2001 post. www.xprojectmagazine.com/archives/paranormal/brnmntlights.html.

Russell, R., and J. Barnett. "Belinda and the Brown Mountain Lights." In *Mountain Ghost Stories and Curious Tales of Western North Carolina*. Winston-Salem, NC: John F. Blair, 1988.

Sakowski, C. *Touring the Western North Carolina Backroads*. 3rd ed. Winston-Salem, NC: John F. Blair, 2011.

Salisbury (NC) *Evening Post*. "Mysterious Light Visible from Top of Blue Ridge"; *Morganton Messenger*, August 31, 1912.

Schlosser, J. "The Queer Lights on Brown Mountain." *Literary Digest*, November 7, 1925. In *Remarkable Luminous Phenomena in Nature: A Catalog of Geophysical Anomalies*. Compiled by William R. Corliss. Glen Arm, MD: Sourcebook Project, 2001.

Schrum, J. "Are Brown Mountain Lights Rising Gases?" Boone (NC) *Watauga Democrat*, January 13, 1992, p. 1.

Scott, W.W. "Linville Gorge and the Mysterious Light on Brown Mountain." Lenoir (NC) *News Herald*, 1915.

Searcy M. "Spectral Light Skepticism." 2012. www.blog.scienceinsociety.northwestern.edu/author/msearcy.

Shelby (NC) *Cleveland Star*. "Mysterious Orbs Confound County." February 27, 2012.

_____. "News in Condensed Form." October 12, 1917.

Shermer, M. *The Believing Brain: From Ghosts and Gods to Politics and Conspiracies; How We Construct Beliefs and Reinforce Them as Truths*. St. Martin's Griffin, 2011.

Shires, W.A. "The Case of the Mysterious Lights." *Gastonia* (NC) *Gazette*, August 20, 1962.

Sparks, J. "Professor Tries to Debunk Popular Mountain Myths." *Winston-Salem* (NC) *Journal*, May 27, 2002, p. 4A.

_____. "Skeptical Professor Tries to See the Light." *Winston-Salem* (NC) *Journal*, May 13, 2002, p. B3.

The State. [Columbia, SC] April 23, 1955.

Statesville (NC) *Record and Landmark*.
  1922, January 12, "Brown Mountain Light Comes into Its Own."
  1922, April 17, No title.

1923, May 14, "Camps on Brown Mountain—Brown Mountain Light Isn't on Brown Mountain."

1927, March 7, "Brown Mountain Light Mystery—The Argument as to the Origin of the Mysterious Light Goes Merrily on Around Blowing Rock."

1928, April 30, "Says Light Not on Brown Mountain."

1961, September 26, "A New Explanation?"

1962, August 16, "Brown Mountain to Be Developed."

1977, August 3, "Theories Advanced."

Tabler, D. "The Brown Mountain Lights, as Told by David Biddix." *Appalachian History*. 2010. www.appalachianhistory.net/2010/10/the-brown-mountain-lights.html.

Taylor, T. "Brown Mountain Lights." In *Weird U.S.: Your Travel Guide to America's Local Legends and Best Kept Secrets*, by Mark Moran and Mark Sceurman. Sterling, 2009.

Taylor, T. "The Brown Mountain Lights, Burke County, North Carolina." *Unexplained America*. 1998 post. www.prairieghosts.com/brownmt.html.

Theriault, R., F. St-Laurent, F.T. Freund, and J.S. Derr. "Prevalence of Earthquake Lights Associated with Rift Environments." *Seismological Research Letters* 85, no. 1 (January/February 2014), 159–178. Including information in the 48-page electronic supplement to the published article available on the Internet. ftp://ftp.mrnfp.gouv.qc.ca/Public/Geologie/Robert_Theriault/SRL-D-13-0059-esupp.pdf.

Trenton (NJ) *Evening Times*. "Brown Mountain Light Is Coming into Its Own as Natural Wonder," November 18, 1921.

Tripod.com. "The Brown Mountain Lights." 2012 post. www.jayboy74.tripod.com/story12.html.

Trivette, J. "More Letters—How About Those Brown Mtn. Lights?" Boone (NC) *Watauga Democrat*, August 13, 2001.

Verne, J. *Master of the World*. Originally published in French in 1904. Published in English in 1911.

———. *Robur le Conquerant*. Originally published in French in 1886. Published in English as the *Clipper of the Clouds* in Britain in 1887 and published as *Robur the Conqueror* in the U.S. in 1887.

Vincent, B. "Strolling with Bert Vincent." *Knoxville* (TN) *News-Sentinel*, 1962.

Wadsworth, E.W. "Brown Mountain Lights." Boone (NC) *Watauga Democrat*, December 13, 1973, p. 17A.

Wagener, H.D., and J.G. McHome. "Uranium Mineralization in the Wilson Creek and Cranberry Gneisses and the Grandfather Mountain Formation, North Carolina and Tennessee." Washington, D.C.: National Uranium Resource Evaluation Report GJBX-191 (82), 1982.

Walser, R. *North Carolina Legends*. Raleigh: North Carolina Division of Archives and History, 1996.

Warren, J. *Brown Mountain Lights: A Viewing Guide*. Morganton, NC: Burke County Tourism Development Authority, 2013.

Warren, J.P. *Brown Mountain Lights Viewing Guide: Tips on How You Can See the Lights*. Asheville, NC: Joshua P. Warren, 2012.

———. "Report on the Cause of the Mysterious Brown Mountain Lights." Asheville, NC: League of Energy Materialization and Unexplained Phenomena Research (L.E.M.U.R.), 2004. www.shadowboxent.brinkster.net/brownplasma.html. (It is also included in Joshua P. Warren's 2012 *Brown Mountain Lights Viewing Guide*.)

Warsing, D. "Project UFO Night Shift." 2009 YouTube Video. www.youtube.com/watch?v=gftfwM9_J0g.

Washburn, M. "Brown Mountain Lights Still Enchanting." *Charlotte* (NC) *Observer*, Saturday, November 3, 2012.

Weir, L. "Brown Mountain Lights Still Seen as Ghosts Walking." *Statesville* (NC) *Record and Landmark*, August 4, 1941.

Whitman, H.A. "Brown Mountain Lights Have Not Disappeared." *Charlotte* (NC) *Observer*, August 11, 1940.

———. "Letter to managing editor of the *Asheville Citizen*." *Asheville* (NC) *Asheville Citizen* (now the *Citizen-Times*), October 11, 1940.

Wichita (TX) *Daily Times*. "The Flame-Clad Mountains," January 15, 1922.

Wikle, J. "Many Mysterious Lights Have Been Seen in WNC." *Asheville* (NC) *Citizen-Times*, March 29, 1959.

Wilson, C.L. "Brown Mountain Light Still a Mystery and a Deeper One." *Lenoir* (NC) *News*, December 14, 1915.

Winston-Salem (NC) *Western Sentinel*.

1912, February 14, "Asks Uncle Sam to Hunt Ghost in North Carolina."

1912, October 3, "Mysterious Light in the County of Burke."

1962, August 3, "Famed Lights Cause Feeling of Dizziness."

2001, July 3, "Researcher Videotapes, Tries to Explain the Legendary Brown Mountain Lights."

2005, July 10, "ASU Professor Chases After 'the Lights.'"

WNC Interactive. "Brown Mountain Lights." WesternNCAttractions.com. 2000 post. www.westernncattractions.com/BMLights.htm.

Zepke, T. "Mystery of the Brown Mountain Lights." In *Best Ghost Tales of North Carolina*. 2nd ed. Sarasota, FL: Pineapple, 2006.

Index

Numbers in *bold italics* indicate pages with photographs.

Abbot, Dr. C.G. 40
Adams Knob 45; *see also* Adams Mountain
Adams Mountain 21, 23, 38, 44–46, 49, 51, 62, 116, *126*, *127*, *134*, *141*, 155, *156*; *see also* Adams Knob
Adventures in the Wilds of the United States and British American Provinces 27
airplanes *98*, 138, *139-142*, 145, *152*, *165*, 166, 167, *169*, 173, 182
airports 6, 138, *142*; *see also* Foothills Regional (Morganton-Lenoir) Airport; Hickory Regional Airport; Statesville Regional Airport
Alabama 87, 89, 112
Albatross 42
Alden, Andrew 83
Alexander, N. 23, 96
Alexander County 69
aliens 5, 24, 63, 81, 82, 164
American Geological Institute 85
American Meteorological Society 51
Andes light 7, 23, 49, 51, 52, 54, 74, 109, 110; *see also* ball lightning; electrical discharge; lightning
anti-crepuscular rays 7, 103, 182; *see also* crepuscular rays
Appalachian State University 15, 18, 19, 24, 26, 58, 75, 78, 114, 167–170
Appletos' Hand-book of American Travel: The Southern Tour 27, 29
Argosy 62
Arkansas 113
Armstrong Creek 19, 96
Asheville 36, 57–59
Asheville Citizen 26, 33, 59, 66
Asheville Citizen-Times 60
Asheville Times 57, 58
Athens 19
Aurora Borealis 100, 103, 182
Avery County 113

Babington, R.K. 23, 30, 37, 55, 155
Bailey, Herbert 24, 59, 62
Baity, Jim 60–63, 75, 96
Baker's Mtn *136*
Baldwin, J. 33–35
Ball, E.M. 22, 23, 57, 58, 74, 77
ball lightning 61, 109, 110, 182; *see also* Andes light; electrostatic discharge; lightning; St. Elmo's fire
Ballad of the Brown Mountain Light (aka "Legend of the Brown Mountain Lights") 35, 36, 172
Balsam Groves of the Grandfather Mountain 27
banded iron formation 93
Bandera, J. de la 25
Bandy Cove Mountain 58, 60, *137*, *138*
Barnett, J. 34
Bear Rocks 128, *131*, *140*, 148, 160, *161*, 163, *164*, *165*
belief-dependent realism (realities) 10, 81, 180
Believing Brain 9, 10, 81
Bell, W.M. 43, 49
Big Dipper firefly 113, *see also* Eastern firefly; fireflies; *Photinus pyralis*
Bird, M.A. 38, 40, 49
Bixler, M. 116
Blount County 113
Blowing Rock 52–55, *160*
blue ghost firefly (BGF) 13, 14, 46, 47, 66–68, 72, 73, 78, 82, 110–116, *117*, *118*, 173, 179, 181, 182; *see also* fireflies; *Phausis reticulata*
Blue Ridge Parkway 13, 113, 117
Blue Ridge Rambler: Descriptions of Local Mountains 27
Bob Brown's Science Circus 58
Boone 15, 19, 58, 78, 114, 167
Bradford Mtn. *108*, *141*, *142*
Brahm, W.G. de: *General Survey in the Southern District of North America* 21, 23, 29–30, 55
Braly, R. 65
Brevard 113; college 113; fault 87

Brown, Bob 22, 23, 58, 59, 62, 63, 74, 79
Brown, F.C.: *Monumental Folklore of NC* 25
Brown Mountain Club 51
Brown Mountain Lights Heritage Festival 24
Brown Mountain Light Symposium 17, 24, 32
Brown Mountain Lights: What's the Explanation? 26
Brown Mountain Off-Highway Vehicle Recreation Area 148
Brown Mountain Overlook (Highway 181) 4, 20, *101*, *104*, *106*, 121, 124, *125-127*, 128, 131, *132*, *134*, 136, 139, *141*, 147, 148, *151*, 153, 155–157, 159, 160, *168*, 197
brush fire 6, 7, 97, 98, 172, 181
brush lightning 23, 49, 74, 109, 110; *see also* electrostatic discharge
Bryson, Rube 45
Buck Creek 96
Buncombe County 112, 113
Burgin, Brent 26
Burke County 3, 17, 24, 26, 28, 29, 34, 113, 180, 201
Burke—The History of a North Carolina County, 1777-1920 26, 27
Bynum's Bluff 28

Cabarrus County 113
Caldwell County 13, 113
Caldwell County Memorial Hospital 139, *143*, *144*
California 41, 81, 176
campfires 6, 7, 14, 26, 32–35, 51, 85, 86, 97, 100, 146, 147, *159*
Canada 41
Cantrell, Henry 19
Carroll Bird 23, 34
Catawba: river flood 21, 23, 38, 43, 44, 51, 75, 76; town 53
Catawba Cave 27
Catawba County 112
Catawba Indians 21, 26
Catawba River 29, 41

Index

Catawba Valley 11, 22, 23, 27–29, 36, 37, 40, 44, 48, 75, 76, 77, 155, 171, 172
Caton, Dr. Daniel 15, 18, 19, 24, 75, 78, 109, 167
Charleston 43, 91
Charlotte Observer (Charlotte Daily Observer) 34, 39, 51, 66
Chatham 94
ChemLights™ 158
Cherokee 21, 25, 26
Chestnut Gap 160, 163, 164
Chestnut Mountain 60, *133*, *134*, 147, 155, 159, *160*
Chestnut Ridge Park 97
Chimney Rock Falls 28
Chimney Rock Pass 28
chimneys 28, 147
Christie, Agatha 42
Christmas Star (Hibriten Mountain) 124, *127*, *129*, *141*, *142*, *145*, 165; *see also* Easter cross
Civil War 24, 33–35, 55
Clark, J. 37
Clark, L.R.: *Indians of Burke County and Western North Carolina* 26
Clarke County 113
Claywell, R.T. 21, 38, 39
Claywell, Sarah 39
Clingman, T. L. 27
Clipper of the Clouds 42
Coffey, Collett 45
Coffey, Dr. L.H. 22, 45, 46, 51
Coffey, Monroe 54
Cold Mountain 34
Cold Springs 21–23, 37, 38, 40, 43, 49, 50–52, 54, 74, 76, 79, *131*
Coleman, J.S., Jr. 57, 58
Collettsville 45
Colton, H.: *Mountain Scenery* 27, 28
Comet 8, 100
Concord 39
Concordia College 45
Conley's Cove 35
Connelly Springs 13, 23, 40, 53, 76, *136*, 138, 153, 155
Conover 45, 53, 112
Cranberry Iron Mine 93
Crane, Carol 33
crepuscular rays 7, 100, 103; *see also* anti-crepuscular rays
Crichton, Dr. Michael 81

Davidson County 113
Derieux, J.B. 23, 75, 77
Dismals Canyon 112
Dixie County 113
Dixon, A.A. 23, 75, 77
Dogback Mtn *159*
Drexel 13, 53, 77, *124*, *136*, 138, *139*, 153
Dugger, S.M. 23, 34, 55; *The Balsam Groves of the Grandfather Mountain* 27
Dunning, B.: *The Brown Mountain Lights: What's the Explanation?* 26

DuPont State Forest 112, *117*
Durham 19

earthquake 27, 88–91, 95; lights 8, 83, 92
Easter Cross (Hibriten Mountain) *107*, 124; *see also* Christmas Star
Eastern firefly 112–114, 116, *118*; *see also* Big Dipper firefly; fireflies; *Photinus pyralis*
Edgemont 147
Elam, C. 38, 49
electricity, first arrival 6, 10–21, 22, 25–31, 37, 51, 54, 55, 69, 76, 171
electromagnetic 24, 84, 85, 94, 95
electrostatic discharge 109, *110*, *111*; *see also* ball lightning; brush lightning; heat lightning; lightning
Ellychnia corrusca 78
Emerald Mine Road 113
enigma 75
eternal flames 97
evergreen 19, 93
Eye of the Skeptic 32

Farah, Annette 19
Feiss, P.G. 93, 94
Festinger, Leon 3
fireflies 6, 13, 14, 46, 47, 51, 78, 82, 11–116, *117*, *118*, *119*, 182; *see also* Big Dipper firefly; blue ghost firefly (*Phausis reticulata)*; Eastern firefly (*Photinus pyralis*); synchronous firefly (*Photinus carolinus*)
fireworks 6, 7, 18, 120, 150, *152*
Fischesser, Mike 18, 159, 160
Florida 25, 113
Flood of 1916 23, 38, 43, 44, 49, 51, 54, 75, 76, 172
Foothills Regional Airport (Morganton-Lenoir) 138
forest fire 1, 7, 8, 97, *98*, *99*, 113
Fort Bragg 166
Foster, Dr. Kevin 48
foxfire 6, 7, 51, 56, 112; *see also* mushrooms
Frank, Adam 48
Franklin, David 28
Franklin, T.C. 28
Frick-Rupert, Jennifer 113, 115
fungus gnat 111, 112; *see also Orfelia fultoni*

Gaither, B. S., 23, 37, 50
Gastonia Gazette 34
Gates of Hell, Turkey 97
General Survey in the Southern District of North America 21, 23, 29–30, 55
geologic faults 83–91, 95
Georgia School of Technology 40, 49
ghosts 5, 23, 24, 34, 55, 68, 81–82
Gingercake Acres 18, 27, 128, *131*, *137*, 153

Gingercake Mountain 52, 53, 66, 67, 79, 129
Gingercake Rock 28, 29
Glass, Alex, PhD 19
Glia, Serra 48
Glossary of Geology 85
Glover, Alex 17, 18, 93
glowworms 7, 110–112, 182
Good Men Project 3
Google Data Center *108*, *128*, *129*, *141*, *145*
Grandfather Mountain 28; thrust fault 87, *88*
Granite Falls *138*, 153, *156*
Grants Mountain 128, *130*
Great Eyrie 41, 42
Great Eyry 11, 42
Great Smoky Mountain National Park 112, 116, 118
Greenville County 112, 113
Gregory, Rev. C.E. 23, 37, 50, 52–54
Grosscup, B.: *The Heart of the Alleghenies, or Western North Carolina* 27–29

Hackett, David K. 78, 116
Haentzschel, Rev. A.I. 45
Hall, E.H.: *Appletos' Hand-book of American Travel: The Southern Tour* 27, 29
Hall, Harriet 174
hallucinations 7, 32, 73, 84, 85, 94, 95
Hanks, Micah 83
Harris, Col. W.H. 37–40, 51
Haskin, F.J. 55, 77
Hawkbill 28
Hawkins, Lee 19, 58, 78, 114
Hawk's Bill 27, 29
Hawksbill 28
Hawksbill Mountain *101*, *102*, 113, *140*, 150, *152*, 155, 158
Haywood County 112
Heart of the Alleghenies, or Western North Carolina 27–29
heat lightning 109, 110, 182; *see also* electrical discharge; lightning
helicopter 1, 6, 9, 14, 18, 120, 138, 139, *143*, *144*, *152*, 167, 173, 182
Henderson County 112
Hibriten Mountain 78, *107*, 124, *126*, *127*, *129*, *141*, *142*, *145*, 155, *157*; *see also* Christmas Star; Easter Cross
Hickory 11, 13, 22, 37, 40, 69, 76, 132, *136*, *137*, 138, 166, 171; Regional Airport 138, 166
High Peak *124*, *125*
Highway 181 overlook 79, 124, 128, 148, 150, 153, 155, 156, 159; *see also* Brown Mountain overlook
Hildebran 138
Hill, Sharon 176
Hite, C.H. 23, 34
Hogan, Sallie 39
Holler, Cato, Jr., DDS 19, 24, 27–29, 41, 42, 65, 75, 111, 160, *161*, 162, *163*, 201, 202

Holler, Chris 19, 162, *163*
Holley Springs Branch 88
Hollifield, Clyde 19, 65, 109, 112
Honeycutt, Mr. 39
Hudson 23, 74, 77, *137*, *138*, 153, *156*
Hume, David 174
Humpback Mountain 28
Humpheries, W.J 23, 49, 51, 74, 109; see also Humphreys, W. J.

Icard *136*, 138, 153
Ignis Fatuus 96
illuminated clouds 100, 182; *see also* iridescent clouds; nacreous clouds; noctilucent clouds
India 100
Indians of Burke County and Western North Carolina 26
International Space Station 100
iridescent clouds 103, 182; *see also* illuminated clouds
Irish, Brian 24
Isla, Frater: *Eye of the Skeptic* 32

James, Sonny 63
jet aircraft vapor trail 7, 103, 120, 182; *see also* rocket vapor trail
Jonas Ridge 15, 18, 34, 37, 59, 63, 66, 79, 128, 131, 137
Joy 23, 39, 40, 76, 155
Jupiter 7, 47, 100, *101*, 104, *106*, 182

Kahan, Dan 3
Kane, M. 109
Kansas 41
Kp index 94, 95

Lael, Ralph 22, 24, 35, 63, 67, 82, 84, 115, 164; alien encounters 69–73; *The Brown Mountain Lights* 69
Lael's Rock 70–72, 104, *108*, *142*, *145*, 164, *165*, 166
Lafreniere, G. 84, 94
Lake James 13, 138, *159*
Lancaster 26
Lanman, C.: *Adventures in the Wilds of the United States and British American Provinces* 27; *Letters from the Allegheny Mountains* 27
Lapace, Pierre-Simon 174
Larson, Art 19, 93
laser lights 6, 7, 120, 150, *151*, 158
Laurel Knob *158*
Lawndale 74
LEMUR 24
Lenoir 9, 13, 23, 24, 40, 45, 54, 75–77, *106*–*108*, *127*, 128, *129*, *133*, *134*, *137*, 138, 139, *141*, *142*, *145*, 153, 155
Lenoir News 43, 76
Lenoir News Herald 45
Lenoir Topic 45
lens flare 61, 62, 78, *104*, *105*, *151*, *168*
Letters from the Allegheny Mountains 27

Lick Mtn. *108*
light pillars 2, 100
lightning 1, 6, 7, 23, 30, 56, 60, 61, 63, 75, 97, 104, 109, *110*, *111*, 113, 167, 179, 181, 182; *see also* Andes light; ball lightning; electrostatic discharge; heat lightning; St. Elmo's fire
Lindville Pinnacle 27
Linville Caverns 28
Linville Falls 22, 24, 27, 28; thrust fault 87, 88
Linville Gorge 11, 13, 15, 18, 19, 22, 24, 28, 30, 35, 36, 42, 55, 58, 60, 77, 78, 88, 86, 89, 91, 94, 97, 112, 138, 146, 147, 159, 162, 167, 170, 172, 173, 181; Wilderness Area 100, 146, 147
Linville River 28, 147, 150
Little, Dr. Greg 24
Little Switzerland 18
Little Table Rock Mountain 147, *157*; trail 147
Loftus, Elizabeth 176
Lost Cove Cliffs 13
Louv, R. 110
Loven, Earl 53
Loven, George Anderson 37, 38, 39, 43, 49, 76
Loven, Joseph L. 22, 23, 43, 50, 53, 55
Loven, Robert 39, 53
Lucidota atra 78
Lucidota corrusca 78, 116
lumen 121, 156–160, 162–164
Lyman, Dr. H. 23, 51, 109

Maddry, John 19
Madison County, Georgia 113
Madison County, Wisconsin 19
Magee, Bryson 28
man-made lights 6, 7, 75, 120–166, 181, 182
Manning, G.H. 38, 39
Mansfield, G.R. 13, 21, 23, 25, 27, 38, 40, 41, 43–47, 49–59, 74–79, 94, 109, 116, 171, 172; *see Origin of the Brown Mountain Light in North Carolina*
Marion 19, 57, 128, *130*; Country Club 138, *159*
Mars 7, 47, 100, 104, *107*, 182
Martin, H.C. 22, 23, 38, 44–47, 49, 51, 53, 54, 59, 75, 79, 116, 155
Master of the World 11, 12, 21, 23, 41, 42, 171, 179, 180
May, F.H. 54
Mays, P. 66, 67
McAfee, H. 14, 23, 26, 33, 34, 55
McCoy, George William 59, 60
McCurry, Joel C. 59
McDowell County 13, 89, 96, 113, *117*
McGowan, Fred 45
McHome, J. G. 94
McKinney Mine Road 113
McRaney, David 17
Means, Bell 39

Means, Col. Paul 39
Mecklenburg County 113
MedEvac helicopter 1, 9, 139, *143*, *144*, *152*
Mercury 104, *106*, 182
meteor lights 6, 7, 15, 100, 104, *108*, 167, 179, 182
methane 96
Miller, Gen. 28
Miller, R. 11, 41
Millner, H.L. 50
mineral plasmas 84, 93–95
mirages 46, 59, 75, 78, 79, 80
misinformation 4, 6, 14, 179, 180
Mitchell County 113
Monumental Folklore of NC (Brown Mountain Lights) 25
moon 7, 23, 47, 58, 68, 100, *102*, *104*, *105*, *137*, *168*; *see also* moonbows; moonlight
moonbows 103, 182; *see also* night sundogs; parhelic circle; parhelion light
Mooney, J.: *Myths of the Cherokee* 25; *Sacred Formulas of the Cherokees* 25
moonlight 6, 7, 60, 68, 72, 103, 104, *108*, 114, *168*
Moosa, Tauriq 74
Morganton 11, 12, 17, 19, 21, 23, 24, 28, 30, 31, 36, 38–43, 50, 69, 76, 116, 132, 138, 171, 179; Fishing Club 23, 37, 50
Morganton News-Herald 34, 45, 75
Mortimer 71, 147
Mount Chimaera, Turkey 97
Mount Pisgah 112
Mountain Scenery 27, 28
Mountains-to-Sea Trail 147, *162*
Mulberry Creek 53
mushrooms, luminescent 6, 110, 112, 182; *see also* foxfire
Myths of the Cherokee 25

nacreous clouds 103; *see also* illuminated clouds
National Geographic Society 23, 49, 51
National Weather Service 104
natural gas 8, 97
nature deficit disorder 110
Nature of Consciousness 3
Nicholson, S. 24, 33
night sundogs 103; *see also* moonbows
noctilucent clouds 7, 103, 182; *see also* illuminated clouds
North American Jules Verne Society 41
North Bandy Cove Mountain 58, 60
North Carolina *Folklore* 34, 35, 55
North Carolina Geological Survey 89
North Cove 13, 27, 28
North Fork 28
North Harper Creek 94, 113
North Muddy Creek 113
Norway 9

Nova Scotia 87, 89
Novella, Steven 83

Oak Ridge 77
Oconee County (SC) 113
Oklahoma 113
Orfelia fultoni 111, 112; *see also* fungus gnat
Origin of the Brown Mountain Light in North Carolina 25, 27, 45, 46, 50–56, 77, 94, 116, 181
ORION (Oak Ridge Isochronous Observatory Network) 24, 75, 77, 78, 79, 109, 116, 155
Orion constellation **98**, *106*
Outer Space Rock Shop Museum 69

Pakistan 100
Pandolfi, Lauren 19
paranormal 1, 3, 8, 14, 73
Pardo, Capt. Juan 25
parhelic circle 100, 103; *see also* moonbows
parhelion light 100, 103; *see also* moonbows
Parke Creek 54
Parris, John 35, 36, 38, 44, 49
Patterson, George 39; wife of 39
Pearson, P.E. 26
Pearson, W. 38, 45, 49, 54, 59, 75, 116
Penland, J.S. 22, 37
Pennsylvania 113
Perry, W.G. 38, 40, 49
Persinger, M.A. 84, 94
Pewam 71, 72
Phausis reticulata 46, 78, 112, 115, **117**, *118*, 173, 179, 182; *see also* blue ghost firefly
Phifer, W.W., Jr.: *Burke—The History of a North Carolina County, 1777–1920* 26, 27, 29, 34
Photinus carolinus 116, **117**; *see also* synchronous firefly
Photinus pyralis 112, 113, 116, *118*; *see also* Big Dipper firefly; Eastern firefly
Pickens County 113
Piedmont Springs 29
piezoelectric 84–86, 93
Pinch-In Trail 162, *163*
Pittsylvania County 94
Planck, Max 176
Pleasant Garden 41
Powell, Elisha 45
prankster lights 1, 9, 149, 150, **151**, *152*, 172, 182
Pressnell, Russell 45
Pribble, Martin S. 81
pseudoscientific explanations 85–95

radioactivity 66, 83, 84, 93–95
Ramsey Library at the University of North Carolina–Asheville 57, 58
Randi, James 32
Rattlesnake Knob 39

Revolutionary War 24, 33
Richter Scale 89, 91, 92
Ripshin Ridge 51, **108**, **128**, **132–135**, **141**, **142**
Roan Mountain 27, 28
Robur le Conquerant 11, 12, 41, 42
rock plasma 84
rocket vapor trail 7, 103, 182; *see also* jet aircraft vapor trail
Rocky road **122**, **123**
Rogers, Will 167, 171
Rose, Jim 66
Rose, Paul 22, 24, 63–69, **64**, 71, 73, 115
Rosen, Joshua 113, 115
Roundtree, Fannie 39
Rowe, Sam 19, 24, **64**, **65**, 75
Ruggles, F.D. 23, 77
Russell, R. 34
Rutherford College 13, 23, 40, 76, **136**, 138, 153, 155
Rutherfordton 19, 28

Sacramento 41
Sacred Formulas of the Cherokees 25
Sagan, Carl 174
St. Elmo's fire 7, 23, 49, 52, 54, 74, 109, 110; *see also* Andes light; ball lightning; electrical discharge; lightning
Salisbury 30, 35, 36, 43
Salisbury Evening Post 37, 38, 40, 76
satellite 6, 7, 13, 14, 100, 120, 154, 167, 173, 182
Saturn 7, 47, 100, 182
Savage, Adam 3
Schiffman, Richard 74
Schoolcraft, H. 26
Schumacher, Francois 75
Scott, W.W. 37, 51
Sevier County 113
Sharpe, Bill: *A New Geography of North Carolina* 58, 59
Sherrill, Rev. A. 50
Shermer, Michael: *The Believing Brain* 9, 10, 81; *The Good Men Project* 3
Shortoff Mountain 147, **159**, **162**, **163**
Sitting Bear Mountain 155
Smithsonian Institution 23, 40, 49, 51
Smokestack 145, **146**
Smoky Mountain National Park 112, 116
snow 6, 104, **108**
Soper, Benita 19, 201
Soper, Will 19
South Carolina 26, 27, 30, 43, 112, 113
South Mountains 37, 39, 121, **122–124**, **139**, *159*
Speer, E. 15, 15, 24, 162, **163–165**, 166
Spence Ridge Trail 147
spirits 26, 33, 34, 81–82
Spruce Pine 54, 93

staged light tests 153–166
star lights 100, 104
Statesville **138**, **142**, 153
Statesville Landmark 77
Statesville Record 55
Statesville Regional Airport 138, 139, **142**
Steels Creek 60
Sterrett, D.B. 12, 21, 23, 39, 40, 44, 48, 49, 51, 74, 76
supernormal lights 1, 8, 14, 82, 180, 198
Swain County 113
swamp gas 72, 96, 181
Swanson/Coles Hill uranium deposit 94
synchronous firefly 6, 116, **117**, 118; *see also* fireflies; *Photinus carolinus*

Table Rock Mountain 11, 27–29, 42, 58, 97, **98**, **102**, **137**, 146, 147, 150, 156, **157**, **158**
Taylorsville **141**, 153
telluric currents 8, 94
Tennessee 77, 113
Texas 113
Theriault, Robert 92
Thompson, Ken 60, 61, 75
thrust faults 87, **88**, 91
thunder 27, 30, 49, 50, 61, 91, 109
Timbered Branch 69
Tower (Paul Rose's) on Brown Mountain 63–68
Transylvania County 112, 113, **117**
Travel Channel 24
Trenton Evening News 109
Trenton Evening Times 50
Turkey 97
Turkey Cove 28
Tyson, Neil deGrasse 17, 182

UFO 8, 11, 24, 41, 42, 62, 81, 82, 100
Underwood, Bob 65
Union County 113
U.S. Air Force 139, **145**, **165**, 166
U.S. Forest Service 3, 49, 51, 54, 63, **132**, **133**, 146, 147, 148, 150, 159, **160**, **161**
U.S. Geological Survey 10, 11, 14, 21, 31, 38, 39, 40, 41, 45, 46, 48, 50, 51, 60, 74–77, 92, 94, 116, 121, 171, 181
U.S. Weather Bureau 23, 49, 51, 54, 74, 109
University of South Carolina 26
Upper Creek 39, 51, 88, 113, 166

Valdese 13, 121, **122**, 123, **124**, **136**, 138, **139**, 153
Valkenburg, Allen van 74
Venus 47, 63, 69, 71–73, 100, **101**, 104, **107**
Verne, Jules: 11, 12, 21, 41, 42, 171, 179, 180; *see also Clipper of the Clouds*; *Master of the World*; *Robur le Conquerant*
Virginia 29, 94, 113

Index

Wade, Kimberly: *Why Does the Human Brain Create False Memories?* 32
Wagener, H.D. 94
Walton, General 28
Ward, Robert 53
Warren, Charley 45
Warren, Joshua P. 32, 109
Warsing, Dean 24
Washington 42, 48, 51, 116
Watauga Democrat 33
Watts, Alan: *The Nature of Consciousness* 3
Webb, Joe S. 45
Webb, Robey 45
Western Sentinel 21, 37, 38
Whitman, Hobart A. 23, 59, 60, 74, 77
Whitworth, Ron 116
Why Does the Human Brain Create False Memories? 32
Whyte, T. 26
Wildcat Branch 69, 70
Wildcat Knob 69, 70, **108**, **142**, 159, 160, **161**
Wildcat Ridge **156**
Wildwood Gallery 112
Wilkesboro 153
Will-o'-the Wisp 8, 51, 56, 96
Wilmington 34, 87
Wilson, Dr. C.L. 23, 37, 38, 40, 49, 76, 155
Wilson, Robert Anton 32
Wilson Creek 13, 45, 88, 147, 150; National Wild and Scenic River area 147
Winston, Patrick Henry 32
Winston-Salem Journal 38, 39, 66
Wiseman, Lafayette (Fate) 21, 22, 23, 30, 31, 35, 36, 44, 171, 172
Wiseman, Scott Greene 24, 35, 36, 44, 63, 172; see also Ballad of the Brown Mountain Light
Wiseman's View 19, 22, 24, 30, 35, 36, 38, 49, 57, 58, 60, 62, 79, **101**, **102**, 109, 111–113, 121, 124, 128, 129, 132, 135, 137, 138, **140**, 146–148, 150, 152, 153, 155–157, **158**, 159, 171
Wolf Pit Trail 147, **162**
Woody, Steve 19
World War I 40

The X-Files 24

Yadkinville 153

Zeigler, W.: *The Heart of the Alleghenies, or Western North Carolina* 27–29
Zodiacal light 7, 100, 103, 182